POST-INTELLECTUALISM AND THE DECLINE OF DEMOCRACY

The Failure of Reason and Responsibility in the Twentieth Century

DONALD N. WOOD

Foreword by Neil Postman

PRAEGER

Westport, Connecticut
London

Library of Congress Cataloging-in-Publication Data

Wood, Donald N.
    Post-intellectualism and the decline of democracy : the failure of
reason and responsibility in the twentieth century / Donald N. Wood
; foreword by Neil Postman.
        p.   cm.
    Includes bibliographical references and index.
    ISBN 0–275–95421–8 (alk. paper).—ISBN 0–275–95661–X (pbk. :
alk. paper)
    1. Mass media—Social aspects—United States.   2. Social problems—
United States.   3. Democracy—United States.   I. Title.
HN90.M3W63   1996
301—dc20   96–10420

British Library Cataloguing in Publication Data is available.

Library of Congress Catalog Card Number: 96–10420
ISBN: 0–275–95421–8
        0–275–95661–X (pbk.)

First published in 1996

Praeger Publishers, 88 Post Road West, Westport, CT 06881
An imprint of Greenwood Publishing Group, Inc.

Printed in the United States of America

The paper used in this book complies with the
Permanent Paper Standard issued by the National
Information Standards Organization (Z39.48–1984).

10 9 8 7 6 5 4 3 2 1

To Andrew, Graham, Blake, Dillon, and Taylor

. . . for they shall inherit the twenty-first century

Contents

Figures and Tables

Foreword

I recently reviewed a book which was about the electronic revolution and its relationship to democracy. The author was enthusiastic about how computer technology would restore the concept of participatory democracy by allowing citizens to participate in continuous plebiscites and by giving them direct access to legislators. He compared this situation to the kind of democracy that existed in the fifth century B.C. in Athens, and he didn't seem to think that there was much difference between a nation of 250 million people spread across a continent and a city-state of about 5,000 slave-holding citizens. As a consequence, he spent a good deal of time delighting in our good fortune. Technology, he believes, has come just in time to save us.

Donald Wood sees things more deeply than this. He understands that the threats to a democratic way of life cannot be so easily defended against by technological innovation; in fact, cannot be defended at all by technological innovation. He quotes Lewis Lapham telling us the following: "The hope of democratic government descends from the ancient Greeks by way of the Italian Renaissance and the Enlightenment, but no matter how often it has been corrupted and abused . . . it constitutes the only morality currently operative in the world." Professor Wood's book is about the kind of morality that democracy stands for, how it came to be, what the dangers are to it, and how we might proceed to preserve it. To accomplish such a task, one must have a deep understanding of history as well as a keen sense of contemporary social, technological, and political trends. This is exactly the sort of knowledge Professor Wood possesses, and there is no other phrase for what he has accomplished than tour-de-force.

I am confident that readers of this book will take seriously Professor Wood's arguments, will come to fear and disdain the post-intellectual age, and will be cheered by Professor Wood's sensible remedies to the failure of reason and responsibility.

Neil Postman
New York City, 1996

Preface

My professional field is media—specifically, media theory and criticism. My strongest social concern is environmental deterioration. As I started to work on the early drafts of what was to evolve into this book, it slowly became apparent that these two dissimilar areas of interest were interrelated. In fact, all our culture's social concerns and problems are interrelated. They all are manifestations of the phenomenon that I began to define as *post-intellectualism*.

Post-intellectualism is the theory that explains how we have evolved beyond the intellectual foundations of our nation's beginnings. The Intellectual Age dawned around four hundred years ago. The Enlightenment was clearly established about three hundred years ago. The United States, founded on the firm intellectual ideals of the Enlightenment, was well under way two hundred years ago. And our nation was at the peak of its intellectual and industrial glory about one hundred years ago.

The intellectual underpinnings of modern democracy were based on the elegant ideal that men and women are rational enough and responsible enough to manage their own affairs, that they could create a new form of participatory government and establish a true democracy. An enlightened citizenry could comprehend and control its social, economic, political, and scientific environments and reach informed and selfless decisions about the governance of its affairs. Indeed, for the better part of a century or two, it looked like we were succeeding.

This intellectual heritage was characterized by a populace that would seek knowledge, would think rationally, could engage in meaningful social criticism, and was dedicated to a broad, liberal arts, cultural perspective. It would be literate, analytic, competitive, morally clear-headed, and determined to make the system work as a collaborative coming together of reasoning individuals.

However, since the end of World War II—most clearly in the last three decades—Americans have gradually and imperceptibly slipped into a *post-intellectual* culture. Our social and scientific environment has gotten so complex that we mere citizens no longer can comprehend what is going on. The citizenry no longer is enlightened enough to make selfless and long-range decisions for the good of society. The populace no longer sufficiently values knowledge, reason, social analysis, or the liberal arts. Literacy, privacy, self-sufficiency, individualism, ecological coherence, and morality fall by the wayside. Citizens stand aside and turn the government over to the special interests and specialized technocrats. We survive not as independent individuals, but as members of tribal lobbying groups. This is the reality of a post-intellectual culture.

Due to my professional background, I am particularly concerned throughout the book with the roles played by the media in advancing our post-intellectual mindset. Pictorial media contribute to our declining literacy rates; media and related computer technologies nibble away at our privacy on several levels; the media are the primary founts of our information overload; they contribute to our isolation and alienation; they contribute to our deteriorating moral infrastructure (although not necessarily in the way that critics assume). And the media complicate the problems of both democratic and autocratic governments in their attempts to govern the masses.

This book is just an introduction to the theory of post-intellectualism. I barely touch on some of the concerns with schooling problems, privacy, social chaos, technological determinism, deterioration of the inner city, economic folly, environmental despoliation, violence in the media, racism and affirmative action, biotechnology and genetic engineering, international turmoil, and related issues. Society would benefit tremendously from a deeper examination of our political malaise in terms of a post-intellectual analysis. There is much more to be explored in a post-intellectual investigation of our cultural dystopia. This work is but a start.

I do have a confession to make at the onset. Despite my mounting concerns over technological determinism—a prevalent theme throughout the book—I cannot claim to eschew all technological help in this day and age. I am using a computer to write this book (two computers, in fact). I do drive a car (two, actually). I have used antibiotics; on extremely hot days I turn on the air conditioning. And I do have an e-mail address. I enjoy the comforts and conveniences of the late twentieth century. But I try not to become too complacent, too cozy, too relaxed with the technologies. This is the danger against which we must guard.

In pulling together the ideas and specifics of this book, I owe a great deal to numerous scholars, writers, students, colleagues, friends, and family members who have inspired, challenged, questioned, and supported me over the past several years. I am heavily in debt to the numerous philosophers, social critics, and neo-Luddites who furnished material that contributed to my synthesis.

Most specifically, I want to thank Neil Postman for his insights and inspirations gleaned over the decades. On a personal level—although I could not attempt to mention everyone who helped me—I do want to acknowledge the following who were especially instrumental in providing information, assistance, and encouragement: Jason Azze, Jean Hamilton, Ants Leps, Brad Loomis, Ruth Loring, Maureen Melino, Nina Pearlstein, George Rebane, Eric Rigney, Marie Vayo, and Brian and Kellie Wood. To all, I express my thanks. But I insist on taking full credit for all the mistakes, misinterpretations, and shortcomings the reader may find.

PART 1

Orientation: The Concept of Post-Intellectualism

We are living and acting at one of the epoch-making turning points of human history, when one fundamental form of culture and society is declining and a different form is emerging.

• P. A. Sorokin
The Crisis of Our Age

Social and literary critics have identified our age as post-industrial, post-modern, and post-literate (among many other labels). But we are actually undergoing a metamorphosis much more sweeping and all-inclusive than these terms imply; ours is a *post-intellectual* era. We are experiencing a cultural transformation that is reversing four hundred years of intellectual evolution.

Contemporary democracy is but a shell of the intellectual ideal that Americans adopted over two centuries ago; the libertarian dream of a rational and responsible self-governing populace no longer appears to be a viable paradigm. The individual no longer can function as an independent being; the collective citizenry no longer can manage its own affairs. This is the phenomenon of post-intellectualism.

1

Our Intellectual Foundations

The television screens may be bright and our comfortable homes may be warm; but outside it is beginning to grow dark and cold.

• William Lederer
A Nation of Sheep

Something is seriously wrong today. The communist monolith has broken up, but global tensions and international mayhem continue to escalate. We have interlocking multinational economic alliances, but the economies of most developed countries continue in a decades-long slump. Scientific and medical breakthroughs multiply, but more and more people despair in poverty and disease. Increasing numbers of students are attending our institutions of higher education, but our colleges and universities operate at a high-school level. Our global environment is deteriorating as we exploit and consume our planet's resources at a non-sustainable rate. Our legal system cannot guarantee justice, our churches are ridden with scandal, our financial institutions cannot protect our finances.

All this cultural turbulence stems from one primary phenomenon: the intellectual underpinnings of the developed world are crumbling—not just our schools and universities, but our entire institutional and philosophical infrastructure. Our governmental systems, educational establishments, legal arrangements, economic and corporate organizations, and media structures are all intellectual ideas. The political and economic foundations of the Great American Experiment were conceived as an intellectual outgrowth of the Enlightenment. But this intellectual legacy withers. This collapse of our intellectual heritage has resulted in our transition to a *post-intellectual culture*.

Our newspapers, television screens, and bookstores are filled with reports and investigations of our mounting cultural and social problems—violent crime, faulty schooling systems, racial inequities, government corruption, drug abuse, bureaucratic ineptitude, declining emotional health, a decaying urban infra-structure, escalating national debt, family disintegration and moral degeneracy. Countless reporters, social critics, media pundits, and government officials analyze and agonize over these multiplying woes.   But all our handwringing misses the underlying connectedness—the fact that virtually all these crises of our age are related. They are all symptomatic of our post-intellectual transfor-mation.

THREE INTELLECTUAL PERIODS

Human history can be roughly traced through three ages—the *cyclical culture*, the *linear culture*, and the *web culture*. These correspond generally to what I shall define as the *pre-intellectual* period, the *intellectual* period, and the *post-intellectual* period.

Pre-Intellectual *Cyclical* Culture

Early human society is often identified as a *cyclical culture,* in which each individual is reared to perpetuate the culture of his or her parents—through countless succeeding generations. There is no political, economic or scientific incentive for expansion and progress.   Indeed, a cyclical culture reflects an instinctive aversion to change. Historian L. S. Stavrianos defines this mindset:

Primitive humans were basically ahistorical and nonevolutionary in their attitudes towards themselves and their society. They assumed that the future would be identical to the present, as the present was to the past. Consequently there was no notion of change, and hence no inclination to criticize or to tamper with existing institutions and practices.[1]

This corresponds to a *pre-intellectual age*. Stretching from our neolithic ancestors through the evolution of the alphabet and the earliest stirrings of literacy, this pre-intellectual culture is characterized by an absence of critical thinking, an acceptance of the status quo, tribal allegiances, group identity, religious rituals, social stagnation, superstition, and a barter economy.

The Oral and Pictorial Tradition. The pre-intellectual cyclical culture was characterized by the spoken word and the pictograph. Education consisted of the simplest and most fundamental survival skills—hunting, some agriculture, food preparation, safety tips, religious training—and was easily handled with oral instruction. Even cave paintings were rudimentary and uncomplicated—depicting family trees, religious ceremonies, and records of successful hunts. There was little abstract thinking or philosophical musing.

No thought was given to the acquisition of knowledge above and beyond what was needed for social maintenance and survival. This is one reason it took thousands of years for the idea of the alphabet to emerge; it simply was not needed. If necessity is the mother of invention, then lack of need is the barrier to invention.

Intellectual *Linear* Culture

However, random discoveries gradually altered our ways of perceiving the world; agriculture slowly evolved; population pressures demanded different social patterns. And a new historical perspective emerged—one that has been termed a *linear culture*. Society would evolve and grow in a ceaseless linear fashion—always moving ahead, developing new tools and technologies, expanding, finding new horizons, new challenges, new markets.

Four hundred years ago, Francis Bacon encouraged the citizenry to seek knowledge and follow the promise of scientific investigation. The idea of *progress* became an accepted model for civilization. Intellectual research, geographic exploration, colonial expansion, missionary zeal, scientific development, free enterprise economics, and a participatory democracy: these are all features of this linear culture.

This gave rise to the *intellectual age*—originally conceived in Classical Greece and nurtured in the Renaissance, blossoming during the Enlightenment and attaining maturity in the Industrial Age. The intellectual mindset embraces the pursuit of knowledge, analytic means of inquiry, willingness to question the status quo, and interest in all the liberal arts. Humanism and rationalism became significant factors.

The Written Word. The oral tradition was displaced by the written word. And with the revolutionary technology of the alphabet, our social fabric was completely rewoven. The scribe's pen replaced the memory of the village elder; the secular administration of the government supplanted the authority of the church. Marshall McLuhan and Quentin Fiore colorfully sum up the impact of the written word:

The goose quill put an end to talk. It abolished mystery; it gave architecture and towns; it brought roads and armies, bureaucracy. It was the basic metaphor with which the cycle of civilization began, the step from the dark into the light of the mind. The hand that filled the parchment page built a city.[2]

The printing press in the mid-fifteenth century magnified tremendously the power of the written word. The resulting societal upheavals were unparalleled. The widespread printing of books in vernacular languages (French, Italian, Spanish) instead of the classic languages (Hebrew, Greek, Latin) gave rise to a new sense of *national identity* and the eventual creation of new nation-states throughout Europe.

Placing books directly in the hands of individual scholars and researchers fostered the intellectual ideas of *privacy* and *individualism;* it was now possible to read original sources unconstrained and in private. This gave rise to independent thinking, social criticism, the Reformation, and eventually the

Enlightenment.

The printing press was the catalyst that facilitated the linear culture. The stability and authority characteristic of the oral tradition were superseded by the ferment and challenge of the printed word: its encouragement of individualism and elitism, the quest for knowledge, critical thinking, the exchange of ideas, and the spirit of exploration of new worlds—geographically, scientifically, socially, and intellectually.

Post-Intellectual *Web* Culture

We have now, however, evolved into a *post-intellectual era*. The beginnings of post-intellectualism can be seen in the Luddite movement and in the Romanticism of the nineteenth century; many elements were associated with post-industrialism of the early twentieth century; the turning point may well have been the transition from the 1950s to the 1960s.[3]

This third period of cultural orientation is what I would label the *web culture* (see Table 1.1). In this model, we are entangled in a confusing snarl of shifting relationships, ephemeral links, impermanent ties, cyber-networks, social ambiguities, information anarchy, temporary jobs, technological domination, and diffused responsibilities.

Table 1.1
Three Cultural Periods

Cyclical Culture	Linear Culture	Web Culture
Pre-Intellectualism	*Intellectualism*	*Post-Intellectualism*
(The Oral Tradition)	(The Written Word)	(The Electric Media)

We make this connection, then that. We are concerned with this alliance, then that. New patterns are perceived, explored, then abandoned. We are pulled this way, then that way. We are not sure where we should be headed as we explore our web in this direction, then that. We relocate geographically with a rapidity that would have been inconceivable to earlier generations. We co-habit, marry without commitment, then walk out when it gets uncomfortable. We switch careers at the drop of a training program. We capitalize a new venture, declare bankruptcy, then move on.

We have few lasting connections, personal responsibilities, or enduring values. The web culture represents rootlessness, mobility, a sense of impermanence, and a loss of orientation. We are no longer able to move straight ahead in a linear fashion, either economically or geographically.

The Electric Media. The web culture is intensified by what McLuhan labeled "the electric media"—referring ultimately to the telegraph, telephone, movies, audio recordings, radio, television, cable TV, satellites, videocassettes, computers, faxes, cellular phones, e-mail, digital data, fiberoptics, and related computer-based technologies. We are immersed today in a whirling, dazzling, reeling display of colors, images, sounds, impressions, and disconnected data. Spontaneity and intuition have pushed aside contemplation and rational discourse.

The oral culture was a tribal culture. Print, with its individualizing tendencies, served to pull apart the tribal structure. Television, on the other hand, tends to retribalize human connections—with everybody living in the same "global village." According to McLuhan, the speed of the electric media returns us to the nonprint, nonlinear, nonanalytic "all-at-onceness" environment of the oral period.

The clearest manifestation of the electric web culture is the computer network—CompuServe, Prodigy, America Online, and a hundred thousand different databases and bulletin boards. We can continuously roam the cyberspace web of specialized gossip channels, information sources, opinion vehicles, stock market analyses, shopping tips, dating services, entertainment leads, pornography, and so forth.

The Internet is a continually evolving paradigm of the web culture. It encompasses all other communication links; it includes all other databases. The Internet deliberately has no center, no coordinating authority, no administrative structure, no bureaucratic hierarchy. No one is in charge. It is the consummate definition of cyberspace. It is everywhere and nowhere. It exists only as tens of millions of users make temporary connections with anybody and everybody else. It is a nonstructured agglomeration of fleeting contacts. Cliff Stoll, former computer guru turned skeptic, writes that "the Internet has become a wasteland of unfiltered data."[4]

When I use the term *web culture*, however, I am referring not just to the Internet and millions of World Wide Web (WWW) sites. I am referring to the web of all our temporary connections and transient relationships—corporate mergers and splits, temporary employment patterns, shifting government policies, educational reforms, neighborhood transitions, religious upheavals, and nontraditional families. The quivering strands of our jittery web culture provide no firm foundation or secure footing—no sense of values from which we can get our bearings.

The cyclical culture was typified by *one-to-one* interpersonal communication; virtually all discourse was conducted on a face-to-face personal level. The linear culture introduced *one-to-many* communication; mass communication was facilitated with the printing press. With the web culture, we have entered an era of *many-to-many* communication; everyone is trying to communicate with everyone else. We are pulled in numerous directions simultaneously. Our focus is constantly shifting. We are now living in a *Placeless Society*, according to

William Knoke in *Bold New World*. We are entering the Age of *Everything-Everywhere*.[5] Post-intellectual computer-bulletin-board-roaming represents an aimlessness, a lack of direction; it is flipping the pages of an almanac rather than seeking out a coherent linear message.

In a pre-intellectual cyclical culture, we always knew what we were doing (the same things our ancestors had done). In an intellectual linear culture, we always knew where we were headed (straight ahead). In today's post-intellectual web culture, however, we have little idea where we are headed (wandering around in cyberspace, trying to figure out what to do next).

Post-intellectualism has replaced the printed word with pictorial media, has rejected personal responsibility in favor of collective security, and has replaced individual identity with tribal consciousness. It is more concerned with sensitivity and emotional comfort than with scholarly pursuits; it values cooperation rather than competition; it has substituted equality for achievement. We are now a culture that cannot discriminate between trivia and valuable knowledge, that relies more on intuition than on reason, that rewards the specialist and scorns the generalist.

I am not arguing that all intellectual activity is dead—that there are no surviving intellectuals. Obviously, there always have been, and always will be, a number of intellectual minds. What I am arguing is that we cannot today maintain the fiction that we are a society guided by the rational and responsible consensus of its populace. The intellectual democratic dream was that the citizenry (not just a few intellectual elitists) could behave rationally and responsibly; the mass culture could be an intellectual culture. It is the end of that dream that concerns me.

POST-INTELLECTUALISM AND THE PROGRESS PARADOX

Democracy is facing a crisis of confidence. Political columnist Kevin Phillips writes in 1994: "Voters have become convinced in the last four to six years that the American dream is fading. . . . Six or seven Presidents and a dozen Congresses in a row have offered hollow explanations and hollower economic promises. None have reversed the fear of the future that gnaws at American households."[6]

Post-intellectualism is an attitude—not only a loss of open-mindedness and intellectual inquiry, but a loss of hope and faith in the future. During the nineteenth century, America vibrated to the promises of expansion, progress, and new frontiers. Even during the Great Depression of the 1930s and throughout World War II, we were a people who had confidence in the future; we faced tomorrow with a resolve, a sense of vision, and faith in our national destiny and our elected leaders. We knew that better days lay ahead. We still believed in linear growth and progress.

Today, that confidence has dissipated. We fear that our best days and strong leaders are behind us; we no longer believe that a new century will guarantee us a golden destiny. We face budgetary shortfalls at all levels of government. Our cities are decaying. Domestic violence is out of hand. Materialism is letting us down. We increasingly sense that our current problems and tribulations are only going to get worse. Concerned with our postwar apathy and ignorance, William Lederer wrote *A Nation of Sheep* in 1961, in which he metaphorically laments, "The television screens may be bright and our comfortable homes may be warm; but outside it is beginning to grow dark and cold."[7] Richard Goodwin, the principal architect of Lyndon Johnson's Great Society, writes,

The underlying facts are now beyond dispute. In the early 1970s, following a quarter of a century of steady increase, the income of the average American began to decline. And it is still shrinking. At the same time, other conditions that contribute to the quality of life have deteriorated: Public schools are worse than ever; college education is priced out of reach; our streets are streaked with violence, our communities plagued by fear.[8]

Giving us more of a historical perspective, P. A. Sorokin writes in *The Crisis of Our Age* more than fifty years ago:

It is a crisis in . . . art and science, philosophy and religion, law and morals, manners and mores; in the forms of social, political, and economic organization, including the nature of the family and marriage—in brief, it is a crisis involving almost the whole way of life, thought, and conduct of Western society. More precisely, it consists in a disintegration of a fundamental form of Western culture and society dominant for the last four centuries.[9]

Defining the Progress Paradox

This is the paradox of progress: *the more progress we make, technologically and materialistically, the more problems we create.* Ironically, the more we accomplish with instant electronic communications, computer advances, materials development, transportation breakthroughs, genetic engineering, and medical miracles, the more we also witness the escalation of our numerous social problems.

For four centuries, Western civilization has been dedicated to the idea that as we continue to evolve and progress, technologically and materialistically, everyone will eventually benefit. Unfortunately, however, progress has not led to a better life for all. Progress is an intellectual concept; however, the rate of our scientific and materialistic progress is accelerating at such a staggering tempo that our intellectual development has not been able to keep pace with our technical development.

Progress leads to new complexities, more information to comprehend, more options to deal with, confusing relationships, escalating disorder, more rules, multiplying inequities, swelling population pressures, and increased personal dislocation and debilitation. We do not understand the new situation, our new environment, our new responsibilities. As a result, we become more disoriented, more distraught, more alienated, and increasingly disenfranchised from the system.

Virtually all our cultural and social problems are symptoms of the Progress Paradox. They are not superficial issues that can be easily solved by shifting tax burdens or redistributing social benefits and entitlement payments. Rather, they represent a deep misalignment of societal values, directions, and technologies; they epitomize a decline of the intellectual culture that we have been espousing since the Enlightenment. After two hundred years of experience and progress, we sense that the American Dream no longer holds the promise it once did.

The institutions that should nurture our children, inspire our youth, provide security for our elders, enlighten the citizenry, and give purpose and direction to our leaders seem not to be functioning as they should. The system has become intellectually bankrupt. Our commitment to progress and the scientific method, our belief in democracy, our free enterprise economics, our egalitarian legal system, our faith in universal education, and our dedication to personal freedoms—these are all intellectual responsibilities that we have not handled well. The result is our post-intellectual dystopia.

A democratic society cannot persist unless the majority of the people—the masses—can understand and participate in the political, technological, economic, ecological, and intellectual infrastructures that have evolved. If the people do not understand the system and contribute to its functioning, it is inevitable that the system—our fragile shell of civilization—will continue to disintegrate.

Fritjof Capra is a physicist who warns us that we have embraced science and technology too zealously. He begins his thoughtful investigation of our dilemma, *The Turning Point,* with this rather strong analysis:

> At the beginning of the last two decades of our century, we find ourselves in a state of profound, worldwide crisis. It is a complex, multi-dimensional crisis whose facets touch every aspect of our lives—our health and livelihood, the quality of our environment and our social relationships, our economy, technology, and politics. . . . a crisis of a scale and urgency unprecedented in recorded human history.[10]

THE INTELLECTUAL LEGACY OF THE ENLIGHTENMENT

From the period some ten or fifteen thousand years ago when our ancestors began seriously to debate philosophy, religion, ethics, morals, politics, and psychology (although not in a very structured academic format at that time), there undoubtedly was an argument over the basic nature of human beings. One side of the debate—the *authoritarian*—maintains that human beings are essentially weak and irrational, subject to animal drives and instincts, prone to corruption, and incapable of governing themselves. As Ayn Rand has one of her antagonists proclaim in *Atlas Shrugged,* "Men are not open to truth or reason. They cannot be reached by rational argument."[11]

The other side of the debate represents the *libertarian* viewpoint—holding that men and women are inherently honest and just, basically rational, able to control their animal drives, and capable of self-government. This belief is the basis of an intellectual society—maintaining that the citizenry can act collectively with reason and responsibility. Rationality is central to the concept of a free society. Summarizing the position of the eminent German philosopher Jürgen Habermas, Steven Seidman writes that "the defense of reason is inseparable from the project of promoting a democratic social order."[12]

The evolution of post-intellectualism can be traced in the interplay between these antithetical concepts of authoritarianism and libertarianism.

Authoritarian Thinking

Democracy is not the natural order of things. Throughout most of human history, authoritarian philosophy has been the dominant means of organizing human society. From the earliest tribal priests and village chiefs to contemporary autocrats and despots, authoritarian leaders have prevailed.

This philosophy holds that authoritarian structures are needed because the people—if left to their animalistic drives—would not have the intelligence and self-control necessary to run their own affairs. *Humans are not to be trusted to form their own conclusions, to fashion their own opinions.* Critical thinking, alternative lifestyles, and nonconformist social ideas cannot be allowed. Individuality cannot be tolerated in an authoritarian society.

From Plato to Karl Marx and beyond, thoughtful writers and philosophers have maintained that men and women are not trustworthy enough to engage in collective decision-making, to handle the responsibilities of freedom. In the *Republic*, Plato argues that humans, with their irrational drives and appetites, cannot be trusted to govern themselves.

Niccolo Machiavelli gives us a succinct summary of authoritarian political philosophy: "Whoever desires to found a state and give it laws, must start with assuming that all men are bad and ever ready to display their vicious nature, whenever they may find occasion for it."[13] Thomas Hobbes paints an equally pessimistic picture of human nature, arguing that "The condition of man . . . is a condition of war of everyone against everyone."[14]

Marx—in promoting a post-Enlightenment form of socialism—actually was anticipating a post-intellectual reaction to intellectually based capitalistic democracy. *Communism is a post-intellectual concept.*

The Ages of Reason and Enlightenment

Meanwhile, the human spirit yearns to be free. During the fifteenth and sixteenth centuries, a flood of emancipating technologies and discoveries and ideas conspired to undermine the foundations of the existing authoritarian establishment.

Johann Gutenberg's press (mid-1400s) swept the European continent with the printed word, igniting the liberalizing fires of nationalism and independence. Both the modern nation-state and individualism are intellectual inventions.

Scientific revelations, beginning with Copernicus and confirmed by Galileo, increased our knowledge of the universe—undermining the anthropocentric authoritarianism of the church. Explorers, typified by Columbus, confirmed that the world was not flat, that the authorities were wrong, and that new lands lay waiting to be exploited. Mercantilism took root, defining the concept of capitalism, establishing a new middle class, and challenging the privileges of the nobility. The Protestant Reformation, which was spread by the ubiquity of the printing press, freed the individual from the dogmas of the priesthood and unseated the pope as the source of all religious authority.

This surely was a heady period of intellectual turmoil and ferment, of anticipation and excitement. The old order was crumbling. New ways of thinking emerged—new ideas, new philosophies, new scientific horizons, new economic arrangements, new political structures; these were exhilarating times indeed. This was the Age of Intellectualism—of belief in the rational capabilities of the human mind.

Enlightened Thinkers. As one of the earliest thinkers to equate knowledge and scientific inquiry with progress, Bacon in effect defined the intellectual mind. In his *Meditationes Sacrae* (1597), he gave us his famous slogan, "Knowledge is power." He argued that scientific investigation and the pursuit of knowledge could advance human society. His philosophy glorified the modern concepts of progress and power.

Following Bacon by a generation, René Descartes also regarded science as a practical means of gaining mastery over nature for the benefit of society. As the founder of modern philosophical rationalism, Descartes was concerned with the scientific method as a universal approach to all logical investigation. His *Discourse on Method* (1637) was one of the earliest statements on rationalism and intellectual inquiry (*cogito, ergo sum*—"I think, therefore I am").

John Milton's *Areopagitica* (1644) is a classic essay on the nature of truth. In it, he enunciated three basic arguments against licensing or censorship: (1) licensing was the evil offspring of a repressive church (much of Milton's life was spent fighting the church); (2) licensing was impractical (there simply were not enough good moral censors to be found); and (3) licensing frustrates the search for truth. This was the clarion intellectual argument that would echo through the centuries: *let all voices be heard, let them clamor for our investigation, let all opinions clash, and ultimately truth will triumph over falsehood.* "And though all the winds of doctrine were let loose to play upon the earth, so Truth be in the field, we do injuriously, by licensing and prohibiting, to misdoubt her strength. Let her and Falsehood grapple; who ever knew Truth put to the worse, in a free and open encounter?"[15]

This thinking formed the cornerstone for the Enlightenment. Let us be free to reason for ourselves, to investigate and seek new information, to search for truth; let us be free to challenge the establishment. With such intellectual freedom we will be able to govern our own affairs, make our own decisions—and thus maintain our independence.

If one date were to be selected as the beginning of the Enlightenment, a strong nomination would be 1687, the year that Isaac Newton published his *Philosophiae naturalis principia mathematica* (mathematical principles of natural philosophy). This monumental tome—summarizing Newton's pioneering work in calculus, gravitation, and optics—conceptualized and organized all the laws of the physical universe. It was a landmark that dominated intellectual and scientific thinking for more than two centuries. Not only was Newton's genius testimony to the rationality of the *Homo sapiens* mind (his cerebral reach demonstrated the heights to which the human intellect could soar), but the *Principia* itself was hailed as confirmation that truth could be ascertained by rational means—as long as humans are free to debate, to experiment, to search uncensored.

What Newton was to the scientific world, John Locke was to political philosophy. Locke agreed with Hobbes that the state was a necessary creation, but he disagreed as to its nature—due to his belief that men and women are rational and have enough common sense to work together for their own mutual good. This viewpoint is woven throughout many of Locke's writings—most notably in his *Second Treatise on Civil Government* (1690).

In reviewing Locke's intellectual contributions to libertarianism, three elemental principles are evident. First, although human beings may be self-centered, they are essentially rational and just. This is the foundation of the entire libertarian movement, the fundamental basis of the Enlightenment, the third point that Milton voiced in the *Areopagitica*. If men and women are allowed to freely argue, investigate, challenge authority, and engage in open discourse, reason guarantees that truth will eventually emerge. Jean Jacques Rousseau in *The Social Contract* agrees: "When the voice of duty takes the place of physical impulses and right of appetite . . . [the individual] is forced to act on different principles, and to consult his reason before listening to his inclinations."[16]

Second, Locke argued that human beings are endowed with basic natural rights. In a natural (that is, ungoverned) state, their inalienable rights include life, freedom, the right to hold property, and the right to express themselves uncensored. This sentiment is found repeated, in altered form, in both the American *Declaration of Independence* and the French *Declaration of the Rights of Man and of the Citizen*.

Third, government exists only at the pleasure of the people who create it. People come together freely to establish a state in order to accomplish certain civic works that cannot be achieved individually—building roads, maintaining a school system, establishing a militia, setting up a mosquito abatement program. Moreover, the state has no right to impose any obligations on the people other than what the people ask the state to do. This anti-authoritarian tenet of Locke's is the cornerstone of every free democratic system of government.

Turning to libertarian economics, it was Adam Smith who defined modern capitalism. His landmark work, *An Inquiry into the Nature and Causes of the Wealth of Nations* (1776), has long been the classic inspiration for all free enterprise theorists. Keep the government out of the marketplace, he argued. Allow the laws of supply and demand to guide our economic destiny. Let every individual work to better his or her own condition and strive to gain the highest amount of profit; society will be well served by such open competition. This economic theory has become a basic cornerstone of libertarian thinking—one of the signposts of an intellectual society based upon reasoned and responsible competition.

These key voices of libertarianism—among numerous other philosophers, scientists, artists, political theorists, economists, and assorted writers—provide the underpinnings for the intellectual culture that we have been trying to hold together for the past two centuries. These were the bold voices that sparked the Enlightenment, created individualism, defined humanism, established modern science, sanctified open economic competition, glorified the acquisition of knowledge, stimulated progress and social change, furthered a print-oriented critical attitude, promoted individual responsibility, and instituted modern democracy.

THE FAILED INTELLECTUAL PROMISE

These two qualities, then, are the hallmarks of an intellectual culture—reason and *responsibility*. An intellectual society is one in which the populace can rationally analyze any given societal issue or dilemma and then act responsibly in the long-term best interests of the society. However, if the people as a whole cannot think through a problem with reason and act with responsibility, they have lost any intellectual pretensions.

Today our cultural and political affairs are dominated, not by the voices of the Enlightenment, but by voices that represent a post-intellectual mindset—those who renounce intellectual responsibility in favor of collective security, those who ignore the long-term needs of the community in order to reap immediate profits, those who disregard the welfare of the greater society in order to maximize benefits for their particular tribal constituencies, those who worship data but cannot find knowledge, those who embrace the idea of technology but have lost a personal analytic perspective.

One underlying trait of intellectualism was the belief of the idealistic minds of the Enlightenment that the benefits and freedoms available to the elites should be enjoyed by all the populace. The irony of intellectualism is that the elites wanted the proletariat to share the opportunities valued by the elites. The thinkers and artists and scientists wanted to open the doors to thinking and art and science to everyone on an equal basis. Christopher Lasch sums up this intellectual potential: "Once the masses enjoyed leisure, affluence, and education, they would become discriminating consumers of art, letters, and ideas."[17]

But the masses failed to respond to the challenge. They did not accept the invitation to join in a collective intellectual culture. They do not excel in academic matters, they do not think scientifically, they do not appreciate fine art, they do not react intelligently to advertising messages, they do not vote or otherwise meet their obligations to participate in a self-governing democracy. And to a distressing degree, they do not want to accept the responsibility for their own lives: *my lack of success is somebody else's fault; society owes me a living; my welfare checks aren't big enough.* In short, the citizenry has not accepted the responsibilities of the Intellectual Age. The apathy and intellectual shortcomings of today's populace would seem to affirm the position of the authoritarian philosophers: humans may not be capable of governing themselves—especially in today's complex society.

Distended-Intellectualism and Counter-Intellectualism

Post-intellectualism actually consists of two separate and generally distinct phenomena. On the one hand, we have what might be termed a protracted, unchecked *distended-intellectualism*—the irresponsible, unbridled, linear extension of intellectual endeavors without consideration of ultimate consequences. Progress without restraint. Exploitation without moderation. Freedom without responsibility.

Many examples of unplanned distended-intellectualism are evident in society today: the information overload, technological determinism, numerous forms of economic manipulation, occupational specialization, bureaucracy and institutionalism, personal isolation, mediated reality, rampant urbanization, environmental exploitation, moral deterioration, and political anarchy. These are all unintended consequences of unconstrained extensions of intellectual ideas without responsible rational control. This is distended-intellectualism. This is the Progress Paradox.

A second aspect of post-intellectualism is the deliberate reversal of intellectual directions. This is *counter-intellectualism.* Often this is an intentional reaction to out-of-control distended-intellectualism. Such a mindset has dominated much of our cultural development from nineteenth-century Romanticism to the *love-in* generation of the 1960s. Some examples of counter-intellectual reaction to the excesses of intellectual progress include New Age mysticism and astrology (reacting to unbridled science and technology), ecological awareness (in reaction to economic exploitation), reliance on pictorial media (as a substitute for the printed word), a "new morality" (replacing traditional standards of cultural behavior), retribalization (rejecting the intellectual nation-state), a loss of privacy and individualism (as we de-emphasize individual responsibility), sensitivity and affirmative action (in response to individual competition and manipulation), and socialism (reacting to capitalistic excesses).

Life is a tour, a visit to a continually evolving new land. We are always encountering new sights, strange environments, novel experiences. The pre-intellectual tribal tourist goes through life on a tour bus—being herded about by a tour guide who selects the destinations and vista points, dictating where everyone will sleep and eat. The intellectual traveler, on the other hand, does his or her own planning—selecting objectives, mapping out a route, deciding what to experience, creating an individual itinerary, and moving about independently. And the post-intellectual tourist wanders about the evolving web landscape aimlessly—looking at whatever is of momentary interest, buying souvenirs and trinkets, having little idea of what tomorrow will bring. In today's muddled terrain, the *counter-intellectual* wayfarer wants to get back on the tour bus; and the *distended-intellectual* tourist seeks out a place of refuge, a museum or temple or specific dogma to explore in depth, experiencing little of the larger picture.

The Basic Syllogism

Every society—tribal or modern, authoritarian or libertarian—must create an institutional framework of some sort. It will have to establish procedures and bureaucracies for *governance* (political structures, national defense, municipal services), *justice and law enforcement* (police, judicial system), *economics and business* (agricultural agreements, trade arrangements, monetary and banking systems), *social services* (how to take care of the ill, the elderly, impoverished and handicapped), and for *education* (both formal schooling and general information for the populace).

Such an institutional infrastructure can be established along either non-intellectual or intellectual lines. In the non-intellectual framework—a tribal or authoritarian culture—we turn to dictatorship (for governance), a police state (for law enforcement), socialism (for an economic system), welfare practices (for social services), and a rigid schooling system (for education) based on propaganda and indoctrination. The authorities are in charge; the common people do not have to worry about making decisions or maintaining the institutional integrity of the system.

In an intellectual framework, however—a libertarian concept—we turn to democratic ideals (for governance), protection of civil rights (for justice), capitalism (for an economic system), private insurance plans (for social protections), and a liberal arts philosophy (for education). The people are in charge; the citizens have to act with reason and responsibility.

Specifically, the institutions in an intellectual culture are set up with two essential criteria in mind. First, the citizens must work for the *greater common good*—for society as a whole, for the concept of a social contract that commits them to a social grouping larger than their village. They are part of a city, rather than a community; part of a nation, rather than a tribe. This is an intellectual concept.

Second, citizens in an intellectual state must be dedicated to the *long-term good* of their culture—to the next fifty years, not to the next profit-and-loss sheet or the next election. Short-term, immediate gratification will not sustain an intellectual society. This consideration of the long-term benefit of society is part of the intellectual mindset. It is when we fail in our commitment to the larger social construct and to the long-term welfare of society that we fail in our intellectual endeavor.

Therefore, the thesis for this book could be summed up in one syllogism:

Major Premise: *Democracy is an intellectual idea.* Our entire cultural infrastructure is founded on the intellectual premise that human beings are rational and responsible enough to handle participatory self-government; they can join in a social contract to work for the greater good of society and for the long-range good of future generations. All the underlying foundations of our democratic culture are intellectual ideas—the concept of freedom of speech, egalitarian guarantee of civil rights, commitment to science and technology, free enterprise, universal education, and equal justice under the law.

Minor Premise: *America has now entered into a post-intellectual era.* Despite two hundred years of democratic effort, we have moved further and further from our intellectual roots. Without realizing it, we have evolved beyond a state of intellectual competence. We are emerging into a post-intellectual state that still pays lip service to an intellectual ideology, but in fact is no longer able to sustain the values and attitudes of an intellectual mindset.

Conclusion: *Therefore, democracy in America is not working.* We are not maintaining our intellectual infrastructure. All the problems we discuss throughout the book result from our intellectual backsliding. Put in its simplest terms: the ideal of democracy was based on reason and responsibility; as we individuals continue to act without reason and responsibility, we will find ourselves no longer able to maintain the ideal of democracy.

Much of our cultural gloom reflects the darkening of the American spirit—a state of societal disorientation and political debilitation that permeates most of our contemporary civilization. We find ourselves today discarding the intellectual ideals of the Age of Reason as we become increasingly entwined in the tangled strands of a post-intellectual web culture.

NOTES

1. Stavrianos, 1982, p. 9.

2. McLuhan and Fiore, 1967, p. 48.

3. For a thorough history of the Luddite movement with an insightful and detailed examination of neo-Luddite activities, see Sale, 1995.

4. Clifford Stoll, "The Internet? Bah!" *Newsweek,* 27 February 1995, p. 41.

5. See Knoke, 1996.

6. Kevin Phillips, "The Angry Majority," *Los Angeles Times,* 16 October 1994, p. M1.

7. Lederer, 1961, p. 192.

8. Richard N. Goodwin, "Economic Justice Dies a Slow Death," *Los Angeles Times,* 18 October 1995, p. B13.

9. Sorokin, 1941, p. 17.

10. Capra, 1982, p. 21.

11. Rand [1957], 1985, p. 183.

12. Habermas, 1989, p. 1.

13. Niccolo Machiavelli, *Discourse upon the First Ten Books of Livy,* 1513, book 1, ch. 3.

14. Thomas Hobbes, *Leviathan,* 1651, pt. 1, ch. 4.

15. Milton [1644], 1952, p. 409.

16. Rousseau [1762] book 1, ch. 8, 1952, p. 393.

17. Lasch, 1991, p. 346.

2

Emergence of Post-Intellectualism

We're biased against brains. For a variety of convoluted reasons, this nation is anti-intellectual to the core, and every kid we tell to stay in school knows it.

• Joe Robinson
Los Angeles Daily News

How did we arrive at this post-intellectual state? This is the irony of intellectualism: the adoption of intellectual ideals—such as egalitarianism, universal education, scientific progress, capitalism, and democracy—involves a commitment to embrace the non-intellectual populace. If we succeed in our intellectual idealism, we will actively include all the citizenry in running the affairs of culture. But this inevitably then results in a decline in the average ability, motivation, and intelligence of those participating in the culture.

As Matthew Arnold forewarned us 135 years ago, "The difficulty for a democracy is, how to find and keep high ideals. The individuals who compose it are, the bulk of them, persons who need to follow an ideal, not to set one."[1] Once the masses are involved in the operation of the system, the cultural level of the system declines. Institutions falter, problems proliferate, and a post-intellectual state emerges. Indeed, it may well be that the very concept of democracy is an oxymoron.

DEFINITIONS OF POST-INTELLECTUALISM

To understand the idea of post-intellectualism, it may be helpful to define *intellectual*. I introduced the concept of intellectualism in Chapter 1 in terms of *reason* and *responsibility*. To be more specific, there are four related interpretations gleaned from dictionary definitions and literary usage. One dictionary stresses "the capacity for knowledge"—simply the search for truth and the *acquisition of knowledge*. Another dictionary denotation involves "the ability to reason or understand," that is, critical thinking or *problem-solving*.

Third is a familiar connotation that has been in general usage for several decades—*social criticism*. Richard Hofstadter writes, "The meaning of [the] intellectual life lies not in the possession of truth but in the quest for new uncertainties."[2] Such a quest surely challenges the status quo. The search for truth is the antithesis of the authoritarian assertion that truth is revealed only to the authorities.

A final dictionary definition stresses breadth of interest: "given to pursuits that exercise the intellect"—a continuing study of philosophy, history, science, art, literature, and the *liberal arts*. This implies the mindset of the generalist rather than that of the specialist or narrowly focused professional.

My definition of post-intellectualism, therefore, consists of four attributes that are opposite of the above definitions: (1) a *decrease of effectual personal knowledge* (despite a proliferation of information); (2) a *decline of analytic thinking* (or problem-solving skills); (3) a *reluctance to challenge the status quo* (due to our growing inability to determine exactly what the status quo is); and (4) *specialization* (loss of a broad perspective). These four attributes (summarized in Table 2.1) are examined in depth in Chapter 3.

Table 2.1
Definitions of Intellectualism and Post-Intellectualism

INTELLECTUALISM	POST-INTELLECTUALISM
1. Search for Knowledge	1. Ignorance (loss of effectual personal knowledge)
2. Critical Thinking	2. Dumbth (a decline of analytic thinking)*
3. Social Criticism	3. Establishmentism (reluctance to challenge the status quo)
4. Broad Liberal Arts	4. Specialization (loss of a liberal arts orientation)

* The term "dumbth" was coined by Steve Allen in his book of that name (1989).

Evolution of a Post-Intellectual Mindset

The American democratic experiment was initiated as the ultimate test of the intellectual theories of the European Enlightenment. America's founding fathers were writers, philosophers, lawyers, scientists, men of broad perspective, schooled in classical learning—who used their education in history, politics, and literature to establish a fresh and intellectual basis for self-government. Neil Postman writes sardonically, "America was founded by intellectuals, from which it has taken us two centuries and a communications revolution to recover."[3] The "recovery," of course, is the transition to a post-intellectual environment.

The onset of post-intellectualism is not an easily discernible event. It has no clear starting point, no underlined date on anyone's calendar. There is no anniversary to celebrate. Post-intellectualism has sneaked up on us over the better part of two centuries.

Post-intellectualism resulted from the dilution of universal education in the 1870s; it contributed to the labor movement of the 1880s. It inspired the Bolshevik revolution. The pictorial content of movies and television added to the gradual intrusion of a nonverbal, post-intellectual mindset in the twentieth century. Following World War I, liberals and other intellectuals became increasingly disenchanted with the prospects for effecting positive social change—disillusioned by wartime censorship, Prohibition, and reactions to the postwar communist scare. Confidence in rationality declined; misology—the distrust of reason—escalated. Post-intellectualism was on the rise.

In the arts-and-scholarship battlefield, post-intellectualism is represented by some post-modernists and deconstructionists who argue that our intellectual self-evident truths are but traditional cultural biases that perpetuate self-serving social, racial, and gender interests. *All communication and literature mask an underlying cultural elitism. We cannot rely on reason to overcome our inherent biases and prejudices.* This is a post-intellectual perspective. The intellectual ideal, on the other hand, is typified by Jürgen Habermas whose Enlightenment-inspired faith in reason and open communication has led to his theory of "communicative action," which argues that "we can reason out solutions to our problems, that just institutions can lead to a fairer society."[4]

The passage from the 1950s to the 1960s was probably the period when post-intellectualism emerged full-blown. This two-decade transition represents a convergence of the information overload, technological determinism, the pictorial domination of television, the communist cold-war challenge to the intellectual concept of capitalism, an intensification of urban disintegration, an awareness of serious environmental degradation, and the incipient movement toward affirmative action and political correctness in dealing with racial inequities, feminist issues, and gay rights.

We entered into the Dwight Eisenhower 1950s with confidence in America's vision and sense of linear progress. We exited the 1960s with an embattled Lyndon Johnson and soon-to-be disgraced Richard Nixon; we were disillusioned and confused, never again to return to the clarity of purpose and intellectual leadership that characterized our idealistic first two centuries as a nation. The web culture had replaced the linear culture.

Positive Values of Post-Intellectualism

In developing my thesis, I am not arguing that a pure intellectual society based exclusively upon rationality, competition, skepticism, and exploitation is necessarily the best way to go. We tried that, and it is not working. Indeed, it is the pursuit of intellectual goals—capitalism, urbanization, universal education, scientific research, growth and progress—that has led to much of our cultural turmoil. It is when these goals are pursued without restraint that we wind up with the negative consequences of distended-intellectualism. We have not shown ourselves to be far-sighted enough to handle the responsibilities of an intellectual society.

Conversely, not all aspects of post-intellectualism are necessarily negative. Many non-intellectual characteristics represent positive values—personal sensitivity, cooperation, charity, civil rights legislation, religious faith, respect for tradition, appreciation of a glorious sunset. Popular novelist Dean R. Koontz phrased it well: "Some people think only intellect counts: knowing how to solve problems, knowing how to get by, knowing how to identify an advantage and seize it. But the many functions of intellect are insufficient without courage, love, friendship, compassion and empathy."[5] There are numerous positive attributes of a post-intellectual culture—especially counter-intellectual precepts—that should be embraced and encouraged. Some of these we will explore in Part 5.

SUMMARY CHARACTERISTICS OF POST-INTELLECTUALISM

In order to understand the scope and implications of post-intellectualism, it may be helpful to summarize briefly some post-intellectual characteristics in several different fields of human activity—many of which will be discussed in the chapters to follow. Table 2.2 outlines some of the attributes of pre-intellectualism, intellectualism, and post-intellectualism.

Technology and Progress

In his book *Technopoly*, Postman identifies three distinct technological cultures: the *Tool-using culture*, the *Technocracy*, and the *Technopoly*. In the tool-using culture—pre-intellectual society—people used basic tools (weapons, cooking utensils, simple machines) to solve problems of their daily existence and further the direction of their particular culture. The tools did not intrude on the shape and function of their society.

Starting roughly in the sixteenth century, European societies moved into a technocratic stage and began to use tools to define and shape their cultures. Francis Bacon gave us the idea that knowledge is power, progress is good, and science is to be used to improve society. Technology equals progress. This cornerstone of intellectualism led to the concept of *technocracy,* which has dominated Western culture for the past four centuries.

Table 2.2
Comparison of Three Intellectual Periods

PRE-INTELLECTUALISM	INTELLECTUALISM	POST-INTELLECTUALISM

Technology and Progress

| Tool-using culture | Technocracy | Technopoly |
| Social stability | Progress | Social chaos |

Media and Communication

| Oral tradition | Written word | Electric media |
| Ethos/charisma | Rational appeals | Emotional appeals |

Art and Education

Folk art	Fine art	Popular art
Crafts	Elitism	Universal education
Vocational	Liberal arts	Specialization
Practical	Scholarly	Social relevance
Collective wisdom	Individual truth	Information anarchy

Science and Religion

Astrology	Scientific method	New Age mysticism
Tradition	Analytic thinking	Intuition
Religious faith	Humanism	Revivalism

Economics and Law

Feudal economy	Capitalism	Socialism
Communal	Free enterprise	Exploitation
Cooperation	Competition	Affirmative Action

Politics and Governance

Tribal	Nation-state	Regional alliances
Authoritarianism	Libertarianism	Social Responsibility
Dictatorship	Democracy	Communism
Aristocracy	Meritocracy	Mediocracy
Group security	Self-reliance	Victimization

Society and Culture

Cyclical	Linear	Web culture
Yin (feminine)	Yang (masculine)	Yin/yang balance
Group identity	Individualism	Ethnic retribalization
Ideational	Sensate	Idealistic
Gemeinschaft	Gesellschaft	?

As we move into a *technopoly,* however, we enter a post-intellectual stage—a culture where the technologies have determined their own place in society and define their own roles. Postman defines technopoly or "totalitarian technology" as "the submission of all forms of cultural life to the sovereignty of technique and technology."[6] Jerry Mander refers to the same concept as *Megatechnology* in which computers, television, satellites, corporations and banks, space technology, genetics, nanotechnology, and robotics intersect and merge with one another so that "they are forming something new, almost as if they were living cells; they are becoming a single technical-economic web encircling the planet."[7]

Just as the automobile, television, the split atom, the satellite, and the computer shaped the twentieth century, so will the information superhighway, genetic engineering, alternate energy sources, virtual reality, superconductivity, and other unforeseen technologies dictate the direction of the twenty-first century. This distended-intellectual phenomenon—technopoly, megatechnology, or *technological determinism*—is a key underlying consideration throughout the book.

Media and Communication

The three broad periods of communication technology—the *Oral Tradition,* the *Written Word,* and the *Electric Media*— reflect our intellectual journey. Oral communication predated our ability to think symbolically and abstractly. Human intellect was greatly handicapped by the absence of printed symbols. The pre-literate Oral Tradition was pre-intellectual.

It was not until the age of the Written Word—with the innovation of the alphabet, and especially the invention of the printing press—that the concept of intellectual inquiry was spread throughout the Western World. Postman explains, "To engage the written word means to follow a line of thought, which requires considerable powers of classifying, inference-making and reasoning. . . . In a culture dominated by print, public discourse tends to be characterized by a coherent, orderly arrangement of facts and ideas."[8] This is the essence of our definition of intellectualism.

The third period of communication technology is the Electric Media. Walter Ong, Harold Innis, Marshall McLuhan, and others point out that with the movies, radio, and television, we evolved from an analytic, inquiring, intellectual means of discourse into a sophisticated form of oral/pictorial exchange. This is post-intellectual communication—a noncognitive manipulation of images and passions, motion and sensations, entertainment and fantasy. It is a non-literate, post-intellectual means of connecting with others—substituting feelings and emotion for analysis and critical thinking.

The written word represented an intellectual *cognitive* society—with an emphasis on analysis and sequential processing of information. The electric media have transported us into a post-intellectual *affective* culture—with an immersion in interactive, multimedia, sensory experiences.

Art and Education

Created originally either for functional purposes (furniture, pottery, quilts) or ceremonial purposes (religious chants and dances), *folk art* is basically a pre-intellectual form of expression. It does not involve analytic or critical intellectual processes. Nor does it recognize the personal achievement of individual artists—an elitist concept that arises with fine art.

Fine art has always been associated with intellectual criticism, analysis, and elitism. In fact, the concept of elitism—the belief that some persons can aspire to greater heights and achieve more significant goals than others—is an integral theme of intellectualism. In the world of fine art, only a limited number of artists, musicians, poets, and dramatists can be recognized as contributors to the body of accepted art. And only a relatively small number of intellectuals and elitists can truly appreciate great works of art. A taste for high culture is acquired only through years of study and intellectual effort.

Popular art, on the other hand, is a completely different entity—a post-intellectual phenomenon. It is designed to be consumed by the masses, not appreciated by the elites. Its only criterion is popularity. The success of post-intellectual pop art is measured by the cash register, the box office, and ratings services. The appeal to an intellectual elite is considered a snobbish remnant of an increasingly irrelevant culture. More than a century ago, America's acclaimed "poet of the people," Walt Whitman, penned a stirring appeal in defense of such a post-intellectual, popular, democratic art that would break with the aristocratic standards of elitist cultures:

I should demand a program of culture, drawn out, not for a single class alone, or for the parlors or lecture rooms, but with an eye to the practical life, the west, the workingman, the facts of farms and jack-planes and engineers. . . . I should demand of this program or theory a scope generous enough to include the widest human area . . . and not restricted by conditions ineligible to the masses. The best culture will always be . . . aiming to form, over this continent, an ideocracy of universalism.[9]

Formal Schooling. Pre-intellectual education was confined largely to vocational instruction, crafts, and survival skills—whether in agriculture, pottery making, weapons fabrication, the healing arts, or even training for the priesthood. Apprenticeships were more common than formal education.

As Europe moved out of the Dark Ages, intellectual education was marked by the classical liberal arts curriculum of the *trivium* (grammar, rhetoric, and logic) and the *quadrivium* (music, arithmetic, geometry, and astronomy). Education up through the Reformation could be identified as an elitist intellectual pursuit, reserved almost exclusively for a chosen handful of scholars.

John Amos Comenius in the seventeenth century issued the first calls for a universal education for all children—girls and boys, poor and rich, rural and urban. These politically correct reforms are the earliest seeds of a post-intellectual culture. Comenius believed that education should emphasize pragmatic knowledge, not just the classics and intellectual matters. He compiled *The World in Pictures* (1659), which attempted to present in pictorial form all the practical activities of life. His attempts foreshadowed our modern concerns with picturization and contemporary "dumbed-down" textbooks fluffed out with handsome graphics and attractive illustrations.

It was in the United States in the nineteenth century that universal education became a reality. By 1870, the pressures on American high schools to accommodate increasing numbers of students led to the decline of classical education and an expanded emphasis on practical and vocational education. The post-intellectual mindset prevailed. According to Frances FitzGerald in *America Revised,*

Administrators and teachers put increasing faith in the notion that vocational training was the democratic alternative to the academic elitism of the European secondary schools. . . . The ideology of the teachers, however, merely reflected the fact that the community at large had no interest in providing intellectual training for the mass of high-school students; its concern was to train skilled workers for industry.[10]

This post-intellectual emphasis on practical and vocational curricula can be seen today in the pervasive cries for educational reform that will meet the need "to regain an economic advantage," "to train tomorrow's workers," "to better compete with Europe and Asia." This is the *distended-intellectual* aspect of post-intellectual education—*schools exist primarily as a training center for the corporate establishment and for economic competition.* We have forsaken the liberal arts in favor of vocational education; we have abandoned the generalist and embraced the specialist.

Another aspect of post-intellectual education is the *counter-intellectual* trend toward "progressive" education centering on the child's ability to feel positive about him- or herself—"feel-good" education aimed at promoting self-esteem, self-discovery, and self-acceptance. *Social relevance* and *political correctness* both have evolved from this concern with equitable treatment of all individuals. It may well be, in this day of cultural turmoil and ethnic inequities, that such an emphasis on self-esteem is indeed a needed function of schooling. However, it is not an *intellectual* function. (As stated earlier, not all post-intellectual trends are to be interpreted as negative developments.)

Joe Robinson adds another dimension to our understanding of the anti-intellectual bias that percolates throughout our educational system:

We're biased against brains. For a variety of convoluted reasons, this nation is anti-intellectual to the core, and every kid we tell to stay in school knows it. . . . We're men and women of action—not talk. Just do it. We're not class snobs like the Europeans. Our stoic Protestant roots and pursuit of classlessness, with a big assist from modern media, have produced a national ideal that celebrates not an intelligent citizenry, but one where educated people have to pretend they're not.[11]

Students today are encouraged to appear average—not stand out intellectually. In matters of higher education, the situation is no better. Concerned as they are with obtaining tenure, securing research grants from the establishment, and defending their particular specialized academic turf, faculty members today seldom dare to venture very far into the quagmire of idea mongering. Those who dare to raise questions and challenge the orthodox or to expand their inquiry beyond their narrowly prescribed academic specialty do not get very far in our contemporary post-intellectual educational milieu. The academy today is the center of the government and defense research industry. The intellectual search for universal knowledge has been superseded by the post-intellectual, commercial search for corporate largess.

Science and Religion

Early pre-intellectual "science" consisted largely of superstition and astrology. Decisions were generally based on tradition. There was little effort to discover truth or to challenge established thinking. With Bacon, Galileo, and Descartes, however, there evolved a commitment to the scientific method. Critical thinking and reason were the hallmarks of the intellectual; empirical evidence and experimentation became the tools of the period.

As we move into the post-intellectual mindset, we witness a return to the supernatural and mysticism of the pre-intellectual period. New Age philosophies, pyramid power, channeling, magic crystals, and psychic readings replace scientific thinking. Astrology and the occult are revived. Intuition replaces analysis and reasoning. In school districts across the country, vocal citizens' groups insist on incorporating Creationism into the curriculum on a par with scientific theories.

In a recent survey of two thousand adults, only 6 percent qualified as "scientifically literate."[12] A 1990 Gallup survey confirmed our non-scientific state of mind: about half of all Americans polled believe in UFOs, extrasensory perception, and psychic healing; while more than a quarter believes in ghosts, astrology, and haunted houses.[13] And a 1995 survey by the International Center for the Advancement of Scientific Literacy revealed that less than half of American adults understand that the earth orbits the sun yearly, that electrons are smaller than atoms, or that dinosaurs were extinct before humans appeared.[14]

Evolution of the Church. In virtually every pre-literate (oral tradition) society, mysticism/religion was based on an unquestioning belief in a system of gods that ruled all aspects of human activity. Such beliefs eventually evolved into a monotheistic, but still pre-intellectual, unchallenged faith in the God of Moses, Buddha, Christ, and Muhammad.

The first significant intellectual challenge to established religious authority came from the printing press—Martin Luther's ninety-five theses, posted in 1517. The ensuing intellectual ferment resulted, not only in the Protestant Reformation, but also in various humanistic alternatives to established religion. The first four presidents of the United States were deists, and Thomas Jefferson even wrote a deistic translation of the New Testament in which all references to miracles are deleted and Jesus of Nazareth is portrayed essentially as an inspiring teacher and leader—not as the divine Son of God. Humanism, deism, and various liberal Protestant sects are all manifestations of an intellectual period in religious thinking.

The clearest post-intellectual movement is the growth of evangelistic and charismatic religions. Membership in the three largest Pentecostal churches—Assemblies of God, Church of God (Cleveland, Tennessee), and the United Pentecostal Church International—more than doubled in the twenty-year period from 1970 to 1990. Authoritarian denominations such as the Roman Catholics, Southern Baptists, and Latter-day Saints have also had increases; whereas membership in the mainline Protestant denominations has been falling over the same period. These trends reflect a post-intellectual, nonanalytic, noncognitive approach to religion.[15]

Conservative, fundamentalist religious zealots (whether Christian, Jewish, Muslim, Buddhist, or Hindu)—just like New Age mystics—are all searching for some post-intellectual meaning, some direction, now that the promise of intellectual humanism and rationalism has failed to sustain our culture.

Economics and Law

Pre-intellectual economic affairs consisted largely of bartering and trading. Capitalism, as defined by Adam Smith, is essentially an intellectual concept. The ideas of competition, profit, individualism, and elitist success are all intellectual precepts—what Max Weber calls "the modern rational organisation of capitalistic enterprise."[16]   Today, however, we have evolved into a post-intellectual period of materialism and economic exploitation that supersedes a rational and responsible free market system.

Classic capitalism assumed a degree of honesty and rationality by the purveyors and advertisers of goods, and it also assumed an equally intellectual sense of reason and discrimination on the part of the buyer. Up until the end of the nineteenth century, advertising was still considered an informational and rational process. But, according to Postman, "By the turn of the century, advertisers no longer assumed rationality on the part of their potential customers. Advertising became one part depth psychology, one part aesthetic theory."[17] This has resulted in a post-intellectual system of commercialism based, not on the value of goods and services, but on perceptions and images that can most effectively be pushed into consumers' consciousness and subconsciousness.

Retailing operations reflect post-intellectual trends. The impersonal, credit-card, assembly-line retail establishments, typified by giant supermarkets and warehouse membership outlets, represent *distended-intellectualism*—an institutionalized technological marketing enterprise. However, we can also see a *counter-intellectual* reaction to such massive merchandising endeavors—the swap meets, arts-and-crafts fairs, yard sales, and farmers' markets that recall a more personal and informal retail environment.

Employment patterns also typify our transformation into a post-intellectual culture. The security of an intellectual contractual arrangement between employer and employee has been obliterated by corporate downsizing and lay-offs. Today's job scene is characterized by outsourcing, free-lancing, "temp" agencies, and outside contracts—all manifestations of the transient relationships and temporary connections of the web culture.

Equality and Affirmative Action. Matters of justice and legal equity pose an interesting dilemma. The assumption of equality under the law—egalitarianism—is essentially an intellectual concept; *all persons should be considered equal and should be treated the same.* But individualism and competition are also intellectual concepts; *all persons should be allowed to compete freely and rise as far as their talents and abilities will carry them.* Some individuals are better equipped to succeed than others (that is, they have more intelligence, perseverance, talent, strength, or resources) and should be allowed to reach their full potential. If we allow unchecked elitist competition to flourish, however, other persons will be hurt—due to socioeconomic deprivation, lower intelligence, physical handicaps, racial prejudice, gender discrimination, lack of academic motivation, inadequate financial resources, or other factors.

In his 1939 work, *Knowledge for What?* Robert Lynd questioned the intellectual assumptions of libertarianism and capitalism. Christopher Lasch sums up one of Lynd's main points:

But most Americans still clung to the political culture of individualism. . . . They refused to admit that individuals varied in their capacities and that many of them inevitably lost out in the "individual scramble for wealth." Egalitarian dogma thus led in practice to radically inegalitarian results. Only the state could correct the inequalities generated by competitive capitalism and protect the weak against the strong.[18]

Therefore, we pass civil rights laws and establish affirmative action quotas to guarantee some degree of equal treatment. We embrace politically correct policies on school enrollment ratios, ethnic studies, sexual harassment abuses, and cultural diversity. In so doing, however, we undermine the intellectual concepts of individualism, self-determination, open competition, freedom of assembly and association, and even freedom of speech. In a 1992 article, noted black author Shelby Steele points out the irony of trying to legislate equality:

The black power movement . . . rejoined race and power—the very "marriage" that civil rights legislation had been designed to break up. . . . When you demand power based on the color of your skin, aren't you saying that equality and justice are impossible? Somebody's going to be in, somebody's going to be out. Somebody's going to win, somebody's going to lose, and race is once again a source of advantage for some and disadvantage for others.[19]

By initiating affirmative action to defend the rights of suppressed groups—racial minorities, females, AIDS victims, the religiously persecuted, Vietnam veterans, homosexuals, the physically handicapped, or any group that claims (whether justified or not) to be a victim of an oppressive society—we are implementing a post-intellectual remedy. *Political correctness is actually counter-intellectual sensitivity.*

Actually, in an ideal intellectual culture, there would be no need for any politically correct remedial legislation or judicial action because the populace—exercising reason and responsibility—would not engage in any discriminatory practices based on race, gender, or other irrelevant characteristics. The need for affirmative action quotas and regulations is evidence of the failure of intellectualism.

Politics and Governance

Several intellectual concepts, when implemented, have resulted in post-intellectual consequences. *Universal education* is an intellectual idea, but when implemented, it has resulted in both a distended-intellectual vocational curriculum and a counter-intellectual "feel-good" emphasis on self-realization; the intellectual goal of liberal arts has been abandoned. *Egalitarianism* is an intellectual ideal, but it has been achieved by mandating a post-intellectual politically correct mediocrity; intellectual competition has been thwarted. *Capitalism* is an intellectual theory, but when put into practice, it results in distended-intellectual exploitation; the intellectual free marketplace has been replaced by manipulation and materialism.

So it is with *democracy*. Participatory government is an intellectual concept. But like universal education and advertising and popular art, democracy—the intellectual ideal—by definition must be practiced by the masses. Therefore, when implemented, it is executed on a non-intellectual level. As sound bites, slander, balloons and buffoonery become the norm in modern politics, we drift further and further into a post-intellectual political arena. National political conventions have evolved into nothing more than flag-draped pep rallies; character issues have replaced serious debate; and "dirty tricks" have replaced discussion of social policies.

After the convincing defeats of the intellectual Adlai Stevenson in 1952 and 1956, presidential candidates have been careful not to appear too intellectual. Although John Kennedy surrounded himself with intellectual advisors, his election was due primarily to his own charisma (and Nixon's unpopularity). And Nixon later won two elections partially because of the more analytical and intellectual tone of his opponents (Hubert Humphrey and George McGovern). The qualities that have been most successful in recent elections are represented by the non-intellectual earthiness of Johnson, the informality of Jimmy (not James) Carter, and the folksy humor of Ronald Reagan.

The 1992 presidential campaign was not between the Yale-educated eastern elitist (George Bush) and the intellectual Rhodes scholar (Bill Clinton); it was between the images of the good ol' boy who calls Texas home and the saxophone-toting Arkansas traveler. It is indicative that both Bush and Clinton continually evoked the image and the home-spun qualities of Harry Truman. (Lewis Lapham points out, however, that "sometimes they [both] made the mistake of being seen to think.")[20]

The masses do not want to be intellectually convinced by analytic arguments; they want to be comforted and reassured by folksy post-intellectual images. The citizenry today no longer can or will accept the intellectual challenge to *think,* to assume responsibility for its own destiny. The intellectual climate of the Enlightenment has been replaced by a culture that has gotten too complicated for the common person to handle.

One attribute of post-intellectual political activity is the increase in the politics of victimization. The political halls, academies, and coffeehouses today are populated, not by open-minded intellectuals debating broad-based political philosophies, but by narrow-interest ideologues and political activists—civil rights champions, gay and lesbian proponents, and feminist spokeswomen— championing their specific causes. From the 1960s on, specialized political victims have replaced the generalist social critics and bohemian intellectuals of the 1950s and earlier.

Today's two major political parties reflect the two opposing strands of post-intellectualism. The Republicans represent the *distended-intellectual* approach. *People must assume responsibility for their own destinies and pull themselves up by their bootstraps; eliminate welfare; encourage competition and self-reliance; rely on unrestricted free enterprise.* This is a commendable libertarian political position that made sense for much of the nineteenth century.

The Democrats, on the other hand, represent a *counter-intellectual* approach. *Since society has gotten too complicated and unbalanced for the average citizen to handle, the state must assume responsibility for rectifying the situation with welfare programs, affirmative action legislation, safety regulations, and other social programs.* This authoritarian political philosophy accepts the fact that as individuals we can no longer manage an intellectual political system; we must now rely on the technocrats and bureaucrats to run things for us.

Society and Culture

A pre-intellectual culture was based on the tangible groupings of the tribe and the community; people understood and cared for those immediate family members and friends whose lives they touched on a regular basis. An intellectual culture, on the other hand, was to be based on the artificial structures of the city and nation-state; people would work with, and support, those whom they did not know personally and directly. Intellectual *Homo sapiens* could order their lives and relationships based on social contracts, legalistic arrangements, business agreements, and institutional obligations. It is this higher level of abstract social organization that defines an intellectual culture. However, we have not handled these intellectual abstractions well during the past few decades.

Many theories and observations of classic sociologists can be analyzed in terms of pre-intellectual and intellectual forces: Auguste Comte's concern with overspecialization; Herbert Spencer's evolutionary model of society; Ferdinand Tönnies' definitions of *Gemeinschaft* (pre-intellectual) and *Gesellschaft* (intellectual) societies; Emile Durkheim's explanation of mechanical (pre-intellectual) and organic (intellectual) solidarity.[21] We have already discussed Postman's breakdown of society into tool-using, technocratic, and technopoly stages.

Fritjof Capra analyzes our current turmoil in terms of the interplay between the Chinese concepts of *yin* and *yang*. Yin characterizes a more feminine, cooperative, sensitive, introspective, passive culture; while yang represents the masculine, competitive, aggressive, expansive, active culture. Using this paradigm, yin corresponds to the pre-intellectual mindset. Yang, with its stress on scientific methodology and material progress, is the intellectual force. Capra would argue that the problems arising from the Progress Paradox "are the results of overemphasizing our yang, or masculine side—rational knowledge, analysis, expansion—and neglecting our yin, or feminine side—intuitive wisdom, synthesis, and ecological awareness."[22] What we should be seeking, according to Capra, is a balance between yang and yin, between progress and homeostasis, between intellectual analysis and post-intellectual synthesis.

Pitirim Sorokin also is concerned with balance. He explains that every great society has been dominated by one of three prevailing cultural systems. It is the interplay of these three overriding cultural precepts that explains the historical fluctuation and crises of all great civilizations. The *ideational* society is a "unified system of culture based upon the principle of a supersensory and superrational God as the only true reality and value."[23] Based upon authoritarianism and tradition, this clearly is a pre-intellectual cyclical culture.

The *sensate* civilization, on the other hand, holds that "the true reality and value is sensory. Only what we see, hear, smell, touch, and otherwise perceive through our sense organs is real and has value."[24] This is what gives rise to empiricism, scientific thinking, and materialism—an intellectual linear culture.

A third, synthesizing, culture identified by Sorokin is the *idealistic*. This represents a harmonious blending of the sensate and ideational. Its major premise is that "the true reality is partly supersensory and partly sensory—that it embraces the supersensory and superrational aspect, plus the rational aspect and, finally, the sensory aspect, all blended into one unity."[25]

Sorokin points out that the current worldwide upheaval is essentially the beginning of a planetary transition—the decline of the intellectual sensate culture of the last four hundred years.

We are living and acting at one of the epoch-making turning points of human history, when *one fundamental form of culture and society—sensate—is declining and a different form is emerging.* The crisis is also extraordinary in the sense that, like its predecessors, it is marked by an extraordinary explosion of wars, revolutions, anarchy, and bloodshed; by social, moral, economic, political, and intellectual chaos.[26]

NOTES

1. Matthew Arnold, "Democracy" [1861], in *The Portable Matthew Arnold*, ed. Lionel Trilling (New York: Viking Press, 1949), p. 454.

2. Hofstadter, 1963, p. 30.

3. Postman, 1985, p. 41.

4. Stephens, 1994, p. 26.

5. From *Strangers* (Putnam), quoted in "Points to Ponder," *Reader's Digest*, December 1993, p. 101.

6. Postman, 1992, p. 52.

7. Mander, 1991, p. 51.

8. Postman, 1985, p. 51.

9. Walt Whitman, "From Democratic Vistas," in Rosenberg and White, 1957, p. 38.

10. FitzGerald, 1979, p. 171.

11. Joe Robinson, "Young People Showing Bias Against Brains," *Los Angeles Daily News*, 30 September 1990, *Viewpoint*, p. 1.

12. Reported by Judith Stone, "Ignorance on Parade," *Discover*, July 1989, p. 102.

13. Reported in "Life among the Science-Impaired," *Discover*, January 1992, p. 69.

14. From the Associated Press, "Only 25% of American Adults Get Passing Grades in Science Survey," *Los Angeles Times,* 24 May 1996, p. A22.

15. All data in this section are taken from various annual editions of the *Yearbook of American and Canadian Churches* (Nashville, TN: Abingdon Press).

16. Weber [1920], 1983, p. 26.

17. Postman, 1985, p. 60.

18. Lasch, 1991, p. 427.

19. Shelby Steele, "The New Segregation," *Imprimis* (Hillsdale College), 21, No. 8 (August 1992), pp. 1–2.

20. Lapham, *Wish for Kings,* 1993, p. 159.

21. See, for example, Auguste Comte, *The Positive Philosophy* [1830-1842] (1915); Herbert Spencer, *The Principles of Sociology* (1876); Ferdinand Tönnies, *Gemeinschaft und Gesellschaft* (1887); and Emile Durkheim, *The Division of Labor in Society* (1893).

22. Capra, 1982, p. 42.

23. Sorokin, 1941, p. 19.

24. Ibid., pp. 19–20.

25. Ibid., p. 20.

26. Ibid., p. 22.

3

Four Attributes of Post-Intellectualism

Information tends to drive knowledge out of existence.
• Daniel Boorstin
1994 Interview

On the Chicago-to-Maine leg of a recent cross-country flight, I found myself seated next to a young lady in her mid-twenties. As soon as we were airborne and heading east over Lake Michigan, she turned to me and asked, "Is that the ocean we're flying over?" Dumbfounded, I politely explained that the body of water was one of the Great Lakes and that it was close to a thousand miles to the nearest ocean. She thanked me and then turned back to her reading—the latest edition of the *National Enquirer*. And for the next half-hour, she and her traveling companion absorbed themselves in an intense discussion on one of the pressing issues explored in the tabloid—the evolving hairstyles of Hillary Rodham Clinton over the past decade. That one encounter put into focus for me the post-intellectual state of our society today—the ignorance, the lack of critical thinking, and the trivia that characterize much of our culture.

In Chapter 2, I identified four attributes of post-intellectualism: *ignorance,* a decrease in personal effectual knowledge; *dumbth,* a decline of critical thinking and problem-solving abilities; *establishmentism,* the reluctance to engage in meaningful social criticism; and *specialization,* the loss of a broad liberal arts perspective.

IGNORANCE: LOSS OF KNOWLEDGE

An intellectual perspective is typified by the Search for Truth—adherence to a scientific attitude, uncompromising research, the acquisition of information.

This is our quest for *knowledge*—the belief that we can master our information environment. But today we are slipping further and further from that goal. As much as any other single phenomenon, this defines post-intellectualism.

The Data Explosion

You walk into a strange room; there are some new and interesting items scattered about. There also are two doors, each labeled with a large question mark. You examine some of the interesting new items—gaining a little new information. Then you open one of the doors, and you walk into a strange room; there are some new and interesting items scattered about; and there are two new doors, each labeled with a large question mark. You examine some of the interesting new items. Then you open one of the doors. You find yourself in a strange room. . . . And so it continues—without end. Each new discovery, each new bit of information we find, raises additional questions and exposes us to more of the unknown. In effect, we are continually expanding our horizons of ignorance.

Why is so much information generated? Aristotle said it simply in his *Metaphysics*: "All men by nature desire knowledge."[1] We have an innate drive to explore; we are destined to seek, to invent, to search for the novel, to uncover new information, to build and develop. We have brought on ourselves this information overload. We walk into the strange room with the two doors and we find it impossible to resist opening one (or both) of them.

A conservative estimate is that the world's storehouse of information doubles about every five years.[2] At this exponential rate, the total amount of information in the world increases a thousand-fold every fifty years! Thus, you are trying to cope with a global information environment that is about a thousand times more complex than what your grandparents were facing at your age. This phenomenon of information overload is explored as one of the three underlying determinants of post-intellectualism in Chapter 4.

Expanding Data and Shrinking Knowledge

It is this proliferation of information that leads to ignorance. Vartan Gregorian, president of Brown University and former head of the New York Public Library, warns us of an interesting dilemma: "Unfortunately, the explosion of information is not equivalent to the explosion of knowledge. So we are facing a major problem—how to structure information into knowledge."[3] It is the generation of data, new discoveries, increasing piles of facts and details, larger mountains of information, that lead to the decrease in our personal command of effectual knowledge.

We should distinguish among four terms. We are generating more and more *data* (bits and pieces of isolated details and disconnected facts). These data must then be organized into *information* (data that have been structured and categorized into some sort of systematized and accessible storehouse or library).

This information can then be conceptualized as *knowledge* (the internalization and comprehension of external information by the human brain). And knowledge ultimately may lead to *wisdom* (the discerning and judicious use of knowledge in critical thinking).

The problem is that as more and more data are generated and the volume of information expands, the *percentage* of information that we are able to internalize as knowledge is actually decreasing. That is, the amount of knowledge that an individual is able to conceptualize and comprehend inside his or her head is relatively constant; yet the amount of external information doubles every five years.

Think of the amount of information your brain can comprehend as being comparable to the size of a ping-pong ball. The quantity of known information that existed in the universe 20,000 years ago would fill maybe a tennis ball—how to build a shelter, hunting and fishing techniques, some religious taboos, a few safety tips. Thus, with your ping-pong-ball capacity, you could assimilate a fair amount of what was in that tennis ball—you could internalize as knowledge quite a bit of the world's existing information. Today, however, the amount of information existing in the known world would fill billions of tennis balls. Yet your ping-pong-ball knowledge capacity cannot expand correspondingly. Therefore, as a percentage of the total amount of information that exists, your personal knowledge is shrinking!

In a recent interview, eminent historian and former Librarian of Congress Daniel Boorstin summed up the quandary succinctly: "Information tends to drive knowledge out of existence."[4] Richard Saul Wurman, in his book *Information Anxiety,* comments, "The glut [of data] has begun to obscure the radical distinctions between data and information, between facts and knowledge."[5] Or as John Naisbitt succinctly phrases it, "We are drowning in information but starved for knowledge."[6]

DUMBTH: LOSS OF ANALYTIC THINKING

The second characteristic of an intellectual culture is critical thinking, reasoning, analytic problem-solving. If as a society we have lost either the will or the ability to reason—what writer Michael D'Antonio calls "modern man's flight from reason"—then we have moved from an intellectual state into a post-intellectual culture.[7]

The title for this section is taken from Steve Allen's book, *Dumbth: And 81 Ways to Make Americans Smarter.* He writes, "Mountains of evidence—both in the form of statistical studies and personal testimonies—establish that the American people are suffering from a new and perhaps unprecedented form of mental incapacitation for which I have coined the word *Dumbth.*"[8] Dumbth is the loss of critical thinking.

After listing numerous contemporary problems, Allen goes on, "It is necessary to *think* about such issues, intelligently speculate about them, reason about them, communicate articulately about them."[9] Thinking, intelligent speculation, reasoning, and articulate communication—these are the elements of an intellectual society. Problem-solving or critical thinking, like technology, is an intellectual concept. It is when we fail to use problem-solving techniques responsibly—just as when we fail to use technology responsibly—that we slide into the post-intellectual era.

Problem-solving, decision-making, critical thinking, academic research, the scientific method, management-by-objectives, criminal investigation: these terms are all synonymous. Each of these processes is concerned with applying a basic analytic thinking pattern to a situation or problem where some decision must be made. Whether you are a government bureaucrat recommending a course of action, a scientist in the research lab, or a corporate leader making a business decision, the rational analytic approach is about the same. Critical thinking is the same as problem-solving; problem-solving involves decision-making; decision-making is critical thinking.

Four Components of Problem-Solving

Decision-making or problem-solving consists of four components: agreement that there is a problem, adequate information, reasoning ability, and a commitment to act reasonably.

Recognition and Identification of the Problem. The first step in any problem-solving situation is reaching agreement that there is a problem. All parties involved must recognize and concur that there is an issue and that it is sufficiently serious to warrant our attention. Until there is consensus that a problem exists and it should be dealt with, little headway can be made toward its solution.

In political debates, for example, there are many situations where intelligent leaders could not (or would not) agree on the magnitude and seriousness of a given problem: global warming, civil rights injustices, unemployment, the national debt, AIDS research, welfare needs, protection of the spotted owl. If—for any political, philosophical, economic, or religious reason—a substantial segment of the populace feels that the problem is not serious enough to merit their dollars or their effort, little social action will be taken to solve the situation. Such abdication of responsibility is indicative of a post-intellectual society.

Adequate Information. A second component of decision-making or problem-solving is gathering the needed information. You must have the necessary facts to analyze the nature of the problem—its magnitude, causes, and ramifications. And you must have information about possible approaches to a solution, about alternate courses of action. Decision-making without adequate information is like spinning a roulette wheel to make your life's choices.

If you are traveling down a highway and come to a fork in the road, you have the "freedom" to go left or right; but if you have no information about where each fork leads or the nature of each road, you are not able to make an intelligent decision. You may have the illusion of freedom, but in actuality, you have no true freedom of choice. You are simply flipping a coin. This is not freedom; this is slavery to the whims of fate.

If you want to enjoy the benefits of self-government, if you want to remain free, one obvious responsibility you have is the obligation to remain informed. Albert Speer, one of Hitler's top policy makers, laments the fact that in the early 1930s, he did not seek out information that would have dissuaded him from committing himself to Hitler's political program. He blames himself for not having seen through Hitler's hypocrisies and false panaceas.

Not to have worked that out for myself; not, given my education, to have read books, magazines, and newspapers of various viewpoints; not to have tried to see through the whole apparatus of mystification—was already criminal. At this stage my guilt was as grave as, at the end, my work for Hitler. *For being in a position to know and nevertheless shunning knowledge creates direct responsibility for the consequences*—from the very beginning [italics added].[10]

Reasoning Ability. The third element of the problem-solving process is the actual act of critical thinking, reasoning, processing the collected information, and then making some sort of decision. This is the analytic operation of engaging brain cells and putting them to work—examining, questioning, deliberating, classifying, challenging, comparing, contrasting, judging and evaluating. It takes effort; it is hard work. Thinking is not passive; it is not easy. However, it is an integral component of an intellectual mindset.

There are many problem-solving models—such as the scientific method, the Program Planning and Budgeting System, and Management-By-Objectives. One model I have labeled the *Analytic Thinking Pattern* consists of four steps:

- Definition and analysis of the problem.
- Establishment of criteria or objectives for a solution (if one has no clear criteria, one cannot engage in critical thinking).
- Examination, selection, and implementation of a solution.
- Evaluation (in terms of the stated criteria).[11]

There are many other models; the idea is to adopt and follow some sort of decision-making pattern.

The Will to Reason. The final essential component of successful problem-solving is the will to be rational, the responsibility to act with reason. Often we refuse to tackle our problems with resolution; we refuse to think seriously about them. The effort might get us into trouble, cost too much money, make some influential individuals uncomfortable, disrupt our accepted ways of doing things; it might challenge the established order. Christopher Lasch writes that intellectual liberals "mistakenly put their faith in moral suasion, education, and the scientific method. . . . But science could not provide the *nerve and will* [italics added]" that would enable men and women to solve their problems.[12]

In a democratic government, we have not only the freedom to think, but we have the *obligation* to think. Too often, however, we simply refuse to think critically. Robert Chianese writes,

Refusing to think . . . has become a national pastime. . . . We embrace intellectual mediocrity by choice. . . . The American way of life [is] promoting quick, simple answers to poorly defined problems. . . . Students, parents and teachers have given up the difficult discipline of self-denial that serious study requires; we . . . have no intellectual goals at all.[13]

Intellectualism consists of two factors—the *cognitive* factor (reason) and an attitudinal or *affective* factor (responsibility). The first three components mentioned above—identifying a problem, gathering information, and thinking logically—make up the cognitive factor. The fourth component of problem-solving—the will to reason—is the affective factor, which involves acting with responsibility. These four components of problem-solving, therefore, constitute the two hallmarks of an intellectual society—reasoning ability and the commitment to responsibility. Our post-intellectual society is defined by the decline of reason and responsibility.

Freedom and Responsible Decision-Making

In one of my courses, I ask students to respond to the question, "What do you appreciate most about living in the United States?" Approximately 95 percent of the responses I get include *freedom* in one form or another—"freedom of speech," "the independence to try any job I want," "being able to read any book or view any film I choose," "freedom of the press," "the right to worship as I please." The students' replies usually cover the high points of the Bill of Rights. But they generally give these glib responses with little awareness of the concomitant need for responsibility and civic duty.

Freedom demands responsibility. As youngsters, we earned the freedom to cross the street only after our parents were convinced that we were responsible enough to make the right decisions to cross the street safely. We earned the freedom to take the family car out alone only after our parents were satisfied that we were responsible enough to handle that degree of freedom. Similarly, every degree of independence we gained in school or the workplace was granted only as we showed we could think critically and make decisions responsibly.

So it is with the intellectual concept of democracy; we can hold on to those freedoms we so routinely espouse only if we exercise enough responsibility to make the system work. Put in operational terms, *freedom essentially means the right to make decisions*—and to be able to act upon those decisions. Freedom of speech or freedom of the press means the freedom *to decide* what to say or write and where to say or write it. Freedom of religion translates into the freedom *to decide* what to believe in and to be able to express that belief wherever and however we choose. Freedom of assembly means the freedom *to decide* whom we want to associate with and what we want to spend our time doing. Economic freedom means the freedom *to make decisions* about our employment and marketing opportunities.

If we make good decisions—if we think critically and solve our problems successfully—we will be able to hold on to our freedoms. If we do not make good decisions—if we do not solve our problems—we will see our freedoms gradually dissipating. In that case, either intentionally or tacitly, we will in effect have turned to the government or other authorities and said, "Do the job for us; we no longer can handle it; we cannot cross the street safely; we are willing to sacrifice some of our freedoms if you will solve our problems and take care of us."

Also, our freedoms become restricted as we abuse them—as we act without responsibility. If we yell "Fire!" in a crowded theater, our freedom of speech is taken away. If we start hurling racial insults in the classroom, our academic freedom is curtailed by politically correct campus speech codes. If our media become too violent or pornographic, we risk stirring up enough reaction to restrict our freedoms through various censorship channels. These restrictions on freedom of speech are all counter-intellectual reactions to our inability to handle freedom intellectually and responsibly.

Most of the problems that society faces are the consequences of our inability to handle freedom responsibly in making decisions and solving our problems. In writing about the troubles faced by the embryonic democratic government of Czechoslovakia, Václav Havel voiced a truth that is just as applicable to a senescent democracy such as ours: "If we don't try, within ourselves, to discover or rediscover or cultivate what I call 'higher responsibility,' things will turn out very badly indeed for our country."[14]

We must continually think and act with reason and responsibility if we are to survive in the increasingly complex politico-techno-economic infrastructure we have created for ourselves. A participatory government cannot persist without a commitment by the citizenry to clear thinking.

Problem-Solving and Intellectual Periods. Freedom is an intellectual concept. In a pre-intellectual society, individual freedoms were circumscribed by numerous tribal practices, religious taboos, and established rituals. In such a society, we simply responded to our day-to-day situations by resorting to tradition. We avoided decisions by doing the same things that our ancestors had done for generations. The idea of being free to think creatively and independently was not even conceivable.

When we moved into an intellectual culture, we embraced freedom and independent thinking. We faced our problems with a scientific mindset; we moved ahead in a straightforward, linear, analytical manner. We invented the process of change, which demanded that we make intelligent decisions and act with reason and deliberation. We researched, we analyzed, we weighed alternatives, we attempted to make rational decisions in our problem-solving situations. And we accepted responsibility for the consequences of our decisions.

However, as we make the transition into a post-intellectual society, we find ourselves enmeshed in a web culture that defies simple analysis. We first try this approach, then that; we start a new government program, then abandon it and try something else; we start to work on one issue, but become distracted and turn to work on another problem. Nothing stands still long enough for us to get a fix on it. Our focus is shifted from Somalia to Bosnia to Haiti to Rwanda to Cuba to Oklahoma City, without any methodical analysis or consistent criteria. Our problem-solving efforts too often are knee-jerk reactions, political expediencies, hunches, self-serving compromises, and short-term fixes. The result is increasing confusion and gradual surrender of our freedoms.

ESTABLISHMENTISM: LOSS OF SOCIAL CRITICISM

My favorite bumper sticker states "Question Authority." It is affixed to the side of my classroom briefcase and prominently displayed in each of my classes. This is not to embrace anarchy. I am not advocating capriciously overthrowing those in positions of authority; I merely argue that we must routinely question where we are, what we stand for, and what we should be doing. The intellectual mind is dedicated to making individuals uncomfortable and challenging the accepted way of doing things. This is the third component of our definition of intellectualism.

One of the greatest dangers to freedom is the assumption that goes unchallenged, the practice that goes unquestioned. Intellectual vigilance, of course, is not comfortable. It is difficult. And you do risk the possibility that you may find yourself outside the mainstream. An interesting premise to explore might be that *the intellectual must live outside the establishment.*

What today passes for social criticism or political commentary is largely a mixture of hackneyed party politics (Republican versus Democrat, liberal versus conservative), exhortations for specific causes (AIDS research, housing for the homeless), politically correct pleas for victimized groups (the racially oppressed, homosexuals, women), and other single-issue concerns. Instead of analytic social criticism, we resort to superficial special-interest crusades.

Our establishment voices (political leaders, editorial writers and media commentators, racial spokespersons, campus radicals) all argue for a modified rearrangement of the status quo. This is what I refer to as the concept of *Establishmentism*—the unquestioning acceptance of our basic social arrangements, without thinking through the deeper issues and long-term implications. John Kenneth Galbraith describes it as "the bland leading the bland":

These are the days when men of all social disciplines and all political faiths seek the comfortable and the accepted; when the man of controversy is looked upon as a disturbing influence; when originality is taken to be a mark of instability; and when, in minor modification of the scriptural parable, the bland lead the bland.[15]

To a great extent, the phenomenon of establishmentism exists simply because no one is sure where to begin any meaningful criticism. The big picture has become so blurry, our institutional entanglements so complex, our social commitments so burdensome, that no one has the audacity or perspective to suggest tinkering with the system to any appreciable extent. No one knows any longer what the exact nature of the system should be.

Schools as Non-Change Agents

The intellectual is one who can assess the social situation and critique it openly and objectively—without feeling obligated to defend the status quo. To prepare future citizens for this role is one task of the school in an intellectual culture. Neil Postman and Charles Weingartner state, "We believe that the schools must serve as the principal medium for developing in youth the attitudes and skills of social, political, and cultural criticism."[16]

However, schools too often are administered from the opposite perspective—reverting back to a cyclical culture. Many believe that schools are primarily instruments of social conformity and continuity. *Authority is to be respected, not challenged.* Education is to teach youth how to fit into their elders' culture; there is no thought of questioning the status quo. Youngsters should be taught how to adapt to existing cultural norms, how to gain the skills needed for a job in today's workplace. Students should not be encouraged to question, to challenge, to stand out as being different. This is the point that George Leonard makes in *Education and Ecstasy:* "Do not blame teachers or their administrators if they fail to educate, to change their students. For the task of *preventing* the new generation from changing in any deep or significant way is precisely what most societies require of their educators."[17]

In higher education, the directive against change is even more pronounced. With a fairly clear-cut post-intellectual mandate, most institutions of higher learning are predominantly asked to provide trained professionals to supply the needs of various corporate interests. The last thing that is wanted by engineering, business, education, law, medicine, and other fields are intellectually oriented graduates who will think for themselves and challenge the ongoing practices of the particular profession. The job of our colleges and universities is to provide sycophants who will slip right into the pre-defined slots of the bureaucratic establishment.

There are fewer and fewer intellectual opportunities for scholars and theorists to question the programs, to challenge the professional standards, to argue how things ought to be done. As Postman and Weingartner put it a quarter-century ago, educators "are acting almost entirely as shills for corporate interests, shaping [students] up to be functionaries in one bureaucracy or another."[18] There are relatively few corners of the ivory tower where unfettered intellectuals are invited to throw stones at the establishment.

Another manifestation of post-intellectual higher education is the broad acceptance of diverse value systems—without any consideration of critical standards or universal truths. (Critical thinking is not possible without recognized criteria; rational analysis means thinking in terms of stated criteria.) Evoking the image of the web culture, Lasch observes that as we embrace pluralistic diversity, we support "the contention that academic life should reflect the variety and turmoil of modern society instead of attempting to criticize and thus transcend this confusion. The very concept of criticism has become almost universally suspect."[19]

Cultural Priorities and Materialism

Many aspects of establishmentism could be selected for examination, for serious social criticism. At this point, let me focus on just one underlying cornerstone of establishmentism, one issue that exemplifies our post-intellectual lack of social criticism—the largely unchallenged acceptance of, and devotion to, a growth-oriented economic system that promotes a deleterious, materialistic mindset.

Our free enterprise, capitalistic system has provided the stimulus for most of our technological and materialistic achievements. However, as the theme of this book indicates, these scientific and economic achievements have resulted in the confounding Progress Paradox that we face. Our runaway economic engine has resulted in a rampant materialism that dominates our cultural value system. We have worshiped too long and too faithfully at the altar of economic growth.

As defined by Adam Smith, capitalism started out as an intellectual idea. However, it has since degenerated into a distended-intellectual obsession with excessive profits and materialistic consumption. Our whole economic enterprise rests upon the twin foundations of exploitation and gluttony. From the perspective of Corporate America, the primary function of the U.S. citizen is simply to be a *good consumer*. As long as each of us fulfills our role as a "happy shopper," the system shall continue to function splendidly. Consumption for the sake of consumption dominates our economy today. Lasch reports on a recent survey of shopping mall visitors that indicates only 25 percent of the shoppers come to a mall with a specific item in mind to buy.[20] Shopping becomes an end in itself.

As early as 1775, Richard Jackson wrote to Benjamin Franklin that "luxury and corruption . . . seem the inseparable companions of commerce and the arts. . . . Steady virtue, and unbending integrity, are seldom to be found where a spirit of commerce pervades every thing."[21]

Our increasing emphasis upon materialistic satisfaction obviously is not contributing to our individual feelings of happiness and self-worth. Nor is rampant materialistic achievement contributing to a lessening of the cultural problems with which we are concerned.

We are bound up in a bottom-line, short-term-profit-above-all-else, establishment mentality that does not allow for long-term planning and broader cultural values. Our whole economy is driven by a development/growth syndrome that impels us forward with its own money-making institutional momentum. Materialism has dulled our sensitivities; greed has weakened our sense of community; consumerism has overshadowed our spiritual values. And establishmentism robs us of the ability to challenge the materialistic ethic we have adopted.

SPECIALIZATION: LOSS OF PERSPECTIVE

Our modern technological and economic society is based increasingly upon specialization in professional and occupational pursuits. This is one of the four features of post-intellectualism—the loss of a broad liberal arts perspective.

Smith, in his monumental *Wealth of Nations,* used the example of pin-manufacturing to illustrate the principle of the division of labor—or specialization—in the Industrial Age. The making of common household pins is divided into "about eighteen distinct operations." Smith points out that ten men, each responsible for only one or two of the operations, could manufacture upward of 48,000 pins a day. On the other hand, one man, working by himself, "could scarce, perhaps, with his utmost industry, make one pin in a day." Smith continues: "The division of labour . . . so far as it can be introduced, occasions, in every art, a proportionable increase of the productive powers of labour."[22]

Every wage earner increasingly is involved with the expanding needs and information demands of his or her specific sphere of expertise—every accountant, dressmaker, insurance sales person, teacher, medical specialist, corporate attorney, and chemical engineer. We know and practice more and more about less and less. Specialization is one inescapable attribute of the information explosion and technological growth that characterize a distended-intellectual society. As we lose the ability to cope with the totality of our social environments, we entrust the management of society to the specialists and the technocrats. We have little choice.

Inevitability of Specialization

As soon as humans left the hunting and gathering stage, we became specialists—some turning to goat tending and cattle raising, while others became sowers and reapers. Specific crafts and trades soon evolved to support the farmer—the butcher, wagon maker, road builder, shoemaker, and mason. Religion was institutionalized, with its priestly caste. Astronomy and meteorology developed to guide the farmers through the seasons. Permanent residences resulted in the art of architecture. Money changers and merchants were needed to handle the increasingly complex finances of the community. Bureaucrats and lawyers emerged to run the affairs of the citizenry. Teachers and scribes were needed to handle the expanding information load. Leisure time facilitated the promotion of the arts—visual decoration, poetry, philosophy.

Leo Moser points out that increased specialization was inevitable as people continued to move into the city: "Crowded into a small area, often walled for defense and economic advantage, the members of various specialized artisan groups and social classes went their own way through life, perpetuating their own fragment of the total pattern."[23] Specialization is one of the six interrelated principles identified by Alvin Toffler as an integral component of the linear culture: "Accelerating the division of labor, the Second Wave [Industrial Age] replaced the casual jack-of-all-work peasant with the narrow, purse-lipped specialist and the worker who did only one task . . . over and over again."[24]

Fears of Isolation and Alienation

Many social observers have expressed, in the words of Lasch, "the fear that specialization would undermine the social foundations of moral independence."[25] Early in the nineteenth century Auguste Comte, the founder of modern sociology, wrote about "the mischievous intellectual consequences of the spirit of specialty which at present prevails." He went on to state that specialization "tends to extinguish or restrict what we call the aggregate or general spirit."[26]

Alienation and isolation unavoidably follow on the heels of specialization. The wheels of industry may spin faster and with more precision as we increasingly rely on specialization, but the human spirit tends to wither even as the mind specializes. Moser describes both the individual and family deterioration that were a predetermined result of specialization and urbanization:

The urbanite had ceased to live the whole life. The family was no longer a self-reliant unit. The individual was dependent on a larger group, whose members were not all known to him and the interrelations of which were too complicated to understand fully. Urban dwellers dealt with each other in terms of highly segmented roles, rather than as whole persons.[27]

Men and women were no longer complete individuals. We became specialized parts of the societal whole, segments of the economic establishment. We no longer were self-sufficient human beings. This is one aspect of what economist Robert Heilbroner refers to as "the de-humanizing requirements of an industrial system."[28] As we entered the Industrial Age, Toffler points out that "the human costs of specialization escalated accordingly. Critics of industrialism charged that highly specialized repetitive labor progressively dehumanized the worker."[29] Any industrial, high-tech, computer-based society is inherently dehumanizing.

In discussing Thomas Carlyle, Lasch points out that as we become more specialized, "The 'whole man, heaven-inspired,' recedes from view, and partial men stand in his place, incapacitated alike for intelligent action and for original thought."[30] Even Smith recognized that continued specialization or division of labor would eventually have deleterious effects upon the individual worker:

The man whose whole life is spent is performing a few simple operations, of which the effects too are, perhaps, always the same, or very nearly the same, has no occasion to exert his understanding, or to exercise his invention in finding out expedients for removing difficulties which never occur. He naturally loses, therefore, the habit of such exertion, and generally becomes as stupid and ignorant as it is possible for a human creature to become. The torpor of his mind renders him, not only incapable of relishing or bearing a part in any rational conversation, but of conceiving any generous, noble, or tender sentiment, and consequently of forming any just judgment concerning many even of the ordinary duties of private life.[31]

What Smith mentioned as a potential problem has ballooned to unmanageable dimensions as all segments of society grow increasingly fragmented and alienated from each other. The more specialized the worker becomes, the less he or she is able to *think*. The deeper the cardiologist, the corporate lawyer, or the international economist becomes embroiled in his or her specialized field, the less he or she will be able to contribute to the running of the democracy.

Throughout the rest of the book, I will be concerned with more particular considerations and consequences arising from these four attributes of post-intellectualism: *ignorance* (a decrease in functional personal knowledge); *dumbth* (deterioration of our analytic thinking and rational problem-solving skills); *establishmentism* (our lack of commitment to meaningful social criticism) and *specialization* (our loss of a broad liberal arts perspective).

NOTES

1. Aristotle, *Metaphysics,* book 1, ch. 1.
2. Some estimates state that information is doubling every four years. See Leyden, 4 June 1995, p. 2T.
3. Interviewed in Moyers, 1989, p. 182.
4. Quoted in Rick Vanderknyff, "Creating Drama with History in One Easy Lesson," *Los Angeles Times,* 23 March 1994, p. E6.
5. Wurman, 1989, p. 37.
6. Naisbitt, 1984, p. 17.
7. Michael D'Antonio, "Science Fights Back. Is It Winning? The Answer Is NOT in the Stars," *Los Angeles Times Magazine,* 11 February 1996, p. 18.
8. Allen, 1989, p. 15.
9. Ibid., p. 27.
10. Speer, 1971, p. 48.
11. See Wood, 1996, Chapter 3.
12. Lasch, 1991, p. 370.
13. Robert Chianese, "The Future Revisited: Hatred in Orwell's 1984 and the Decline of Thinking," *Perspective* (California State University, Northridge), 2, no. 1 (Spring 1986): 11; referring to an article by Raymond A. Schroth, "Education: Mediocre by Choice," *Los Angeles Times,* Opinion sect., 24 May 1983, p. 5.
14. Havel, 1992, p. 1.

15. Galbraith, 1984, p. 4.
16. Postman and Weingartner, 1969, p. 2.
17. Leonard, 1968, p. 7.
18. Postman and Weingartner, 1969, p. 14.
19. Lasch, 1978, p. 149.
20. Lasch, 1991, p. 522.
21. Quoted in ibid., p. 201.
22. Smith [1776], 1952, pp. 3–4.
23. Moser, 1979, p. 134.
24. Toffler, 1980, p. 49.
25. Lasch, 1991, p. 195.
26. Comte [1830–1842], 1915, p. 293.
27. Moser, 1979, pp. 135–36.
28. Heilbroner, 1980, p. 94.
29. Toffler, 1980, p. 49.
30. Lasch, 1991, p. 237.
31. Quoted in Gay, 1966, p. 106.

4

Underlying Determinants of Post-Intellectualism

But lo! Men have become the tools of their tools.
> • Henry David Thoreau
> *Walden*

We cannot rebuild our societal infrastructure by merely patching the potholes—it is not enough simply to hire more teachers, put more cops on the street, recycle all our trash, build shelters for the homeless, and seal off our borders. Such superficial stopgap measures will do nothing to solve our long-range problems. To come to grips with the web culture, we must examine the underlying determinants of our current post-intellectual disarray. The causes of our cultural disorder are not our failed educational institutions, not drug abuse or street violence, not the breakup of the nuclear family, not the decay of our inner cities, not a loss of moral values, or too much pornography. All these problems are but surface symptoms.

A deeper analysis reveals three underlying determinants that explain our transition to a post-intellectual culture: the exhaustion of the intellectually based policy of *linear growth and expansion;* the phenomenon of the *information overload;* and our surrender to *technological determinism.* Before examining these three underlying determinants, however, we must look at one other primary consideration—the limitations of human intellect and reason.

ONE PRIMARY CONSIDERATION: LIMITATIONS OF HUMAN INTELLECT

We emerged from the Enlightenment aroused by the words of Bacon, Descartes, Milton, Locke, and Jefferson. *Authoritarianism is dead; long live*

Libertarianism! Elated with a new-found philosophy that decreed we were clearheaded and responsible enough to run our own affairs, we plunged into the American and French revolutions to prove that common citizens could control their own destinies. But to understand what went wrong, we need first to reconsider the basic nature of *Homo sapiens.* Herbert Spencer observed over a hundred years ago that "The Republican [i.e., representative] form of government is the highest form of government: but because of this it requires the highest type of human nature—a type nowhere at present existing."[1]

Reason and responsibility—the two R's of an intellectual culture—are the prerequisites for participatory self-government. A key component in our definition of intellectualism is analytical thinking. Yet humans are not by nature rational beings. Jeremy Campbell points out in *The Improbable Machine* that "some compelling research in cognitive psychology has shown that we are logical only in a superficial sense; at a deeper level we are systematically illogical and biased."[2] We are driven by our short-term greeds for immediate profits, sensual satisfactions, lusts for power, and advantages to be gained at the expense of others. As Jean Jacques Rousseau wrote over two hundred years ago, "When the citizens are greedy, cowardly, and pusillanimous, and love ease more than liberty, they do not long hold out against the redoubled efforts of the government."[3]

Although we are not inherently rational creatures, virtually all our civil institutions—our political structures, legal contracts, economic arrangements, schools, commercial enterprises, and media systems—are constructed on the assumption that human beings are reasonable and intellectual. We insist on perpetuating what Reinhold Niebuhr called "the modern illusion that human reason will be able to become the complete master of all the contingent, irrational, and illogical forces of the natural world which underlie and condition all human culture."[4] We want to believe in the supremacy of divine reason, the premise that we can overcome our animal passions. But we find ourselves still dominated by our basic instincts. Barbara Tuchman refers to this paradox in *The March of Folly*:

The theory was comforting, but . . . "divine reason" was more often than not overpowered by non-rational human frailties—ambition, anxiety, status-seeking, face-saving, illusions, self-delusions, fixed prejudices. Although the structure of human thought is based on logical procedure from premise to conclusion, it is not proof against the frailties and the passions.[5]

When times were less complicated, a modicum of reason was good enough to get by. But in today's increasingly complex technological culture—with our information explosion, bewildering scientific environment, shaky economic structures, extended urbanization, ecological complications, and suffocating bureaucracies—a modicum of intelligence will no longer suffice. In today's culture, we must manifest an even stronger commitment to reason and responsibility. But we fail to do so.

Our Genetic Heritage

Despite our imposing technological environment and our impressive monuments to culture, the veneer of civilization is exceedingly thin. Indeed, civilization—starting with the agricultural revolution—is a fairly recent phenomenon. And human beings have yet to adapt biologically to this intellectual lifestyle. Contemporary *Homo sapiens* is genetically still in the Stone Age. Technologically, we may be able to dissect the atom and send rockets to the stars, but our paleolithic genes are still programmed for a life of hunting and gathering.

As Boyd Eaton, Marjorie Shostak, and Melvin Konner point out in *The Paleolithic Prescription,* if we were to look back far enough, we would find that our prehistoric forebears were biologically the same animals that we are: "We would discover the linkage continuing, generation upon generation, back through unimaginable lengths of time, through war and famine, through ice ages and thaws, through geographic and political change, . . . to a time and place 40,000 years ago."[6]

Our cave-dwelling ancestors were what Neil Postman described as a tool-using culture. Their intellectual achievements may not appear very impressive by today's computer-society standards. Nonetheless, they made full use of their spears, stone knives, simple levers, and fire. And they developed the oral tradition. With brain structures and throats similar to ours, they did have fully human speech. Biologically and anatomically, they were essentially modern human beings.

If we were to take one of these uncivilized beings, transport her 40,000 years up to the present, give her a bath and a modern hairdo, and clothe her in contemporary garb, she could walk down Fifth Avenue or Main Street completely unnoticed—a modern *Homo sapiens* in virtually every aspect. Indeed, if raised from infancy in a twentieth-century environment, our paleolithic forefather could take his place in any modern research lab or corporate board room.

The basic animal drives and instincts that guaranteed our survival as hunter-gatherers are still programmed into our genetic makeup. Our need to store food for the lean months has evolved into a greed for excessive corporate and personal profits. The desire for satiation and enjoyment of sensual pleasures results in overeating, in alcohol and drug abuse. Our innate territorial nature has been translated into a deleterious nationalism. Our hereditary drive for dominance of the pack is manifest in cutthroat corporate competition and personal ego trips. And our instinctive biological drive for survival of the species has become an intensified lust for sexual gratification.

Human beings are fundamentally animals. We are still governed by our animal instincts.

Altering the Gene Pool

Even as we contemplate the intellectual limitations of our basic animal makeup, we must also consider that we may actually be weakening our genetic heritage. As a species, we may be gradually becoming less rational and less intelligent, less capable of coping. In ages past, it was the strongest and brightest who managed to survive and raise large families—Darwin's concept of the survival of the fittest. For thousands upon thousands of years, *Homo sapiens* continued to strengthen its gene pool through natural selection.

However, we may have reversed that trend a few generations ago. Looking at the work of contemporary biologists and geneticists, Christopher Wills writes, "Natural selection once ensured that only the fittest survived and reproduced. Now almost everyone in the industrialized Western world can grow up to have children."[7]

Birthrates. The data indicate that today our social policies and practices tend to encourage those who have inherently lower intellectual capabilities to multiply more rapidly than those with more intelligence, better education, and greater social consciousness. For example, in 1992, among all American women (between the ages of fifteen and forty-four), those who had not completed high school had 67 births per 1,000 women; those who had completed high school had 65 births per 1,000; those who had completed at least one year of college had 60 births per 1,000; and for those who had a graduate or professional degree, the figure dropped to 55.[8] The correlation with income is even more striking (see Table 4.1). Families with an annual income under $10,000 have 95 births per 1,000 women; the figures generally drop through the income brackets, bottoming out at 43 births per 1,000 women in families with income over $75,000. The implication is that those who are educationally and socioeconomically most capable of raising and nurturing the next generation are not the ones having the babies. One encyclopedia source states:

In general, the lower the social, economic, and educational level, the higher the birth rate, which means that the persons who can least afford to raise and educate them have the most children. This is a cause for concern among those who believe that economic and social status reflects intelligence, and who fear that mankind is deteriorating because the brighter people are not breeding as fast as the others.[9]

It makes us uncomfortable to speak of such matters—but they cannot be ignored. Our well-meaning social support and entitlement programs—as compassionate and humane as they are—have repealed the law of survival of the fittest. We are now encouraging expansion of the weakest.

Concern in this area is what motivated the eugenics movement, what led to Hitler's crude breeding experiments, what inspired the genetic factories described by Aldous Huxley in *Brave New World*, and what encourages some of the eyebrow-raising experimentation of our contemporary genetic engineers (touched upon in Chapter 16). It is a sensitive and disturbing issue, but it is hard to deny that—from an intellectual viewpoint—we are encouraging, generation after generation, the proliferation of individuals who are less capable of handling the responsibilities demanded by an increasingly complex technological environment.

Table 4.1
Births per Income Level

Family Income	Births per 1,000 Women: 1992*
Less than $10,000	95
10,000 – 19,999	70
20,000 – 24,999	66
25,000 – 29,999	57
30,000 – 34,999	61
35,000 – 49,999	58
50,000 – 74,999	53
75,000 and over	43

*Total births for all women, aged 15 to 44 years old.
Source: U.S. Bureau of the Census, *Current Population Reports,* series P20-454, reprinted in *Statistical Abstract of the United States: 1995* (115th ed.), Washington, DC, 1995, p. 79.

Disabled Babies. Another growing concern is the increasing number of babies born with impaired intellectual and emotional abilities due to alcohol and drug abuse by the mother during pregnancy—the 300,000 or so babies born each year with drug-related problems. One study indicated that up to 11 percent of all American infants tested positive for either alcohol or cocaine the first time they had any blood drawn.[10] It is estimated that up to 20 percent of all babies born at the University of Southern California Medical Center in Los Angeles are "crack babies."[11] Although the numbers may be relatively small, they are growing; and they do add up to a significant impact on our societal resources.

These crack babies and alcohol-abused children, who are now making their presence fully felt in our schooling system, are, according to author Michael Dorris, "consistently described as 'remorseless,' 'without a conscience,' passive and apparently lacking that essential empathy, that motivation toward cooperation, upon which a peaceful and harmonious classroom—and society—so depends."[12] Twenty years from now, these will be the adult citizens affecting the decisions that govern our society.

Another disturbing consideration is the possible role played by environmental pollutants and toxins. How might we be altering the genetic structure of future generations? Starting with concern over Strontium-90 in the 1950s, continuing through Rachel Carson's 1962 eye-opening indictment of the pesticide DDT in *Silent Spring*, and on into the 1990s, scientists and geneticists continue to raise worrisome questions about the impact of the hundreds of chemical and toxic elements being injected into the biosphere.

It may be decades before we can accurately assess the cumulative hormonal impact of agents such as dioxin, kepone, triazine herbicides, polychlorinated biphenyls (PCBs), diethylstilbestrol (DES), styrenes and the alkyl phenols found in some detergents and plastics. A 1994 *Time* report states, "Now, even as the cancer debate continues, environmental groups are pointing to a different, previously unrecognized threat. Chemical pollutants, they say, can interfere with one of the most basic of biological functions: the ability to reproduce."[13] Donella Meadows warns that infinitesimal quantities of these chemical "endocrine disrupters" can "derail development, change the sex or sexuality of the unborn child, or, most insidiously, affect its future ability to generate sperm or egg cells."[14]

All these factors contribute to the primary consideration leading to postintellectualism—limitations of human intellect. We continue to embrace the ideals of the libertarian egalitarian society and press forward with the framework of a democratic culture—even as we become less and less capable of handling such an intellectual enterprise with reason and responsibility. Starting from this primary consideration, there are three broad underlying determinants of postintellectualism to examine. These are the three inescapable factors that increasingly shape our web culture.

LINEAR EXPANSION AND GROWTH: THE FIRST DETERMINANT

The first determinant is the failure of *linear expansion and growth* to sustain our economic environment. This is one result of our unchecked distendedintellectual faith in progress—unrestrained linear growth, progress without restriction, without a sense of direction. Progress today is more a source of societal turmoil and conflict than it is the scientific panacea that was envisioned four hundred years ago.

Legacies of the Linear Culture

The Enlightenment gave us a linear culture based on science and technology, on progress and development—the concept of continually moving forward in a straight line. We were to push onward with an unswerving faith in perpetual economic growth. In his classic *Wealth of Nations*, Adam Smith set down in concrete the definition of modern, free enterprise capitalism based upon unending growth and expansion. Fritjof Capra summarizes this position: "Within a nation Smith thought that the self-balancing market system was one of slow and steady growth, with continually increasing demands for goods and labor."[15]

Our economic structures have been built, for centuries, on the assumption that our planetary resources are inexhaustible. Every social enterprise, every political plan, every financial move has been predicated on the ideology that there would always be more—more territory to explore and conquer, more resources to mine and exploit, more trees to cut down, more land to plow, more room to build cities and industries, more products to manufacture and sell, more babies to clothe and feed, more children to send to more schools, more industries, more employees, more taxpayers, and more customers—year after year. (The fallacy of this policy is explored in Chapter 10.)

This push for economic growth and progress has been the root cause of many of our social and ecological problems for the past century. The exploitation of our natural resources, the resulting global pollution, and spiraling worldwide population pressures are all evidence of our dependence on continued linear growth and expansion—with little consideration of our responsibility for future generations.

A pre-literate cyclical culture is much closer to nature than is a linear culture, aiming as it does to maintain an equilibrium among all living and nonliving things. Only when humans evolved from the cyclical culture to the linear culture, when the printed word became paramount, when progress became god, did men and women feel they had the right—the mandate—to change things, to "improve upon" nature and exploit its resources. The linear mindset—growth and development—is the essence of P. A. Sorokin's *sensate* culture: believe only in what you can perceive and grasp; put your faith in science; hold onto the tangible. "A fully developed sensate system of truth and cognition is inevitably *materialistic*, viewing everything, openly or covertly, in its materialistic aspects."[16]

Economic and Ecological Limits

However, the end to linear expansion had to come at some point. Within the last few decades, this linear culture has bumped into the ecological and economic realities of a world that has physical limits and finite resources. The straight line of progress and expansion has come to an end. Capra writes that "Smith himself predicted that economic progress would eventually come to an end when the wealth of nations had been pushed to the natural limits of soil and climate, but unfortunately he thought this point was so far in the future that it was irrelevant to his theories."[17]

Today, it is no longer irrelevant. The future has arrived. Rufus Miles, in *Awakening from the American Dream,* observes that "the twin gods of growth and progress . . . [are] not performing their duties properly."[18] It becomes more and more apparent that we cannot continue forever on a straight line of increasing growth and development.

Many societal problems are triggered directly by the failure of linear growth to sustain us indefinitely. Problems of the exploited, the unemployed, the homeless; the deteriorating inner cities; widespread poverty; our debilitating welfare system; crime in the streets: these are all attributable to the fact that economic development and employment opportunities eventually reach a finite limit. The economy stops expanding; the promise of eternal progress falls short. And millions find themselves without jobs, without homes, without a secure environment, without hope for the future.

The promise of unending expansion has failed us. The economic cornucopia has stopped flowing. Old financial aphorisms no longer ring true; the platitudes fall on numbed ears. We wander aimlessly in a fiscal dystopia.

THE INFORMATION OVERLOAD: THE SECOND DETERMINANT

As discussed in Chapter 3, it is the proliferation of information that leads to ignorance. This information overload is the second of the three determinants of post-intellectualism.

Think of all the world's information as being contained inside a gigantic balloon. And everything outside the balloon is the unknown, ignorance, stuff that we do not know. As we discover more data and facts, we pump more and more information into the balloon. And it expands. However, as our balloon fills up, its skin stretches and the surface area where we interface with the unknown keeps increasing. We come into contact with more and more stuff that we do not know. As our information store is expanded, we are ever more aware of our ignorance. An ever-increasing number of new questions are asked. And we are driven to generate more information.

In a cover essay for *Newsweek,* Steven Levy summarizes how the data explosion is defining our post-intellectual culture: "The [information] revolution has only just begun, but already it's starting to overwhelm us. It's outstripping our capacity to cope, antiquating our laws, transforming our mores, reshuffling our economy, reordering our priorities, redefining our workplaces, putting our Constitution to the fire, shifting our concept of reality."[19]

You must constantly learn to cope with new information about genetic manipulation, Asian trade practices, recycling requirements, AIDS research, new tax revisions, European politics, 500-channel cable TV systems, the latest nutritional research, new WWW sites, the inner city homeless, high-impact plastics, religious cults, satellite transponders, famine in Africa, data compression, the hole in the ozone layer, domestic terrorism, new cancer treatments, electric automobiles, junk bonds, superconducting ceramics, desktop video conferencing, new professional legal entanglements, and on and on and on. Make your own list.

Information Retrieval

The media have engulfed the American citizen in a cornucopia of facts and data, both significant and trivial, structured and unstructured: TV commercials, newspaper headlines, radio jingles, political sound bites, weather reports, billboards, magazine ads, book jackets, movie previews, music videos, magazine covers, transit ads, storefront posters, consumer tips, station-break news summaries, and so forth.[20]   Various studies indicate that we are exposed to anywhere from 500 to 1,500 advertising messages a day.   A Bell Labs report stated that in a single day's edition of the *New York Times,* there is more information than an individual man or woman would have had access to in his or her entire life in the sixteenth century.[21]

This is what Alvin Toffler refers to as the *blip culture:* "On a personal level, we are all besieged and blitzed by fragments of imagery, contradictory or unrelated, that shake up our old ideas and come shooting at us in the form of broken or disembodied 'blips.' We live, in fact, in a 'blip culture.'"[22]   About 75,000 new books are published in the United States each year.   Between 6,000 and 7,000 scientific articles are written *every day.*[23]   The Library of Congress is adding between 7,000 and 10,000 new items to be catalogued every day.[24] However, about one-third of the library's treasure is uncatalogued; incoming material piles up faster than the library staff can keep track of it.

How do you sift through all this material to find the precise information you need? More and more, according to John Naisbitt, the answer is that you cannot: "This level of information is clearly impossible to handle by present means. Uncontrolled and unorganized information is no longer a resource in an information society. Instead, it becomes the enemy of the information worker."[25] Even with all our modern information storage-and-retrieval sophistication— extensive on-line databases, computer-based catalogs, the Internet, data compression technologies, high-density storage formats, CD-ROM libraries, computer-accessed indexes to indexes of indexes—it is increasingly difficult to keep track of human information. With all the technological tools at our disposal, we continue to lose ground in the information race.

The value of any commodity is lessened as it is produced in great quantities—oil, wheat, coal, housing, academic research, or TV talk shows. The more we have of any given product, the less each individual item is worth. We simply cannot treasure anything of which there is too much. Information overload leads to *information desensitization.*   Boston columnist Mike Barnicle writes, "This is the America of drive-through windows where we get what we want, when we want it and if we don't like it we simply dispose of the item in the trash: Food, marriages, information, it does not matter so long as it is quick."[26]

Our Broken Information-Control Systems.   One way to think of society is in terms of information systems. Who controls what information? Who can generate information? Who can gain access to information? In *Technopoly*, Postman suggests that most of our social institutions can be thought of as "information-control" systems. He describes technopoly as "what happens to society when the defenses against information glut have broken down."[27]   The family, schools, religion, political parties, business corporations, military units, government agencies, medical systems, libraries, and the media all are concerned with processing information for us. Each information-control agency compiles, organizes, filters, and interprets information for us (as each institution perceives our needs) and tries to shield us from other information.

However, as the total information load becomes heavier than these institutions can handle, they no longer can funnel the appropriate information to us. Our information-control mechanisms go astray—and we become lost.

One needs only to look at our schools. In the past forty years, the quantity of new discoveries, facts, theories, and practical developments has been overwhelming. Students today seem to know much less about history, geography, basic science, or international relations than students in previous generations for the simple reason that in generations past, there was much less history, geography, basic science, and international relations to know about. Classics professor Stephen Bertman points out that as time passes, "more and more factual information has accumulated in the storehouse of history. Its sheer bulk makes it difficult to distinguish what is worth knowing."[28]

Simultaneously, the schools' educational efforts are continually diluted as they are mandated to assume an increasing nonacademic burden—driver education, homemaking skills, safe-sex education, job-training programs, parenting classes, sensitivity and self-awareness, psychological and family counseling, medical services, nutrition programs, and security concerns. Consequently, children complete their formal schooling today with less command of basic subjects than their parents and grandparents had a few decades ago. The school as an information-control system has broken down.

In a post-intellectual society, overwhelmed by the magnitude of the information overload, it may be that we ordinary citizens cannot command the knowledge to participate in the decision-making process. It may be inevitable that we have to rely on the specialists and bureaucrats to make the decisions for us. In which case, we are no longer taking part in a participatory democracy.

A Crisis of Epistemology

Epistemology is the branch of philosophy that investigates the basis of human knowledge—how we determine what is Truth, how we verify reality, how we comprehend our information environment. In the cyclical culture, we found knowledge by listening to our elders; truth was handed down from generation to generation. In the linear culture, we found truth by scientific analysis and logical thinking; rational inquiry dominated our epistemology.

In the post-intellectual web culture, we are not sure where to turn for knowledge. The blip culture offers us no coherence. We no longer trust science, or religion, our political leaders, the police, what we read in the papers, or what we see on the tube. We all looked at the videotape of the police beating Rodney King and came away with conflicting versions of truth—our own definitions of police brutality, resisting arrest, justice, racism.

The O. J. Simpson murder trial stretched our traditional epistemology to the breaking point. In what one defense attorney called "maybe the most over-whelming circumstantial case in the history of American jurisprudence," the legal system was not able to determine truth—in spite of the devastating physical evidence, the numerous laboratory reports, the corroborating witnesses, and the disingenuous defense counter-charges.[29] We have pushed the intellectual idea of social criticism into the abyss of information anarchy. Healthy skepticism evolves into ugly cynicism. In the web culture, we no longer know how to de-termine truth; *we no longer know how to know.*

TECHNOLOGICAL DETERMINISM: THE THIRD DETERMINANT

The third root of the Progress Paradox, the third underlying determinant of post-intellectualism, is what is broadly labeled *technological determinism*—the recognition that our technologies have taken on an existence and direction of their own. This is Postman's *Technopoly*, Jerry Mander's *Megatechnology.*[30]

This phenomenon involves many considerations other than hardware. It entails the way we structure our institutions, the way we tackle our prob-lems. Technological determinism is a major factor in virtually all the post-intellectual consequences explored throughout the book—communication foul-ups, educational shortcomings, hyper-urbanization, bureaucratization, the in-vasion of privacy, debilitating automation, personal isolation and alienation, information anarchy, economic failures, and our democratic deterioration.

Technology Defined

Properly defined, *technology* includes more than just science apparatus and machinery. I use the term in its broadest sense to mean *the application of sci-entific knowledge and principles, utilizing a combination of human and non-human resources, applied in a methodical and systematic manner, in order to achieve specific practical ends.* This defines technology as a systems approach to problem-solving. Moreover, it uses both human and nonhuman resources—brains as well as hardware, intellectual constructs as well as science labs, bureaucratic institutions as well as machines.

The alphabet is a technology. So is the calendar, a legal contract, the jury system, the city zoning commission. The city itself is a technology. Therefore, when I use the word *technology,* I am referring, not just to the complex equip-ment and resource-intensive machinery, but also—and most importantly—to the systems and institutions we have created in the implementation of our linear, progress-oriented culture.

Technopoly/Megatechnology

Technological determinism is the phenomenon of *allowing research and bureaucracy to determine for us where society is headed.* Kirkpatrick Sale, author of *Rebels Against the Future,* writes that "It is not just that the machines seem to be beyond our individual control, . . . but that, separately and collectively, they seem to be beyond anyone's control, operating at such speed and complexity that it defies human competence to manage them regularly and infallibly."[31]

The proliferating branches of science and social engineering develop a thrust, a momentum, a dynamism of their own. Instead of being merely our servants and assistants, the machines and automated systems and research labs and government bureaus now dictate their own directions. As industrial, communications, and computer-based technologies become increasingly sophisticated, our engineering and legalistic infrastructure takes on its own sense of destiny and control.

As soon as the technology of agriculture had been developed, for example, it was predetermined that the city would have to be invented. Once Gutenberg had assembled the components for his crude printing press, it was inevitable that the authority of the church would be challenged, that nations based on vernacular languages would be established, that individualism would be fostered, and that books would dictate the necessity of creating schools.

Once the automobile was let loose upon the road, it was foreordained that we would soon have suburbia, interstate commerce, new courtship traditions, new corporate structures, freeways, air pollution, new family relationships, new occupational opportunities, Middle East battles over oil supplies, fast-food chains, and shopping malls. When the Wright brothers first propelled their flimsy powered glider over 120 feet of Kitty Hawk sand dunes, it was determined that ultimately close to 20,000 commercial airline flights would take off from U.S. airports every day. After the first atom was split at the University of Chicago, there was no way that we could have halted the realization of the atomic bomb.

After television was invented, it was destined that all of our social, leisure, economic, political, and informational patterns would be drastically rearranged. Once the Soviet Union managed to balance *Sputnik* in its tenuous orbit, it was inevitable that one day, cable would be delivering hundreds of channels of video entertainment and trivia into our living rooms. After the first integrated circuit was etched onto a silicon chip, it was guaranteed that the computer would alter every aspect of contemporary society.

As Henry David Thoreau succinctly observed nearly a century and a half ago, "But lo! men have become the tools of their tools."[32] This is technopoly; this is megatechnology. Postman emphasizes, "to be unaware that a technology comes equipped with a program for social change, to maintain that technology is neutral, to make the assumption that technology is always a friend to culture is, at this late hour, stupidity plain and simple."[33]

Strictly speaking, of course, it is not the machines and the institutions that make these decisions. The ultimate decisions are up to the human beings who operate the computers and manage the systems. However, seldom, if ever, have humans come up with a new scientific wonder and then decided not to implement it. Operant conditioner Roger McIntire observes, "History tells us that whenever we develop a technology we inevitably use it."[34] Humans are no longer exercising their responsibility. This is technological determinism.

Technological Totalitarianism

We are engulfed by *technological overload*—the result of the incomprehensible rate at which new technological developments are unveiled and thrown at us in a number of fields: medicine, nuclear fusion, lasers and fiberoptics, molecular chemistry, superconductivity, materials engineering, video compression and data transmission, subatomic physics, genetic engineering, and, of course, computers.

We are developing optical computers that use laser beams instead of wires, X-ray lasers that could shrink electronic circuits to one-thousandth of their present size, and organic computers that use bacteria as central processing units (CPUs).[35] The advanced electron scanning tunneling microscope uses a beam almost as small as an atom—to drill a trillion holes in an area the size of a pinhead. Physicists are working to increase data transmission by a factor of 10,000.[36] Genetic engineers now routinely implant animal genes into human beings.

Theoretically, as enlightened and involved citizens of the democracy, it is our job to keep abreast of these developments. We must remain on top of all this emerging wizardry. We are to set the policies and dictate the directions that our technological society is to follow. *Practically,* there is little realistic hope that we mere citizens can keep up with it all.

Our cumulative scientific advances have resulted in a techno-industrial society that has outstripped our intellectual and emotional capabilities to comprehend and control what mankind hath wrought. Step by small step, we seem to have a grip on what we are doing; individual researchers and technologists understand what they are working on. But in the aggregate, nobody has a clear picture of the totality of what is happening. We are unable to grasp the impact of technological progress as a whole. The loss of a broad intellectual perspective is the fourth component of our definition of post-intellectualism.

The trouble, of course, is that no one knows where our technological thrust is leading us. We have little idea in which direction we should head. Like the deer frozen in the sudden glare of oncoming headlights, we are so transfixed by the dazzle of today's technology that we do not know in what direction to run. René Dubos stated, "Life is an adventure . . . where man himself, like the sorcerer's apprentice, has set in motion forces that are potentially destructive and may someday escape his control."[37]

We are consumed by the scientific environment. Our ways of thinking, our business structures, our legalistic mindset, every aspect of our communication and transportation systems are dictated by this technological totalitarianism. Like fish unable to discern the nature of water, we are so thoroughly immersed in our techno-habitat that we do not even recognize it.

Science has become the metaphor for all that is rational and logical. Capra comments that "Such 'technological determinism' seems to be a consequence of the high status of science in our public life—as compared to philosophy, art, or religion."[38] As long as something can be proven in the lab, confirmed with a computer simulation, and quantified with statistical treatments, it is legitimate; otherwise it must be suspect. Blind faith in the scientific approach thus becomes the stairway to technological totalitarianism.

In one of the clearest and most forthright pieces written by a politician on the subject, Representative George E. Brown, Jr., as chair of the House Committee on Science, Space and Technology, succinctly sums up the fallacy of our unquestioning faith in science and, at the same time, eloquently describes the role that technology plays in creating the Progress Paradox:

> The promise of science . . . may not serve society as advertised. Indeed, the promise of science may be at the root of our problems, because it is easier—politically, economically, socially, scientifically—to support more research than it is to change how we behave. . . .
>
> As the pace of technological development continues to accelerate, so does the speed with which we encounter new, unanticipated crises. The current debates over issues such as global climate change; energy production, consumption, and conservation; endangered species and disposal of hazardous waste all hinge on the expectation that science will provide the data and the technologies needed to overcome these challenges, many of which were caused by technological innovation in the first place. But there has never in human history been a long-term technological fix; there have merely been bridges to the next level of societal stress and crisis.[39]

Science has provided us with an exhilarating technological joyride; our scientific and engineering miracles have provided the engine for a thrilling excursion. The problem is that we lack a clear idea as to where we are headed. Our vehicle accelerates faster and faster, but we have no road map. We have become so enamored with the methodology and tools of science that we have allowed our technology to run out of control.

I am not anti-science. We obviously cannot turn our backs on communication technologies, computer-based management systems, medical research, transportation advances, and new materials synthesis. We must continue to promote the rational problem-solving mindset. However, we must also adopt a renewed sense of self-restraint and responsibility. Without a clearer vision of purpose and perspective, our distended-intellectualism will continue to undermine our heritage from the Enlightenment.

The Three Determinants and Future Directions

Reason plays less of a role in the governance of human affairs in the late twentieth century than it did in the eighteenth century. One has but to look at our schools, our advertisements, our political campaigns. Despite the number of people living in squalor two hundred years ago, the elites—the decision-makers—were dedicated to a culture of reason and civility. Today, we live in a world less governed by reason, less committed to individual responsibility.

Americans seem to have lost control of our civic institutions for three reasons: traditional dependence on unabated growth and development no longer works *(the fallacy of linear expansion);* we are overwhelmed by an incomprehensible glut of data *(the information overload);* and our technological environment has grown so complex that we can no longer comprehend where it is going and what we can do about it *(technological determinism).*

Our problems are becoming more complicated at the same time that our ability to handle these problems is deteriorating. In 1928, in the *Future of an Illusion,* Sigmund Freud stated the progress dilemma in classic simplicity: "While mankind has made continual advances in its control over nature and may expect to make still greater ones, it is not possible to establish with certainty that a similar advance has been made in the management of human affairs."[40] Or in the contemporary words of Jonathan Schell, "human power has outrun human knowledge."[41]

These three underlying determinants are unyielding realities of the late twentieth century; they are the inevitable, irrational outgrowths of research, expansion, and progress. There is nothing we can do to reverse the end of linear growth, to dismiss the information overload, nor to eradicate our technological dependency. No amount of government effort, educational reform, or revitalization of traditional values is going to dismantle this post-intellectual labyrinth in which we find ourselves.

NOTES

1. Herbert Spencer, "The Americans" in *Essays,* 1891.

2. Campbell, 1989, p. 14.

3. Rousseau [1762] (book 3, ch. 14), 1952, p. 421.

4. Quoted in Lasch, 1991, p. 375.

5. Tuchman, 1984, p. 380.

6. Eaton, Shostak, and Konner, 1988, p. 2.

7. Christopher Wills, "Has Human Evolution Ended?" *Discover*, August 1992, p. 22.

8. U.S. Bureau of the Census, *Current Population Reports,* series P20–454, reprinted in *Statistical Abstract of the United States: 1995* (115th ed.), Washington, DC, 1995, p. 79.

9. Marston Bates, "Population," *The Encyclopedia Americana*, International ed. (1970), s.v.

10. Dorris, 1990.

11. "Doing Drugs in the Womb [editorial]," *Los Angeles Times,* 18 September 1993, p. B17.

12. Dorris, 1990.

13. Michael D. Lemonick, "Not So Fertile Ground," *Time,* 19 September 1994, p. 68.

14. Donella H. Meadows, "A Chemical Whirlwind on the Horizon," *Los Angeles Times,* 31 January 1996, p. B11.

15. Capra, 1982, pp. 200–201.

16. Sorokin, 1941, p. 93.

17. Capra, 1982, p. 201.

18. Miles, 1976, p. 7.

19. Levy, 1995, p. 26.

20. For a delightful and overwhelming accounting of the television torrent of trivia, see Bill McKibben's *The Age of Missing Information,* 1992.

21. Cited in Moyers, 1989, p. 182.

22. Toffler, 1980, pp. 165, 166.

23. Naisbitt, 1984, p. 16.

24. In the video *Memory and Imagination,* various sources from the Library of Congress actually place the estimate anywhere from 3,000 new items per day to 30,000 items per day (Krainin Productions, Inc., New York, 1990).

25. Naisbitt, 1984, p. 17.

26. Mike Barnicle, "We Tune Out Daily Slaughter," *Boston Globe*, 3 July 1994, p. 27.

27. Postman, 1992, p. 72.

28. Stephen Bertman, "Modern Values and the Challenge of Myth," *Imprimis* (Hillsdale College), 22, no. 3 (March 1993), p. 2.

29. Quoted in Neal Gabler, "How We Know What We Know: Logic Meets Illogic at Simpson Trial," in *Los Angeles Times,* 6 August 1995, p. M6.

30. See Postman, 1992; Mander, 1991.

31. Sale, "In Industrial Revolution II," 1995.

32. Thoreau [1854], 1942, p. 30.

33. Postman, 1985, p. 157.

34. Quoted in Packard, 1977, p. 329.

35. See David H. Freedman, "Bytes of Life," *Discover*, November 1991, pp. 67–72; and Will Hively, "X-Ray Dreams," *Discover*, July 1995, pp. 70–79.

36. Presently, it takes something like 500,000 electrons to represent one digital *bit*—the combination of one's and zero's that form the language of all digital communication; but two physicists at Cambridge University have built a circuit that uses just 50 to 100 electrons per bit—and Haroon Ahmed and Kazoo Nakazato feel there is a good chance that they can ultimately devise a system that will work with one-electron bits!

37. Dubos, 1987, p. 1.

38. Capra, 1982, pp. 218–19.

39. George E. Brown, Jr., "It's Down to the Last Blank Check," *Los Angeles Times*, 8 September 1992, p. B9.

40. Quoted in Lasch, 1991, p. 145.

41. Schell, 1989, p. 47.

PART 2

Personal Consequences of Post-Intellectualism

Consider the auk;
Becoming extinct because he forgot how
*   to fly, and could only walk.*
Consider man, who may well become extinct
Because he forgot how to walk and learned
*   how to fly before he thought.*

• Ogden Nash
The Private Dining Room and Other New Verses

The next twelve chapters are divided into three parts—personal, social, and political effects. Under these three (somewhat arbitrary) headings, we explore twelve identifiable problem areas that can be defined as consequences of post-intellectualism: illiteracy and the dominance of mediated reality, loss of privacy, cognitive deterioration and the demise of analytic thinking, psychological isolation and dependency, urban deterioration, economic exploitation, environmental degradation, moral collapse, retribalization, the decline of freedom, the disintegration of democracy, and worldwide anarchy.

5

Illiteracy:
The Brave New Mega-Mediated World

I am convinced that Mars used to be inhabited by rational human beings like ourselves, who had the misfortune, some thousands of years ago, to invent television.

• Robert Hutchins
"Points to Ponder," Reader's Digest

About ten years ago, one of my television graduates landed a production job with a major TV network. Dave worked his way up rapidly and now holds a highly responsible production management position. We frequently call on him for our "career days" seminars to share the secret of his success with current undergraduates. Besides other leadership and creative abilities, Dave attributes his rapid rise to one quality—*he could read*.

This is not to say that other production personnel could not read the words in various instructions, memos, manuals, union newsletters, and technical reports—but Dave could read and comprehend, analyze, and interpret. His fellow workers would receive a three-page document and typically react by saying, "Let Dave read it and tell us what it's all about." His supervisors recognized that he was a young man with a special talent—the intellectual ability to understand and master the written word.

THE COLLAPSE OF THE PRINT CULTURE

A participatory democracy is dependent upon an enlightened, informed, and literate citizenry that understands its nation's history and governmental procedures, is aware of current issues, can analyze opposing political arguments, and participates in public debates. This level of enlightenment and involvement demands a high standard of literacy.

The writers of the U.S. Constitution assumed that the citizenry of the new republic would be competent in handling the printed word. Joshua Meyrowitz writes that it was "unthinkable in a print society to have non-literates become actively involved in the governing process because they had neither access to the 'public forum' created by books and newspapers nor the skill necessary to make a significant contribution to the 'discussion.'"[1] It would not do to allow only a certain class of people—readers like Dave—handle all the reading and analyzing and interpreting for the rest of us. All the citizenry is to be involved.

From time to time, civil libertarians and concerned librarians warn us about impending censorship threats and the cancer of a growing book-burning mentality. The danger, however, is not that books will be censored, burned, or otherwise kept out of the hands of an eager and intellectually hungry citizenry; the danger is that the citizenry no longer will care enough to seek out books and ideas. In comparing George Orwell's *1984* and Aldous Huxley's *Brave New World*, Neil Postman observes, "What Orwell feared were those who would ban books. What Huxley feared was that there would be no reason to ban a book, for there would be no one who wanted to read one."[2]

Around 1900, the U.S. literacy rate was holding steady at almost 90 percent.[3] Until well into the twentieth century, Americans were still a literate culture. However, during the last three or four decades, we have seen our literacy decline precipitously.

Contemporary Illiteracy

Compiling data from a multitude of federal reports, national studies, and independent books over the past two decades, the following profile can be compiled: sixty million Americans (about one-third of the adult population) are totally or functionally illiterate (that is, they cannot read a want ad, address a letter, understand the poison warnings on a pesticide can, or fill out a job application). Young adults between the ages of eighteen and twenty-three read, on the average, at the level of a ninth-grader. About one-third of American youth are "ill-educated, ill-employed, and ill-equipped to make their way in American society."[4]

More than 50 percent of the nation's prison inmates are not able to read newspaper headlines or understand written instructions. Eighty-five percent of all juveniles who appear in court are functionally illiterate. The result is significantly higher costs for all of us in terms of welfare payments, bigger law enforcement bills, medical care for the indigent, increased insurance premiums, and the like.

There is an emerging class of literate readers and thinkers, like Dave, who assume leadership positions because of their ability to master the written word. This was not the situation 150 years ago when it was assumed that *all* citizens could handle the written word equally. The irony is that in today's post-intellectual, quasi-egalitarian culture we are witnessing the rise of a new class elitism in America—based on literacy and technological know-how—the journalists, computer programmers, and technocrats who do the thinking and decision-making for all of us.

Falling SAT Scores. Many educators point to falling scores on the Scholastic Aptitude Test (SAT) and other standardized exams as evidence of our nation's declining verbal literacy. As indicated in Figure 5.1, the average SAT verbal scores for college-bound high school seniors hovered between 470 and 480 throughout most of the 1950s. Then a decided decline became apparent, from the early 1960s through about 1980. From that point on, scores have leveled off around 420 to 430.[5]

Figure 5.1
Average SAT Verbal Scores: 1951-52 to 1993-94

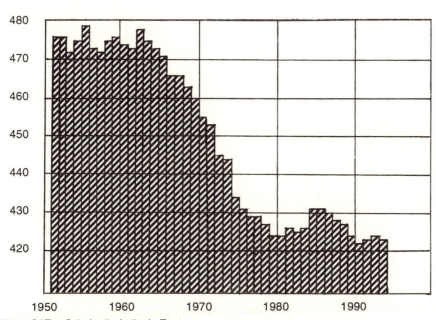

Note: SAT = Scholastic Aptitude Test

Several explanations are frequently offered for this drop: an increasing number of immigrants who speak English as a second language are taking the test; a larger number of inner-city students who have not had adequate elementary and secondary education are going on to college; more students are suffering emotional stress triggered by today's societal uncertainties.

None of these reasons explain, however, why the decline began to level off in the early 1980s. Within a single generation, literacy scores fell from a standard around 470 to 480 down to a new standard around 420 to 430; and they have stabilized at that point. What is unique about that twenty-year period?

One inescapable observation is the correlation of the drop in scores with the period when the TV generation came fully of age. Starting in the early 1960s, we were processing each year a new group of high school graduates who had spent yet one more year in front of the television screen. By sometime around 1972, the average high school graduate had spent his or her entire life with the tube. For the next several years, viewing time increased, cognitive patterns changed, and school systems slowly adapted to a gradual decline in intellectual competencies and expectations. By the end of the 1970s, the transition was complete.

Whatever the reason for the falling scores, the one incontestable fact is that today's college-bound high school graduates are less intellectually prepared for higher education than preceding generations. And our colleges and universities have compensated for this decline with remedial programs and correspondingly lower standards. We are adapting to the post-intellectual culture.

Degeneration of Writing Skills. Marshall McLuhan contends that the electric media are returning us to the oral and pictorial tradition.[6] As a result, the average citizen is less able to express him- or herself in writing. Fewer and fewer of us write diaries or journals any more; we pick up the telephone rather than write a letter; truncated e-mail blurbs replace carefully constructed thoughts. Educators decry the decreasing ability of students to write a well-ordered essay—formulating a thesis, building an argument, expressing intelligible ideas in writing.

Students entering college exhibit such diminished writing skills that institutions of higher education have to devote more and more of their resources to remedial courses. At City College of New York, two sequential preparatory courses are offered *before* a deficient student can be admitted into Remedial English![7] Colleges and universities across the country have had to institute "writing proficiency exams" to ensure that college graduates will at least be able to write two or three coherent paragraphs in a row before they can get their degree.

CAUSES OF ILLITERACY

Numerous social, economic, and political factors could be examined as reasons for our rising illiteracy—the breakup of the nuclear family, increasing immigration problems, inner-city deterioration and gang warfare, economic uncertainties and frustrations, and many more.

Declining budgets, for example, are a major cause. It is easy to overlook library and school needs as other pressing social problems (crime, welfare,

public health, garbage collection) demand our urgent attention. (A munici-
pality cannot afford to let its police, fire protection, or trash collection go
unfunded for more than a couple days—but a community can let its schooling
system slide for a couple decades before seeing the results. We are now seeing
the results.)

Across the nation, we see educational finances slipping—in higher education
as well as elementary and secondary levels. In 1970, the state of California
spent twice as much on the University of California system as it did on prisons.
Twenty-five years later, this ratio has been reversed; the state now spends twice
as much money putting people behind bars as it does putting people through the
University of California. From 1989 to 1993, the California Department of
Corrections added 8,600 persons to its payroll, while the State's colleges and
universities lost 10,300 positions.

Regardless of obvious social and economic causes, however, much of the
problem stems from our changing attitudes toward education in a post-intellectual climate.

The Education Dilemma

An enlightened citizenry requires universal education. But if universal
education is to accommodate the masses, it inevitably means a deterioration of
academic standards—lowering scholarly expectations so that the greater populace can be included in the system. The subtitle of Christopher Lasch's landmark 1978 *The Culture of Narcissism* is *American Life in an Age of Diminishing
Expectations*. Concerning lowered expectations in education, he writes, "The
whole problem of American education comes down to this: in American society,
almost everyone identifies intellectual excellence with elitism. This attitude not
only guarantees the monopolization of educational advantages by the few; it
lowers the quality of elite education itself and threatens to bring about a reign
of universal ignorance."[8]

Starting with the flood of European immigrants in the 1890s, schools
become de facto welfare institutions—stressing remedial English, health education, home economics, occupational instruction, and citizenship training. We
simply are asking our schools to assume too many responsibilities—as surrogate
parents, medical clinics, welfare kitchens, law enforcement agencies, and sensitivity-training centers. Gone are any intellectual aspirations.

Shifting Educational Priorities. The 1918 report of the National
Education Association, *Cardinal Principles of Secondary Education*, listed seven
main objectives for American high schools: health, "worthy home membership,"
vocational education, citizenship, "worthy use of leisure," ethical character, and
"command of fundamental processes." Only the last goal stressed any academic
content at all. There was a deliberate lack of emphasis on intellectual achievement or mastery of traditional scholarly disciplines. This report became one of
the most influential educational documents of the twentieth century and, right or

wrong, helped to propel us into the post-intellectual culture.

During the turbulent 1960s, we decided we were serious about self-esteem education. One study of the American education system traced the roots of the decline to "a shift in social and educational values during the 1960s which led to a massive cut in the number of basic academic classes, less strenuous graduation requirements, and an overall emphasis on less demanding elective courses."[9] Schools were to stress the counter-intellectual goals of self-realization, multi-culturalism, sensitivity, and self-esteem—rather than intellectual and scholastic pursuits.

Our Anti-Intellectual Bias. Even more disturbing is the overt anti-intellectualism that pervades our contemporary culture. Society glorifies the macho hero and the sex goddess, while belittling those who are concerned with affairs of the mind. We reward our entertainment celebrities, professional athletes, and top corporate executives with extravagant incomes, while our nation's school teachers, poets, philosophers, writers, and other intellectual toilers subsist barely a notch above the official poverty line. Alumni of outstanding institutions of higher learning such as The University of Michigan, UCLA, Duke University, and Notre Dame identify more with their football and basketball teams than they do with their research labs or Nobel Prize winners.

Such an anti-intellectual attitude contributes to the endorsement of mediocrity as our standard. This viewpoint was summed up by columnist Roger Simon in a mock graduation speech he wrote for the graduating class of 1990: "Why be more than mediocre when mediocrity is all that life demands of you? Mediocrity will get you through. It always has. It got you through high school and through college and, let me assure you, it will get you through the job market."[10]

Academic achievement is perceived as being inherently anti-democratic. Students get the subliminal message that, in the spirit of democratic egalitarianism, they should not aspire to rise above the average; it is somehow unfair to achieve a position of intellectual competence. Columnist George Will writes, "Indeed many teachers now consider the traditional idea of teaching to be intellectually suspect and morally offensive because it is tainted by the authoritarian idea that there are defensible standards and by the inegalitarian idea that some people do things better than others."[11]

Pictorial Media as the Culprit

We could examine many of these causes of illiteracy in some detail; my primary concern in this section, however, is the impact of pictures. We live in a society dominated by television, movies, billboards, corporate logos, posters, magazine layouts, advertising displays, newspaper charts and graphics, textbook illustrations, and cash registers that work with pictures rather than numbers. Television has eliminated the need to learn to read for basic survival activities. One can get one's entertainment, news highlights, political sound bites, and product information from the tube. Why bother to learn to read?

Even with our computers, keyboard literacy has been replaced by graphical interfaces, windows and icons, pull-down menus, mouses, touch-screen technologies, and voice commands. "User-friendly" is to be interpreted "computer systems for the semi-literate."

The amount of time that children spend with the TV set is an especially worrisome matter—considering the formation of their intellectual attitudes and cognitive learning styles at an early age. Although surveys and studies differ, one may conservatively say that the average child watches television more than four hours a day. As a consequence, today's young people are spending less time reading than ever before. This dominance of the TV tube is reflected in the deceasing emphasis on reading material in the home. A 1994 biennial report from the National Assessment of Education Progress "found a sharp decrease in the amount of reading materials such as encyclopedias, books and magazines in homes over the last two decades."[12]

The less one uses a given technology—print, for example—the less proficient one will be with that technology. Skills do not develop unless one practices and masters a given craft; this is true whether one is learning to play the piano, hit a golf ball, or read a book. The less time a child devotes to reading, the less competent he or she will be in the future when dealing with printed symbols, abstract ideas, and linear argumentation. Judith Van Evra comments, "By narrowing word use or substituting jingles for thought, we may limit rational capacity, which is especially important for young viewers who are just starting to internalize language."[13]

Another consideration is the alteration of brain-wave patterns. Many studies confirm that while watching television there is an increase in alpha waves (characteristic of relaxation and minimal brain activity) and a decrease in beta waves (which indicate an aroused, active state of mind).[14] As Jerry Mander sums it up, "The longer the set is on, the slower the brain-wave activity."[15] The more one watches television, the less one's brain is challenged.

Many writers have drawn a parallel between drug addiction and television addiction, suggesting that we become narcotized by the heavy media dosage we routinely ingest. Daniel Goleman writes in the *New York Times:* "The proposition that television can be addictive is proving to be more than a glib metaphor. The most intensive scientific studies of people's viewing habits are finding that for the most frequent viewers, watching television has many of the marks of a dependency like alcoholism or other addictions."[16]

Pictures and Pacing: Killing Concentration. In discussing comparative video games, my six-year-old grandson once proclaimed, "My friend Ryan has such an old and slow Nintendo game that it's like looking at a book." Youth learn early to expect an intense level of visual excitement and stimulation from their video experiences—whether from computer games, TV cartoons, adventure shows, or even educational programs.

The media, of competitive necessity, have to rely on sensory bombardment and overstimulation rather than intellectual reflection and analysis. We have been conditioned to expect short, snappy presentations of all types—special effects, quick-cut editing, continual camera movement, fast-paced action, flashy colors, pounding music, and any other means to intensify the visual and aural excitement. In a 1984 speech, newscaster Robert MacNeil summed up this attribute of the television experience:

> The trouble with television is that it discourages concentration. . . . Programmers live in constant fear of losing anyone's attention—anyone's. The surest way to avoid doing so is to keep everything brief, not to strain the attention of anyone but instead to provide constant stimulation through variety, novelty, action and movement.
>
> . . . Consider the casual assumptions that television tends to cultivate: that complexity must be avoided, that visual stimulation is a substitute for thought, that verbal precision is an anachronism. It may be old-fashioned, but I was taught that thought is words, arranged in grammatically precise ways.[17]

There is little time for deliberation and literate analysis in today's media: shorter segments in news programs, mini-documentaries inserted into newscasts, MTV videos, one-minute prime-time news breaks, political debates in five-second sound bites, rapid-fire rap records, the frenetic pace of *Sesame Street*, the fifteen-second commercial, and the three-column-inch stories of *USA Today*. In an essay on contemporary culture, Pico Iyer writes, "Increasingly, in fact, televisionaries are telling us to read the writing on the screen and accept that ours is a postliterate world. . . . MTV, *USA Today*, the PC and the VCR—why, the acronym itself!—are making the slow motion of words as obsolete as pictographs."[18]

Perceiving the world through sound bites and fragmented pictures results in the lessening of our ability to think logically, sequentially, and abstractly. We have become increasingly impatient when it comes to analyzing and solving our problems—we want answers now. This is one indication of our immersion in the web culture.

Picturization and Hemisphericity. Research indicates a difference in function between the right and left hemispheres of the brain. The *right hemisphere* is predominantly concerned with pictorial input, nonverbal communication, holistic and nonlogical processing of information. It is more clearly identified with the non-intellectual processes of feelings and instinct. Interpreted by the right hemisphere, television and film look at the world sensually, artistically, bringing us a world of images, sound, and motion. Oral and pictorial messages involve us instantaneously and emotionally; we are swallowed up in the communication experience; we cannot stand back and examine it; we are immersed totally; we must react immediately and intuitively—without analysis and reflection.

The *left hemisphere* of the brain is more involved with logic and reasoning, analytic processing of information, the sequential treatment of data, the manipulation of verbal symbols, written communication. The left hemisphere represents our intellectual leanings—objective investigation and the scientific method. Print—exercising the left hemisphere—brings to us a world of ideas and exposition, reason and linear argumentation, cause-and-effect relationships, and rational discourse. Print allows the reader to stand back and examine the message objectively, to think about it, to make comparisons and contrasts.

Freedom, democracy, progress, economic theories, scientific concepts: these are all ideas and abstractions. One must be able to handle the printed word in order to understand and contemplate and debate these topics. The more time we spend in the right hemisphere—watching pictures, listening to music, and approaching life with an intuitive or holistic attitude—the less our brains will be able to manipulate written words and mathematical symbols; the less we will be able to deal with ideas, theories, abstractions, and analytic chores; the less we will be able to handle the intellectual demands of a democratic government. The problem is not that television brings us bad programming (which is what concerns most critics); the problem is that television brings us good pictures.

Oral and pictorial communication can be interpreted as both *pre-intellectual* and *post-intellectual*. Print involves *intellectual* activity. A society that processes most of its data orally, or in pictorial format, develops a completely different culture from the society that learns to rely on written symbols. One develops sensually, intuitively, artistically; the other develops symbolically, analytically, intellectually. The former develops compassion; the latter develops computers.

MEDIATED REALITY

Today's mass media play a pervasive role in shaping practically every aspect of our post-intellectual culture—our family, political, economic, educational, religious, and entertainment institutions. All media substitute words and pictures and recorded sounds for the real world. Post-intellectual media have constructed their own reality, their own substance.

When you climb a tree, play softball, pet your dog, practice your guitar, or engage in sexual intercourse, you are experiencing reality firsthand. However, when you are looking at a nature program, watching the Yankees on television, reading a dog-care manual, listening to a CD, or viewing a porno movie, you are not experiencing reality. Instead, you are experiencing a mediated reality—a synthetic substitute that is brought to you through media channels. Mander describes the creation of this artificial environment:

Most Americans spend their lives within environments created by human beings. . . . Natural environments have largely given way to human-created environments.

What we see, hear, touch, taste, smell, feel and understand about the world has been processed for us. Our experiences of the world can no longer be called direct, or primary. They are secondary, mediated experiences.[19]

What we see and hear is real to us. And if what we see and hear are printed words, moving pictures, and recorded sounds, then these symbols and mediated images become our reality. Most of our experiences, our information, our knowledge about the world is brought to us through mediated channels. Less and less do we encounter reality directly. Perceiving the world by looking at a two-dimensional flickering picture framed in a 25-inch box is, after all, a pretty weird way to experience one's environment. And, of course, neither does surfing around from one World Wide Web site to another on a 15-inch computer monitor do much to build a coherent picture of reality.

We become further dehumanized as we distance ourselves from personal involvement in life. As we go through the years with fewer and fewer real experiences—not attending athletic events, discussion groups, church services, live instructional sessions, nightclubs, nature hikes, poetry readings, or political rallies—our identity as a unique human being is diminished. Our individuality disappears as we all watch the same news summaries, laugh at the same sitcoms, and listen to the same recordings. Acceptance of this homogenized mediated reality contributes significantly to our loss of identity (discussed in Chapter 8).

The Medium as the Message

Perhaps the clearest post-intellectual manifestation of media reality is the concept that *the medium is the message;* we experience the mediums themselves—regardless of the specific artistic, informational, or persuasive content. Although many media critics have voiced variations on this theme, the slogan is generally associated with McLuhan.[20]

For example, the act of watching television in the evening is what is significant; that is the cultural message to which we must pay attention—not the particular programs that happen to be on the tube. What matters is that individual family members are each involved, in a one-on-one basis, with that flickering tube in the semi-darkened bedroom, kitchen, or living room. Socially, it does not matter if each particular viewer is watching a sitcom, a football game, a serious drama, a game show, a talk show, a PBS documentary, or MTV videos. What counts is that each individual is focusing, for the better part of the evening, independently and singly on that medium.

The fact that you wake up to your alarm clock/radio each day is the significant message—not the particular piece of music that happens to be playing. The act of reading the newspaper with breakfast every morning is the message—not the particular headline on any given day. Logging on to the Internet for an hour or two every day is the message—not the specific WWW sites you happen to hook up with. Going out to the movies on a date is the important message—not the particular movie that happens to be playing this week. The habit of reading a book before you drop off to sleep at night is the message—not the particular novel you happen to be reading this month.

It is the way we use the media—the way we allow them to shape our lives—that is the significant message. That is the essence of technological determinism; the media—the technologies themselves, and not their content—mold our culture. Imagine what a different society we would have without the telephone, the television, the computer. They are our reality. McLuhan and Fiore sum up the concept in this passage:

Societies have always been shaped more by the nature of the media by which men communicate than by the content of the communication. . . . The alphabet and print technology fostered and encouraged a fragmenting process, a process of specialism and of detachment. . . . It is impossible to understand social and cultural changes without a knowledge of the workings of media.[21]

Author Cliff Stoll adds, "In short, the medium in which we communicate changes how we organize our thoughts. We program computers, but the computers also program us."[22]

Media Confirmation of Reality

There was a cartoon in the British humor magazine *Punch* many years ago that showed a group of vacationers at the oceanside; each one was intently looking at his or her personal portable TV set displaying a picture of (what else?) the ocean. It is as if nothing exists except as we read about it or see it portrayed on television. We take our transistor radios to the ballpark to listen to the game—to confirm what we are actually seeing. People attending the Rose Parade in person for the first time often remark, "We should have stayed home and watched it on TV; we could have gotten a better view."

Today's current events do not really exist until they are covered by the news media. Famine in Africa, celebrity trials, political scandals, and anti-abortion demonstrations become social realities only when televised. Of course, many such events are staged only for the news coverage; the demonstrators do not bother to pick up their placards and start to march until the cameras arrive. Real things do not even happen unless the media are there; pseudo-reality is created for the cameras. Ernst Cassirer makes this observation in 1956—at the dawn of the Information Age:

Physical reality seems to recede in proportion as man's symbolic activity advances. Instead of dealing with the things themselves, man is in a sense constantly conversing with himself. He has so enveloped himself in linguistic forms, in artistic images, in mythical symbols or religious rites that he cannot see or know anything except by the interposition of an artificial medium.[23]

Fictionalized Reality. The worlds of dramatic fiction and entertainment have always provided a mix of actuality and mediated reality. Our neolithic forebears undoubtedly entertained their peers around the evening fire with exaggerated retellings of the glories of last year's hunt. Homer poetically weaved myth and reality in his narration of the Trojan Wars in the *Iliad*.

Throughout history, powerful novels have played a significant role in creating our views of reality. From the boost given to the abolitionist movement by Harriet Beecher Stowe's *Uncle Tom's Cabin*, to the muckraking exposé of the meat-packing industry by Upton Sinclair in *The Jungle*, to Margaret Mitchell's portrayal of the South in *Gone with the Wind*, the novel has shaped our perception of what the world was actually like.

Consider the extent to which our interpretation of historical events has been shaped by the movies and television fiction—from the racism of *Birth of a Nation* to the Roman spectacle of *Ben-Hur* to our impression of the Korean War in *M*A*S*H*. What about the accuracy of hundreds of biographical films and televised life stories? How have Oliver Stone's *Platoon* and *JFK* and *Nixon* influenced our collective perceptions of contemporary events and leaders?

Docudramas, "reality programming," tabloid television, and the re-creation of actual events on newscasts and magazine programs further add to the confusion between what really happened and what we are told happened. What dialogue was actual and what was scripted? How much is actual footage and what has been re-staged? Who are the real characters and who are the actors?

The public, of course, greatly adds to its own confusion. During his peak popularity in the early 1970s, TV's fictional Dr. Marcus Welby received up to five thousand letters per week from anxious viewers seeking medical advice. Author Robert James Waller has gone to great lengths to try to convince his many readers that *Bridges of Madison County* was a total fiction.

Reality was further bent when Vice President Dan Quayle chastised fictional TV news personality Murphy Brown for having a baby of wedlock. (This occurred after an episode of the sitcom in which Murphy Brown had a baby shower attended by real-life news anchors and reporters Katie Couric, Faith Daniels, Joan Lunden, Mary Alice Williams, and Paula Zahn.) The fictional Murphy Brown then responded to the real Dan Quayle on her make-believe TV newsshow-within-the-sitcom by parading real-life single mothers on the air, while the vice president watched the fiction in a room peopled with his chosen real-life single mothers (all captured on real videotape, of course).

Commenting on the O. J. Simpson trial, Chicago columnist Bob Greene writes about "the queasy drift of our society as we increasingly become a nation of citizens who watch anything and everything as if it is all a show." He continues, "It's not that we can't tell the difference between entertainment and reality; it is that entertainment and reality have somehow become the same."[24]

Marie Winn adds that "The separation between the real and the unreal becomes blurred; all of life becomes more dreamlike as the boundaries between the real and the unreal merge."[25] If a person spends four hours a day watching fictional characters on a video screen or reading a novel about imaginary people, do we categorize this time period as reality (what a real person is doing with a real life) or as fantasy (the four-hour period is devoted entirely to an unreal media experience)? If someone spends two hours cruising the Internet, do we consider the time spent in cyberspace as real or illusory? Within the web culture, fantasy becomes reality. Reality is devoted to fantasy.

SPREADING MEDIA TENTACLES

Media saturation can only increase. With the escalation of digital technologies, fiberoptics, video compression, continuing miniaturization, direct satellite broadcasting, personal cellular communications, and optical recording techniques, we are going to be locked ever more tightly in the grasp of the media macrocosm.

One example is the increasing ubiquity of *place-based television,* "the migration of television out of the home and into places where consumers eat, wait, study, shop, play, work and travel."[26] The idea is to place TV receivers and closed-circuit messages wherever people are standing or sitting with any time on their hands—no need to allow idle minds to daydream, or work on something creative, or, worse yet, read a book, when they can be saturated with lively pictures and relevant sales pitches.

In the 1980s, Whittle Communications introduced its controversial satellite-based Channel One service for schools (bringing news summaries and commercial messages into the classroom). Since then, place-based sales and propaganda channels have popped up wherever a captive audience could be found: doctors' waiting offices, airport lounges, maternity wards, health clubs, subway platforms, record and video stores, private hospital rooms, truck stops, supermarket checkout lines, clothing stores, post office lobbies, waiting lines for amusement park rides, fast-food restaurants, beauty salons, movie theater lobbies, banks, the gas pump at your local service station ("How about a car wash?" "Tried our snack shop?"), and wherever else people might be standing around for a moment or two. Robert Kubey is among the critics who are concerned that "wherever we go we're targeted as consumers who need to be sold something."[27]

Information and the Channels Explosion

The explosion in potential media channels is awesome. The leap into the future involves the use of fiberoptics to transmit digitized, compressed information modulated onto laser beams. At the incredibly high frequency rates of light waves—in the neighborhood of *1,000 trillion* vibrations per second—these laser beams can carry an unimaginably large quantity of data. Utilizing the full bandwidth of fiberoptics potential, such broadband services can theoretically provide a bandwidth of 25,000,000,000,000 hertz—the equivalent of some 2.5 billion AM radio stations! Or over 4 million TV channels!

This could bring to every consumer boundless video and print multimedia information, entertainment, advertising, on-line databases, reference works, business communications, personal audio and video communication devices, retail purchases, financial transactions, medical assistance, education and training, security surveillance, games, polling, political interactivity, and so forth. This is the essence of technological determinism: (to paraphrase the theme from the movie *Field of Dreams*), "Make the channels available, and we will fill them."

Interactive Media

Starting with the introduction of coin-operated "Pong" games in the mid-1970s, the public has been increasingly seduced into the world of interactive media. The video consumer was now able to exercise control over the images and happenings on the video screen—flipping paddles, firing rockets, clobbering bad guys, obliterating space aliens, maneuvering objects, choosing pathways, and answering questions. No longer would the TV viewer be at the mercy of network programmers and distant advertisers. However, the more insidious impact was largely ignored: the appeal of interactivity lured us further and further into a mediated environment.

Social critics were quick to condemn the darkened environment and aggressive nature of the video arcades and their violence-prone games, comparing them to the dens of iniquity frequented by earlier adolescent generations—pool halls and bowling alleys. The difference, however, is highly significant: in taverns and pool halls, the interaction and competition was between individuals; whereas in the newer arcades, the interaction and competition is between human and machine. We are pulled deeper and deeper into the vortex of mediated reality. Stoll, a well-known computer enthusiast and hacker, voices some second thoughts about the computer environment in *Silicon Snake Oil:* "How sad . . . The only sensations are a glowing screen, the touch of a keyboard, and the sound of an occasional bleep. All synthetic."[28]

One of the more intriguing developments is *interactive movies*. Distributed on a CD-ROM format, this technology allows the viewer to interact and choose plot paths throughout the story—in effect, building a different story line every time one goes through the video. Another layer of interactive clutter was added to our mediated reality when cable services such as MTV and the Sci-Fi Channel added on-line capabilities to some of their regular programming.

Multimedia interactive formats and presentations are increasingly used in every aspect of contemporary culture—for entertainment, instruction, shopping, games, business, finances, politics, and anywhere else people communicate. Users are conditioned to push buttons; select icons; pursue this path, then that; intuitively try this, then that. See what works, then try something else. This is the very definition of the web culture—the antithesis of a linear approach.

In an intellectual culture, a storyteller such as Shakespeare or Poe or Agatha Christie would masterfully craft a linear, sequential tale that would be hard to top. Today, however, we construct our own interactive storylines, we create movie screenplays by committee, and we devise our educational entertainments by bouncing around and seeing what grabs our interest. Steven Levy writes, "Considering the sorry state of literacy, there's real danger in even a partial abandonment of narrative forms and rigorous modes of thought associated with logical arguments, where A leads to B. *Multimedia's forte is not reason, but hot emotional impact* [italics added]."[29] We abandon the cognitive culture and embrace the affective experience.

Communal Interactive Media. And now we have theatrical, *communal* interactive movies. At crucial decision points during the film, the theatergoers are polled en masse (through electronic pistol-grip handles on each armrest) to decide what path the drama should take. The audience is given numerous opportunities to dictate the course of events by consensus, so that dozens of possible plot twists can actually be pasted together.[30]

The significant feature of this theatrical interactive participation is the communal nature of the event. In other interactive experiences, the viewer or participant is a solitary traveler, encountering his or her mediated event as a lone individual. However, in this theatrical interactive activity, the individual is swallowed up as part of a collective decision-making entity. Such a communal experience is part of the retribalization with which we are concerned in a post-intellectual environment.

We have been playing in the MUDs (multi-user domains) for several years, with players at distant terminals chasing each other through medieval mazes. One potential application for the 25,000 gigahertz broadband fiberoptics technology is the possibility of such communal interactivity on a hitherto unfathomable scale. Imagine, if you will, an ongoing computer-based video game that pits some 100,000 players from the Pacific Northwest in a massive strategic battle against a similar number of players from New England. The more players/soldiers each team can recruit for its side of the battle, the better its chances of winning the nationwide simulation.

A less fanciful application of communal interactivity is the concept of *desktop video conferencing*, also known as "team computing" or "document conferencing." This process enables multiple users, located anywhere in the world, to work simultaneously on the same document, technical drawing, or electronic painting. The *groupware* package drives all the computer screens synchronously. Any entry or change made by any one of the users anywhere on-line will instantaneously be reflected on all the networked computer screens. Again, the tribalizing impact of numerous persons working in a group-think project runs counter to the individual creativity nurtured in the Intellectual Age. We are pioneering a kind of post-intellectual, communal, electronic folk art.

Virtual Reality

Evolving from early applications of the "Super Cockpit" flight simulator into an encyclopedia that becomes a walking tour through a virtual museum, and virtual buildings that allow architects and prospective clients to wander through simulated rooms, virtual reality (VR) has become today's most captivating extension of technological reality (without getting into a discussion of computer implants, wired mind-machine neural connections, and brain-actuated technologies).[31] By the early 1990s, we were hosting art exhibits featuring virtual reality environments, installing VR games in video arcades, and sponsoring musical concerts on virtual instruments. At NASA's Ames Research Center in Mountain View, California, you can walk around the virtual surface of Mars (recreated from satellite data).

Telepresence is the use of VR-controlled robots that operate in dangerous or remote environments while the human operator, located some distance away, functions in virtual reality, seeing what the robot sees and guiding the robot's movements and hand maneuvers via the operator's gloves and other gear. Technicians can safely manipulate highly toxic or radioactive materials in a hostile environment; workers can manipulate equipment in extremely high-temperature conditions; an operator in Tokyo can operate a spray-painting robot in Paris; and a surgeon sitting in a comfortable console in Boston can use a virtual scalpel to deftly remove a diseased gall bladder in rural upstate Vermont.[32]

Ultimate Considerations. Writing in 1914, the brilliant English author and essayist E. M. Forster penned an insightful short story, "The Machine Stops," in which the protagonist, Vashti, lives in a futuristic, underground cubicle that is a model for a modern virtual residence:

> There were buttons and switches everywhere—buttons to call for food, for music, for clothing. . . . There was the button that produced literature. And there were of course the buttons by which she communicated with her friends. The room, though it contained nothing, was in touch with all that she cared for in the world.[33]

All of us become increasingly, insidiously, immersed in an ever-expanding network of mediated experiences. This is inherent in the web culture of a post-intellectual period—a culture in which we willingly give up literacy, independent thinking, and a sense of individuality. We eagerly embrace the images and recorded sounds that define for us a new homogenized reality—a technological environment that frees us of the need to experience the natural world firsthand. We sit isolated in our segregated information cubicles, like Forster's Vashti, mesmerized by the blips and information fragments displayed on our computerized video screens.

Thoughtful observers question some of the potential effects of such progress. Michael Heim, a computer programmer/philosopher, asks, "So how do we deal with this electronic layer that has come between man and what used to be considered *real* life? What does it do to the mind, to the concept of what is real and what is not, to the essential connections between human beings, and to the connection between man and machines?"[34]

One of the most delightful, tongue-in-cheek, cynical views of what television can do to the human mind came from the very fertile mind of one of the mid-century's greatest intellectuals, Robert Hutchins:

> The horrid prospect that television has opened of nobody speaking and nobody reading suggests that a bleak and torpid epoch may lie ahead. If it lasts long enough, it will gradually, according to the principles of evolution, produce a population indistinguishable from the lower forms of plant life.
>
> Astronomers once detected something on Mars that looked like moss growing. I am convinced that Mars used to be inhabited by rational human beings like ourselves, who had the misfortune, some thousands of years ago, to invent television.[35]

NOTES

1. Meyrowitz, 1985, pp. 160–61.

2. Postman, 1985, p. vii.

3. Lukacs, 1984, p. 291.

4. Data for these conclusions were drawn from the following sources: the 1977 Adult Performance Level project of the University of Texas; the 1979 Carnegie Council of Policy Studies in Higher Education (source of the quotation); the 1983 National Commission on Excellence in Education; Kozol, 1985, pp. 4–5; Meyrowitz, 1985, p. 75; and the 1987 survey by the National Assessment of Educational Progress.

5. U.S. Department of Education, National Center for Education Statistics. *The Condition of Education*, 1995 (Washington, DC: Government Printing Office, 1995), p. 68.

6. See McLuhan, 1964.

7. See James Traub, "Annals of Education: Class Struggle," *New Yorker*, 19 September 1994, pp. 76-90.

8. Lasch, 1978, p. 145.

9. Allen, 1989, p. 45.

10. Roger Simon, "Words to the Class of '90: 'Dare Mighty Things,'" *Los Angeles Times,* 10 June 1990, p. E4.

11. George Will, "Writing Isn't Taught Anymore," *Honolulu Advertiser*, 3 July 1995, p. A10.

12. "Better Math, Science Grades? [editorial]" *Los Angeles Times*, 24 August 1994, p. B14.

13. Van Evra, 1990, p. 45.

14. See, for example, ibid., p. 39.

15. Mander, 1978, p. 207.

16. Daniel Goleman, "How Viewers Grow Addicted to Television," *New York Times*, 16 October 1990, p. C1.

17. MacNeil, 1984.

18. Iyer, 1990.

19. Mander, 1978, p. 55.

20. See, for example, Chapter 1 of McLuhan, 1964.

21. McLuhan and Fiore, 1967, p. 8.

22. Stoll, 1995, p. 46.

23. Cassirer, 1956. p. 43.

24. Greene, 1994.

25. Winn, 1985, pp. 104–05.

26. Mahler, 1991, p. 1.

27. Quoted in Mahler, 1991, p. 29.

28. Stoll, 1995, pp. 43–44.

29. Levy, 1995, p. 29.

30. Victor F. Zonana, "This Movie Requires a Pistol Grip," *Los Angeles Times,* 22 December 1992, p. A1.

31. See Bennett Daviss, "Brain Powered," *Discover,* May 1994, pp. 58–65.

32. See Gary Taubes, "Surgery in Cyberspace," *Discover,* December 1994, pp. 85–94.

33. Forster [1914], 1928, p. 20.

34. Quoted in Bettijane Levine, "Philosopher Bytes Off More Than Most of Us Can Chew," *Los Angeles Times,* 2 August 1992, pp. E1, E7.

35. "From a Speech," quoted in "Points to Ponder," *Reader's Digest,* April 1989, p. 165.

6

The Fishbowl Society: Loss of Privacy

Invasion of privacy is perhaps the most serious problem associated with information societies.

* Jerry Salvaggio
The Information Society

Privacy is an indispensable attribute of freedom. Without the right to travel unchallenged, seek information unhindered, buy products anonymously, meditate in seclusion, and talk to friends in private, there can be no freedom.

In the pre-literate oral tradition, there was no privacy. Everyone shared a common, collective tribal consciousness. There was no space for privacy; there was no technology to allow people to experience private thoughts. Privacy was created by the printing press; it is the invention of an intellectual culture.

In our post-intellectual culture, however, we witness an alarming erosion of personal privacy. The electric media, by facilitating both a retribalization mindset and computerized data gathering, are breaking down the walls of privacy. In his book, *The Information Society,* Jerry Salvaggio concludes that "Invasion of privacy is perhaps the most serious problem associated with information societies."[1] *Time* reporter Richard Lacayo sums up the extent to which we feel our privacy threatened today:

> Open up in there. The census taker wants to know what time you leave for work. Giant marketing firms want to know how often you use your credit cards. Your boss would like your psychological profile, your bill-paying history and a urine sample. Is that enough to make you feel like hiding in a corner, muttering to yourself about invasions of privacy? Forget it—the neighbors might be videotaping.[2]

The loss of privacy diminishes our sense of individuality and identity—that unique, singular world of values, dreams, secrets, and distinctive characteristics that defines who we are. We lose our concept of *self*. We are assimilated into one uniform collective entity. Tribal collectiveness is a pre-intellectual trait; individuality and privacy are intellectual qualities; retribalization and a loss of privacy are post-intellectual characteristics.

SIX CATEGORIES OF PRIVACY INVASION

Our privacy is whittled away, sliver by sliver—public records, government files, computer transactions, routine surveillance, business activities, personal security measures. Cliff Stoll observes that "Individually, each of these droplets of data isn't much of a threat. Collectively, though, the entire ocean becomes a serious threat to anonymity and privacy within our society."[3]

Media Publicity

When loss of privacy is mentioned, many people think first of the popular press and its hounding of both public and private citizens. Whether it is through a bizarre fabrication of some supermarket tabloid ("Extraterrestrial Gives Advice to Ross Perot") or a muckraking exposé on *60 Minutes* or *20/20*, those who have sought public recognition or acclaim—politicians, entertainers, sports figures, business leaders—must live with the public consequences of notoriety. Stalked both by professional videopaparazzi and amateur camcorder-wielding wannabes, they have lost the right to be left alone.

A more disturbing issue involves media coverage of private citizens who, through some inadvertent happenstance, have been shoved into the news—the victim of an accident, the spouse of a murder suspect, the couple whose house has just burned to the ground, the parents of a missing child. The result is often a flagrant disregard for the individual's right to be left alone, the right to private grief. As the media thrust their cameras and recorders into every nook and cranny of our daily experience, we are removing part of the veneer of civilization and returning to an open-to-all tribal existence.

The Sixth Amendment guarantee of a public trial is intended to protect citizens from a contemporary version of the Spanish Inquisition or the English Star Chamber. However, the effect is often to generate pretrial publicity which may be so sensationalized that the accused loses any chance for an unprejudiced court hearing. Boston lawyer and columnist John J. McGivney recounts the pretrial publicity of one of the most sensational trials of our century:

> The media swarmed over the story, emphasizing evidence that tended to incriminate [the defendant] and pointing out discrepancies in his statements to authorities. The sources of their stories were police officers, prospective witnesses and the lawyers for both sides, all of whom released leads and other information to the media. Much of it was inaccurate and groundless, . . . There were also stories about [the defendant's] "Jekyll-and-Hyde" personality and his "fiery temper," his late wife's fear of him before her death and blood found in his garage after the murder.[4]

Sound familiar? McGivney is describing the notorious 1954 trial of Dr. Sam Sheppard. Forty years later, the obvious parallel to O. J. Simpson is inescapable. However, the Simpson media spectacle eclipsed anything the country has ever seen. To what degree can the First Amendment protection of a free press, the Fourth Amendment prohibition against "unreasonable searches and seizures," and the Sixth Amendment guarantee of a speedy and public trial ever be satisfactorily reconciled?

Government Databases

There are about a thousand federal data banks, monitoring every conceivable aspect of your life: educational, financial, criminal, judicial, credit, health, welfare, employment, motor vehicle ownership, housing, travel, military records, and every other area where you have ever signed a piece of paper.[5] Plus the Census Bureau. Supposedly, the Census data are strictly confidential, but on at least two occasions government agencies have used the data for their investigative purposes: in 1917 to track down those who had not signed up for the draft, and in 1942 to locate Japanese-American families to be interned.[6]

In the past, we jealously guarded the confidentiality of our Social Security number. Originally, it was to be our private code to be used purely for social security benefits. Today, it is shared by the IRS, the military services, U.S. Civil Service, and the Bureau of the Census, among many other federal agencies; several states use it for voter registration, driver's licenses, and welfare and social services programs; and it is used by private agencies such as retail credit bureaus. We willingly divulge it to just about anyone who asks for it.

The next step would be an encrypted national identification card. Seen as an aid in fighting both terrorism and illegal immigration, such a card would be welcomed by many citizens as a positive security step; they would argue, "Surely we can sacrifice a little privacy for the benefits to be gained from law enforcement and defense protections." California Senator Dianne Feinstein envisions such a card which "could include a magnetic strip or microchip containing a digitized form of each citizen's vital statistics, photograph, voiceprint and retina scan. The card would be linked to massive new federal computer databases, and would be presented whenever an American applied for employment or government benefits."[7] How about an under-the-skin tattoo? A surgically implanted microchip? A bar-code ID number etched on every citizen? These and many other identification measures have been proposed—all in the name of security and fiscal efficiency.

Smart Cards Plus. Several years ago, a government study investigated *(purely as a theoretical exercise)* the ways in which a government *(if it so desired)* could exercise totalitarian control over its subjects. The study concluded that total domination could most effectively be achieved by the use of *financial smart cards*—the initiation of a totally cashless society.

Under such a system, all your salary, tips and gratuities, interest earnings, welfare checks, bond dividends—in short, all income—would be deposited in a single master personal account. All cash transactions would then be declared illicit; physical dollar bills and coins would be illegal; all bartering *(Will work for food)* would be outlawed. Everything you would ever purchase—your daily newspaper, time on a parking meter, coffee from a vending machine, the tip added to your restaurant bill—would be immediately transacted by your *super smart card*. With this record-keeping system, your every move would be traceable. You could not make a single purchase, take a trip, contribute to a charity, or subscribe to a magazine, without *them* knowing exactly where you were and what you were up to. All vestiges of personal privacy would be swept away.

Government Surveillance

When most citizens think of the government and invasion of privacy, they envision covert surveillance—spying. The menacing image of George Orwell's Big Brother (from the novel *1984*) remains the classic description of total-itarianism at its most invasive: "The telescreen received and transmitted simultaneously. Any sound that Winston [the protagonist] made, above the level of a very low whisper, would be picked up by it; moreover, so long as he remained within the field of vision which the metal plaque commanded, he could be seen as well as heard."[8]

We have today microphones the size of pinheads, video cameras slightly larger than a sugar cube, transmitters the size of a pea. Infrared film and telephoto lenses make it possible to photograph anybody anywhere (including inside their own homes), day and night. Voices inside a room can be picked up a half mile away by bouncing a laser beam off a window. An electronic sur-veillance truck can determine from the street what TV channel you are watch-ing. Cities have installed telephoto video cameras on buildings for random pub-lic surveillance. School districts are using video cameras on school buses.

In late 1995, cities started experimenting with "gunfire detection systems"—sophisticated microphones placed atop tall buildings and utility poles to pick up any gunshots and instantaneously report their location on a computer map at police headquarters. Such a surveillance system promises significant security benefits. And every official involved invariably will reject any suggestion that such a system would ever be used to pick up any street conversations.

Traffic Control and Movement Surveillance. We are moving ahead with development of the "Intelligent Vehicle Highway System" (think of it as a bar code on every vehicle, to be read by roadside scanners). Initially to be used to replace tollbooths on interstate highways, it can be adapted to monitor traffic, catch speeders, and otherwise keep track of who is driving where. In Los Angeles, the Automated Traffic Surveillance and Control (ATSAC) system will eventually have up to four thousand cameras located at various intersections and traffic hot spots, ostensibly solely for traffic control purposes. (No tie-in with law enforcement agencies is planned at this stage.) However, as law professor Jonathan Turley warns, "Very few people seem to understand that cameras are part of a collective movement that is putting a great deal of pressure on our collective rights. They kill our sense of privacy. What we are slowly becoming is a fishbowl society."[9]

Many local police departments have initiated the use of dashboard-mounted camcorders to record all their routine operations—traffic violations, domestic disturbances, street fights, and other calls. Get stopped by a cop and you wind up on *Candid Camera*.

We also see the growing usage of miniaturized electronic transponders utilized as personal tracking devices. Used to confine a convicted felon to house arrest or to monitor the activities of someone on probation, these sophisticated transmitters—which are virtually tamper-proof—constantly report on the whereabouts of the individual under surveillance. If we can track grizzly bears in the wild, why not disreputable characters in the city?

The danger, of course, is that once such a technology becomes routinely accepted as legitimate, its insidious spread is hard to curtail. If it is okay to monitor and track the movements of someone on bail or on probation, why not also keep track of ex-convicts, known criminals under suspicion for drug trafficking, gang members suspected of violent activities, neighborhood troublemakers, fathers behind in their child-support payments, political activists, leaders of religious cults, people who subscribe to the wrong magazines, or anybody else we simply do not trust? Where do we draw the line? It is so easy to use the technology that it becomes harder and harder not to use it—and abuse it. Technological determinism.

Eavesdropping on the Information Superhighway.   The federal government has outlawed unbreakable private encryption or encoding systems that would allow individual citizens or corporate officers to talk to each other or send private data without fear of being spied on. The FBI, CIA, and other agencies, do not want private individuals (that is, *suspected lawbreakers*) to communicate freely without the possibility of legitimate law-enforcement agencies being able to monitor suspicious communications. The federal government instead offers us schemes such as the controversial "clipper chip," a sophisticated system that would allow any two private parties to communicate in secret, but also would allow the federal government *(with proper authorization of course)* to intercept any message.

Even as the national *information superhighway* is being designed, law enforcement and security agencies are poised to make sure that they can gain access to every bit of information carried on that highway. Brock Meeks warns, "Are you getting this? If the FBI gets its way, the entire *next generation* of communications networks—from your hand-held 'call anywhere phone,' to your personal digital assistant, like Apple's Newton—will come with wiretap capability *pre-installed.*"[10]   The tribal chiefs want the right to know what is going on in their provinces.

Private Sector Data Files

Author Sheldon Wolin warns that "In terms of the extension of control over individual lives, private concentrations of power are as much of a problem now as governmental agencies."[11] Our privacy is increasingly compromised by banks, credit bureaus, market researchers, insurance companies, direct-mail marketers, and other financial and retail operations. Thomas Rosenstiel writes,

Americans are potentially under surveillance—watched, videotaped and digitally monitored—for most of their waking hours. . . . It isn't necessarily the government doing the watching. Often it is employers, doctors, insurers and merchants—seeking security or gathering information in an invisible universe of mostly unregulated databases, the memory bank of the electronic culture.[12]

These same agencies and institutions then turn around and sell the collected data to others. Jeff Rothfeder reports, "As insurance companies, banks, doctors, and substance-abuse treatment centers put their data online, any attempt to keep your private life private will be in vain."[13]

All our educational records, job applications, IQ and aptitude tests, financial and credit records, bank statements, medical reports, political affiliations, and insurance accounts leave an increasingly detailed paper trail. Every month Equifax, TRW, Trans Union, Chilton, CSC, and about 1,200 other credit bureaus in the United States update their files on us with new data from banks, retailers, public records, and other credit sources.

In addition to the authorized appropriation of our personal records, we must consider also the unauthorized invasion by computer hackers and inveterate voyeurs. All government and private-sector files, no matter how presumably secure they may be, are subject to electronic incursion by computer savants with the right equipment and know-how.

Marketing Intrusions. Kroll Associates, with access to 700 on-line databases, is the country's largest manipulator of marketing information. Companies such as The Behavior Bank, CDB/Infotek, Information America, National Credit Information Network, Tracers Worldwide, and TRW's P$ycle Financial Markets offer for sale to anyone detailed demographic and financial breakdowns of 95 percent of all U.S. households. Both America Online and CompuServe have offered their subscriber lists to marketers.

The Direct Marketing List Source offers for sale to marketers some 12,000 different categories of lists—everything from "born-again doctors who donate" to "Bill Moyers Journal transcript buyers."[14] "Fax broadcasting" can reach up to 10,000 consumer targets with a single message. Jeff Slaton, the self-proclaimed "spam king" of the Internet claims to have amassed a database of 6 million e-mail addresses, which he offers for sale to any direct marketer.[15]

Every time you make a purchase through a cable channel, order an item from a mail-order catalog, phone certain 800 and 900 numbers, respond to a magazine or telephone poll, donate to a political campaign, or log on to an

Internet WWW site, you are potentially adding information to your permanent record of individual preferences, leisure activities, political leanings, and cultural tastes. Your supermarket purchases are increasingly tracked. Combine your credit card number with bar-code scanners and a permanent record of your purchases is established.[16] Any time you use a "membership card" for some bargain in a membership-club store, your purchase is permanently linked with your consumer record.

It may be one thing for an agency to take a survey about your views on birth control and sex education; it is quite a different matter to keep a record of your condom purchases. Such information can be used to build an accurate and detailed consumer profile—telling prospective market manipulators what advertising appeals work best on you, what kind of foods you are likely to buy, when you are in the market for new clothes, and how to talk you into buying a new car. Not only is your privacy being invaded, but your behavior is being manipulated without your knowledge.

Media researchers are becoming increasingly sophisticated in their exploration of what makes their audiences tick. Both A.C. Nielsen and Arbitron are experimenting with high-tech, passive audience measurement devices to tell them not only what is playing on your TV set, but who is watching, who left the viewing area to go to the bathroom, who fell asleep, and what commercials you like best. Nielsen is working on one system that would use a "camera-type monitoring device with a lens trained on family members as they watch TV."[17] One Nielsen executive offered, "I don't think we're talking about Big Brother here at all."

And you certainly are not alone at your computer terminal. The NPD Group is the first research outfit to accurately keep tabs on your computer usage. Its PC-Meter device traces your Windows usage, other software preferences, and Web site visits—to link your demographic profile with your specific computer usage patterns.

Corporate Surveillance

Chances are that you do not know much about firms such as Krout & Schneider of California, Business Risks International of Tennessee, or Creative Services of Massachusetts—but they may know quite a bit about you. They are part of a growing professional field of investigative services involved with corporate snooping.

A 1994 report by a United Nations agency states that up to 80 percent of U.S. employees in banking, telecommunications, and insurance jobs are "subject to telephone or computer-based snooping by their employers." Michelle Jankanish, a co-author of the report says, "It doesn't matter whether you work in a factory, in an office or as a highly paid engineer or professional—you are very likely under observation . . . by computers or machines controlled by your boss."[18] Individual phone lines can be routinely tapped; computer keyboard operations and entries can be systematically recorded.

Many companies track the movements of their delivery trucks to monitor where their drivers are actually going and how much time they spend on doughnut breaks. Office furniture is manufactured that can measure the extent of employee wiggle to determine how workers are performing. There is increasing use of video cameras in restrooms, employee lounges, and locker rooms to make sure no illegal activities are going on. In fact, the corporate war on drugs involves an implicit suspension of Fourth Amendment rights as employees are assumed guilty of something illegal—until they are proven innocent.

Within our retail environments, we are tacitly aware of the extent of increasing surveillance—with security cameras in banks, office buildings, retail stores, shopping malls, parking lots, and other obvious locations. Long before the new Denver International Airport got its computerized baggage-handling system working right, it had its 1,500 closed-circuit cameras fully operational. We just go about our business, accepting the fact that we are being observed wherever we move.

Private Personal Surveillance

With modern surveillance tools, it is becoming increasingly easy for private individuals to snoop into the affairs of family members, neighbors, friends, and associates. Consider even conventional familiar equipment—the telephone, for instance. Modified radio scanners (and earlier over-the-counter models) can pick up both cordless and cellular phone transmissions.

The ubiquitous answering machine is used to record incoming messages for all members of the family—although any other family member may be the first one to pick up those messages. (More sophisticated models now offer separate "mail boxes" for individual household members.) Answering machines also can easily and discretely record any and all telephone conversations. Incoming fax messages may be read by anybody.

Caller ID displays for any customer (who has purchased the service) the phone number of the person who is calling. However, there are many justifiable instances when the person initiating a call deserves to retain his or her privacy: the whistle-blower calling anonymously to report a safety violation; the physician, lawyer, or professor returning a call to a patient, client, or student from his or her private residence. Caller ID is potentially one more little incursion into our private lives, innocuous enough in its initial application—but creating one more dent in our armor of personal privacy. The phone companies are obliged to offer "Caller ID blocking" to any customer who wants to maintain a modicum of privacy. But it is indicative that the burden of action is on the customer; it is accepted that your privacy will be violated unless *you* take the initiative to stop the intrusion. The assumption is with those who want your number.

Household and Neighborhood Surveillance. Specialized surveillance boutiques and mail-order spy catalogs offer to the private consumer items such as hidden-camera video systems, microrecording and bugging technologies, vehicle-tracking systems, night-vision equipment, and other electronic-surveillance "personal security devices." Such snooping gear can be furtively placed around the house to record suspicious behavior of your youngsters, your babysitter, your spouse.

We start with audio surveillance of the nursery. Like virtually every technological advance, the first uses are enthusiastically accepted as a worthwhile step toward more convenience, security, and peace of mind. Being able to place an inexpensive audio monitor in your infant's nursery and hear his or her nighttime murmurings and cries of distress while you are in the living room is undeniably a valid convenience. You also can put an inexpensive surveillance camera in your one-year-old's bedroom to make sure he or she is all right both day and night. And you can leave it there to monitor your two-year-old, your five-year-old, your twelve-year-old. All you have to do is indoctrinate your child early in life to the idea of having no privacy, no place to hide: "Don't worry, dear, Mommy and Big Brother will always be watching to make sure everything is all right."

The innocuous electronic pager has added another useful instrument to the toolbox of family surveillance and security. Your teenager is compelled to wear the beeper at all times while out on a date—for his or her own safety and security, of course: "Whenever I beep, Honey, you call home—or you're grounded for a month!"

The ubiquitous camcorder is another tool in our personal surveillance kit. We might not think of the camcorder as an invasion of privacy (except that Aunt Mary does not want you shooting her overweight fanny); it is just there—like the personal camera has been for close to a century—to record family celebrations and travels. However, with the ever-present camcorder readily available to an increasing number of Americans, it has become a de facto amateur surveillance device for domestic troubles, law enforcement problems, community vigilante programs, and a host of other situations. One only has to recall the impact of George Holliday's spur-of-the moment, late-at-night recording of the Rodney King incident. Court battles of the future may well hinge on whose surveillance videotape the jury believes—the victim's or the police officer's.

Attend a parade, ride the Chicago subway, join a campus demonstration, get caught in a freeway traffic jam, argue with a homeless panhandler, or visit a topless bar, and you just may find yourself on somebody's video and end up on a national hookup—or in the courtroom.

VOLUNTARY SURRENDER OF PRIVACY

We increasingly accept the fact that anywhere we go, someone may be recording us on videotape or be eavesdropping on our conversations. One of the most ominous signs of our post-intellectual culture is the gradual acceptance of increasing intrusion into our privacy—the willingness to tolerate inch by inch additional infringements, the insidious surrender of a little information here, a phone number there. Peter McGrath writes in a *Newsweek* essay: "In the end, we compromise ourselves. We leave traces of our lives in databases everywhere. Computers are built to recognize patterns, to find coherence in individually insignificant details. If we lose our privacy, it's because we volunteered." [19]

Insidious Tolerance of Government Surveillance

We compliantly accept the fact that every government bureaucracy has the right to know our Social Security number, our income, our educational background, our military record, our driving offenses. *Harper's* editor Lewis Lapham reminds us that "With scarcely a murmur of objection, [the majority of Americans] fill out the official forms, answer the questions, submit to the compulsory urine or blood tests, and furnish information to the government, the insurance companies, and the police." [20] In this piecemeal fashion we are willing to let go of our privacy, our freedom, one little chunk at a time—for increased personal safety, for peace of mind, for convenience. Salvaggio comments:

> The most serious setback for maintaining privacy in an information society is not the growth of technology or the difficulty of passing legislation, but the fact that invasion of privacy is so easily rationalized. As we have seen, privacy is often sacrificed for more valued commodities—profits, efficiency, and productivity. When two concepts cannot coexist, the one that is most valued survives. [21]

People want, not only profits, efficiency, and productivity, but also security. In order to feel safer, we willingly surrender some of our independence, our privacy. We support random drug testing in the war against drugs; we welcome the idea of state trooper roadblocks in order to crack down on drunk drivers. We rationalize: *these are good things and a little erosion of our Fourth Amendment protections against "unreasonable searches and seizures" seems a small price to pay for security and peace of mind.*

After all, is it not a good thing for law enforcement agencies to know who the drug addicts are? Should not our local cops know what is going on in the crack houses and brothels in our communities? Should they not know what is going on in the basement of my suspicious-looking neighbor? (And therefore, of course, do they not also have the right to know what is going on in my basement?)

Piecemeal Acceptance of Marketing Intrusions

Bit by bit, we find ourselves more and more exposed—our credit balances, our political choices, our drinking record, our eating preferences. We are continually polled, recorded, investigated, queried, sampled, and surveyed. And we do not seem to mind. I barely react when my monthly telephone company newsletter blandly informs me that "When you call an 800 or 900 number, your phone number may be disclosed to the subscriber of that number as part of the billing information we provide."[22] In actuality, since 1989, our telephone numbers (and other demographic data) have been routinely captured by a system known as Automatic Number Identification and sold to hundreds of eager marketing and political solicitors.

Should we not enjoy the convenience of shopping via cable channels or mail order catalogs? Should we not communicate through e-mail? Should we not let the ratings company know what TV programs we enjoy? One little incursion at a time will not hurt, will it? Gerald Silver makes the point that one way we lose our privacy is from "individuals so accustomed to divulging their personal affairs that they lose privacy out of ignorance or sheer lack of interest."[23]

There are so many opportunities to let others do things for us, to make life a little more convenient. All we have to do is let them into our private lives a little more. A company called Consumer Financial Institute will handle all my money matters for me, making all sorts of wise investments for my future; all I have to do is turn all my personal fiscal information over to the firm and let it run my private financial life. Similarly, a service called Comp-U-Card will be glad to handle all my shopping for me, making the best possible deal for any major purchase I wish to make; all I have to do is let it know exactly what I want.

Voluntary Personal Surveillance

Many of our personal and residential monitoring and security devices are simply extensions of the electronic conveniences we increasingly embrace each year: burglary and alarm systems wired into a private security firm or police department, fire and smoke detection systems monitored by the fire department, life-sign indicators for the elderly and shut-ins to ensure that they are alive and mobile each day, telephone paging and call-forwarding services to keep track of our daily travels and meanderings, computer modems to hook us into the Internet and our Web-site sanctuaries. The conveniences far outweigh the negligible surrender of a little of our independence, our self-reliance, our privacy.

How about the emerging Brave New World of personal communication networks (PCNs) or personal communication services (PCS)—combining advances in fiberoptics, satellites, and cellular technologies? Instead of being tethered to phone numbers that are linked to instruments at fixed locations, you will have a unique PCN identifying number (perhaps your financial smart card or national ID number?) that ties you in with a vast, integrated digital web. This PCN system (such as Motorola's *Iridium* project or the Microsoft-McCaw *Teledesic* network) will then locate you via satellite, wherever you happen to be—in your car, camping in the Rockies, in a plane, in your lover's apartment—and ring your miniaturized radiophone. In its ads, AT&T is promising us a strap-on wrist telephone "in the near future."

Of course, if you wanted privacy you could just leave your PCN phone at home in your bedroom closet, right? Experience shows, however, that once we are given this kind of technological advance, we are unable to resist the temptation to use it. Who would take a chance on missing an important call? We welcome the constant tribal communion—the voluntary surrender of solitude and privacy in order to enjoy the security of a collective consciousness.

Earlier, I mentioned the use of miniaturized electronic transponders as personal tracking devices. We are already finding voluntary applications for such technology. Weighing about as much as a dime, the *Real Time Champion Chip* was first introduced at the 1994 Berlin Marathon. And at the 1996 Los Angeles Marathon, over 20,000 runners were outfitted with this tracking device—to record precise running times as well as to monitor every runner's whereabouts to ensure that each one did, indeed, run the full course. If it is cost-effective to adopt this technology on such a widespread scale, can routine tracking of students, patients, family members, and employees be far behind?

Lanny Ross, president of Rockwell International's telecommunications group, foresees the day when surgically implanted transponders can be sewn into every individual to monitor their whereabouts by using the pinpoint-tracking technology of the 24-satellite Global Positioning System (GPS): "I think somewhere beyond the year 2050, this will be embedded in you and your location will be known at all times."[24] *Think of the marvelous advances in personal security and communications—when everybody knows precisely where everyone else is at all times!*

The giant Japanese monopoly, Nippon Telephone & Telegraph, is working on several other futuristic ideas to enhance our personal security and convenience. How about programmable robotic or wall sensors that would allow you to recognize who was in your home (in what room and with whom) while you were not there? How about "mind-link" thought sensors that could actually read brain waves to accomplish basic communication tasks? How about the ultimate in hands-free technology—surgically implanted mini-telephones?

We are all absorbed into the Global Village. We are all part of the tribal community. We welcome the assimilation into a greater, post-intellectual communal sensibility.

Effects of a Surveillance State of Mind

The danger is not simply that we may be spied upon, but that we might *believe*, and consequently *act*, as if we were being spied upon. For if we suspect our movements are being monitored and our thoughts are being detected, we are as imprisoned as if we were actually confined to a cell. Self-censorship is no less onerous than physical confinement. In many ways it is even worse, because it means we have ceased to fight; we have accepted the limitations on our freedom. Orwell describes the effect of the potential for random surveillance: "But at any rate they could plug in your wire whenever they wanted to. You had to live—did live, from habit that became instinct—in the assumption that every sound you made was overheard, and, except in darkness, every movement scrutinized."[25]

Leaving the world of fiction, former Justice William O. Douglas warns of such a real-life scenario: "Our citizens will be afraid to utter any but the safest and most orthodox thoughts, afraid to associate with any but the most acceptable people. Freedom as the Constitution envisages [it] will have vanished."[26] We will all conform to a post-intellectual tribal group-think; no one will have the courage or intellectual insight to think original thoughts, to express the non-conventional, to challenge the status quo, to resist establishmentism. If citizens utter nothing but the "most orthodox thoughts," all intellectual aspirations are gone. We will have eased into a post-intellectual collective consciousness. And we will feel good about it.

NOTES

1. Jerry Salvaggio, "Is Privacy Possible in an Information Society?" in Salvaggio, 1989, p. 128.

2. Lacayo, 1991, p. 34.

3. Stoll, 1995, p. 35.

4. John J. McGivney, "A Murder, an Accused Husband, a Press Frenzy," *Boston Globe*, 3 July 1994, p. 58.

5. Hoobler, 1986, p. 15.

6. Tony Knight, "Census Necessary, Not Nosy, Bureau Says," *Los Angeles Daily News,* 26 March 1990, pp. 1, 10.

7. Ron K. Unz, "Big Brother, Make Room for Big Sister," *Los Angeles Times,* 12 June 1995, p. B11.

8. Orwell [1949], 1961, p. 6.

9. Quoted in Hugo Martin, "Officials Say Police Not in the Picture," *Los Angeles Times,* 4 April 1993, p. B4.

10. Meeks, 1994, p. 51.

11. Interviewed in Moyers, 1989, p. 100.

12. Rosenstiel, 1994, p. A1.

13. Rothfeder, 1995, p. 61.

14. See Rosenstiel, 1994, p. A12.

15. "Spamming" is the process of indiscriminately flooding the Internet with a given message or advertisement. See Daniel Akst, "Coming to a Computer Near You: Junk E-Mail," *Los Angeles Times,* 1 November 1995, p. D4.

16. For a full discussion of marketing intrusions and privacy concerns, see Erik Ness, "BigBrother@cyberspace," *Progressive,* December 1994, pp. 23–27.

17. Adam Buckman, "'Passive' Meter Plan Draws Active Approval," *Electronic Media*, 5 June 1989, p. 2.

18. Cited in Slobodan Lekic, "Employers Spying More on Workers," *Honolulu Advertiser,* 2 August 1994, p. C1.

19. Peter McGrath, "Info 'Snooper-Highway,'" *Newsweek,* 27 February 1995, p. 61.

20. Lapham, 1990, p. 56.

21. Salvaggio, 1989, p. 129.

22. *Pacific Bell Calling,* October 1995.

23. Silver, 1979, p. 316.

24. Quoted in Vartabedian, 1994, p. D4.

25. Orwell [1949], 1961, pp. 6–7.

26. Quoted by Nat Hentoff in LeMond, 1975, p. xxi.

7

Cognitive Chaos: The Data Daze

*The acceleration of change compels us to perceive life
as motion, not as order;   Change is scary;
uncharted change demoralizing.*

• Arthur Schlesinger, Jr.
The Cycles of American History

The single most overwhelming issue facing Western Civilization? It is not the
starving masses; not gangs in the inner cities; not our national debt; not the
breakup of the Soviet empire nor the breakup of the American family. The
most awesome reality of the late twentieth century is the crushing information
overload we are facing, the unmanageable rate at which new data are being
generated and thrown at us—adding information to the world's storehouse at
such a bewildering pace that no single individual, corporate entity, think tank,
government agency, or super-computer can comprehend the totality of what is
going on.

This is what Alvin Toffler identified as the Third Wave (the Agricultural
and Industrial Revolutions being the first two): "Humanity . . . faces the
deepest social upheaval and creative restructuring of all time. Without clearly
recognizing it, we are engaged in building a remarkable new civilization from
the ground up. This is the meaning of the Third Wave."[1] The 1950s sanctioned
television as our dominant cultural influence; it was the decade that saw
widespread introduction of the transistor, the videotape recorder, the computer,
the commercial jet, the office photocopier, and the launching of the first
satellite. The Industrial Age had peaked and ebbed. We were now catapulted
into the blur of the Information Age.

THE ACCELERATION OF CHANGE

My mother, born in 1896, was an infant when the first horseless carriage chugged into her small Indiana town. She was seven when the Wright Brothers demonstrated powered flight at Kitty Hawk. She was twenty-four when radio broadcasting became a popular reality, and fifty-two when she owned her first television set. Before she died in 1980, she saw the atom bomb used, flew in jet planes, watched men walk on the moon, and witnessed computers restructuring our corporate environment. There is no way that as a youngster she could have begun to imagine the revolutionary changes she would live through. Similarly, there is no way that we can conceive of the enormous upheavals we will experience in the next half century.

There is no governor on our technological engine, no brake pedal on our rocket to tomorrow. Arthur Schlesinger, Jr., points out that "The pace of change grows ever faster. . . . The acceleration of change compels us to perceive life as motion, not as order; . . . Change is scary; uncharted change demoralizing."[2] Regardless of what index you use—urban growth, energy consumption, research projects, patents awarded, transportation leaps, communication advances, computer processing speed, genetic breakthroughs--the results are the same: incomprehensible acceleration of progress and change during the past few decades.

The Agricultural Revolution took thousands of years—roughly from 10,000 to 5,000 B.C. And the Industrial Revolution took two or three hundred years. However, the third revolution, the *Information Revolution,* has taken but a couple of decades.

The Reasons for Change

Why did our early ancestors take so long to make any substantial changes? And why is change exploding in our faces today? First, during our vast preintellectual past, tradition was to be cherished; change was to be abhorred. This was the ethic of the *cyclical culture:* do nothing different from what our ancestors did. Most of human history has been spent with rigid class patterns that rewarded conformity and constancy. It is only in the last couple centuries that we have witnessed the kind of intellectual, economic, and social environment that provided any reason to challenge the status quo.

Second, until population pressures increased to the point where social problems began to pile up, there was no need to turn to technology to solve civilization's problems. Housing, road maintenance, clothing and food requirements, all our needs were handled relatively easily up through the eighteenth century—with no demand for any vast improvements or technological miracles. However, as our lives have gotten more complicated, the need for technological solutions has increased. Change was mandated.

The main reason for the acceleration of change, however, is that technology breeds more technological thinking. As Jacob Bronowski writes, our technological culture "is a multiplier of ideas, in which each new device quickens and enlarges the power of the rest."[3] The more technological progress we make, the more opportunities we see for additional advancements. Once we discovered electricity, we could invent things to do with electricity. The more we find out about the nature of quarks, the more we want to dig deeper into the atom. The more we find out about DNA, the further we have to delve into genetic mapping.

This helps explain the continuing information explosion (introduced in Chapter 3). In the accelerating pace of contemporary society, each new scientific breakthrough or technological discovery seems to lead to several more. Every bit of information we discover, every answer we get from research, raises two more questions. *(There are two doors, each labeled with a large question mark. . .)* Thus, we are compelled to push just a little further into the unknown.

The Accelerating Cycle. We are caught up in an ever-accelerating cycle of forced adaptation and alteration of our environment. Imagine a circle with three points located equidistant around the perimeter (see Figure 7.1). Start with our *altered environment;* our world today is quite different from what it was five years ago; because our environment is altered we *need to adapt* to it; we adapt by uncovering *new information* that will help us understand our environment; as we add to our information store, we have altered our overall environment; as our environment is altered we must adapt; we adapt by uncovering new information; this new information changes our environment and we must adapt; we adapt by uncovering new information that alters our environment . . . We keep spinning faster and faster in this never-ending cycle of altered-environment-need-to-change-new-information-altered-environment-need . . .

Of course, this cycle of Alteration-Adaptation-Information has always been with us. The plow altered our environment, forcing a need to adapt to new farming methods and demanding new agricultural information. The steam engine changed our environment, forcing us to adapt to new transportation possibilities and demanding more applications information. The examples continue through every advance that humans have made.

The difference today is that we no longer have the luxury of generations, or even years, to adapt to new situations. New communications technologies, new computer chips, new materials fabrication, new genetic manipulations, new WWW sites: these all demand immediate response, adaptation, and additional research and information. We no longer have the leisure of deliberately examining where we are headed. Returning to the Third Wave paradigm, Toffler explains, "As a result, people and organizations continually crave more information and the entire system begins to pulse with higher and higher flows of data."[4]

Figure 7.1
The Acceleration of Change

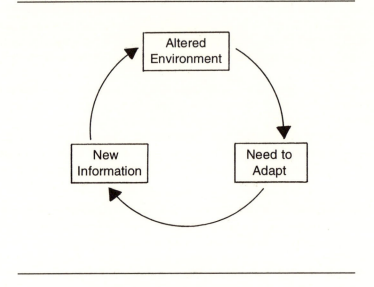

THE GENERATION OVERLAP

The transition from the 1950s to the 1960s was a crucial point in the emergence of post-intellectualism. The decade of the 1960s was remarkable for one phenomenon: it produced the *Generation Overlap*.

The Transition to Adulthood

Part of normal maturation involves rebelling against authority. Adolescents revolt against their parents, their teachers, their clergy. They must prove themselves and find their own answers. Then as they display the ability to make responsible decisions, they gain increasing independence; until finally they are deemed to be adults and can go off on their own—to march in their parents' footsteps.

For, in generations past, behind all rebellious teenagers—even while they struggled against the reins and restrictions of the establishment—there was always the subliminal knowledge that parents and teachers really did know what was right. The elders had been there; they knew how the world was organized; they knew how to make things work. No matter how mutinous and defiant adolescents may have been, there was always the certainty that when they grew up, they would be living in the same world that their parents had come to terms with. There was always that certainty, that security. Until the 1960s.

The Hippie Generation and Post-Intellectualism

The decade of the 1960s launched the *hippie generation* and the age of free speech, freedom to drop out, use drugs, find yourself, and "do your own thing." It fostered demonstrations against racial injustices and other social inequities. Women came out of the kitchen and homosexuals came out of the closet (but neither group knew what to do in the new rooms in which they found themselves). It was the decade of disillusionment with U.S. involvement in Vietnam. It was the shock of assassinations of political and civil rights leaders—Jack, Bobby, Martin and Malcolm were gunned down as we watched, horrified and numbed. It was the beginning of environmental awareness and challenges to traditional, capitalistic business-as-usual. The Esalen Institute of Big Sur, California, triggered sensitivity-training movements throughout the country.

In terms of P. A. Sorokin's analysis, the 1960s represented a rebellion against sensate truth. We began to lose our faith in material things. Technology, intellectual competition, scientific progress, and economic growth began to lose their age-old attraction. Mysticism, astrology, love-beads, incense, and group awareness all represented a groping toward new insights, a new synthesis.

Post-intellectual educational reform was promoted. Frances FitzGerald writes that "because the New Romantics saw the technocracy—intellectual and otherwise—as the main enemy, they tended to look upon all intellectual pursuits as narrow, 'academic,' and stunting to the psyche." Their goal was "to make education larger and more generous; they called for free play, creativity, authenticity, direct experience, and joy."[5] The flower-child decade saw the blossoming of post-intellectualism.

The Eisenhower-Kennedy Transition. Dwight Eisenhower's administration—coincidental with the onset of the Information Age—marked the transition from an intellectual society to a post-intellectual society. Eisenhower won World War II for us—a decidedly linear victory of Good over Evil. But Eisenhower's administration then saw an unsatisfactory standoff in Korea; we no longer clearly understood what we were supposed to do. We had moved from the linear culture to the muddled web culture.

As president, Eisenhower represented the culmination of an intellectual, capitalist dedication to linear expansion and growth—giving us nuclear energy and the interstate freeway system. No president since has achieved any comparable domestic accomplishments of such distinct linear development and expansion—with the possible exception of the space program in the 1960s, which represents the last serious thrust of an intellectual/scientific culture. Major domestic programs of following administrations, from the Great Society to Medicare, would be post-intellectual welfare and entitlement efforts—not triumphs of linear exploitation and progress.

However, Ike also presided over the beginnings of our post-intellectual political disorientation. During his administration, authors such as John Ken-

neth Galbraith, C. Wright Mills, and William H. Whyte, Jr., began to alert us
to the suffocating entanglements of the web-like government-corporate bureaucracy.[6] And, at the end of his second term, Eisenhower himself warned of
the growing hegemony of the military-industrial complex.

John Kennedy, for all his intellectual trappings, ushered in an era of post-
intellectual charisma and confusion. His was the first in a continuing series of
"can't-do" administrations. And it was under his leadership that we got
hopelessly bogged down in Vietnam. The Age of the Enlightenment expired
around 1960. *Camelot* (the nickname for JFK's administration) was, after all,
from a pre-intellectual medieval culture.

The 1960s spilled over into the 1970s as continued governmental deception
and public cynicism resulted in the extraordinary spectacle of an American
president being forced to resign. To the established order, it was a time of
values run amok, a loss of societal direction.

Why did all these disparate unsettling happenings come together at this
time? Why did our post–World War II political idealism degenerate into the
quagmire of Vietnam and Watergate? Why did the flower-child generation blos-
som in this particular season? Why was there such unprecedented cultural
turmoil in so many aspects of our civilization? Why were young people coming
of age in the 1960s so out of sync with the preceding generation?

Dawning of the Age of Information

I submit that what we witnessed in the 1960s was not exactly the Age of
Aquarius—not just drugs, nudity, and social awareness. What we witnessed in
this tumultuous decade was *Information*—more precisely, a whirling disorientation brought on by the angst and alienation of the information overload.

This was the decade when white collar information-processing workers
outnumbered blue collar industrial wage-earners for the first time. Television
dominated our culture; this was the first full decade of the videorecorder and
color television. Names such as Xerox and Polaroid impacted our collective
consciousness—along with the transistor, the satellite, and the computer. The
information genie was out of the bottle.

Reality of the Generation Overlap. This was the decade when the
Generation Gap was erased—to be replaced by the *Generation Overlap*. As
noted above, every generation of adolescents moved into adulthood by rebelling against its elders—only to accept the values and institutions of its elders
once it passed the rites of maturation. However, when the 1960s generation
rebelled against the authority of its elders—the elders did not know what to do.
For the first time in history, young people emerged into a culture that was alien
to their parents and teachers and priests. The "love-in generation" would not
be inhabiting the same world that their parents had governed; the older institutions, economic patterns, and social systems were being drastically altered by
new informational and technological realities. Computers in the home? Nuclear

fusion? Multinational corporate monoliths? Genetic cloning? The Internet? Where were we headed?

Confidence in the older generation disappeared. Youth realized that the emerging technologies were bypassing the elders; their parents did not know where technology was headed. (Nobody did.) Therefore, the older generation was irrelevant. The ordered transformation from adolescence to adulthood was obliterated. From the 1960s on, every succeeding generation would be raised within a culture fundamentally different from the culture shaped by the preceding generation. The gradual transition from one generation to the next—that passage that had endured since the beginning of evolution—had been annihilated.

In a cyclical culture, youth followed precisely in their elders' footsteps. In the linear culture, youth confidently pushed ahead in the direction pioneered by their elders. In the emerging web culture, everybody headed in whatever direction they felt like.

Schlesinger points out that this societal shift placed traditional roles and institutions "under severe and incomprehensible strain. It has cast off reference points and rituals that had stabilized and sanctified life for generations. It has left the experience of elders useless to the tribulations of the young."[7]

Institutions were shifting from an industrial base to an information base, and neither generation knew what to do about it. In all areas of society, traditional institutions and relationships were radically altered to reflect the new "youth culture"—marketing and corporate strategies, financial patterns, church services, school curricula, family structures, and even politics, as the back-room political bosses found themselves pushed aside by populist primaries and state caucuses.

Thus, the 1960s were the decade when post-intellectualism emerged—the period when it became apparent that we were setting out on a new and uncharted course. Our path would be dictated by evolving technologies and the information surfeit, not by the experience and wisdom of the elders. In this post-intellectual ferment, analytic thinking was thrown out and feelings were in; competition was out and sensitivity was in; intellectual achievement was out and relevance was in; individuality was out and communal living was in; economic growth and exploitation were out and environmental awareness was in. Confidence in the intellectually conceived American dream began to falter seriously for the first time in two hundred years—when the Generation Overlap became a reality in the 1960s.

The Disappearance of Childhood

Prior to the sixteenth century, the concept of childhood did not exist. Historian J. H. Plumb writes "There was no separate world of childhood. Children shared the same games with adults, the same toys, the same fairy stories. They lived their lives together, never apart."[8] As soon as a small person learned to speak, that boy or girl entered society as a diminutive man or woman, ready to live in the adult world, assume economic responsibilities, and participate in adult pastimes. Barbara Tuchman explains "If children survived to age seven, their recognized life began, more or less as miniature adults. Childhood was already over."[9]

There were no nursery schools, no kindergartens, no elementary schools, no driver-training programs, no boy scouts or girl scouts, no preparation programs for adulthood. There was no training period for adulthood because there was nothing for which to train. Adults had no specialized occupational skills. Adults were not charged with any responsible civic duties. Most significantly, adults could not read; literacy in the working class was virtually nonexistent. There was no need for a formal period of schooling because no one was schooled. It required no intellectual skills to move into adulthood.

This all changed after the invention of the printing press. Books led to schools which led to the idea of a formal educational period in one's life. Childhood was an inevitable consequence of literacy. Schools were needed to train adolescents both for the civic responsibilities of a libertarian society as well as for specialized occupations that emerged with the industrial age.

In the late twentieth century, however, the electric media are eradicating childhood. Television, radio, the movies, cassettes and CDs, Nintendo and Sega, icon-driven computer programs, and virtual reality games all are non-linguistic. We are returning to a nonliterate age that requires no special schooling. We are returning to an oral and pictorial tradition. My five-year-old grandson often bests me at one of our favorite video games because he deciphers the pictorial icons and reacts intuitively while I am still reading words and trying to follow written cues.

We have also obliterated the line between what is intended for children and what is intended for adults. Everyone can play the same video games and view the same television programs. People of all ages watch *Sesame Street, Roseanne, Star Trek* or *Rescue 911* with equal enthusiasm and enjoyment. Literacy and intellectual maturity are no longer prerequisites for participation in today's pastimes.

The generational line continues to blur. Adults wear jeans and sneakers to the corporate office. Adults play children's video games, while the kids are organized into highly structured Little League baseball and AYSO (American Youth Soccer Organization) competitions. One president refuses to eat his broccoli and his successor popularizes MacDonald's fast food. Neil Postman describes this blending as the creation of the "adult-child." He explains that we are creating a new generation of citizens who will "remain like television's adult-child all their lives, with no sense of belonging, no capacity for lasting relationships, no respect for limits, and no grasp of the future."[10]

The abolition of childhood helps to explain many of our concerns expressed thus far in the book—the limitations of human intellect, the turn to escapism, exploitation based upon immediate gratification, and the collapse of literacy. The disappearance of childhood is part of the Generation Overlap. It is a consequence of post-intellectualism.

PROBLEMS WITH OUR PROBLEM-SOLVING

Critical thinking, or problem-solving, is one of the components of an intellectual mindset. Regarding our failure to solve our post-intellectual societal problems, there is one comprehensive hypothesis that explains everything that is going wrong. My simplified tautological explanation is this: *The basic reason for all our societal problems is that we are not doing a good job of solving problems!* What an insight! If only we could master the decision-making or problem-solving process, perhaps we could do a better job of solving problems.

Problem-solving, as discussed in Chapter 3 (reasoning in terms of stated criteria or objectives), is virtually the same as the definition used for *technology* in Chapter 4 (applying scientific principles in a systematic manner to achieve specific practical ends). Both are concerned with systematic, reasoned approaches, using available resources or data, in order to achieve specific objectives. Technology *is* problem-solving.

Problem-Solving Shortcomings

There are many explanations for our problem-solving deficiencies.[11] Some stem from the *limitations of human reason* (the primary consideration underlying the three determinants of the Progress Paradox). Our political and social motivations are often dictated by personal greed, short-term interests, pride and ego protection. It must be conceded that logical thinking is not natural. Discussing the work of Gottlob Frege, Jeremy Campbell concludes that "logic is unnatural, and we ought to accept it as such wholeheartedly."[12]

One related factor is *mental rigidity.* This is a throwback to the cyclical culture. Trust the elders. Rely on tradition, established customs, and our institutional rituals; make decisions as we have always made them. Such a mentality—a refusal to research, analyze, and criticize the status quo—is the antithesis of an intellectual approach.

Institutional fragmentation is an outgrowth of specialization. We are hampered by our limited bureaucratic perspectives. Few societal or governmental agencies have the charge to stand back and look at everything that is going on in a broad perspective. The intellectual tradition of social criticism is lost in the maze of post-intellectual specialized institutionalism. Educational problems, for example, are caused by immigration troubles, drug abuse, family breakdowns, racial intolerance, unemployment, urban-planning policies, law enforcement difficulties, population crowding, the information overload, and technological determinism. However, no educational agency is in charge of these factors.

Another shortcoming with our current problem-solving efforts is that we are *not setting the right goals.* We organize our planning commissions, school districts, and medical institutions to deal with short-range goals and immediate crises. How do we deal with this year's budget shortfall? How can we best respond to our competitor's new product? Seldom do we ask the long-term, anti-establishment questions with which an intellectual culture should be dealing. What kind of society do we want to see in twenty-five years? How can we maintain a viable economic system that does not depend upon continual material growth year after year?

One specific difficulty in goal-setting is the *influence of parochial constituencies*. The role of lobbyists and special-interest groups in Washington is an extension of our personal greed and shortsightedness. As examined in Chapter 15, lawmakers are forced to respond to the immediate pressures of local groups and moneyed interests. Examining the phenomenon of "special-interest gridlock" in politics, Jonathan Rauch gives us a definition of the web culture in his book *Demosclerosis:*

> Problem-solving capacity is precisely what seems to have been shrinking for the federal government. Political activity has become a kind of flailing which creates frenzy but does little good, or even makes problems worse. Wheels spin and gears mesh, but the car goes nowhere, or goes everywhere at once, or shakes itself to pieces. More problems seem to be created than solved.[13]

Turning Solutions into Problems. One reason that "more problems seem to be created than solved" is that virtually *all problems started out as solutions to previous problems*. Almost all problems can be viewed as the results of human attempts at problem-solving.

First, consider this: virtually every problem we have is the result of something that humans have done (perhaps the only two exceptions are natural disasters and diseases). Every economic difficulty, every social injustice, every war and urban riot, every drug problem, every traffic accident: all are caused by something men and women have done.

Second, consider that everything humans do is in response to some felt need; every action we take is an attempted solution for some perceived problem. Every tool, every building, every committee, every article of clothing, every institution and bureaucracy, every bit of pornography, every ice cream cone: everything human beings have ever done or created has come about in response to some specific problem or need.

Therefore—since all problems are caused by human actions and all human actions are attempts to solve some problem or meet some need—*virtually every problem we have is a consequence of a solution to some prior problem!* Stated conversely, anything we do to solve a problem today is likely to compound problems in the future. This phenomenon helps answer the question posed by Rauch: "Why does 'getting things done' in the short run often make problem-solving more difficult for the government in the long run?"[14]

As simplistic as this interpretation may appear, an extended analysis would support this thesis as a valid explanation. Most of our problems are caused either by putting in place an ill-considered solution to some problem (trade sanctions, immigration restrictions, get-rich-quick schemes) or by failing to anticipate the *unintended consequences* of some implemented solution (smog, drug addiction, unemployment, and so forth). In this post-intellectual climate, we just do not do a good job of working through our problems rationally.

Technology and Problem-Solving

The shortcomings outlined in the prior section could be discussed at some length, but my main concern at this point is how problem-solving specifically is complicated by technology. As Ogden Nash whimsically reminds us, man "learned how to fly before he thought."[15] Franco Ferrarotti writes, "According to the technocrats, machines resolve all problems."[16] Cliff Stoll elaborates: "The key ingredient of their silicon snake oil is a technocratic belief that computers and networks will make a better society. Access to information, better communications, and electronic programs can cure social problems. I don't believe them. There are no simple technological solutions to social problems."[17] All technology is problem-solving. But we do not do a good job of using technology to solve problems. The irony is that technology—whether it succeeds in solving a specific problem or not—causes additional complications.

Technology and Problem Acceleration. The more technology we use, the more it breeds a technological state of mind. We are thrust into a labyrinth of self-generated scientific leaps without adequate planning and deliberation. Technology enables us to come up with "solutions" faster and faster; but, as noted earlier, since each solution tends to create more problems, we are simply *creating more problems faster and faster*. Technology has not made us any smarter; we are just faster—quicker at creating new problems!

In turn then, we must rely on technology to solve the new problems. In so doing, however, we are digging ourselves deeper and deeper into a technological hole—counting on promised technologies to be delivered tomorrow. *Throw together a combination of money, task forces, commission reports, research and engineering, and we will come up with a temporary stopgap measure*—and worry about straightening out the long-term problem later. We will also take care of the problems caused by our stopgap measure later. We see no way out of our immediate dilemma but to continue borrowing against the future in this way—thus compounding tomorrow's problems.

Theodore Roszak defines a "mature technology" as one that "finally generates as many problems as it solves." He explains:

The railroad and the automobile "solved" the problem of rapid transportation—only to finish by depleting our store of nonrenewable fossil fuels, fouling the air, and destroying the integrity of cities. Modern medicine "solved" the problem posed by numerous infectious diseases, only to finish by giving us the population explosion, ever-more-resistant strains of bacteria, and the ethical dilemma of protracted senility.

The computer "solved" the problem of fast, cheap data processing in a business culture drowning in red tape and paperwork, only to finish by destroying the rights of privacy, concentrating the political and commercial control of information in ever fewer hands, mesmerizing our children with bad art and pernicious nonsense, and menacing us with "computer errors" vast enough to paralyze whole societies.[18]

Roszak concludes, "Every mature technology brings a minimal immediate gain followed by enormous long-term liabilities."[19]

Technology and Information Processing. Successful decision-making and problem-solving are dependent upon having access to needed information. We must have enough information to make an intelligent decision or select the best solution. However, the irony is that an overabundance of irrelevant data can also thwart intelligent decision-making. One major difficulty with many of our problem-solving efforts is not that of having too little information, but rather, that of having *too much information.*

As technology—computers, research labs, academic journals, think tanks, federal projects, the proliferation of media channels—makes more and more information available, it becomes increasingly difficult to sort out and analyze all the data. Seldom do we ever have enough time and resources to examine and evaluate all the facts and details we have accumulated. The plethora of data so overwhelms us that we cannot sort out the needed information from the insignificant, the useful data from the trivial and peripheral.

Earlier, we used the example of two forks in the road. If you know nothing about the two choices, you cannot make an informed decision. On the other hand, suppose you had access to all the following information about each alternate road: mileage to your destination; width of the road; number of lanes; width of shoulders; condition of shoulders; average grade; steepest grade; percentage of road that is gravel, oil-sealed, asphalt, or concrete; number and severity of curves; speed limits; extent of police patrolling; population density (rural, suburban, urban); general terrain (wooded, bushy, desert, wild, culti-vated farmland); scenic highlights; roadside attractions; service stations; avail-ability of food and water; number of rest areas; cleanliness of restrooms; num-ber and depth of potholes; overall need for maintenance; frequency of repair crews; length of road under repair; number of detours; traffic density; number of intersections, stop signs, and traffic signals; use by truckers, motorcycles, farm equipment, and bicyclists—and every other factor you can think of.

Now, with all these data available, would you have the time to analyze thoroughly all the possible combinations of factors that would enable you to make the best decision? Overwhelmed by the task of sorting out the trivial from the significant, you still are not capable of making the best decision. You would exist in a condition of dysfunctional bewilderment. In *Technopoly*, Postman summarizes our current state: "Information has become a form of garbage, not only incapable of answering the most fundamental human questions but barely useful in providing coherent direction to the solution of even mundane problems."[20]

One response to this information glut is the emergence of "information agents," also called *knowbots* or *cyberservants.* In its simplest manifestation, such an electronic agent would be a form of defensive buffer or filter—a computer-based personal assistant to help replace the broken information-control systems discussed in Chapter 4. Katie Hafner explains: "As they are envisioned by computer scientists, within the next decade agents will be our alter egos, culling information for us, reading, sorting and sending e-mail on our behalf, placing calls and performing dozens of routine tasks."[21]

A more advanced version would consist of self-replicating intelligence agents that would reproduce themselves as needed to scour all the known databases in the cyberuniverse to bring to you all the relevant information you should know about. Your cyberservant would be able to sort the data for you, arrange your personal itinerary, manage your professional life, and handle your basic decision-making chores. (That is, if you do not mind turning your life over to your electronic alter ego.)

Diminished Problem-Solving Skills and Will to Reason. All technology is designed to solve our problems and ease our lives. But each advance simply leaves us *individually* more debilitated, more dependent upon additional technology, less able to cope on a personal level. When Stoll's friends and computer enthusiasts tell him that computers are tools to help us think and solve problems, Stoll replies, "Ouch. We need a tool to spare us the effort of thinking? Is reasoning so painful that we require a labor-saving device? What is it we're trying to avoid?"[22]

Whenever a technology actually succeeds in solving a particular problem, it creates a different troublesome side effect. *Technology—successful technology—is dehumanizing*. Sewing machines, bulldozers, photocopying machines, calculators, electric bread-makers, word processors, and information agents have all greatly increased our capacity to get more work done, to move more material, to cover more ground in a shorter period. However, each advance also has enervated the individual—made us more dependent upon even more technology. We have increased our ability to get more work done; but in the process, we have also diminished our own personal capabilities.

As technology succeeds, we lose some of our own self-reliance. We have less of an idea as to what is going on inside our computers, in our business contracts, under the hood of our car, or in the halls of Congress. As our environment gets more complex, we give up trying to deal with it. We assume less responsibility for our own welfare. To a great extent, technology has robbed us of our will to reason. Roszak explains that the computer, for example, "has been cast in the wishful role of a benign angelic protector that will relieve us of adult responsibilities that have become too burdensome."[23]

The computer can most efficiently diagnose our medical symptoms, design a car with less drag, and build a winning stock portfolio. Why should we even try? After all, relieving us of responsibilities is one of the goals of a post-intellectual culture. Postman sums up Aldous Huxley's vision in *Brave New World:* "people will come to love their oppression, to adore the technologies that undo their capacities to think."[24] To the extent that we turn over our decision-making tasks to technology, we have lost some of our sense of humanness.

Freedom is dependent upon responsible decision-making and successful problem-solving. An intellectual culture consists of a command of one's environment, an ability to cope. As unsolved problems pile up in our post-intellectual culture, we find ourselves having to rely on others—the specialists and technocrats—to handle our information-processing and problem-solving chores. And, as a consequence, we surrender some of our independence, our freedoms. The intellectual is one who solves his or her own problems. The post-intellectual is one who calls in consultants and specialists to solve the problems.

NOTES

1. Toffler, 1980, p. 10.
2. Schlesinger, 1986, p. xi.
3. Bronowski, 1973, pp. 73–74.
4. Toffler, 1980, p. 167.
5. FitzGerald, 1979, p. 200.
6. See John Kenneth Galbraith, *American Capitalism: The Concept of Countervailing Power*, 1956; C. Wright Mills, *The Power Elite*, 1956; and William H. Whyte, Jr., *The Organization Man*, 1956.
7. Schlesinger, 1986, p. xi.
8. Quoted in Postman, 1988, "The Disappearance of Childhood," pp. 149–50.
9. From *A Distant Mirror*, quoted in ibid., p. 150.
10. Postman, 1988, "The Disappearance of Childhood," p. 160.
11. For a fuller discussion of communication and problem-solving see Wood, 1996, ch. 3.
12. Campbell, 1989, p. 41.
13. Rauch, 1994, pp. 11–12.
14. Ibid., p. 5.
15. Ogden Nash, "A Caution to Everybody," in *The Private Dining Room and Other New Verses* (Boston: Little, Brown and Company, 1952), p. 22.
16. Ferrarotti, 1985, p. 70.
17. Stoll, 1995, p. 50.
18. Roszak, 1994, pp. xlii–xliii.
19. Ibid., p. xlvi.
20. Postman, 1992, pp. 69–70.
21. Katie Hafner, "Have Your Agent Call My Agent," *Newsweek,* 27 February 1995, p. 76.
22. Stoll, 1995, p. 44.
23. Roszak, 1994, p. 39.
24. Postman, 1985, p. vii.

8

Isolation and Loss of Direction: Disoriented We Despair

We created the Machine, to do our will,
but we cannot make it do our will now.
. . . The machine develops—but not on our lines.
The machine proceeds—but not to our goal.

• E. M. Forster
The Machine Stops

One overriding reality of the web culture is a loss of direction. We have lost our sense of purpose, our system of cultural values. Technopoly breeds detachment. Specialization leads to isolation. We have become so segregated and fragmented that we no longer can comprehend our own affairs nor direct our own destinies.

We are increasingly at the mercy of authorities and bureaucracies who know much more than we do about our business arrangements, automobiles, legal matters, appliances, personal financial investments—even our own bodies. We are losing our humanistic faith that individuals can handle their own concerns and control their own futures. This unintended consequence of distended-intellectualism leads to disorientation, alienation, psychological debilitation, loss of perspective, and loss of self-sufficiency.

MASS MEDIA AND ISOLATION

In a web culture, we have more superficial contacts and connections—but fewer real relationships. Media technologies, which would seem to bring us together, ironically have the perverse effect of separating us into isolated cells. Individuals increasingly are cut off from each another. Cliff Stoll writes,

"Electronic communication is an instantaneous and illusory contact that creates a sense of intimacy without the emotional investment that leads to close friendships."[1] Speaking specifically of computers, he later observes, "Kids that interact with computers rather than their parents miss out on the most important part of growing: being close to their families."[2]

Virtually every advance in communication technology during the last century has paradoxically resulted in increased isolation. Rural Free Delivery (RFD) mail service brought the mail directly to the farmer's house—eliminating the trip to the post office/general store, a socializing event. Farmers became more isolated as a result of the communications advance.

The telephone eliminated face-to-face contact for much of our social intercourse. Today, we use our answering machines, push-button banking services, computer-generated telephone sales pitches, and voice mail to avoid even having to talk to a live person on the telephone. ("Hello. You have reached Acme Conglomerate. Your call is important to us. For a listing of this week's marketing specials, push 'one.'")

Radio brought performers into our homes, eliminating the chautauqua and vaudeville circuits as a community attraction. The movies further isolated us from live events such as the theater, the carnival, and the circus.

Television not only replaced the movie house as a community center, but by giving all household members their personal receivers in their separate viewing areas, it has splintered the family. Video rentals of Hollywood films isolate us even further from the neighborhood theater; videocassette sales and rentals now bring in more revenue than do theater box office receipts. Television has become our personal entertainer, electronic babysitter, teacher, preacher, and talk-show conversationalist. As we insulate ourselves further, we confuse isolation with privacy.

Personal portables (radios and cassette players) provide another layer of isolation from those around us. One of my students tells of an experience that she and another eleven teenagers once shared on the way to a religious camp. The twelve of them sat huddled in a van, each cocooned in his and her own headsets connected to their personal "Walkman" portables, saying not a word to each other for the two-hour journey.

Most recently, the computer has substituted bulletin boards and chat rooms for live interpersonal contact. We turn increasingly to computer games, newsgroups, video arcades, Nintendo and Sega games, and virtual reality experiences. As we become more sophisticated with our communication and computer devices, we become ever more isolated from personal interactions. Jeremy Rifkin observes,

Already, the sense of isolation wrought by the introduction of the computer is being felt. As people rely on the computer as both a form of communication and a time frame through which they relate to their fellow human beings, they are finding it more and more difficult to slip back into face-to-face interchange.[3]

In their research, Elizabeth Perse and Alan Rubin cite many other studies that explain how media are used to replace human contact: "Mass media can complement, supplement, or substitute for interpersonal interaction. . . . Without [higher levels of social support], media use may become a substitute for personal interaction."[4] Or as Stoll puts it, "What a lonely way to spend an evening."[5]

ANXIETY AND MALAISE

Henry David Thoreau 140 years ago observed that "The mass of men lead lives of quiet desperation. What is called resignation is confirmed desperation. . . . A stereotyped but unconscious despair is concealed even under what are called the games and amusements of mankind."[6] The sense of assurance and self-determination we enjoyed in the linear culture had begun to fade even by the mid-nineteenth century. Today, in our post-intellectual environment, we lead lives of increasing resignation and quiet desperation. Christopher Lasch writes that "The structure of modern experience gives . . . encouragement to a sense of helplessness, victimization, cynicism, and despair."[7] The web culture leads to psychological debilitation.

Alienation and Apprehension

Ours is an age of simultaneous *ennui* and *anxiety*. We are bored and hyper-stimulated at the same time. On one hand, we are weary and resigned to the fact that the future is out of our control; we are anesthetized by our inability to cope. On the other hand, we are restless and fidgety; the more we are bombarded, the more anxious we are to see what happens next. Commenting on our reactions to the O. J. Simpson preliminary hearing, Chicago columnist Bob Greene writes, "Because we demand our world to move at warp speed these days, the Simpson story seems somehow old already, even as we wait for new developments. Dichotomy of dichotomies: As the public appetite waits impatiently to be fed, it already feels full."[8]

Three Anxieties. Every age has had its doomsayers and prophets of the apocalypse. But the generation born in the last half-century senses, if only subconsciously, that it is confronting potential catastrophes on a scale never before faced by the human race. This is part of our post-intellectual malaise.

The most obvious anxiety is the *threat of a nuclear holocaust*. Every thinking person has carried in the back of his or her mind since the end of World War II the fear that a handful of madmen could push some red buttons and virtually wipe out civilization as we know it. Even today the possibility of a nuclear outbreak may be increasing. Citing "nihilistic terrorists, unratified chemical and biological treaties, a growing rich-poor gap, rogue nations, chaos in Russia, and a world awash in legitimate and black market plutonium and warheads," the Board of the Bulletin of Atomic Scientists, in 1995, pushed the hands of its infamous Doomsday Clock forward to 11:46, fourteen minutes before nuclear midnight.[9] This was the first adjustment of its symbolic assessment of the likelihood of a nuclear confrontation since 1991, when the hands had been set *back* to 11:43.

Another web-culture fear is that of total economic breakdown—*the threat of worldwide monetary collapse*. We sense today, for the first time in history, that the world's economic structure is such an interdependent house of plastic cards and overextended credit slips that it would not take much to bring the whole planetary debt-ridden fiscal structure crashing down. In 1994, Americans owed more than $256 billion just on their Visa and MasterCard accounts (up 24 percent from only a year earlier)—and that figure does not include home mortgages, car payments, or other credit cards.[10] Our total national debt is now more than $5 trillion. How far can the extended chain of IOU's stretch? What happens when Third World countries start defaulting on their massive debt payments?

A third gnawing anxiety is the growing suspicion that complete global environmental collapse may be a possibility for the first time in human history—*the threat of irreversible ecological annihilation*. We realize that we are now on the verge of unalterably destroying major components of our planetary ecosystem. We have it within our technological power actually to make it impossible for human beings to inhabit the planet.

These nagging subliminal uncertainties linger deep in the background of our gray matter—haunting us and reminding us that we are not necessarily sure about everything we are doing. We fear that our unquestioning faith in progress and technology has led to changes and directions we did not intend. We suspect we have lost control, and the awareness is rather unsettling.

Loss of Identity

As we rely increasingly on technology, we experience a loss of identity and individuality. We lose both our perception of self-worth (mental castration) and our significance as distinct human beings (social castration).

Mental Castration. Gordon Pask defined *mental castration* as "fear of being outdone in those areas in which we most pride ourselves." This is the frustration, the hollowness, of feeling that we have nothing worthwhile to contribute—the realization that machines, computers, and robots, can do the job better than we. Why try to memorize facts when so much more can be stored in a digitized database? Why try to figure out a problem when a computer can do it so much faster? Pask argues that "mental castration might lead to a total loss of feelings of individual identity and worth. If and when machines can emulate and even surpass us in every measurable area of human endeavor, what uniquely human pursuits will be left to us?"[11]

In *The Micro Millennium,* Christopher Evans speculates that artificial intelligence may result in Ultra-Intelligent Machines that would, in effect, represent the final step in our evolutionary path. "And then what happens to Man, poor Man who set the whole thing in motion?"[12]

Social Castration. Another major factor contributing to loss of identity is *social castration* or depersonalization—removing oneself from society. We are cutting ourselves off from other humans, eliminating interpersonal contacts as an intentional strategy to cope with our increasingly complex culture.

We purchase our goods, conduct our business, entertain ourselves, handle our financial affairs, and meet numerous diverse cultural needs without face-to-face contact with other human beings. We play computer chess and video games rather than compete with other individuals. We listen to recorded music or watch MTV rather than attend vaudeville or a concert. We videoconference rather than hold regional sales meetings. We browse the Internet rather than gossip over our backyard fences.

For education, we turn to computer-based programmed instruction, the TV teacher, computer simulations, distance-learning systems, and interactive CD-ROM multimedia instruction. We get our cash from automated teller machines (ATMs). We get our coffee, candy bars, soup, and sandwiches from vending machines. We buy our newspapers and pornography from curbside dispensing boxes. We purchase our clothes, electronic gadgets, jewelry, furniture, camping supplies—virtually everything we want—from cable channels and mail-order catalogs. We rent videos rather than attend a theater filled with other people. Rather than talk *live* over the telephone, we solicit business with computer-generated recorded sales messages; we screen calls with our answering machine; we respond with e-mail.

As population pressures intrude more and more, as neighbors crowd in closer, as freeways become more impacted, as business contacts become less civil, and as we feel the streets becoming less secure, we find ourselves increasingly welcoming the social castration of machine transactions. We deliberately seek this anonymity, this feeling of welcome seclusion.

Thus, we sacrifice those human relationships that give us identity and individuality. We have lost the warmth, the spontaneity, and the challenge of human contact. To some extent, our self-image is but a reflection of the contacts we have on a routine basis. And as our contacts are increasingly with machines, so our self-image becomes increasingly depersonalized.

LOSS OF THE BIG PICTURE

In our specialized web culture, individuals have trouble seeing the big picture. We have lost the ability to perceive the whole—whether we are trying to make sense of the global landscape or understand the people next door.

Today, our complex society demands such a range of narrow specialists that the nuclear engineer, agriculturist, stock broker, forest products manager, corporate lawyer, architect, accountant, nurse, and computer programmer all speak different languages. We cannot talk together; we cannot comprehend what each of the others is doing. How can we expect to live together in harmony and have a feel for what each of us is about when we cannot understand each other? This is not a new concern, of course. Vartan Gregorian points out that in the early 1930s, José Ortega y Gasset was worried that "we may be producing one-dimensional people who will be insensitive to the total-ity of human experience and the human predicament."[13]

This is one of the perplexities of our post-intellectual political culture. We work independently on our various specialized pieces of the socioeconomic puzzle without fulfilling our intellectual responsibility to put all of the pieces together. How do we get all these occupational specialists and narrowly focused professionals to debate and collectively decide international treaties, economic controls, environmental protection, welfare reform, educational goals, and crime prevention? How can we expect to manage a global social/political enterprise that is so complex that no one can grasp the whole? Author Lewis Coser warned, "more and more people will research, discuss and defend ideas in so narrow a compass that American culture as a whole will no longer be able to assess its own condition."[14]

Isolated in Cyberspace

Hunkering over their keyboards, staring intently at their glowing screens, and planning where to stack their next peripherals, millions of computer zealots and hackers have sequestered themselves in their dimly lit cyber-closets. Hooked into the Internet, they embrace thousands of databases and newsgroups as substitutes for human interaction. Roaming the millions of WWW homepages and web sites for idle chatter and disconnected factoids, they have abandoned any intellectual orientation.

In examining this electronic cyber-culture in Japan, Karl Greenfeld de-scribes the *Otaku,* or "techno-kids," who have "fashioned a world driven by trivia—and barren of human contact." He then quotes magazine editor Abiko Seigo, who explains how isolation contributes to today's lack of moral sub-structure: "Where they are coming from is a world where all the usual per-spectives—like whether something is good or bad, smart or stupid, etc.—are irrelevant, because all of those things are judgments based on social relations. If you don't socialize, you don't have much sense of morality."[15]

Many of the brightest minds of the next generation have shut themselves off from any sustained human contact. Isolated in their electronic asylums, they lose all perspective and all sense of what is significant in the real world.

Isolated in the Present

We are also isolated, lost, in time. Men and women today are so concerned with specialized professions, immediate obligations, institutional entanglements, and electronic entertainments that few individuals—even among the educated elite—have the time or inclination to delve into the philosophers, essayists, poets, and other thinkers of yesterday. Consequently, we have a limited grasp of the journey of mankind. We have cut ourselves off from the past.

Simultaneously, our culture is evolving so fast that we have no idea where we are headed; we have no reliable insight into the future. The Generation Overlap cuts us off from tomorrow. If a society has no concept of the consequences of its immediate decisions, no sense of obligation to future generations, how can it expect to act with reason and responsibility?

We have no sense of our history; we have no sense of the rapidly evolving future. Therefore, we experience historical detachment. *We are isolated in the present.*

If young people today are not reading history and understanding their place in the story of humankind—and if they have little faith and hope for the future—then they have nothing left but the present. They are frozen in a time warp that offers them no sense of connection, no grasp of who they are or where they are in history—where they came from or where they are headed—nothing for a value system but immediate gratification. *We have neither the security of the backward-looking cyclical culture nor the confidence of the forward-looking linear culture.* We are running in place on the treadmill of the web culture.

LOSS OF SELF-SUFFICIENCY

Ralph Waldo Emerson was one of the most eloquent nineteenth-century voices crying out against the rising tide of conformity and specialization. In his famous essay, "Self-Reliance," he proclaims that the only happy man is he who holds his destiny in his own hands. "Welcome evermore to gods and men is the self-helping man. For him all doors are flung wide; him all tongues greet, all honors crown, all eyes follow with desire."[16]

How would Emerson react to today's Age of Specialization and Dependency? We have lost a sense of self-sufficiency; our fortune no longer is in our own hands. We sense that we no longer have jurisdiction over our personal environment because we no longer understand our personal environment. Our lives, our professions, our financial affairs, our medical problems, our schooling, and our households have become so complicated that we cannot cope on our own.

My grandfather used to rebuild his auto engine as needed. My father meticulously handled every aspect of his car's routine maintenance. But I (frustrated by electronic fuel injection, vacuum hoses, air-conditioning apparatus, power lines, air pollution controls, power-assisted steering, numerous onboard computers and monitoring gizmos) cannot even *see* my oil filter—let alone try to wrench it free for an oil change.

Legal and Financial Machinations

Thirty years ago, when we bought our first house, my wife and I decided on the house we wanted, talked it over with the seller and agreed on a price, and then went to our bank for a loan. The deal was done. Today, there is no way we would sell or buy another house without a realtor/broker to guide us through the required paperwork: listing agreement, multiple-listing service agreement, termite inspection form, other pest control reports, earthquake and other environmental hazard reports, smoke detector compliance form, real estate transfer disclosure, potential disturbance disclosure, other various disclosure statements, escrow papers, title report, affidavit of nonforeign status, water conservation retrofit certification, geology report, loan application (requiring up to forty signatures), physical inspection, credit statement, financing disclosures, seller financing form, four-page deposit receipt, eight-page purchase agreement, federal tax report, state withholding exemption certificate, attorney's agreement, loan agreement, certification by transferee, various amendments, insurance authorization, closing statement, assorted specialized forms for condominiums, farms, vacation property, and on and on.

I used to handle my income taxes myself. My taxes are—or should be—a relatively uncomplicated affair; I am involved in no complex stock transactions, no arcane tax shelters, no sophisticated tax write-offs, no major land deals. Nonetheless, it typically takes twelve or thirteen different forms and schedules just to satisfy the IRS bureaucracy. The IRS Code and accompanying Regulations fill 200 volumes—just to collect a designated percentage of my income for government support. We have passed the point where an intelligent taxpayer with the aid of a clear conscience and reliable calculator can confidently figure it out for him- or herself. So we call in the specialists.

You think you need an attorney? What kind do you need—criminal defense (drunk driving, immigration, assault), personal injury, divorce, estate planning, bankruptcy, eviction, medical malpractice, workers' compensation, insurance, construction law, adoption, probate and wills, corporate and business, discrimination/harassment, or whatever? Lawyers have turned specialization into an art form. One early expression of distrust of the legal profession was penned by Sir Thomas More in 1516 when describing his *Utopia:* "They have no lawyers among them, for they consider them as a sort of people whose profession it is to disguise matters."[17] In today's post-intellectual legal labyrinth, lawyers represent an increasingly frustrating layer of specialization and complexity—to the point that it becomes impossible to conduct any business without engaging the services of a lawyer for interpretative purposes.

Financial experts, like lawyers, have managed to create specialized environments in which we mere mortals dare not tread. In years past, it was possible for a person of moderate means and reasonable intelligence to devise a secure retirement program by putting some money in the bank and then investing in a few stocks or bonds. Today, however, few among us would try to negotiate without the aid of a consultant the arcane world of investment options: zero-coupon bonds, debentures, futures contracts, junk bonds, custom-designed certificates of deposit, high-risk derivatives, limited partnerships, convertible bonds, margins, stepped certificates, commercial paper, closed-end options, treasury securities, and dozens of other esoteric investment opportunities. We are at the mercy of the financial specialists—the stock brokers, bankers, economists, accountants, advisors, agents, traders, arbitragers, and other pecuniary high priests.

Medical and Educational Specialization

The medical field is another area where we have substituted faith in the technology of drugs and specialists rather than act with responsibility in preserving our own good health. Ivan Illich argues that "professional medicine may be causing more harm than good. . . . [Modern medicine] has separated people from knowledge about keeping themselves healthy, a knowledge that once was ingrained in the culture."[18] I recall an informal lecture by an elder Hawaiian who was explaining the medicinal powers of various natural plants and herbs and the importance of personal knowledge: "Hey, I go way up in the valley, along with guys from Harvard and Yale. We get caught in big fire and get burned real bad. Me, I'm gonna survive okay. Those guys, they gonna die." As we turn ourselves over to medical technology, we have lost control of our own physical well-being—and we feel increasingly guilty and estranged.

Who are these dozens of specialists with the unpronounceable labels who are probing, picking, and prying into every crevice of my being? My orthopedist knows my bones; my otologist knows my ears; my optometrist knows my eyesight; my optician knows my eyeglasses; but I need my ophthalmologist to understand my eyes; my orthodontist knows my teeth; my oncologist knows my cancer cells; and my otolaryngologist understands my sinuses. But who knows me—the whole person?

In the post-intellectual educational arena, we have fallen victim to the need, the reverence, for specialization. The problem is what Coser calls, "the fragmentation, specialization, and bureaucratization of the American mind."[19] Especially in higher education, the problem is compounded. We have *undergraduate* courses such as "Diagnostic Instrumentation Imaging," "Metal and Jewelry Design Surface Embellishment," "Clerkship in Physical Therapy," "Experimental Tailoring," and "Utilization of Radioactive Tracers in Biology."[20]

These are valuable topics, all. They represent the kinds of expertise we have to master in today's society. But in our commitment to train young professionals for today's myriad occupations, what is it we are omitting in our undergraduate program? What are we not covering in Western and Eastern civilizations, philosophy, ancient history and contemporary geography, consumer science and technology, arts and literature, the basics of our economic and political systems, communication abilities, ecological understanding, critical thinking and reasoning? In his critique of our educational system, *Education and Ecstasy,* George Leonard writes, "No need for obscure psychological explanations for modern man's fragmentation; that is what his schools teach."[21]

As we become more specialized and isolated, we become even less knowledgeable (as explained in Chapter 3). Wendell Berry compares our internalized knowledge with that of our less sophisticated forebears: "In living in the world by his own will and skill, the stupidest peasant or tribesman is more competent than the most intelligent workers or technicians . . . in a society of specialists."[22] L. S. Stavrianos gives us a more extended example:

To the present day, an Australian aborigine can take a piece of broken glass, fashion it skillfully into an arrow head or spear point, fit it to a spear thrower or to a bow that he has strung himself, set forth and kill his game, prepare his dinner with due attention to ceremony, and, after dinner, round out the day with storytelling, sharing his adventures with the stay-at-homes. In this manner the Paleolithic hunter was a "complete man" to a degree that has not been approached since the agricultural revolution.[23]

Technological Dependence

We lose our feelings of self-reliance as we depend increasingly on technology to do our research, ensure our safety, handle our communication and transportation logistics, fight our battles, manage our financial transactions, and provide our entertainments. Lasch makes the point, "One important effect sophisticated technology has is to mystify; people grow too dependent on it. In some respects, technology could become the 'magic of the 1990s' that tends to make people feel lost in the world."[24] Why try to do things for ourselves when we have the computers and the specialists to handle things for us?

We enjoy the continual improvements and conveniences—the portable cellular phone, the self-programming videorecorder, the desktop printer-copier-fax—and we do not see how these benign pieces of progress serve to entrap us and make us ever more dependent upon each succeeding technological refinement. The more complex we build our technological environment, the more committed we become to increasing technological dependence. We no longer have the option of breaking free of our technological addiction.

The Vehicular Example. The automobile is but one illustration of how dependent we have become on technology to handle our information and safety concerns. We now rely on flashers, buzzers, beeps, dashboard readouts, and recorded voices to remind us to fasten our seat belts, to release the parking brake, to turn on the headlights, to check for an open door, to take the key out of the ignition, and to turn off the headlights. We now have autos that lock all doors and turn on the headlights as soon as you turn on the ignition; vehicles that automatically slide into four-wheel drive when slippery pavement is sensed. Increasingly, we are relieved of our decision-making responsibilities.

We now can rely on the satellite and cellular-based GPS navigation technology to tell us where to go; the location of the geographically challenged driver can be pinpointed within a few feet. We even have the "talking navigator" that will tell us orally how to find our way without looking at any kind of map or readout. Technologies on the way will link our cellular phones with "vehicle local area networks" that will tie in our air bags, laptop computer, fax, GPS system, alarm devices, and engine computers for a complete electronic monitoring and diagnostic system.

Futurists anticipate the day when we will have automated, computer-based traffic control systems: universal navigation schemes to determine the least congested pathway and mandate vehicular routing, radar-regulated spacing between cars and speed-supervision controls, imbedded radio-beacon tracking controls in the roadway—an expanded Intelligent Vehicle Highway System (introduced in Chapter 6).

Great progress is being made in the move to relieve untrustworthy drivers of the responsibility of handling their own autos. Some critics have even questioned whether antilock brakes and air bags might not subconsciously allow people to drive a little more carelessly—since they know they will be protected by the technology. Our technologies handle our decision-making for us; they relieve us of our own intellectual obligations. Our technologies debilitate us.

The Self-Engendering Process.   Historian and former Librarian of Congress Daniel Boorstin notes that "The irony is that the very power of technology means those who unleash it don't have much control over where it goes."[25] The next step for our automated technological systems occurs, then, when these systems begin to shape their own sense of direction—when, like the neural networking computers, they begin to determine their own pathways and solutions that were not envisioned by their human creators. Writing over a quarter-century ago, Jacques Ellul observes that "Apparently this is a self-generating process: technology engenders itself."[26]

All of which reinforces the concept of technological determinism—Mander's *Megatechnology,* Postman's *Technopoly.* Due to our demand for short-term palliatives and immediate profits, we have surrendered control over where we are headed. Using the metaphor coined by Stewart Brand in his chronicling of *The Media Lab* at the Massachusetts Institute of Technology, we have let technology become the steamroller. "Once a new technology rolls over you, if you're not part of the steamroller, you're part of the road."[27] And today we are letting the steamroller determine where the road is to be built.

We may debate whether the twentieth century turned out better or worse because of the automobile, the television set, nuclear energy, and the computer; however, there is no question that it turned in directions that business and political leaders never could have envisioned back in 1900. The technologies have determined where we are today.

One of the dangers is that we slip into a cultural malaise—a sense that we might as well coast along and enjoy the hedonistic pleasures and securities that progress hath wrought. John Buchan, writing over fifty years ago, describes such a world—satiated with material wealth and worldly pleasures:

In such a world everyone would have leisure. But everyone would be restless, for there would be no spiritual discipline in life. . . . Everybody would be comfortable, but since there could be no great demand for intellectual exertion everybody would be also slightly idiotic. Their shallow minds would be easily bored, and therefore unstable. Their life would be largely a quest for amusement.[28]

Buchan's prose captures the simultaneous ennui and anxiety of the post-intellectual age.

In summarizing the psychological consequences of post-intellectualism, Leo Moser asks, "For good or bad, we have emerged into a new and strange world. Can we survive the secondary effects of life in a manmade world long enough to adjust to it? Or are we, in frustration and despair, likely to destroy ourselves before we can do so? Are we already entrapped by our technologies?"[29]

We contribute to our own dehumanization. We need to ask, *Can we turn off the machines if we wanted to? Could we reassert our human authority if need be?* At what point have we lost control? In the process of "mastering" our personal technologies, we ourselves become peripherals, the add-on components. We come back to Thoreau, "But lo! Men have become the tools of their tools."

Warning of increasing technological dependency in E. M. Forster's "The Machine Stops," the son of the story's protagonist cries out,

Cannot you see, cannot all your lecturers see, that it is we who are dying, and that down here the only thing that really lives is the Machine? We created the Machine, to do our will, but we cannot make it do our will now. It has robbed us of the sense of space and of the sense of touch, it has blurred every human relation and narrowed down love to a carnal act, it has paralysed our bodies and our wills, and now it compels us to worship it. The Machine develops—but not on our lines. The Machine proceeds—but not to our goal.[30]

INSTITUTIONALISM AND BUREAUCRATIZATION

In the 1920s and 1930s, America actively debated the merits of Technocracy—the economic-political theory that would turn all economic and governmental planning over to an elitist corps of scientists, economists, and engineers who could best judge how to guide and structure our civic institutions. Government by technical experts. Today we tacitly accept the concept (without the terminology). We submit to a government with decisions being made by the Federal Reserve Board, the Pentagon experts, congressional staffers, lobbyists, the research labs, think tanks, government commissions, the corporate consultants, the lawyers and engineers and bureaucrats. As Rousseau put it, "the State is governed by clerks."[31] Popular participation in societal decision-making is but a vestigial myth.

This is one more isolating factor in our post-intellectual culture—*bureaucratization*, with all segments of society becoming increasingly institutionalized.

As society grows ever more complex—as our problems get more involved, as technology becomes more incomprehensible, as economic matters get increasingly convoluted—we turn to bureaucratic defenses and institutions to handle things for us. In *Company Man,* Anthony Sampson reminds us that corporate bureaucracy is "both the blessing and the curse of Western civilization."[32] It takes big institutions to cope with big problems.

In effect, we willingly surrender our individual freedoms for the security of an institutional bulwark against bigness and change; we ask for more bureaucracy as a shield. As a result, however, the individual becomes even more isolated and debilitated. We become less self-sufficient, less of a whole being. Within the context of the bureaucracy, we become only specialized parts. We have voluntarily contributed to our feelings of dehumanization.

Pervasiveness of Bureaucracy

When we speak of bureaucracies, we are not referring solely to the government. Bureaucratization has long been the dominating institutional force among businesses, schools, labor unions, philanthropic foundations, environmental groups, and every other public or private organization. John Lukacs emphasizes this sameness among governmental and private-sector bureaucracies: "By the 1950s the mental attitudes, the inclinations, procedures, aspirations, and the very language of a government bureaucrat was not one whit different from that of a college administrator or foundation official or corporation executive."[33]

Fritjof Capra points out also the similarities in growth of institutions and the effects of such bureaucratic evolution: "Whatever the original purpose of the institution, its growth beyond a certain size invariably distorts that purpose by making the self-preservation and further expansion of the institution its overriding aim."[34]

This bigness, this tendency toward perpetual growth, is one of the most pervasive threats to the sanctity of the individual. The bigger our bureaucracies and corporate institutions become, the more dehumanized the individual becomes. Our personal identities are diminished as we see our cities, our budgets, and our bureaucracies get larger and larger. Theodore Roszak, in his provocative work, *Person/Planet,* underscores the threat to both the individual and our planetary ecosystem: "I believe . . . that both person and planet are threatened by the same enemy. *The bigness of things.* The bigness of industrial structures, world markets, financial networks, mass political organizations, public institutions, military establishments, cities, bureaucracies."[35]

Institutional Momentum and Collapse

Another characteristic of bureaucracies is Institutional Momentum (IM)—the inertia that keeps institutions and bureaucracies moving in the same direction long after their original purpose and reason for existence have been completed or forgotten. Legislatures keep passing laws (whether or not they are needed); professors keep publishing research articles (even if they have nothing substantial to say); committees keep meeting (whether or not there is anything to accomplish); banks keep making loans (even when they are on the verge of bankruptcy); and judges keep on sentencing criminals to jail terms (even if the prisons are overflowing and criminals are immediately released to the streets). All this is due to the IM factor. We simply do not know what else to do—so we keep on doing what we have always done. Whether or not it makes any sense.

Military and defense activities are especially prone to IM tendencies. For example, according to Lukacs, "with the thoughtless momentum so characteristic of the bureaucratized military," under President Johnson, our "political, financial, and even military involvement in Vietnam increased bit by bit"— virtually without any initial clear mandate or deliberate policy.[36] It was simply the IM factor. Barbara Tuchman explains that "bureaucracy, safely repeating today what it did yesterday, rolls on as ineluctably as some vast computer, which, once penetrated by error, duplicates it forever."[37]

Institutional momentum is, in effect, one specific aspect of technological determinism. Bureaucracy is technology—a systematic way of applying human and non-human resources in an attempt to solve some problem. And when the technologies, the bureaucracies, take on a direction and momentum of their own, they become Technopoly. Jerry Mander explains how the IM factor inevitably leads to technological determinism on the part of corporate bureaucracy:

The corporation is not as subject to human control as most people believe it is; rather, it is an autonomous technical structure that behaves by a system of logic uniquely well suited to its primary function: to give birth and impetus to profitable new technological forms, and to spread techno-logic around the globe.[38]

As computer systems, for example, are installed and integrated into an organization's structure, it becomes that much more difficult to drastically alter the direction and function of the organization. Therefore, the bureaucracies themselves mandate that they generate more paperwork and more detailed computations and more complex reports—merely because they have the computer power to generate such paperwork and analyses.

John Kenneth Galbraith points out that there is an institutional malaise—a senility, if you will—that grows out of the IM factor. And this bureaucratic decay applies to both the political and corporate worlds. Initial entrepreneurial vigor "gives way to contented, well-rationalized but senile bureaucracy and to the tendency to measure achievement by the number of one's subordinates, excellence by what most resembles the people already there, wisdom by what most accords with what is already being done."[39]

As institutions and people become set in their ways, it becomes more difficult to jolt them into needed change. This is the third component of our definition of post-intellectualism—the difficulty of engaging in social criticism, the unwillingness to consider needed modifications and alterations, an unswerving dedication to maintenance and continuation of the status quo. Establishmentism.

However, any organization that fails to keep abreast of technological change is a candidate for institutional collapse. Essayist Meg Greenfield writes that "it is not the individual human ability to adapt that is the problem in the new age. Rather, the problem is the ability of our human handiwork to do so: our institutions and economies and societies."[40]

The institutions on which we rely—our schools, churches, political parties, corporations, and cities—were conceived and molded during the intellectual age. They were not designed for our electric technologies, the information explosion, the speed and ubiquity of our contemporary communication systems, or pictorial media. Consequently, it should come as no surprise that our institutions are not functioning well in a post-intellectual culture.

In its broadest context, the danger of institutional entropy and collapse applies to the entire American system. If we are not successful in rethinking our priorities, modifying our political and technological and economic attitudes, and adopting a more reasonable and responsible approach to problem-solving and decision-making, we may not be able to sustain our present freedom-abusing path much longer. Our institutional momentum will keep America going for a while. But not forever.

Isolation and Specialization

How can one establish a sense of direction when one does not know where he or she is coming from (loss of historical perspective) nor where he or she is headed (loss of faith in the future)? The more complicated our environment becomes, the less we can handle on our own. The more technologies we have, the more we must rely on the specialists who understand the technologies and can design the future. There are at least three related issues that we should raise as we get buried deeper and deeper in our bureaucratic quagmire.

First, we are increasingly dazed and disoriented. We have less and less understanding of what is going on around us. We turn to the authorities—the specialists and bureaucrats—to handle our affairs. But to the extent that we do not comprehend what the specialists are doing—with our finances, our technologies, our legal matters, our society, our future—we feel that we are not in control of our own lives. We no longer can grasp what is going on in our own world. Our sense of confusion and disorientation increases as we turn the decision-making responsibilities over to others.

A second major concern is that the specialist and the corporate bureaucracy both contribute to our sense of dependency. *Bureaucratization is a form of retribalization,* a return to group-think mentality, a loss of personal individuality—a theme we will explore in Chapter 13. C. Wright Mills opens his provocative 1956 analysis, *The Power Elite,* with the observation that the lives of ordinary men and women "often seem driven by forces they can neither understand nor govern. . . . The very framework of modern society confines them to projects not their own, but from every side, such changes now press upon the men and women of the mass society, who accordingly feel that they are without purpose in an epoch in which they are without power."[41]

The more we depend upon others—a mechanic to fix our car, an accountant to figure our taxes, a lawyer to draw up our agreements, a bureaucrat to establish our safety standards, a financial planner to set up our retirement program, a priest to save our souls—the more we diminish our sense of self-sufficiency. What happens when we as individuals no longer have faith in our personal ability to handle our own affairs? What happens to our sense of identity? Our sense of uniqueness and self-worth? Our sense of independence?

Finally, we are concerned with the state of our culture once we turn the decision-making over to the experts and specialists. We sense that the various technocrats, each one working within his or her particular fragment of the whole, cannot see the big picture. Each has but a limited grasp of the overall situation and thus is unable to put the problem in perspective. Therefore (as discussed in Chapter 7), their incomplete and ill-conceived solutions are likely to lead to more problems in the future. We feel both isolated and betrayed by the very technologies to which we turn. We feel we no longer can do the job ourselves. Neither do we have faith in the specialists!

NOTES

1. Stoll, 1995, p. 24.

2. Ibid., p. 59.

3. Rifkin, 1987, p. 28.

4. Perse and Rubin, 1990, p. 50.

5. Stoll, 1995, p. 24.

6. Thoreau [1854], 1942, p. 10.

7. Lasch, 1991, p. 386.

8. Greene, 1994.

9. John Beckham, "The Clock is Still Ticking," *Los Angeles Times,* 29 February 1996, p. B2.

10. Kelley Holland with Richard A. Melcher, "Plastic: Are Banks Over Their Limit?" *Business Week,* 6 March 1995, p. 92.

11. Pask, 1982, p. 46.

12. Evans, 1980, p. 243.

13. Vartan Gregorian, interviewed in Moyers, 1989, p. 183.

14. Quoted in Noble, 1987.

15. Karl Taro Greenfeld, "The Obsession of the Otaku," *Los Angeles Times Magazine,* 12 September 1993, pp. 40, 42.

16. Emerson [1841], 1948, p. 748.

17. Thomas More, "Of Law and Magistrates," *Utopia,* 1516.

18. Quoted in Mander, 1978, p. 71.

19. Quoted in Noble, 1987.

20. Examples taken from the 1994–96 Catalog of California State University, Northridge. The undergraduate catalog of any large university would reveal similar course offerings.

21. Leonard, 1968, p. 11.

22. Berry, 1977, p. 20.

23. Stavrianos, 1982, p. 11.

24. Quoted in Michael Schrage, "Where Technology is Taking Us," *Los Angeles Times*, 7 January 1990, p. D7.

25. Quoted in Peter Grier, "Discovery, Science, Technology, and the 'Illusion of Knowledge,'" *Christian Science Monitor,* 2 January 1992, p. 3.

26. Ellul, 1964, p. 87. I have taken the liberty of using the word *technology* where Ellul's translator used *technique*.

27. Brand, 1987, p. 9.

28. John Buchan (Lord Tweedsmuir), *Pilgrim's Way: An Essay in Recollection* (Cambridge, MA: Houghton Mifflin Company/The Riverside Press, 1940), pp. 289–90.

29. Moser, 1979, p. 170.

30. Forster [1914], 1928, pp. 55-56.

31. Rousseau [1762] (book 2, ch. 9), 1952, p. 403.

32. Quoted in Jonathan Kirsch, "Corporate Culture: A Blessing and a Curse," *Los Angeles Times*, 22 November 1995, p. E5.

33. Lukacs, 1984, p. 376.

34. Capra, 1982, p. 220.

35. Roszak, 1979, pp. 32–33.

36. Lukacs, 1984, p. 74.

37. Tuchman, 1984, p. 386.

38. Mander, 1991, p. 120.

39. Galbraith, 1984, p. xxxv.

40. Meg Greenfield, "The Laptop Revolution," *Newsweek*, 27 February 1995, p. 84.

41. Mills, 1956, p. 3.

PART 3

Social Consequences of Post-Intellectualism

*This is modern life: sealed up, walled in, locked up,
locked out. It's lonely and it's sad and it didn't used
to be like this. Don't wait for the new Dark Ages any
longer. They're here.*

• Benjamin Stein
Los Angeles Times

Part Three looks at some social repercussions of post-intellectualism. Many of
the attributes we have touched on in previous chapters also have broader social
implications. However, in these four chapters we specifically want to consider
urbanization, some aspects of our economic structure, broad environmental
concerns, and a few questions relating to media and morality—these are but a
few of the social consequences of post-intellectualism.

9

Hyper-Urbanization:
Losing Our Way in the Concrete Jungle

> *America is becoming the first developed nation in which central cities—cities as traditionally understood—are important primarily as problems.*
>
> • George Will
> *Syndicated Column*

Urbanization is an attribute of the Intellectual Age—an inevitable outgrowth of technological industrialization, competitive capitalism, linear progress and expansion. However, post-intellectual cities globally are decaying: congestion and pollution, increasing crime and gang warfare, escalating poverty and homelessness, deterioration of inner-city neighborhoods, dysfunctional governments, and collapsing physical infrastructures. Urban deterioration is one of the unintended consequences of distended-intellectualism.

THE CONCEPT OF URBANIZATION

As soon as nomads traded in their walking sticks for plows, the idea of *settlement* took root. Once the crops were planted and the cattle and goats were fenced in, the farmers needed a trading post, a source of supplies, and a spot to congregate. As L. S. Stavrianos describes the process,

the agricultural revolution set off a chain reaction of *urbanization*, class differentiation, and social cleavage that undermined the appealing equality of primitive society. But in doing so it also broke the restricting bonds of tribal traditionalism and thereby launched humanity, for good or ill, on the fateful course that was to lead from hunting ground to *megalopolis.*[1]

Urbanization as a Technology

The city is a technology—a systematized means of structuring resources, an organized approach to *solving a problem.* (All technology is problem-solving.) Urbanization was the solution to the problems generated by the coming of agriculture—meeting the needs for the marketplace, financial institutions, defense, industrialization, specialized occupations, education, transportation systems, and mass communication. The city is the ultimate technology, the foreordained end result of linear growth and development.

However, the city-as-solution has given rise to numerous subsequent problems and unintended consequences. (Yesterday's solutions lead to today's problems.) The city is a technology gone amok. The ills we associate with contemporary cities, like most of the other symptoms of the Progress Paradox, have arisen as a result of misapplied technological development. Hyper-urbanization is the result of technological determinism.

Eradicating the Community

The city started out as an extended community. Rufus Miles defines community as "common roots in a place and a common feeling of mutual support among a group that trusts and is basically loyal to one another."[2] In rural villages and small towns, individuals grew up together, went to school together, attended the same church, shopped at the same general store, knew each other's families, and probably worked at the same places. And they cared for each other. They were a community—Ferdinand Tönnies's *Gemeinschaft.*[3]

But in the city, we live by the intellectual social contract—Tönnies's *Gesellschaft.* You do not know your neighbor two doors down the block. You do not go to the same church, possibly not to the same school; certainly you do not work at the same factory or mill. In fact, you probably do your best to shut yourself off from your neighbors—their dogs, lawnmowers, kids, music. The irony is that the closer you live to someone physically, the more you try to protect your space by isolating yourself from that person. *The city has killed the community.*

The tribe or rural community is a *pre-intellectual* social grouping—based on cooperation, sharing, tradition, and clan allegiances. The city started out as an *intellectual* construct—a social unit based on abstract rational and political arrangements, dedicated to industrial progress, change, capitalistic enterprise, and technological advances. However, today's city has evolved into a *post-intellectual,* ill-defined, disordered megalopolis—characterized by exploitation, isolation, specialized roles, and an obvious loss of critical-thinking and problem-solving skills. The intellectual social contract has broken down.

Hyper-urbanization may be defined as the condition in which inner-city problems emerged as the principal feature of urban reality. Columnist George Will observes, "America is becoming the first developed nation in which central cities—cities as traditionally understood—are important primarily as problems."[4]

The numerous urban civil riots of the 1960s serve as the symbolic end of America's long intellectual endeavor. We began to experience the breakdown of the rational linear culture and the impending confusion of a web culture.

Removal from Reality

Science fiction writers give us the vision of the futuristic city that places all civilization under a protective dome—with its climate controls, moving sidewalks, air-rejuvenating systems, personal monorail pods, and synthesized nutrients. Such an environment shields its denizens from the outer world, from all contact with reality. Disney World, Leisure World, shopping-mall-world, and television-world all are transitions to this encapsulated environment of the future.

In such an artificial urban setting, however, there is something deep-rooted in our animal psyche that cries out in rebellion. The synthetic city simply is not a natural environment; it is contrary to our genetic makeup as carried over from our paleolithic hunting heritage. As anthropologist Ralph Linton writes, "We are, in fact, anthropoid apes trying to live like termites, and, as any philosophical observer can attest, not doing too well at it."[5] The whole concept of civilization, Rousseau would remind us, is something alien to our natural state. The idea of an intellectual social construct is foreign to our basic animal instincts.

We deal every day with the mediated reality of television images, computer simulations, marketing messages, bank statements, blueprints, and financial projections. These things are man-made inventions of an intellectual civilization; they do not exist naturally. We confuse the images, the symbols, and the pictures with reality. And we sense that the city, as well, is part of this synthetic creation.

The city additionally conspires with our media technologies to immerse us in an environment of materialistic excess. Hal Himmelstein writes,

Television work is done in New York City and Los Angeles; the images, sound, and pacing of television tend to reflect the distinctive auras of both urban ecologies, which are subsequently embedded in our collective consciousness and which promise excitement, financial success, mobility, visibility, and emotional fulfillment—in short, the Great American Dream—the "good life" as described in the myth of eternal progress and characterized by the perpetual economic expansion of the society and the growth of personal material compensations.[6]

What is it that attracts people to nature, to the out-of-doors, to the forest, mountains, desert, lakes and rivers? Camping. Hiking. Fishing. Visiting our national parks. Renting a cottage at the lake. Our recreational pursuits are geared to nature—horseback riding, bird-watching, gardening, backyard barbecues in the suburbs, and picnics in the park. Even the landed gentry return to nature for their country clubs and golf courses.

The answer is that we sense we are increasingly out of touch with our natural background—our genetic and ecological heritage. We need to confront the real world physically. We are attracted to wilderness (wild-ness) because it represents freedom. In the wilderness, we are on our own to face the elements. We must make our own decisions; we must solve our own problems. On the other hand, civilization—urban living—represents restrictions, rules, regulations, one-way streets, and building codes. In the city, the decisions have already been made for us.

We have chosen the security of the city because we want our uniformed police officers, our medical centers, our street lights, and our welfare offices. But in return we have had to surrender some of our freedoms. And we are not quite sure whether we are content with such a swap. Despite our reclining rockers and deodorized bathrooms, we are not entirely comfortable with the decision to live in a synthetic environment. The freedom and uncertainties of the untamed world still call to us.

With each succeeding generation, however, the untamed real world becomes less accessible. The longer we dwell in cities, the more trouble we have in distinguishing the real from the unreal. We are drawn deeper and deeper into the post-intellectual vortex of concrete and computers. And we become increasingly anxious and uncertain.

URBAN PRESSURES

Along with the excitement, economic opportunities, and stimulation of the metropolis come also the distended-intellectual drawbacks and disadvantages— the tension, noise, crime, congestion, and emotional clutter. Many of our urban problems are due to the deterioration of what might be termed the *human infrastructure* of the city.

Congestion, Crowding, and Confusion

The poet Percy Bysshe Shelley conjured up the urban image as succinctly as anyone: "Hell is a city much like London—A populous and smoky city."[7] Numerous laboratory experiments have demonstrated that rats crowded into an unnaturally dense environment develop emotional problems and eventually turn on themselves to reduce the population numbers. Leo Moser points out the obvious human parallel: "Whether or not we accept that *Homo sapiens* is a 'territorial animal,' we do know that increased population densities can create tensions both within groups and between them."[8]

In 1790, the U.S. population density was 4.5 persons per square mile; in 1990, it was 70.3 persons per square mile—over fifteen times more crowded than when the country was founded.* These figures are averages for the country

---

*Density per square mile is based on the territory encompassed within U.S. boundaries for the given year.

as a whole, including all the mountains, plains and deserts. The average density for large cities varies tremendously—from a low of under 3,000 persons per square mile (generally in the south and southwest) to concentrations between 12,000 and 15,000 per square mile for places like Chicago, Philadelphia, Boston, and San Francisco. New York City tops out with 23,500 individuals assigned to each square mile (which is one-tenth the density of Hong Kong).[9]

Urban residents often try to flee the distress of city living by oozing out into the suburbs. Today, the largest segment of the U.S. population lives in the rapidly expanding sprawl between the city and the farm—the ubiquitous suburban jumble. However, we do not escape the confines of the city; we merely spread out the freeways, shopping malls, industrial complexes, condominiums, parking lots, and housing tracts in an ever-expanding circle of metropolitan congestion and despair. As observed in the *National Journal* in 1993, "older working-class suburbs are starting to fall into the same abyss of disinvestment that their center cities did years ago."[10]

Urban Urgency. There is an accelerating urgency to the pace of life associated with the city—a constant pressure to get things done; cram a myriad activities into 168 hours a week; fill our schedules with something productive in every fifteen-minute slot. With a computer-notebook organizer in our jacket pocket, a personal recorder in our shirt pocket, a cellular phone in our car, a laptop computer on the plane, a fax machine in our office, and a modem in our den, we are constantly productive, continually in touch, eternally meeting deadlines. Ralph Keyes, author of *Timelock*, summarizes our plight: "From telegrams to faxes, one technological innovation after another has met our demands for a faster tempo, then speeded it up some more."[11] The average American now has 37 percent less leisure time than he or she enjoyed twenty years ago.[12]

The computer does not necessarily save us any time; it merely allows us to process more data and do more work in the same amount of time—if we push a little. In Moser's words, "To a great extent, the machine has become the pacemaker of techno-industrial society."[13] The pace of life profoundly influences our self-images, our values, our behavior. We tend to measure our self-worth in terms of how much information we can process in a given amount of time—never mind that the information is half-digested, that we respond in terms of ill-considered proposals, that we deal only with summaries and slogans. *We must move on.*

The irony is that it is our development as a civilization—pushing for more and more technological progress and urban expansion—that has created our current frazzled mental state. This is distended-intellectualism. The eminent historian Will Durant once observed that "no man who is in a hurry is quite civilized."[14]

We are also assaulted by continual urban din: the traffic rumble, emergency vehicles, animals screeching and barking, doors and trash cans slamming, trains and planes, babble of our radio and TV sets, jangling of our telephones and alarm systems, whirring of our computers and air-conditioning units, lawn-mowers and power tools, supermarket background music and pervasive rock and rap, the jackhammer and piledriver celebrating new construction projects. The ubiquitous cacophony surrounds us day and night. Our noise pollution adds to the sense of urgency—reinforcing the breakdown between our inner nature and our technological environment.

Urban Impact on the Individual

As population pressures increase, we retreat into whatever isolation we can find: we hide behind stout fences and tall hedges; we clamp our Sony Walkmans to our heads (adding to the urban soundtrack even as we cut ourselves off from other intrusions). We secure ourselves in gated residential areas, private recreational clubs, and restricted parking structures.

In an article dealing with urban intrusion, Benjamin Stein concludes, "This is modern life: sealed up, walled in, locked up, locked out. It's lonely and it's sad and it didn't used to be like this. . . . Don't wait for the new Dark Ages any longer. They're here." [15] This self-imposed isolation in turn leads to a sense of despondency and impotency. Isolated, disconnected people do not congregate to discuss issues and exercise political clout. Calling on the insights of earlier political observers, Roger Boesche writes,

> With isolation comes powerlessness; isolated individuals are by definition powerless, because they do not meet with fellow citizens to discuss and to organize. In this new world of isolation, each person, Tocqueville maintained, "is instantly overwhelmed by his own insignificance and weakness." Nothing renders us more powerless, Hannah Arendt noted, than modern urban loneliness, which only in the late 20th Century "has become an everyday experience of the ever-growing masses." No wonder men and women believe that they cannot make a difference. [16]

Emotional Imbalance. Among city dwellers, there is a continual struggle to maintain an emotional balance, a sense of coherence. Like the experimental rats in the crowded cage, we sense the ill-defined stress and agitation, without being able to articulate what is happening to us. We do not have the time or space to stand back and gain any perspective on where we are headed.

We can plan utopian space colonies, but we cannot manage our terrestrial cities; we can send teams of explorers to the moon, but we cannot control urban traffic jams; we can transplant human hearts and kidneys, but we cannot deliver rudimentary health care to our indigent citizens; we can send back color video pictures from planets across the solar system, but we cannot speak the same language as our neighbors across the street; we can build huge skyscrapers, mammoth military installations, luxury resort communities, and vast research complexes, but we do not know what to do with the homeless of our inner cities. It is this sense of imbalance that leads to feelings of simultaneous malaise and anxiety, conflicting emotions of dejection and tension.

In 1988, the National Institutes of Mental Health released the results of a major study involving diagnostic interviews with 18,500 subjects. The study revealed that almost one-third of U.S. citizens will experience a severe mental disorder at some point in their lives; and at any given time, almost 15 percent of the nation's population is suffering from some urgent mental illness. These findings indicate an accelerating increase in the rate of mental disease.[17] Although many factors may be implicated as causes, one reason constantly referred to is the stress and pressures of today's fast-paced, technology-driven, urban lifestyle.

Medical Problems. In several ways, we urban dwellers today are actually worse off medically than our paleolithic predecessors. Anthropological and biological studies have shown that our stone-age ancestors had lower cholesterol levels, lower blood pressure, less diabetes, and fewer dental caries than we do. Eaton, Shostak and Konner itemize the toll taken by our *diseases of civilization*—"the heart attacks, strokes, cancer, diabetes, emphysema, hypertension, cirrhosis, and like illnesses that cause 75 percent of all mortality in the United States and in other industrialized nations."[18]

Our paleolithic forefathers did, of course, statistically have a considerably shorter life expectancy than we do; however, this was largely because of childhood diseases and accidents. Once safely beyond childhood, many lived long and productive lives.

One factor obviously is nutrition. The typical stone-age diet consisted of no refined carbohydrates (other than honey), far more nondigestible fiber and complex carbohydrates than what we consume, about one-fifth of our daily salt intake, and wild game that had about one-seventh the fat of our deliciously marbled domesticated beef.[19] Our stone-age parents had one other health advantage that cannot be discounted: they were active physically. They spent very little time sitting behind a desk or curled up on the couch in front of the TV.

Jared Diamond points out also that there was less contagious disease. "Epidemics couldn't take hold when populations were scattered in small bands that constantly shifted camp. Tuberculosis and diarrheal disease had to await the rise of farming, measles and bubonic plague the appearance of large cities."[20]

Our modern medicine, of course, countered many diseases with the technology of wonder drugs. In the 1940s, the marvel of penicillin and a profusion of other "miracle" antibiotics promised to do away with the scourge of bacteria and fungus pathogens. But it now appears that we are backsliding. We failed to reckon with the tremendous capacity of the microbes to alter their genetic structure and develop resistant strains that spread faster than we could map them.

Perhaps no other phenomenon so frighteningly demonstrates the Progress Paradox: *the more wonder drugs we invent, the faster that drug-resistant strains of microbes keep evolving.* Mark Caldwell writes, "Now, 50 years after the first human deployment of antibiotics, bacteria are putting our drugs to rout. Initially antibiotics gained us many easy victories, but their subsequent overuse also gave bacteria ample opportunity to confront our chemical weapons and find ways around them."[21]

Early in 1996, a major federal study revealed that from 1980 to 1992, on a per capita basis, the proportion of Americans who died from infectious diseases had increased 58 percent.[22] Pneumonia, meningitis, gonorrhea, numerous *staphylococcus* infections: the list of drug-resistant diseases grows longer each year. In 1992, we saw the first strains of tuberculosis that are resistant to all eleven of the existing TB drugs. Periodic outbreaks of the bubonic plague cause us to cry out that this isn't supposed to happen in the late twentieth century. The spread of the HIV virus, Ebola outbreaks, and other viral epidemics remind us how vulnerable our post-intellectual medical shields may be.

PHYSICAL AND SOCIAL ENTROPY

In the little mountainous corner of Los Angeles County where I live, our community is served by a fire station that was built in the 1920s and has safeguarded the area since the time when the population was one-quarter of what it is today. I live within jogging distance of a natural park that has been maintained by the county for decades. Today, the fire station is on the list of those that are targeted for closure whenever the county runs low on funds. And the park has been abandoned to transients and drug dealers because the county no longer can afford to maintain or patrol it. Why—as our population expands and the revenue from taxes keeps increasing—can we not maintain the basic services that were the norm fifty years ago?

The Physical Infrastructure Crumbles

Many of our contemporary problems obviously stem from the fact that our nation's physical artifacts are deteriorating—our roads, bridges, tunnels, buildings, canals and aqueducts, water and sewage treatment facilities, prisons, transit systems, trains and planes, schools and hospitals, libraries and parks. All these concrete manifestations of technology and urbanization are growing old. And our cities and counties no longer have the budgets to maintain or replace them. Former governor of Colorado Richard Lamm estimated in 1987 that the cost of rebuilding our country's physical infrastructure would be close to $3 trillion.[23]

Infrastructure problems can be most readily exemplified in New York City, where the congestion is the greatest, the structures the oldest, and the finances the shakiest. The *New York Times* reports:

> The physical infrastructure of the city continues to deteriorate. The bridges, tunnels and streets—the arteries of the system—give way a little more every year. Large portions of the city's steel skeleton are now nearly a century old and need major repair or replacement.

A week seldom goes by without the eruption of some underground facility as a not so kindly reminder that subterranean New York, with its pipes, sewers, wires and cables, will have to be redone in the next decade. Once again, the price tag will run into the billions.[24]

Across the nation, cities large and small report major problems as the concrete crumbles, the asphalt disintegrates, and the bricks come unglued. Citizens are not as well serviced or protected today as they were twenty or thirty years ago. We have reached the end of sustainable growth and development. Our linear culture no longer works.

Unfortunately, this material deterioration of our physical foundations is taking place at a time when the tax dollars needed for repair and replacement are becoming increasingly hard to obtain. According to U.S. Department of Commerce figures, during the last two decades federal spending for public works has dropped from 2.3 percent of the gross domestic product to less than one percent. Government priorities have been shifted. We are focused more on post-intellectual, human-centered social entitlement programs—Social Security, child care, Medicare, Medicaid, food stamps, drug rehabilitation, job-training programs, civil service pensions, and the like—rather than building or maintaining our physical infrastructure. In 1963 such entitlement programs made up 30 percent of the federal budget; thirty years later they accounted for 61 percent of our federal expenditures.[25]

Affluence and Lack of Responsibility. One factor contributing to this entropy is that large numbers of the affluent have dropped out of the public sector. Rather than utilize public schools, libraries, police, parks, hospitals, and public transportation, more and more of the upper reaches of even the middle classes send their children to private schools, use private security personnel, maintain private gated residential communities, take advantage of private and corporate recreation facilities, on-line information services, limousines and helicopters, private hospitals, and catering services.

Seldom do they have to step outside their privately secured environment to mingle with the masses and ride the bus. And therefore, they repeatedly vote not to support those services. They vote against bond measures for new schools and sewers; they vote against city council members who see the need to raise taxes to rebuild the city.

This post-intellectual avoidance of urban responsibility undermines the intellectual democratic commitment to the abstract concept of *society*—the rational compact dedicated to the egalitarian well-being of all persons, as opposed to a narrow provincial concern with one's immediate tribe or community. All citizens must support the public education system, whether or not they have children enrolled in the public schools; all citizens must support public mass transit, even if they choose to drive their own cars. If we are not able to find a way to meet the costs for repair of our public infrastructure, the result will be the collapse of our urban environment. And the ultimate loss is the continuing bankruptcy of the idea of an intellectual culture.

Societal Deterioration

As the quality of urban living deteriorates, individuals find themselves increasingly alienated. Their destiny is dictated by institutional bureaucracies, incomprehensible rules and regulations, faceless manipulators, and establishment decision makers: educators, bosses, rich folks, advertisers, politicians, police. They no longer can figure out where to grab a handle on what is happening to them; they no longer can deal with problems rationally; they no longer can cope. As a consequence, many react out of frustration and pent-up hostilities; they lash out with wanton violence and vandalism against whatever or whomever is at hand—schools, corporations, government agencies, strangers, neighbors, loved ones, or even themselves (with drugs, alcohol, suicide).

Crime statistics fill in the details: in cities (over 250,000 population), robberies occur ten times more frequently than in the suburbs, thirty-five times more frequently than in surrounding rural areas. Similar kinds of comparative data can be provided for murders, rapes, drug abuse, gang-related crimes, suicide, divorce, homelessness, illiteracy, mental illness, unemployment. Pick your favorite social problem; it will be much more prevalent in the city than in rural communities.

In a 1993 speech, "A Cry for My City," Senator Daniel Patrick Moynihan compared New York City today with the same city he grew up in fifty years earlier.[26] In 1943, the city's population was about 2 percent greater than it was in 1993. Yet its welfare rolls increased during that half-century from about 90,000 to over one million; the illegitimacy rate climbed from 3 percent of all births to 43 percent; and the number of gun-related homicides multiplied from 44 murders in 1943 to 1,537 in 1992. These alarming statistics are repeated—perhaps with only slightly less dramatic increases—in virtually every major metropolitan area in the United States.

The Urban Underclass. The city gives us a panorama of materialistic contrasts. Even as some of us grow more comfortable and secure—behind our fences, private guards, and alarm systems—others grow more despondent and disenfranchised. Many of us reap the benefits of advancing technology; others slip further and further into the subterranean world of shadowy subsistence.

Consider the homeless, the illegal immigrants, the chronically unemployed, the drug addicts, the displaced rural workers, the urban rejects, the emotionally wrecked, the AIDS victims, the growing underworld, the neighborhoods where even the police dare not tread. We seem to have accepted the reality of a permanent underclass. Lyndon Johnson unveiled his hopes for the Great Society over three decades ago, in order to eradicate—or at least to bring under control—poverty, homelessness, illiteracy, and violent crime. Richard Goodwin, the White House speech writer who coined the phrase, "the Great Society," stated in 1989 that "All the problems that Johnson was talking about then are problems that we still have now. Only they are worse."[27] Critics differ on the success of individual programs encompassed within Johnson's grand scheme, but there is consensus that for the entrenched permanent underclass, the problems have been increasing.

Analysis of the 1990 census data reveals, for example, that during the 1980s the number of children living below the poverty level increased over 40 percent. The percentage of families on some sort of public assistance rose from 19 percent in 1980 to about 25 percent in 1990—although, when adjusted for inflation, the average annual welfare check had diminished.

Worldwide, the urban crises intensify. A 1996 report from the United Nations Population Fund projected that by the year 2006, more than half of the world's masses will be living in urban areas, "underlining the prospect of ever more crowded, violent and unhealthy cities."[28]

If our urban problems are to be solved, it will not be with piecemeal handouts to patch up separate programs—special education programs, additional counseling, crackdowns on crack pushers, more birth control information, job-training programs, and similar palliatives. Neither can we reform our cities simply by eliminating our urban cores, our economic centers, our industrial base, our communication systems. Nor can we return to the seventeenth century and try again. We need a concerted effort to redefine the modern *city*.

Rousseau pointed out that "houses make a town, citizens make a city."[29] In our technological push toward urbanization, we have populated our cities with too many residents and not enough citizens. We must rediscover citizenship— the reasoned and responsible commitment to the abstract idea of a social contract. The city is an intellectual idea. Our contemporary hyper-urbanized chaos is a post-intellectual perversion of that idea.

NOTES

1. Stavrianos, 1982, p. 14.
2. Miles, 1976, p. 85.
3. See Tönnies, 1887.
4. George Will, "Manhattan Dreams and Nightmares," *Los Angeles Times*, 26 May 1991, p. M5.
5. Linton, 1964, p. 11.
6. Himmelstein, 1994, pp. 19–20.
7. Percy Bysshe Shelley, *Peter Bell the Third,* pt. 3, stanza 1 (1819).
8. Moser, 1979, p. 173.
9. U.S. Bureau of the Census, *Current Population Reports* (Washington, DC: U.S. Government Printing Office, 1990.)
10. Quoted in Mike Davis, "The Suburban Nightmare," *Los Angeles Times,* 23 October 1994, p. M1.
11. Ralph Keyes, "How to Unlock Time," *Reader's Digest,* October 1991, p. 112.
12. According to a Lou Harris poll quoted in Gibbs, 1989, p. 58.
13. Moser, 1979, p. 157.
14. Quoted in Gibbs, 1989, p. 58.

15. Benjamin Stein, "Modern Life: Sealed Up, Walled In, Locked Out," *Los Angeles Times,* 18 August 1989, pt. 2, p. 7.

16. Boesche, 1994.

17. Parachini, 1988, p. 1.

18. Eaton, Shostak, and Konner, 1988, p. 5.

19. See ibid., p. 7.

20. Diamond, 1987, pp. 65–66.

21. Mark Caldwell, "Prokaryotes at the Gate," *Discover,* August 1994, p. 46.

22. As reported in the Journal of the American Medical Association. See Terence Monmaney, "U.S. Infectious Disease Deaths Rise Markedly," *Los Angeles Times,* 17 January 1996, pp. A1, A11.

23. Lamm, 1987, p. A4.

24. Richard C. Wade, "New York's Next Crisis: Worse Than 1975," *New York Times,* 30 September 1989, p. 15.

25. Figures are according to the 1994 report of the Bipartisan Commission on Entitlement and Tax Reform (Washington, DC: U.S. Government Printing Office, 1994).

26. Moynihan [1993], 1994.

27. Quoted in Stanley Meisler, "Can L.B.J.'s Great Society Ever Exist?" *Los Angeles Times,* 14 July 1989, p. 1.

28. "Science in Brief: Half of World's People Will Be In Urban Areas by 2006, Report Says,". *Los Angeles Times,* 30 May 1996, p. B2.

29. Rousseau [1762], book 1, ch. 6, 1952, p. 392n.

10

Economic Destitution: Bankruptcy of Fiscal Theory

Anyone who believes that exponential growth can go on forever is either a madman or an economist.

• Rufus Miles
Awakening from the American Dream

Of all the topics covered in this book, none is more indicative of distended-intellectualism than an economic policy based upon continuing linear growth and development. Capitalism is an intellectual theory. But extended exploitation without restraint is post-intellectual folly. In our financial institutions, our corporate arrangements, our media structures, and all our governmental policies, we tenaciously cling to the illusion that if we can somehow just keep growing and exploiting, we can maintain a healthy economy. We refuse to accept that we have reached the end of the era of unrestrained expansion.

If any confirmation of this failed policy is needed, consider our inability to cope with poverty in the United States. According to U.S. Census Bureau figures, in 1978, 11.4 percent of the U.S. population was living below the official poverty line; in 1992, the figure had increased to 14.5 percent. Or consider that the average pay of nonsupervisory employees in private industry has fallen over 10 percent in the past two decades—from $12.06 per hour in 1973 (in 1993 dollars) to $10.83 in 1993.[1] Analysis of 1993 census data indicates that the inflation-adjusted income of the bottom 95 percent of American families has fallen since 1989.[2]

If it takes two incomes to support a family today—when one income could sustain a family a couple generations ago—something has gone amiss with the system. *Either* our economic system has really failed as a means of providing adequate support for the average household (if one wage earner is no longer adequate) *or* the materialistic demands of the typical family have escalated well beyond a healthy level. In either case, something is wrong.

MEDIA AND MATERIALISM

The American dream should be about more than materialism. But today one would be hard-pressed to find much evidence in Washington for any creed other than greed. Calvin Coolidge is credited with the saying, "The business of America is business."[3] Today, we accept the precept that the business of America is materialism. Richard Goodwin reminds us that the "one consistent thread in the complex tapestry of national policy . . . is the continued support of big business and the affluent over the interests of the nation as a whole."[4]

The mass media play a major role in the promotion of materialism and deleterious consumption. It is only as demand for products and services can be generated by the media purveyors (owners, publishers, advertisers) and paid for by the receivers (readers, viewers, consumers) that the system can succeed.

Lifestyles of the rich and materialistic are dramatized and paraded before us constantly—the fancy cars, plush residences, exclusive restaurants, designer clothes, and expensive entertainments. From *Dallas* to *Melrose Place*, pictures of the Good Life ceaselessly and subliminally reinforce our consumerism mindset. We are constantly setting goals for the *haves* (how to dress, where to live, what to drive, how to enjoy a successful career, how to win big). And we are continually creating more resentment for the *have-nots* (reminding them of what they don't own, what they can't achieve, and where they don't belong).

The Big Business of Media

Within the media industries, the mandate for growth is relentless. Profit momentum, greed, tax incentives, and legal interests of the stockholders all dictate more development, acquisitions, amalgamations, buyouts, and conglomerate consolidation. Mergers result in fewer and fewer companies owning more and more of the communication channels. The number of voices contributing to the media mix is thereby reduced. And the larger the media conglomerates become, the more they stress profits and consumerism-as-usual.

Our web culture is defined by the weekly machinations of the global communications and computer giants announcing new alliances and confederations as they jockey for positions in cyberspace. Who owns whom this week? Who came out on top in the latest round of corporate takeovers—the TV networks, newspaper publishers, cable systems, computer giants, regional phone companies, Hollywood studios, satellite moguls, long-distance carriers, or the software designers? Or is there any meaningful distinction anymore?

Commercial media operations steadily permeate every lane of the information superhighway. By the end of 1995, NBC had established an America Online site, a WWW site, its NBC desktop publishing operation, a financial news service, an e-mail service, the NBC Data Network, an on-line newsletter, and NBC SuperNet on the Microsoft Network. Eight newspaper giants (Advance Publications, Cox, Gannett, Hearst, Knight-Ridder, Times Mirror, Tribune, and the Washington Post) have formed the New Century Network to sell a variety of on-line interactive services.[5]

One component of intellectualism is social criticism. But where do we find the social critics when all are employed by the establishment? Where do we find the cultural perspective from which to examine our interlocking corporate interests when these interlocking corporate interests *are* our cultural perspective? How does our media/corporate/government/educational infrastructure find a podium from which to critique our media/corporate/government/educational infrastructure? This is the essence of anti-intellectual establishmentism—the lack of social criticism. Where do we turn for diverse voices when our media outlets ultimately will all be owned by one monolithic colossus—the ATTimeWarnerDisneABCBSonyGEWestingIBMicrosof Multicorp?

Advertising and Consumerism

Adam Smith's rational free enterprise theory has degenerated into an aggressive manipulative materialism—based on exploitation of a consumer culture. Michael Lerner points out the role of materialistic thinking in today's culture: "The values of 'looking out for No. 1' and 'getting mine' were precisely what was needed to succeed in the capitalist marketplace. Yet those were the very values that taught our children to put material goods ahead of spiritual needs, to develop competitive rather than cooperative skills, . . . The marketplace fostered the development of a narcissistic personality structure adept at manipulating and controlling others."[6]

A basic means of "manipulating and controlling others" is, of course, *advertising*—specifically, the stimulation of excessive consumerism. Advertising, as much as any other phenomenon, explains how the intellectual ideals of Enlightenment thinkers have been distorted into an ugly obsession with materialistic values. Hal Himmelstein explains, "Nothing serves the cause of advanced capitalism more effectively . . . than does advertising. . . . Ads are not only selling us a product or service or politician, they are selling us a style of life. And they have become the engines that drive our way of life."[7]

Consumerism and Establishmentism. Because the media are dedicated to attracting mass, popular audiences, the system stifles expression from any but the middle-of-the-road; it becomes increasingly difficult to give voice to any non-conventional viewpoints. Advertisers and media owners think alike. They are all part of the common establishment; *consumerism is good; materialism is what makes the economy go round*. Advertisers need not dictate editorial policy; their needs *are part of* the editorial policy.

Establishment thinking dictates that the cultural level of the mass media cannot be raised because they would then reach a smaller audience. This results in what we cover in Chapter 14 as "lowest-common-denominator" content. Tabloid news programs, copycat sitcoms, sensational reality programming, exploitative made-for-TV movies, violence-prone Hollywood productions, and inane talk shows are all indications of the degeneration of this mediated culture. Therefore, as Steve Allen observes, "there is never going to be any serious hope for marked improvement in the quality of commercial television, simply because television is primarily an advertising medium."[8]

Advertising, and indeed, our whole materialistic economic philosophy, is predicated upon avarice; this is one of the limitations on our ability to act with reason—the primary consideration underlying post-intellectualism. The media are in business to exploit this basic animal drive; they must capitalize on our greed. To keep the economy energized and growing, it is necessary to stimulate as much consumption as possible. Christopher Lasch states,

The rise of consumerism in this century—in which the individual's self-interest is the *only* good—created a society in which you don't need any public consensus as long as the economy can satisfy people's needs and expand them into ever increasing levels of desire and expectation. . . . Americans came to believe that it was no longer necessary to grapple with underlying issues of justice and equality as long as the goods kept coming.[9]

Consumerism and the Creation of False Wants. Consumerism demands that we must buy great quantities of things we really do not need. Jules Henry explains that "advertising is an expression of an irrational economy that has depended for survival on a fantastically high standard of living incorporated into the American mind as a moral imperative."[10] Without these material acquisitions, how are we to keep ahead of the Joneses? How are we to impress our colleagues and neighbors unless we have the latest and biggest? How are we to define ourselves except by our material possessions?

Referring to Jean Jacques Rousseau as "the first modern philosopher to question the goodness of historical 'progress,'" Francis Fukuyama goes on to summarize Rousseau's explanation of consumerism: aside from basic needs for food and shelter, "all other human wants are not essential to happiness, but arise out of man's ability to compare himself to his neighbors and feel himself deprived if he does not have what they have. The wants created by modern consumerism arise, in other words, from man's vanity."[11]

Take a stroll down any commercial boulevard and ponder the number of retail establishments that cater to our false wants, entertainments, and needless products—amusement arcades, antique stores, auto accessories, baseball cards, beauty shops, donut shops, fancy clothing emporiums, florists, gift shops, health clubs, liquor outlets, manicurists, movie theaters, party favors, pet groomers, record stores, tanning parlors, taverns, video rentals, yogurt parlors, zodiac paraphernalia, and on and on.

This emphasis on consumerism is especially debilitating for those who cannot afford the good life: the rural poor, the urban underclass, the economic misfits. They are demeaned and alienated as they watch the parade of the rich and ostentatious flaunting their possessions in full view. This estrangement contributes to the societal unrest and incipient revolution seething below the surface of every major American city.

Advertising also contributes to our false expectations. It promises a simple solution to every problem. Whether your breath smells, your head aches, your back hurts, or your belly bulges, there is a mint, a pill, a proper mattress, an effortless exerciser, or some other miraculous remedy to make everything all right. Whatever your problem, there is something you can buy to fix it. The crucial thing is that you buy *something*.

Advertising and Dehumanization of the Consumer. Another post-intellectual consequence is the dehumanizing effect of advertising on the media consumer. We are made to feel inadequate, a materialistic failure, if we do not fulfill our responsibility to purchase and consume. Lasch describes the dehumanizing manipulation of the consumer by pointing out that advertising "makes the consumer an addict, unable to live without increasingly sizable doses of externally provided stimulation."[12] This creates a never-ending quest for more and bigger. We are driven by the need to be better consumers.

Jerry Mander explains that we are being psychologically manipulated: "Am I saying this *is* brainwashing or hypnosis or mind-zapping or something like it? Well, there is no question but that someone is speaking into your mind . . . First, keep watching. Second, carry the images around in your head. Third, buy something. Fourth, tune in tomorrow."[13]

Commercial media are in the business of delivering you, the consumer, to the advertisers. *You* are the commodity. *You*, your attention, your time, are being sold to the highest bidders—those who want to inundate you with their messages. You are nothing more than a consuming cog in the wheel of big business. You have no identity other than your Visa or MasterCard number. You have no uniqueness; you have only your demographic profile. Advertising annuls the individual; materialism dulls the intellect. Whereas intellectualism values the individual, post-intellectualism values the consumer.

Homogenization and Establishmentism

Most Americans spend their discretionary time with standardized media fare across the country. We all laugh at the same sitcoms, heed the words of the same media pundits, and enjoy the antics of the same late-night talk jockeys. We are products of our media experiences; and as we all have similar experiences, we begin to reflect the same cultural outlooks. We are casting ourselves into one pedestrian orthodoxy. As exclaimed by Howard Beale, the demented newscaster from Paddy Chayefsky's 1976 movie *Network*, "You think like the tube! You dress like the tube! You eat like the tube!"

The creation of a homogenized culture is an important part of establishmentism. If all media consumers can be molded into a common materialistic orientation, it is much easier to maintain a consumeristic society. A homogenized materialistic culture does not mean that all consumers can be predictably manipulated into making the same product decisions or voting along the same party lines (we aren't all going to rush out and buy the same model Dodge pickup). But it *does* mean that media viewers and readers can be induced to adopt a conforming pro-growth, big-business, exploit-and-consume mentality (we are all going to want to buy *some sort* of new vehicle). Such a mindset cancels one's ability to engage in meaningful social criticism.

In an intellectual society, the media would be used as agents of *social criticism*. In our post-intellectual society—as in a pre-intellectual cyclical culture—the media are used primarily as agents of *social maintenance*. Due to the conservative nature of big business, the media and their sponsors emphasize easy-to-digest, middle-of-the-road news, commentary, and dramatic content that typically reflects and reinforces the viewpoints of the establishment.

In 1989, the watchdog group, Fairness and Accuracy In Reporting (FAIR), released the results of a comprehensive study of ABC's *Nightline* compiled over three years, a total of 865 programs. The FAIR report showed that *Nightline*'s guest list was "heavily weighted in favor of government spokespeople."[14] Over 80 percent were government officials, corporate representatives, or other professionals; 5 percent represented "public interest" constituencies (peace, environmental, consumer organizations); and less than 2 percent were leaders of labor or racial/ethnic groups. The media purveyors seldom present any content that is going to offend a large number of readers or viewers and listeners.

ECONOMIC THEORIES AND THE FALLACY OF INFINITE GROWTH

The capitalistic free enterprise system that has been the driving force of the free world for over two centuries has resulted in unparalleled personal motivation, monetary success, and material well-being. However, capitalism has always had to rely on linear expansion and growth-oriented economic policies. Franco Ferrarotti states simply, "the eighteenth-century lay religion of progress became the pure and simple nineteenth-century mythology of expansion."[15]

Free Enterprise and the Pursuit of Growth

Adam Smith predicated his monumental *Wealth of Nations* on the premise of "slow and steady growth." This model then became the universal touchstone for all succeeding economic thinkers. All economic schools—from the conservative supply-siders to the Keynesian interventionists—are rooted in the pursuit of growth. All economic models have been based on expansion.

Grow and develop, mine and exploit, consume and throw away. Bigger is better. More is necessary. All economic vitality is based on unending growth—more jobs, more consumers, more industrial growth, more of a tax base, more government programs, more stockholders and borrowers, a bigger population to grease the wheels of progress and development. Year after year we must build more houses, more schools, more factories, more roads, and more skyscrapers. And we must make more babies to fill the houses, schools, factories, roads, and skyscrapers. This means continuing economic prosperity for everybody—in the short run. All sectors of the economy benefit—as long as we continue to foster more growth, more expansion, more products, more markets, more development. To remain static is to atrophy and disintegrate.

However, this is a long-range fiscal pyramid scheme. As long as we can count on more people paying into the scheme next year, to cover this year's expenses, the system will hold together for a while yet. It is as if we have been riding a narcotics high since the nineteenth century; as long as the dosages keep getting bigger, we feel great. As long as each succeeding chemical or materialistic fix is bigger than the last, we experience continued exhilaration.

We maintain the enduring political myth that somehow we can cut taxes, increase government spending, and pay for it all with increased economic activity (that is, growth) tomorrow. However, this simply cannot be done. Such fallacious argumentation is not intellectually responsible; it has no place in a society dedicated to reason.

The spend-and-borrow tactics cannot continue forever. In order to support Social Security, for example, in 1950 there were 16 workers paying into the system for every retiree; by 1995 the ratio was 3.2 to one. And the ratio continues to decrease.[16] How long can the system hold together on the promise of *more* tomorrow?

Capitalism and Socialism. In their doomsday novel, *Nature's End: The Consequences of the Twentieth Century*, Whitley Strieber and James Kunetka have one character proclaim, "Capitalism is unworkable without expansion, and so it is the most self-destructive of institutions."[17] We have reached the finite limits of linear growth. With its push for expanded markets and global consumerism, distended capitalism can only add to our planetary problems.

And socialism is not the answer. One needs only to look at the unbelievable economic and environmental mess that is the legacy of communist Eastern Europe and the Soviet Union. Former socialist states are reeling from decades of economic perversion. Unchecked pollution resulting from a desperate attempt at industrial growth and competition has left its killer refuse from the Black Sea to Lake Baikal, from the White Sea to the Black Forest.

As Fritjof Capra pointed out in 1982, the theories of capitalism (an intellectual concept) and communism (a post-intellectual reaction to the excesses of capitalism) are both dependent upon linear expansion. A mutual obsession with growth resulted in a marked similarity between the economies of the United States and the Soviet Union. "Both are dedicated to industrial growth and hard technology, with increasingly centralized and bureaucratic control, whether by the state or by so-called 'private' multinational corporations. The universal addiction to growth and expansion is becoming stronger than all other ideologies."[18]

Economist Robert Heilbroner similarly comments that both capitalism and communism have "been marked with serious operational difficulties; each has overcome these difficulties with economic growth. Each has succeeded in raising its level of material consumption; each has been unable to produce a climate of social satisfaction."[19]

The Finite Realities

Rufus Miles states sardonically that "Anyone who believes that exponential growth can go on forever is either a madman or an economist."[20] Stated simply, *it is impossible to grow to infinity.* Every biologist, every physicist, and—deep in his or her secret soul—every economist knows that continual linear growth in any context is clearly not possible.

In the short run, growth looks good—creating jobs and short-term rewards. But what happens when we exhaust our resources? When there are no more minerals, coal, and oil to pump out of the earth? When our planet runs out of timber and uranium, clean air, and drinkable water? What happens when the globe runs out of space to continually expand? When we no longer have room to build the houses, schools, factories, and skyscrapers? When there are no more spaces for garbage dumps, transportation corridors, toxic waste sites, sewage treatment plants, and elbow room for the earth's inhabitants? When we no longer can feed the increasing number of consumers?

The Warning Voices. Our foremost anti-growth oracle is Thomas Robert Malthus, who in 1798 published his *First Essay on Population,* in which he articulated the Malthusian principle: *population grows faster than the means to support it.* As the global population expands, it will become increasingly difficult to feed the world's hungry. If we are not able to contain our insatiable appetite for growth and expansion, our population will be contained by three factors: warfare, pestilence, and famine. In Malthus's own words:

The power of population is so superior to the power in the earth to produce subsistence for man, that premature death must in some shape or other visit the human race. The vices of mankind [murder and warfare] are active and able ministers of depopulation. They are the precursors in the great army of destruction; and often finish the dreadful work themselves. But should they fail in this war of extermination, sickly seasons, epidemics, pestilence, and plague, advance in terrific array, and sweep off their thousands and ten thousands. Should success be still incomplete; gigantic inevitable famine stalks in the rear, and with one mighty blow, levels the population with the food of the world.[21]

Many economists argue that Malthus failed to consider the role that technology would continue to play in solving our immediate pressing problems. With improved agricultural techniques, hydroponics and aquiculture, miracle fertilizers and super hybrids, we will manage to feed the expanding multitudes. However, adding to the world's population can only result in ultimate deterioration in the quality of life for all; this is an issue we explore in Chapter 11. Many would therefore agree with historian Paul Kennedy who writes that "Thomas Malthus, the overpopulation prophet, rather than Adam Smith, the champion of free markets, has become the more relevant thinker for the times ahead."[22]

Of the contemporary critics who have challenged the fallacy of infinite growth, none has been more outspoken or iconoclastic than Edward Abbey, who points out that the closest analogy to unlimited growth in the natural world is cancer:

Viewing it in this way, we can see that the religion of endless growth—like any religion based on blind faith rather than reason—is a kind of mania, a form of lunacy, indeed a disease. And the one disease to which the growth mania bears an exact analogical resemblance is cancer. Growth for the sake of growth is the ideology of the cancer cell. Cancer has no purpose but growth; but it does have another result—the death of the host.[23]

And in the case of unrestrained economic growth, the host is the planet Earth.

Reaching Our Limits. About the best gauge we have for judging growth is the annual Gross Domestic Product (GDP)—formerly the Gross National Product (GNP). According to the U.S. Department of Commerce, the U.S. GDP increased from $1.973 trillion in 1960 to $2.876 trillion in 1970 (in constant 1987 dollars, adjusted for inflation). It then rose to $3.776 trillion in 1980, and eased up to $4.885 trillion in 1990.

Table 10.1
Increases in U.S. Gross Domestic Product

Year	Gross Domestic Product (in Billions of Dollars)*	Percentage Increase (for the Decade)
1960	$1,973.2	—
1970	2,875.8	45.74%
1980	3,776.3	31.31%
1990	4,884.9	29.36%

*Figures are in constant 1987 dollars.
Source: U.S. Department of Commerce, Bureau of Economic Analysis, *Survey of Current Business,* Vol. 72, no. 2 (February 1992).

In terms of percentage increase, the GDP went up an average of 4.57 percent annually from 1960 to 1970. From 1970 to 1980, the yearly growth was 3.13 percent. From 1980 to 1990, the average increase each year was 2.94

percent. (So far in the early 1990s, the rate remains sluggish.) What this indicates is that the rate of growth of our economy is slowly decreasing.

We are experiencing not just a temporary depression or economic downturn; we are in a period of continued decline of our growth rate—which is now entering its fourth decade. The government bureaucrats and economic forecasters who insist on predicting a turnaround of our financial picture fail to recognize the larger picture: *the distended-intellectual era of unfettered linear expansion is over.*

What is true in the United States is also true throughout the rest of the world. Europe, Japan, and the rest of the developed planet are bumping up against similar economic realities. And the fragile economies of Third World countries, which are dependent on the health and leadership of the industrialized nations, are suffering proportionately. The globe is running out of accessible exploitable resources; we are running of space that can be cheaply developed. We can never return to the expansion potential of the nineteenth century.

CONGLOMERATE MANEUVERINGS AND MULTINATIONAL CARTELS

Like scientific research, universal education, and egalitarianism, the intellectual idea of capitalism has been pursued beyond the limits of rational responsibility. Neil Postman writes that it was in the eighteenth century that capitalism was "demonstrated to be a rational and liberal system of economic life."[24] Capitalism was to be based on honest competition, rational advertising, modest profits, and individual success.

However, honest competition has been replaced by cutthroat monopolistic cartels and protective tariffs; rational advertising was supplanted by psychological and subliminal manipulation; modest profits have been superseded by obscene profiteering; and individual success was outmoded by corporate groupthink campaigns and strategies. Subliminal technology has even invaded video arcades where hidden messages are beamed to video game players. Contemporary capitalism has evolved into a post-intellectual distortion of the original ideal.

The Role of the Multinationals

Citizens of most developed countries believe that their governments exercise sovereign control over all aspects of their nations' affairs. Although the roles of business and market enterprises are obviously important, most citizens would maintain that corporate interests are subservient to government authority. Moreover, national interests certainly take precedence over international entanglements. There is, however, a growing realization that this is no longer the situation—that the multinational corporations increasingly are in control of the world's affairs.

In the introduction to his critique of the morality of multinational corporations, Gerard Elfstrom stresses the significance of the global corporate infrastructure: "Future historians may come to view the economic integration of the globe as the single most important development of the twentieth century, far surpassing the threat of nuclear war, the spread of Marxism or the human disruption of the environment in its broad and continuing influence on human life."[25]

The globe is dominated today not by political ideologies or national boundaries—but by corporate interests. The major players on the world stage are multinational corporations that supersede and dictate the policies of individual countries. There are over two hundred independent nations today; yet only seven of them (United States, Japan, France, Germany, Italy, the United Kingdom, and Canada) have gross domestic products greater than the assets of the largest multinationals.*

In his series, *Listening to America*, Bill Moyers observes, "In the global economy, corporations and financiers move business around the world as if national boundaries didn't exist."[26] Lewis Lapham expands on the issue: "The post–Cold War world begins to look like medieval Europe. The frontiers run between markets and spheres of commercial interest, not along the boundaries of sovereign states. If a company is large enough and rich enough, the company, of necessity, conducts its own foreign policy."[27]

Janet Lowe, in her analysis, *The Secret Empire*, points out the increasing dominance of multinational corporations over global affairs of state: "Some visionary business leaders and social critics say that, for the most part, governments are irrelevant. They only interfere with the unfettered travel, trade, and discourse that will distinguish the next century from earlier eras."[28] The multinationals are clearly in charge.

The irony is that by substituting global financial unions for global political unions, we have surrendered an intellectual idea (a worldwide political federation entered into freely by men and women of all colors and creeds for mutual support and protection) and accepted instead a de facto distended-intellectual economic structure (characterized by the monetary clout of the *haves* and exploitation of the *have-nots*).

Continued Post-Intellectual Corporate Dominance

Like Adam Smith (as discussed in Chapter 4), we would like to believe that the point at which growth has to stop "was so far in the future that it was irrelevant" to today's conditions. So we stick our collective head in the sand and pretend that we can fix today's problems with more growth, more of an industrial tax base to shore up our sagging infrastructure, more public works projects

---

*Russia would be counted among the largest national economies if its financial situation were not in such turmoil.

to cut down unemployment, and more babies this generation to ensure the integrity of the Social Security system for another few decades. No one wants to face the ultimate responsibility for the future.

The result is a growing materialistic obsession with short-term profits and increasing international economic exploitation. However, today's multinational corporation can no more be considered a *laissez-faire* enterprise (as envisioned by Smith) than a city can be considered a community or a nation can replace a tribe.

Elfstrom points out that "If humans were wiser, more far-sighted, more courageous or more saintly, this process of meeting the challenge of multinational commerce may have occurred much more quickly, or its abuses and excesses might have been avoided altogether; but since they are not, it did not."[29] But humans appear not to be wise, far-sighted, or saintly enough to contain their exploitative natures. Consequently, post-intellectual corporate domination distorts the theoretical intellectual concept of responsible free enterprise.

NOTES

1. Cited in Walter Russell Mead, "Economy Keeps Improving, Why Aren't Clinton's Polls?" *Los Angeles Times,* 4 September 1994, p. M1.

2. See Jesse Jackson, "'Class War' Is Real for Those on the Bottom," *Los Angeles Times,* 3 September 1995, p. M5.

3. In an address to the American Society of Newspaper Editors, 17 January 1925, Coolidge actually said, "The chief business of the American people is business."

4. Richard N. Goodwin, "Economic Justice Dies a Slow Death," *Los Angeles Times*, 18 October 1995, p. B13.

5. Lock, 1995, pp. 8–9.

6. Lerner, 1990.

7. Himmelstein, 1994, p. 50.

8. Allen, 1989, p. 226.

9. "Who Owes What to Whom?" 1991, p. 45.

10. Henry, 1963, p. 45.

11. Fukuyama, 1992, p. 83.

12. Lasch, 1991, p. 519.

13. Mander, 1978, p. 169.

14. Cited in Lee and Solomon, 1991, p. 27.

15. Ferrarotti, 1985, p. 1.

16. "As Social Security Turns 60: Do We Have the Will to Save It? [editorial]," *Los Angeles Times*, 30 July 1995, p. M4.

17. Strieber and Kunetka, 1986, p. 409.

18. Capra, 1982, p. 214.

19. Heilbroner, 1980, p. 91.

20. Miles, 1976, p. 11.

21. Malthus [1798], 1965, pp. 139–40.

22. Paul Kennedy, "Population Surge Tilts the Planet," *Los Angeles Times,* 21 July 1994, p. B17.

23. Abbey, 1988, p. 21.

24. Postman, 1985, p. 52.

25. Elfstrom, 1991, p. 1.

26. Bill Moyers, "America: What Went Wrong (Part II)," in the series, *Listening to America*, PBS, broadcast 21 April 1992.

27. Lapham, "Modern Democracy," 1993.

28. Lowe, 1992, pp. 120–21.

29. Elfstrom, 1991, pp. 109–10.

11

Environmental Decay:
Damn the Resources, Full Speed Ahead!

We are within decades of an environmental collapse on this planet.

> • Bruce Babbitt
> *1994 Interview*

Virtually all our ecological deterioration can be traced to unrestrained linear growth and exploitation. This is one of the most tragic consequences of distended-intellectualism. Technological solutions to one set of problems (as pointed out in Chapter 7) often lead to future problems. Our ecological troubles—air pollution, forest destruction, radioactive wastes, acid rain, resources depletion, the greenhouse effect, oil spills, global warming—all stem from human attempts to meet other needs, solve other problems. Our environmental woes are, in virtually every case, either man-made or are seriously compounded by humankind's greed and materialism.

GLOBAL POPULATION PRESSURES

A quarter-century ago, the President's Commission on Population Growth and the American Future stated, "Our country can no longer afford the uncritical acceptance of the population growth ethic that 'more is better.'"[1] This was not the wide-eyed ranting of some extremist environmental group. This was the carefully reasoned conclusion from a commission, appointed by Richard Nixon, chaired by John D. Rockefeller III, and composed of business leaders, academicians, public health officials, politicians, and even a couple economists. The commission continued its summation in *Population and the American Future:* "There is hardly any social problem confronting this nation whose solution would be easier if our population were larger."[2]

The underlying cause of virtually all global social problems is population growth. Deterioration of the inner cities, toxic wastes, gang warfare, poisoned water supplies, inadequate health care, unemployment, traffic congestion, filthy beaches and littered highways: all are caused directly or compounded greatly by crowding too many people into our fragile biosphere. A greater population simply means more mouths to feed, more bodies to house, more energy to be generated, and more trash to be thrown away.

The Global Growth Rate

At the current rate of growth, the planet continues to add over a million persons to its global census every four days! The frightening statistic, however, is the acceleration of the rate at which the world's population is doubling. Estimates are that neolithic *Homo sapiens*—on the eve of the agricultural revolution about 10,000 years ago—numbered around 5 million. With the technologies of farming and urbanization, the human population increased to approximately 250 million by the time of Christ. In the next thousand years, it increased to an estimated 300 million. By 1700, it was somewhat over 600 million; it had taken *700 years* to double. The world's population reached 1.2 billion around 1860; this was a doubling period of only *160 years*. It then bounced up to 2.5 billion by 1950—taking only *90 years* to double. And by 1990, the global people count reached five billion; it had doubled in only *40 years!* We will hit 6 billion about the turn of the century (see Figure 11.1).

Sobering News for the Third World. The highest birthrates continue to be in the less developed countries of Asia, Africa, and Latin America. We are faced with quite a perplexing moral dilemma for the twenty-first century. We in the United States have to tell the emerging nations, *Sorry, but the planet cannot afford to let you exploit the world's resources and pollute the biosphere to the same extent that we Americans have over the past one hundred years; we have enjoyed an exceedingly comfortable standard of living, it's too bad that it isn't ecologically possible for you to do the same.* Charles Birch asks, "Can those who live in the rich world morally justify a way of living that would be impossible for the rest to enjoy?"[3]

Another sobering reality is the observation introduced in our discussion of the information overload (Chapter 4) that the value of any commodity is lessened as it is produced in great quantities. Sadly, this appears to apply to human beings as surely as it does to information. Anything loses value as it becomes more abundant—including flowers, sunshine, rain, diamonds, or people. Whether we are concerned with starving children in Africa, gang members in the inner city, crowded masses in Asia, or too many kids in the classroom, the inhumane reality seems to be that the more people there are, the more difficult it is to care about each one as a separate, unique, sacred human being. With too many bodies to take care of, each one becomes less of an asset and more of a liability.

Figure 11.1
World Population Estimates (in Millions)
(Years Indicated in Italics)

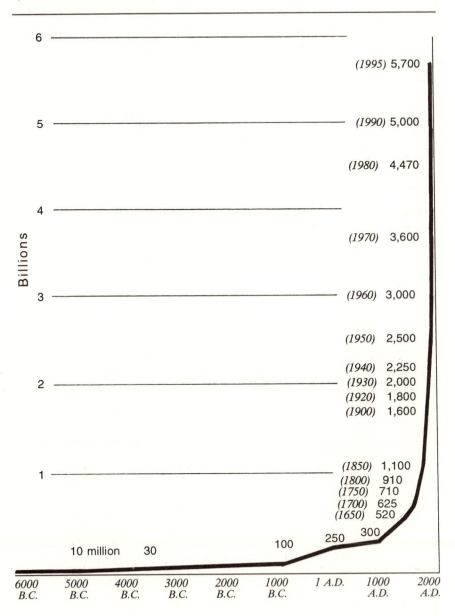

Reaching the Limit

No responsible society can continue to plan on infinitely sustained expansion. Infinite growth simply is not possible. The earth *does* have a finite carrying capacity—although no one knows for sure what it may be. Whether one wants to argue that the planet's maximum population should be 5 billion people (we have already exceeded that level) or 50 billion, 500 billion, 5 trillion, or 5 quadrillion, it must be conceded that at some point it absolutely will not be possible to stack any more living bodies on the planet's surface (or under ground, under the sea, or in the air). At some point, the expansion must stop.

The question is: What do we do *then?* How do we design a viable economic system that does not depend upon continuing annual growth, more bodies, more industry, more taxes, year after year? How do we eventually escape the Fallacy of Infinite Growth?

Even a better question: *Why don't we do that now?* Whatever the ultimate answer is—whatever kind of eventual steady-state economic system we must devise—why do we not start working on that system now? It may be that with technological miracles and genetic breakthroughs, we can feed additional billions of people on this little blue globe; but we must weigh the sacrifices that would have to be made in the quality of life—less breathing room, energy cutbacks, extinction of wildlife, elimination of personal privacy, and loss of open areas.

Also we must consider the psychology of overcrowding. As our population has increased, our collective mood has grown ugly. When we meet a stranger on the road today, we react with suspicion, not charity. When a country sees millions of strangers building up on the other side of its national border, it reacts with hostility, not compassion. The correlation between our increasingly crowded planet and our increasingly ill-tempered public disposition cannot be ignored. To a great extent, the post-intellectual despair and cynicism that pervades our culture is a result of population pressures. How much more can we withstand?

The sooner we stop expanding—the fewer people we add to the planet's load—the more comfortable our offspring will be. Why wait until conditions become even more insufferable? Why wait until humanity is buried in unspeakable discomfort before we decide to do something about it? What is to be gained by any greater population density?

Just because the planet has not yet been rent asunder by some fatal catastrophe does not mean that we can, or should, continue as we are. Just because the system still manages to keep most governmental bureaucracies intact, because borders are still drawn on maps, because committees continue to meet, research centers still get funding, and marketing operations still send out junk mail, we cannot assume that this straining patchwork will continue to hold together indefinitely.

Indeed, many post-Malthusians would look at the world today—ethnic slaughter and terrorism in every quarter of the planet, the spread of AIDS and other viral diseases, permanent famine in sub-Saharan Africa—and easily conclude that Malthus's three agents (warfare, pestilence, and famine) are indeed stalking the globe; we have already exceeded the earth's humane carrying limit. The Institutional Momentum we are experiencing—the sensation of life and vitality—may be little more than the neural reflexes of a decapitated body. *We may have already self-destructed, but just do not realize it yet.*

ECOLOGICAL ESTRANGEMENT

We dwell in the land of aluminum, asphalt, concrete, plastic, styrofoam, silicon chips, and silicon implants. We have strayed from what is real in the world—trees, rocks, animals, mountaintops, salt spray, and wild flowers. We no longer grasp intuitively the basic concept of ecology—the interrelatedness of all things, organic and inorganic.

We walk into a dark room, flip on the wall switch, and the room is filled with light. We give no thought to the vast mining operations, the depletion of our coal reserves, the energy and pollution involved in trucking the fuel to a power plant, the resources and metals used in the construction of the plant and its generators, the air pollution caused by the burning of the fuel, the miles of copper used in transmitting the electricity, the altered landscape needed to accommodate the cross-country transmission lines, the possible side effects of the electromagnetic radiation given off by the high-power lines, and the visual blight of the neighborhood substations. We flip the switch, and there is light. What else do we need concern ourselves with?

We have no appreciation of what happens to nature when we turn a handle to obtain water, twist a key to start our auto engines, turn up the thermostat, pick up a magazine, or eat a hamburger. Urbanized, post-intellectual *Homo sapiens* no longer understands nature because we no longer experience nature. How are we to care about a natural world that is so remote, unseen, and unknown? We have lost all perspective.

In discussing the computer, Theodore Roszak points out that we define reality in terms of the technologies that we have created: "And in this there can be the real danger that we fall prey to a technological idolatry, allowing an invention of our own hands to become the image that dominates our understanding of ourselves and all nature around us."[4] Kirkpatrick Sale writes,

The point is that [technology] dominates and pervades, it is imposed throughout our lives in such a way that it mediates experience to a degree no society before has ever undergone. Less and less is human life connected to other species, to natural systems, to seasonal and regional patterns; more and more [we are connected] to the *technosphere*, to artificial and engineered constructs, to industrial patterns and procedures, even to man-made hormones, genes, cells and life forms.[5]

Our very technological success—which has removed us from our essential natural roots—has left us with a basic ignorance of the order of things.

Arrogance and Nature

Our political and economic leaders have always reassured us that the entire planet and all its resources are at our disposal for our anthropocentric purposes. Rivers exist to be dammed; marshes are to be filled in; deserts are to be irrigated; mountains are to be leveled; forests are to be felled; and plains are to be plowed or paved—whichever reaps the biggest economic benefit.

With our powerful man-made machines and tools, we like to think that we are the ultimate arbiters of the environment. The lumberjacks, construction engineers, farmers, and roadbuilders with their chain saws, cranes, threshing machines and bulldozers: the sense of power courses through our veins—*we can rearrange nature any way we want.* In our distended-intellectual conceit, we believe that with our advanced technologies, scientific know-how, and sophisticated computer simulations, we can somehow improve upon nature's trial-and-error approach. David Ehrenfeld writes, "Our belief in environmental control, approaching omnipotence, is reinforced by repeated demonstrations of the enormous yet precisely directed power we can mobilize against the forces of nature."[6] After all, we can make catalytic converters and genetically alter microbes to make them eat oil. *Can we not do anything we wish?*

Religion, also, has contributed to our human audacity in dominating nature. In primitive cultures, the human impulse to exploit nature was held in check, to some extent, by instinctive pantheistic ecological awe. However, monotheism, as enunciated in Genesis, has removed the age-old restraint. Twenty years ago, Arnold Toynbee voiced concerns about the biblical charge *to go forth and multiply and exercise dominion* (Genesis I:28): "Before the Industrial Revolution, Genesis I read like a blessing on the wealth of Abraham. . . . [Today] it reads like a license for the population explosion and both a license and an incentive for mechanization and pollution."[7]

However, *Homo sapiens* must obey the basic laws of ecology if the species is to survive. It took nature billions of years to work out the careful ecological balance of waters, rocks, soil, bacteria, plants and animals that endured up to a few hundred years ago. *There is no way that any human activity can possibly improve upon the natural global ecosystem!* By definition, anything that we do with our technologies is alien to nature. All we can do with our blueprints and bulldozers is to hasten the deterioration of our fragile biosphere.

Pre-Literate Wisdom. Murray Bookchin writes in *The Ecology of Freedom*, "The notion that man is destined to dominate nature is by no means a universal feature of human culture. If anything, this notion is almost completely alien to the outlook of so-called primitive or preliterate communities."[8] Many pre-intellectual peoples (American Indians, Australian Aborigines, Kalihari Bushmen, Tanzanian Hadza, Iranian Bakhtiari, Lapplanders, Eskimos, Polynesians, and so forth) have a deep-rooted appreciation of nature and instinctive understanding of ecology. Their innate *wisdom* far exceeds our scientific *information.*

Fritjof Capra explains, "Such intuitive wisdom is characteristic of traditional, nonliterate cultures . . . in which life was organized around a highly refined awareness of the environment."[9] Such cultures have respect for the laws of nature. Their very existence depends upon understanding and following those laws. They belong to nature. Douglass Baglin and Barbara Mullins explain, for example, the philosophy of the primitive Australians:

> The first Australians, the Aborigines, took the simple approach: they did not try to tame the land, but came to terms with it, and lived with it in harmony for thirty thousand years. . . . Living in close association with their environment and entirely at its mercy, they were perforce natural conservationists. . . . The bush was their garden and while they did not cultivate it in the accepted sense, neither did they strip a plant entirely of its fruit, nor dig out all the yams. . . . Nature must yield so that man may survive, but man must also discipline himself so that nature may survive.[10]

The cyclical culture of the oral tradition was much kinder to the earth than has been the linear culture of the printing press or the web culture of the electric media. We civilized types push on, craving change and demanding progress. We insist on taming nature. The aboriginal culture lived in harmony with the land for over 30,000 years. How long will our concrete-and-plastic, high-tech distended-intellectual culture endure?

Perhaps we should heed the advice of the Great Law of the Iroquois Confederacy: *In our every deliberation, we must consider the impact of our decisions on the next seven generations.* This is a sobering perspective, one that is utterly alien to our short-sighted, materialistic culture. More typically, society's viewpoint is summed up by Lawrence Summers, chief economist at the World Bank, who wrote, at the beginning of the Rio Earth Summit in 1992, "The argument that a moral obligation to future generations demands special treatment of environmental investments is fatuous."[11]

Herbert Read, several decades ago, gives us an insightful perspective on nature and technology: "Only a people serving an apprenticeship to nature can be trusted with machines. Only such people will so contrive and control those machines that their products are an enhancement of biological needs, and not a denial of them."[12] Our problem today is that too many economists and bureaucrats share Summers's perspective; they have never served such "an apprenticeship to nature."

ENVIRONMENTAL OVERLOAD

Secretary of the Interior Bruce Babbitt solemnly observes, "We are within decades of an environmental collapse on this planet. Our urgent task is to communicate to the American people what it means to live more lightly and respectfully on the land."[13] Although scientists, researchers, naturalists, and government bureaucrats may argue over specific numbers and rates of degradation, there can be no denying that each year throughout the planet our forests are shrinking, the deserts are spreading, our oil reserves are dwindling, our minerals are being used up, the oceans are filthier, the topsoils are getting thinner, the ozone layer is scattering, and biological diversity is diminishing.

Resources Depletion

One aspect of the environmental overload is, of course, the exploitation of our natural capital. Barbara Tuchman asks, "Why does American business insist on 'growth' when it is demonstrably using up the three basics of life on our planet—land, water, and unpolluted air?"[14] Virtually all economic development depends upon using up resources of our physical environment.

Sustainable development may be defined as the use of natural, self-renewing resources (air, water, topsoil, trees, minerals) at a rate that does not exceed nature's ability to replenish and cleanse itself. However, humans have exceeded what may be deemed reasonable and sustainable—taking from the land more than it can replace naturally. Our ever-increasing exploitation of our natural resources can only be described as rapacious and nonrational and, in the long-run, suicidal.

The United States has hundreds of satellites in space—many of which are concerned with finding and mapping the planet's minerals and petroleum, so that we may more quickly deplete the earth's dwindling nonrenewable resources. *Why?* Is this really a rational and responsible thing to do? Once we exceed the level of natural replenishment, we are embarked on a one-way path to the ultimate liquidation of our natural assets, an inevitable annihilation of our ecosystem.

Vanishing Minerals. Coal, uranium, tin, copper, iron ore, bauxite (aluminum ore), and all other minerals and metal ores are finite resources that will eventually be depleted (at least to the point of cost-effectiveness). After a two-century energy binge, we will run out of retrievable petroleum stores sometime in the twenty-first century. And as with any unrestrained binge, one has to pay for one's excesses the morning after. Tom Wolfe has observed that the twenty-first century may well be the hangover of the twentieth century.[15]

In America's farmlands, we are losing almost five tons of topsoil per acre every year. Worldwide, we are destroying between 50,000 and 100,000 acres of virgin rain forest every day. The destruction of the ozone layer also is depletion of a natural resource—the protective layer that has helped to keep all organic things in balance. A 1992 report from the Worldwatch Institute, titled *Last Oasis,* warned that "per capita water supplies have declined by one-third and people have been multiplying faster than irrigated lands can expand."[16]

Rufus Miles writes that this exploitation of our natural resources is a direct result of our linear economic system: "American laissez-faire encouraged the most rapid possible extraction and sale of these treasures by anyone who could get them out of the ground, with no thought given to the future industrial needs of the nation or how long the resources would last."[17]

Disappearing Plants and Animals. We have eradicated tens of thousands of species of animal and plant life. Conservative estimates suggest we are destroying more than twenty species every day. (Some sources calculate that as many as one hundred species are being wiped out daily.)

From a selfish anthropocentric point of view, it is not rational to destroy natural species without even being aware of what medicinal, chemical, or agricultural benefits might be extracted from these plants and animals. We have no idea of the ultimate value of that which we are destroying. To quote Mr. Spock, in *Star Trek IV: The Voyage Home*, "To hunt a species to extinction is not logical."

Moreover, from a *deep ecology* point of view (placing the survival of the planet above the preservation of the human race), we must answer the philosophical argument that human beings have no inherent moral right to destroy that which we can never replace, to eradicate a species that cannot be restored. John Muir asked, "Why ought man to value himself as more than an infinitely small composing unit of the one great unit of creation?"[18]

We are a throwaway society; we even throw away our physical environment. We continue consciously, and willfully, to use up our resources with no thought for the future. We can count the trees destroyed, the tons of topsoil eroded, the animals driven to extinction; we can estimate the barrels of oil remaining. Yet we proceed in a premeditated manner to continue depleting these declining resources. *We are knowingly and deliberately destroying our own planetary life-support system.* Mr. Spock would tell us that is not a rational thing to do. The Iroquois would tell us that is not a moral thing to do. But the economists will tell us that is the profitable thing to do—at least in the short run.

Pollution

If one side of the ecological coin is labeled *diminishing resources,* the other side would be *environmental pollution.* Economic competition dictates that every business must keep costs as low as possible in every step of the operation—including the disposal of its poisons and pollutants. Traditionally, this has meant dumping industrial liquid wastes into the nearest stream, throwing our solid wastes in open landfills and slag heaps, and spewing forth our gaseous pollutants into the skies.

The average American household discards almost two-thirds of a ton of garbage every year; that adds up to a nationwide total of 160 million tons annually—more than enough to fill a fleet of garbage trucks lined up five abreast, bumper-to-bumper, encircling the equator.[19] Despite our incipient attempts at recycling, we are hooked on throwing away trash—paper plates and styrofoam cups, newspapers and computer printouts, disposable cameras, junk mail, old tires, excess packaging, worn-out refrigerators, and about 16 billion disposable diapers a year.

The consequences are tragic—unsafe drinking water, smog, medical wastes and sewage on our beaches, the death of fish-spawning grounds, more than 12,000 barrels of crude oil spilled into the world's oceans every day, dangerous toxic leakages, carcinogenic communities, acid rain, long-lasting radioactive dump sites, the greenhouse effect, and malodorous mountains of garbage (the Fresh Kills rubbish dump on New York's Staten Island now rises over 250 feet in the air). The quantity of garbage that we keep piling up is a legacy to future generations. Richard Lamm points out that we have "inadequately disposed of toxic and hazardous wastes at more than 10,000 various sites that the next generation will have to go back and correct."[20]

The problem simply is that there is no way that humans can manufacture, distribute, use, or dispose of any commodity without having some sort of deleterious impact on the natural environment. No one can total up the entire cost in terms of medical complications and psychological maladjustment. Market theory simply fails to consider the long-term costs of environmental pollution and deterioration.

"The World's Worst Polluter." In a moving personal column, long-time activist Ruth Loring writes that "I have a confession: It is I who am the world's worst polluter. I didn't mean to be. But ignorance is no excuse. I have broken nature's laws. And I can't seem to stop." She continues, implicating us all with her confession:

> The veins of Mother Earth have bled to meet my constant needs for oil and gas, for metals, for coal. To produce my cars and appliances, factories and power plants pour noxious fumes into faraway skies, burning trainloads of dirty coal to make clean electricity. For years after WW II, I sprayed DDT from aerosol cans, killing who knows how many songbirds in my ignorance. . . .
>
> In Central America's lush green valleys, cattle for my hamburgers have displaced native farmers, forcing them up dry, rocky hillsides. And huge plantations growing my breakfast coffee, sugar, and bananas have displaced tangled rain forests. For my tuna sandwiches gill nets over 30 miles long kill multitudes of seals, turtles, dolphins, and sea birds every day. . . .
>
> People around here mostly agree that we need more roads, more skyscrapers, more schools and houses, more shopping malls, more parking lots. Don't forget our kids and their kids and *their* kids will need more cars, more energy, more food and water.
>
> And Third World residents, with mounting birth rates, crowd around their village TV sets, captivated by our extravagant lifestyle displayed in vivid living color. They, too, want it all.[21]

Worldwide Development and Pollution. It is difficult to grasp the global magnitude of the problem. One report estimates that five thousand people die every year in Mexico City (the "World's Most Polluted City") due to the poisoned air.[22] Throughout Eastern Europe, communism "indulged a cult of big production at any cost," leaving a legacy of devastation that is almost incomprehensible.[23] In the former Czechoslovakia, pollution has destroyed over 50 percent of the forests and damaged about 70 percent of the rivers.

In Taiwan, all forty-five rivers in the country are contaminated with toxic wastes, and water pumped from underground wells is so polluted it can be set on fire with a match. In Thailand, a new power plant is being completed near the city of Chiang Mai that will emit more carbon dioxide than all the plants in Western Germany; the coasts have become so polluted that the fishing industry has to send its boats hundreds of miles out to sea to catch uncontaminated fish; clear-cutting of forests has removed 85 percent of Thailand's trees. In mainland China, the industrial city of Benxi is probably "the worst case of pollution in the world"—with 420 factories crammed into 27 square miles, the air is so thick that the city often is invisible to satellites.[24]

The Nuclear Legacy. There are countless examples that could be used to document our environmental insanity. Let me elaborate on just one area—our atomic bequest from decades of nuclear development, experimentation, and accidents. In December 1993, Hazel O'Leary, Secretary of the Department of Energy, revealed that during a forty-five-year period, the United States had conducted over 200 unannounced nuclear explosions.[25] Even more appalling is the extent to which human beings were subjected to nuclear experiments. In thirty-one research tests (that we know about), dating from 1945, secret radiation experiments were carried out on about 600 American citizens who were used as human guinea pigs. Commenting on both our atomic testing and the radiation experimentation, a *Newsweek* article concludes, "It is clear that the U.S. government behaved far more malignly and recklessly than most Americans ever suspected."[26]

Our greatest environmental concern today is the continuing problem of nuclear wastes; over one hundred commercial reactors from Maine to California are producing about 2,000 tons of nuclear refuse a year. We are now a half-century into the Atomic Age, yet we still do not know how to store and properly dispose of our radioactive garbage! Russell Watson writes that "Tons of plutonium from arms factories and spent fuel from nuclear reactors were stored haphazardly and unsafely, sometimes threatening plant workers and nearby residents. The public still has not been told the true dimensions of the toxic mess."[27]

America's mismanagement of its atomic adventure pales, however, when compared to the nuclear legacy from the Soviet Union. According to Grigori Medvedev, prize-winning author of *The Truth about Chernobyl*, the 1986 nuclear accident at Chernobyl released an estimated fifty tons of evaporated fuel, about ten times the amount of radioactive waste generated by the Hiroshima bomb, "creating a colossal atmospheric reservoir of long-lived radio-nuclides: In other words, 10 Hiroshima bombs, without the initial blast and firestorm effects."[28] Other reports state that the radiation released at Chernobyl was closer to two hundred times the amount produced by the Hiroshima and Nagasaki blasts combined.[29] About 20 million citizens of various Soviet republics were exposed to Chernobyl radiation.

A 1994 report by Chernobyl researcher Ludmilla Thorne estimates that "Nearly half of Belarus' 10 million people are still living in contaminated areas and we are just beginning to see the devastating results." She reports "astronomical increases" in thyroid cancer, considerable increases in other cancers, anemias, immune disorders, Down's syndrome, and various respiratory illnesses. She continues, "there have been horrific mutations in humans, animals and plants, including livestock born with extra legs and other body parts and children born with missing limbs and skulls."[30]

Such concerns about nuclear accidents are dwarfed, however, by our increasing knowledge about the effects of atomic-bomb testing. Throughout the Soviet Union, hundreds of atomic bombs were detonated with little or no protection against radiation effects; untold millions of persons have been exposed—sometimes intentionally—to varying quantities of radiation.

In the Siberian town of Talmenka, the "Yellow Children" continue to be born—infants with an initial jaundice condition and permanent congenital defects to their nervous systems and organs. These children are what one researcher has labeled "nuclear mutants," third-generation offspring of a region that was exposed to nuclear fallout from 122 above-ground atomic explosions in the late 1940s and early 1950s. One professor at the Altai Medical Institute proclaimed, "There is evidence of chromosome change due to radiation exposure. Only God knows what we will see in the fourth generation."[31]

Moreover, the residual radioactive wastes continue to pile up in unimaginable quantities. In one stockpile complex, near Chelyabinsk in the southern Urals, the formerly secret weapons-grade plutonium plant of Mayak has accumulated so much radioactive waste—in an open lake, dumps, and storage pools—that if spread evenly over the entire former Soviet Union, it would contaminate every square foot. The total radioactive waste stored at Mayak is equivalent to 240 times the amount of radioactivity released at Hiroshima.

Atomic energy and nuclear weaponry illustrate better than any other modern advancement the phenomenon of technological determinism. Once the atom was split, it was destined that the reality of radiation dangers and toxic residue would haunt us for generations. Yes, it can be argued, it was not the technology that forced us to take the course we did; humans made deliberate decisions every step of the way. However, when technology is coupled with the linear drive for progress and with the innate human lusts for power and greed, the outcome was foreordained.

NOTES

1. Commission on Population Growth and the American Future, 1972, p. 1.
2. Ibid.
3. Charles Birch, "Can Religion Remain Silent Any Longer?" *Los Angeles Times*, 7 March 1990, p. B13.

4. Roszak, 1994, p. 40.

5. Sale, "In Industrial Revolution II," 1995.

6. Ehrenfeld, 1978, p. 47.

7. Arnold Toynbee, "The Genesis of Pollution," *Horizon*, 15, no. 3 (Summer 1973): 4–9.

8. Quoted in Devall and Sessions, 1985, p. 17.

9. Capra, 1982, p. 41.

10. Douglass Baglin and Barbara Mullins, *The Book of Australia* (New York: Paul Hamly, 1973), p. 53.

11. Letter written to the *Economist*, quoted in Peter Cook, "Rio Agenda Sacrifices Consumption for Survival," *Durham Herald-Sun*, 7 June 1992, p. G7.

12. Quoted in Sale, "In Industrial Revolution II," 1995.

13. Bruce Babbitt, "A New Conservation Ethic," *Los Angeles Times*, 1 June 1994, p. B13.

14. Tuchman, 1984, p. 4.

15. Quoted in Moyers, 1989, p. 60.

16. Rudy Abramson, "Group Warns of Worldwide Water Crisis," *Los Angeles Times*, 15 November 1992, pp. A1, A6.

17. Miles, 1976, p. 29.

18. Quoted in Devall and Sessions, 1985, p. 104.

19. Beck, et al., 1989, p. 67.

20. Lamm, 1987, p. A4.

21. Ruth Loring, "I Am the World's Worst Polluter," *Venture Inward*, September/ October 1990, p. 43.

22. Cecilia Rodriguez, "The World's Most Polluted City," *Los Angeles Times*, 21 April 1991, p. M1.

23. Dennis Hayes, "Ravaged Republics," *Discover*, March 1993, p. 70.

24. Charles P. Wallace, "Pollution Is the Price of Asia Boom," *Los Angeles Times*, 15 February 1991, pp. A1, A22-23.

25. See Watson, et al., 1993.

26. Ibid., p. 14.

27. Ibid., p. 14.

28. Quoted in "Chernobyl Syndrome: Are Accidents Waiting to Happen?" [editorial], *Los Angeles Times*, 3 November 1991, p. M4.

29. As reported on ABC's *World News Tonight with Peter Jennings*, 25 April 1996.

30. Ludmilla Thorne, "No Peace for Chernobyl's Victims," *Los Angeles Times*, 29 April 1994, p. B13.

31. Dahlburg, 1992, p. A8.

12

Moral Collapse:
Sex, Lies, Violence, and Videotape

The dream factory has become the poison factory.

• Michael Medved
Hollywood Vs. America

On Wednesday afternoon, 29 April 1992, twelve jurors in Simi Valley, California, determined that four police officers were not guilty of using excessive force in subduing Rodney King thirteen months earlier. For the next seventy-two hours, moral anarchy prevailed. People assaulted and shot each other; citizens robbed and looted at will; Los Angeles burned. Three days of burning, looting, and murder left over 50 people dead, 2,000 wounded and bleeding, about 8,000 separate fires, at least 10,000 people unemployed, and a billion dollars in property damage.

How could this happen? How could civil order be so completely disrupted—in the late twentieth century, in the land of freedom and opportunity? Is society that close to moral chaos? Is the veneer of civilization so thin? Less explosive eruptions in New York, Seattle, Atlanta, and San Francisco reinforced the impression that the moral glue that holds together our culture is losing its binding strength.

Not only must we be concerned today with verbal illiteracy, but we are also confronted with moral illiteracy. To what extent is our apparent moral decline a consequence of post-intellectualism? And—a specific question for this chapter—how are the media implicated?

SOCIETY AND A POST-INTELLECTUAL MORAL BREAKDOWN

A 1990 report from Michael Josephson's ethics institute concludes that there are "undeniable signs that the moral fiber of our country is weakening and that, as this generation takes its place in society in decision-making positions, the situation is likely to get worse." It goes on to state that "an unprecedented proportion of today's young generation lacks commitment to core moral values such as honesty, respect for others, personal responsibility and civic duty."[1] The divorce rate, white-collar crime, decreasing influence of the church, unmarried mothers, senseless violence, looser sexual standards—and many other indications—are all cited as evidence of a morally disintegrating culture.

According to FBI figures, in 1983 there were 1,258,090 violent crimes committed in the United States—these include murders, rapes, robberies, and aggravated assaults. In 1993, the comparable figure was 1,924,190. Factoring in population growth, this is an increase from 538 violent crimes per 100,000 population to 746—an increase of almost 39 percent in one decade![2]

While recent data indicate a slight decrease in overall crime statistics in the past three years, FBI Director Louis Freeh states that "Violent crime, involving young people, both as perpetrators and victims, is on the rise—an alarming indicator of future trends."[3] And John DiIulio points out that most crimes are never reported. According to the Justice Department's own survey, "the actual number of rapes, robberies, assaults, burglaries, and other crimes suffered by Americans was . . . more than three times the FBI's number."[4] Violent crime is on the rise—in America and throughout the globe.

In discussing the Generation Overlap (Chapter 7), I pointed out that starting in the post-intellectual 1960s each succeeding generation has had to discover for itself the scientific, corporate, communication, and political structures that would determine the future. Allan Bloom explains that "Parents do not have the legal or moral authority they had in the Old [pre-1960s] World."[5] Each succeeding generation would have to establish its own rules and criteria that define success.

While this may be true in engineering, manufacturing, and marketing, it should not necessarily be true in the humanities; it should not apply to artistic and moral values. But this sense of emasculating dysfunction carries over into all corners of our culture. The younger generation turns to its elders and says, *We reject your values and morals; you have nothing to offer us.*

Thus, in a post-intellectual age, the church adopts a form of moral relativism rather than reverence; families cultivate an environment of permissiveness rather than discipline; and the schools teach what is "relevant" rather than what is historically significant. Amitai Etzioni comments, "In the '60s and '70s people became reluctant to make moral judgments, to say something was right or wrong. Everything was considered an individual choice, and all values were supposed to be equal."[6]

One important component of an intellectual culture is critical thinking.

Critical thinking means, in essence, reasoning or making decisions in terms of stated criteria. How are we to think critically when there are no criteria by which to judge our actions?

Media and Morality

Many critics and social observers are quick to condemn the media—especially television, movies, and the recording industry—for a general societal breakdown. Film critic Michael Medved writes, "Tens of millions of Americans now see the entertainment industry as an all-powerful enemy, an alien force that assaults our most cherished values and corrupts our children. The dream factory has become the poison factory."[7]

Although the media must be a major focus in any discussion of cultural shortcomings, we should look at them not solely as causative agents, but as mirrors and magnifying glasses that reflect and intensify other societal values. We cannot alleviate our problems merely by subjecting the media to more critical scrutiny and censorship. It is not enough to point to increasing nudity in the media or to more frequent portrayals of extra-marital hanky-panky and claim that we have found the cause of all our woes.

We must examine the underlying factors and ask, Why has there been an increase in the divorce rate? Why are we becoming more materialistic and greedy? Why has the traditional nuclear family taken such a hit? Why is there so much political corruption? Why have we abandoned our intellectual commitment to keep our inherent emotional drives in check? And *then* we can turn to the media and ask, Why is there an *audience* for media portrayals of sex and violence? Why do so many people buy recordings that emphasize hatred and vulgarity? *Why* has the dream factory become the poison factory?

Sociological and Economic Factors

Other than media, there are numerous social and economic causes to be considered in any examination of our moral degeneration. Perhaps the most significant factor is that children today are raised without any overriding societal value system. The church no longer dominates our moral landscape. Humanist values replaced the church as a principal moral philosophy, but we have now given up on humanistic reason and belief in our ability to govern ourselves. Without religion and without humanism, perhaps the only value system we have to go by today is *materialism;* this theme is explored in Chapter 17.

One source of much social unrest is anxiety and alienation born of our *web-culture disorientation.* Today's generation experiences a loss of direction, a lack of self-sufficiency, a diminished sense of identity. With lack of confidence in the future, many turn to *negative retribalization*—gang affiliation, civil warfare, international terrorism, or racial and religious intolerance. These are all post-intellectual rejections of the rational arrangement we espoused in our social contract.

Others fall victim to *victimization*. Criminologist Michael Rustigan writes, "More and more Americans, particularly the young, believe that being a victim entitles them to be violent. . . . If you've been wronged, if something or somebody is holding you back—parents, teachers, bosses, society, whatever—blow 'em away!"[8]

Much of our moral decay may be due to economic factors. Unemployment, homelessness, widespread poverty, immigration frictions, and inner city deterioration all are triggered by our *inability to sustain continuing linear economic growth*. As individuals lose their economic security, so also do they lose their faith in the social and political system. When individuals see themselves as economic failures or cultural dropouts, they turn against the system—with vandalism, graffiti, gang terrorism, and mindless violence. Anarchy and nihilism become social levelers.

Another factor is that today's post-intellectual generation lacks confidence that the banks, the savings and loan associations, the insurance companies, the pension plans, and the Social Security system will be around to meet their needs three or four decades down the road. Therefore, they demand *instant gratification*—immediate sex, synthetic pleasures from chemicals, instant material purchases on credit. Our economic system is too shaky to plan for the future. P. A. Sorokin writes, "Hence the sensate *Carpe diem*, as tomorrow is uncertain; snatch the present kiss; get rich quick; seize the power, popularity, fame, and opportunity of the moment, because only present values can be grasped."[9] This attitude, too, leads to a breakdown of traditional morality.

The *disintegrating family* can be seen as a cause of much of our moral collapse. Michael Lerner writes that "The breakdown of families, the crisis of friendships, the deep trouble people have in finding and sustaining long-term, committed, loving relationships . . . are the central political issues of our time."[10] In 1970, just 11 percent of all births were to single women; by 1980, this figure had increased to 18 percent; and in 1990, a full 28 percent of all U.S. births were to unwed mothers.[11] One major nationwide study of fifty-seven neighborhoods found that the absence of a father at home "was far more important than either race or poverty in predicting high levels of violent crime."[12] Moreover, 1991 census data show that half of all American children no longer are being raised in a traditional nuclear family—that is, living with both biological parents and with no other non-related adults present in the household.[13]

One interesting and disturbing speculation is that violence may be the *unavoidable offspring of an intellectual culture*—a society that stresses freedom rather than restriction, competition rather than cooperation, development rather than stability, capitalistic profit rather than compassion, and individualism rather than group identity. The American Dream is, in part, the dream of besting others. We are a violent society because we are a competitive society—with an emphasis on beating the other guy and getting ahead at any cost.

In an insightful essay examining the role of shame in moderating violent

behavior, James Q. Wilson points out that in the United States we have deliberately forsaken the ameliorating influence of social or tribal pressure in holding
malevolent tendencies in check: "We have more crime, violence, debauchery
and drug abuse than most Americans want, but we have also forsworn the use
of those methods—either a repressive state or group-centered social order—that
might reduce these pathologies."[14] Individualism breeds aggression and violence; group identity, on the other hand, breeds social conformity and tran-
quility.

THE MEDIA CONNECTION

My focus in the rest of the chapter is on the role played by the mass media.
To what extent are we a violent society because of the violence and mayhem
portrayed in our pictorial media? The media must be viewed in several related
contexts.

Media as Avenues of Escapism

The media have always been a source of escapism and fantasy. Conflict,
aggression, and violence have been the mainstays of dramatic entertainment
since the first cave man embellished the tale a bit in relating to his fellow *Cro
magnon* how he fought off the wild boar. As formal drama was institutionalized, the bloody stories became part of our cultural heritage: the conflict and
conquest of Achilles and Aeneas; the paternal murder, incest, suicide, and self-
mutilation of Oedipus; the infanticide and cannibalism of Medea; the sex, greed,
murder, treachery, vengeance, and royal butchery of Shakespeare.

More to the point, the media in recent generations have been used as a
source of adolescent rebellion. For the past century or so, parents have registered alarm about the contemporary media that were turning their children into sex
maniacs and axe murderers—dime Westerns, pulp magazines, silent movies,
jazz, comic books, girlie magazines, swing music, radio adventure serials,
rock'n'roll, television violence, heavy metal, slasher flicks, music videos,
gangsta rap, and whatever comes next. Whether we can always appreciate it or
not, storytelling and art in all media have forever exaggerated horror, violence,
and sexual exploits.

Media as Reflections of Reality

Escapism may be one function of the media, but another role—perhaps the
more important social function—is reporting to us what is going on in the world.
In this role, the media are of necessity going to present a view of the world that
is not pretty. News, by definition, is what happens that is out of the ordinary.
Crops are growing peacefully in Iowa, and almost 20,000 domestic airline
flights took off and landed yesterday without incident. But those items are not

news. However, when the Mississippi River floods or when a plane overshoots the runway at O'Hare Field in Chicago, we then have *news*. Thus, reports of serial killers, civil wars, racial conflicts, starving babies, riots, crooked politicians, terrorism, celebrity murderers, child abuse, and other ugly pictures become our news-of-the-day. This is how our reality is interpreted to us. This is the role of the media.

Consider how television was involved in the entire Rodney King saga: George Holliday's videotape of King's apprehension and beating, live television coverage of the Simi Valley trial, live TV coverage of the unrest (when the message that there were "No fires yet" was an open invitation to trouble), the broadcast of Mayor Tom Bradley's inciteful call to respond ("We will not accept renegade behavior by a few cops"), broadcast appeals for calm from many officials and celebrities, follow-up local and national coverage in news programs and talk shows, coverage of the federal civil rights trial of the four officers a year later, and subsequent coverage of the trial of the youths who attacked trucker Reginald Denny during the riot (and were also captured on videotape).

Many other case studies, from coverage of the Vietnam War to the way we elect our presidents to the O. J. Simpson trial, could be used to illustrate the impact that media have in interpreting reality to us. To what extent might we say that the media's preoccupation with a loosening of moral standards is but part of their job in reporting to us what is happening in society—is but a reflection of reality?

Media as Agents of Free Enterprise

The mass media must also be seen as commercial, profit-making operations. Consequently, they are going to provide a marketable commodity. Whatever the public wants, the media will provide. Speaking specifically of the intensifying emphasis on TV violence and ugly programming, Marie Winn, a decade ago, asks, "Why did television, relatively nonviolent at its start, gradually become the hotbed of crime and mayhem it now is?" She continues,

The answer . . . is simple: people *want* violence on television. The [audience sampling] rating system that effectively controls what appears on national television indicates that the public regularly chooses violent programs over more peaceful alternatives. . . . The advertisers meekly protest they would gladly give the public "Pollyanna" round the clock if that's what people would watch. But the rating system shows that people won't watch "Pollyanna" when they can watch "Hill Street Blues."[15]

Or as columnist Al Martinez writes in his critique of radio personality "shock jock" Howard Stern, "While Stern's may be a voice from the sewer, it has an audience of amazing size and fidelity which, if nothing else, ought to tell us something about ourselves."[16]

Media as Vehicles of Free Speech

It is the "free marketplace of ideas" that makes democracy possible. This is what distinguishes our society from communism, religious fundamentalism, or any other form of totalitarianism. And this is what gives the purveyors of artistic garbage and anti-social messages access to our media. Freedom of speech inherently opens up the channels for excessive sex and violence—if that is what the consumers want.

How are we to draw the line between legitimate, intellectual freedom of expression and perverted, irresponsible, post-intellectual exploitation in the name of freedom of speech? To what extent do we want to try to control or restrain blatant vulgarisms and anti-social messages? Censorship is a pre-intellectual (authoritarian) concept. To call for censorship is to admit that our intellectual underpinnings have failed us. Censorship is what happens when media channels are not used with reason and responsibility; it is therefore a post-intellectual reaction to intellectual irresponsibility. *Censorship reflects a society's lack of confidence in its intellectual competence.*

Media as Reaction to Victorian Puritanism. Pre-intellectual cultures did not cover up naked bodies; privacy was unknown. An intellectual society, however, values privacy and covers up its nakedness. The Victorian Era was the epitome of intellectual reserve, privacy, and social gentility. Our post-intellectual culture reflects a return to the openness and naked state of the pre-literate tribe. Any number of crudities and barbarisms in modern media could be interpreted as a reversion to an uncouth pre-intellectual state; contemporary film and television can be seen as a post-intellectual reaction to Victorian reserve. This helps explain the degree of nudity in today's media.

The most revealing indicator of how far contemporary media have removed us from the Victorian era is in popular music. Contemporary rock and rap groups saturate their audiences with an unending stream of obscenities, sadism, violence, and perversion. For example, an analysis of 2 Live Crew's album, *As Nasty as They Wanna Be* (which sold 1.7 million copies), reveals that in one hour there are 226 uses of the word "fuck," 163 instances of "bitch," 81 mentions of "shit," 87 descriptions of oral sex, and 117 uses of explicit terms for male or female genitalia.[17] We have succeeded in shaking off any remnants of Victorian restraint.

Media as Post-Intellectual Artistic Exploitation. In his detailed *Hollywood Vs. America,* Medved cites examples such as "the estimable and outspoken Annie Sprinkle, who masturbates on stage with various sex toys and then invites members of the audience to explore her private parts with a flashlight" and Kevin Michael Allin (of the rock group the Toilet Rockers) who, in the midst of a 1991 concert, "delighted his devoted fans by defecating on stage and then throwing his feces out to the cheering audience."[18] Both performers defend their actions as expressions of their artistic freedom.

Artists must be free to express themselves and criticize their social environment. *Artistic freedom is a form of social criticism; it is an intellectual underpinning.* Artistic anti-establishmentism is an indispensable corollary of intellectual inquiry. But artistic freedom—like progress, technology, universal education, and urbanization—is an intellectual concept that can be pursued beyond responsible limits. Without self-restraint, the intellectual ideal degenerates into distended-intellectual anarchy.

We—artists, producers, consumers—no longer seem to be able to separate constructive social analysis from license, artistic freedom from debasement, creativity from anarchy. Since the 1960s, we have abandoned any meaningful standards of comparison and criticism. The Generation Overlap has erased our artistic guidelines, our cultural criteria. We confuse nihilism with social criticism. We substitute shock for originality. Artists exploit the sensitivities of their audiences as surely as economic entrepreneurs exploit our natural resources for short-term profit. Artistic exploitation leads to moral bankruptcy as surely as economic exploitation leads to ecological bankruptcy.

EXPLANATIONS OF MEDIA IMPACT

The widespread availability of violence and sexual activity in the media cannot be doubted. The statistics are paraded before us constantly. Between the ages five and fifteen, a typical American child will witness over 13,000 persons violently killed in the media. There are six to eight acts of violence on every channel in each hour of prime-time television. In the average hour of children's programming on Saturday morning, there are between twenty and twenty-five acts of violence.

What impact does this have on society? Despite the many research studies that claim to show a causal relationship between media portrayals of violence and other anti-social activities, a closer inspection reveals that, as stated by William McGuire, the "empirical evidence for massive media impact is surprisingly weak."[19]

Modeling Theories

Most of the explanations that attempt to confirm media's impact are variations of modeling theories. These argue simply that viewers and listeners tend to imitate what they see and hear—*monkey see, monkey do.* Media violence allegedly directly begets real-life violence.

Copycat Crimes and Suicides. There are many crimes and other acts of violence that are unarguably inspired by specific media events. The 1972 movie *Fuzz* inspired a senseless murder-by-burning that was clearly patterned after an incident in the film. The 1974 TV movie *Born Innocent* featured a broom-handle rape that triggered a copycat incident that wound up in the courts.

Charles Manson claims he was influenced by the Beatles. After the 1978 movie *Deer Hunter* was aired on national TV, some twenty-six persons killed themselves playing Russian roulette. Two teenagers put bullets through their heads while repeatedly listening to Ozzy Osbourne's recording of "Suicide Solution." At least two youths were killed emulating a daredevil stunt from the 1993 movie *The Program.* Tragically, hundreds of additional incidents could be recounted.

As lamentable as these instances are, the events must be kept in perspective. Each was, in effect, an isolated happening—in every case committed by an individual who was not emotionally well balanced. In actuality, the percentage of individuals who are motivated to try some copycat crime of violence is close to nil. If we were to try to keep all suggestive dramatic material out of the hands of all individuals who might be tempted to copy some bizarre action, we would have to eliminate everything from Shakespeare to Mother Goose.

Correlation and Causation. Many research studies find some correlation between the watching of mediated violence and subsequent anti-social violence; numerous reports indicate that children who watch a lot of violent television grow up to be aggressive adults. However, establishing a correlation between two events or variables does not, in itself, indicate which (if either) might have been the causative agent.

One prominent admonition among social researchers is that *correlation does not prove causation.* It may be, quite simply and logically, that youngsters who tend to be aggressive (for whatever reasons) turn naturally to television programming that is violent in nature. Violent people watch violent television. That does not prove that it was the act of watching violence on television that made an individual violent. It simply confirms that people who are predisposed to violence are attracted to violent action.

Violence and Aggressive Behavior. Another problem with much of the violence research is the confusing use of the term *aggressive behavior.* Starting in the early 1960s, thousands of studies have shown that violence portrayed in the media can teach aggressive behavior to young children. However, this *aggressive* behavior is not necessarily anti-social *violent* behavior. Showing youngsters how to play aggressively does not mean that they will then go home and deliberately, and violently, hurt a younger sibling. In a 1993 essay, Kurt Andersen pointed out that "most of the observed 'aggressiveness' is bratty boisterousness, not violence."[20]

Most aggression in society is *not* anti-social violence. Indeed, our society rewards aggressive behavior. We offer classes in assertiveness training; we reward those who succeed in beating others; individuals win by pushing competitors out of the way on their climb up the corporate ladder. Our culture awards the prizes to those who are aggressive, not to the wimps. There are many examples of societally approved aggression—sports competition, pushy business tactics, self-defense, slapstick comedy, and even warfare ("national defense"). This is one of the characteristics of an intellectual competitive culture.

Aggression—social criticism, competition, individuality, *yang*—is an intellectual trait. Media content that promotes aggression is not necessarily anti-social.

Thus, in looking for explanations of moral decay caused by media violence, one finds only qualified evidence for media culpability in the research dealing with *modeling theory*. However, if one looks at theories dealing with *desensitization and distorted reality*, one is likely to find more cause for concern.

Desensitization and Distorted Reality

The negative consequences of immorality and depravity in the media come not from isolated dramatic or shocking incidents, but rather from long-term cumulative impact—the desensitizing experience of regular exposure to a mediated reality of chaos, violence, uncertainty, greed, sexual adventures, and vulgarity. Barry Sapolsky and Joseph Tabarlet explain: "A steady diet of television influences viewers' conceptions of social reality such that heavy viewers' beliefs about the real world are shaped by the images of television. . . . Further, heavy consumption of the highly repetitive messages of television can create a distorted picture of social reality."[21]

Our reality becomes that which is constantly paraded before us in the media. It is this long-term exposure—not modeling theory—that helps to explain the media's impact. Even Medved concurs: "I never stress the pernicious power of *one* movie, or one TV show, or one hit song; what concerns me is the accumulated impact of irresponsible messages that are repeated hour after hour, year after year."[22]

Many social observers and writers are especially concerned about the long-term impact of participating in violent interactive computer games. With their powerful weapons, gory dismemberments, torture, and sadism, they put the player directly in control of the carnage. Brian Stonehill points out that "This takes you out of the role of spectator and into the role of murderer. And that's not just a little change, it's a big change."[23] Potentially this has more of a desensitizing effect than passively watching video mayhem.

The "Mean World Syndrome." Much of the research conducted by Pennsylvania State University's George Gerbner over the years has dealt with what he has called the "mean world syndrome." His studies have shown repeatedly that people who view a lot of television tend to see the world as a much more hostile and mean place than do people who watch less television. Heavy viewers tend to have triple locks on their doors; they are more likely to own a serious watchdog; and they are more likely to have a loaded gun stashed in their bedstand.[24]

One danger of such a distorted "mean world syndrome" is that people who are frightened are more likely to surrender their privacy and other civil rights for security and protection. They ask for more law enforcement surveillance and more police presence; they are more willing to give up their own rights guarding against unreasonable search and seizure. This is one clear-cut manifestation of a post-intellectual culture—the surrender of freedom (an intellectual libertarian idea) in order to attain peace and stability (post-intellectual authoritarian goals). The electric media have given us a distorted, confusing, and exaggerated view of what the world is like. We cannot comprehend it; we cannot cope with it; we are scared of it. We retreat.

Desensitization and Narcotizing Dysfunction. Senator Daniel Patrick Moynihan observes that a certain amount of aberrant behavior is to be expected in any society. "But when you get too much—too much crime, too many broken families—you can start to convince yourself it's not really all that bad. Pretty soon you're accepting behavior that a healthy community needs to condemn."[25] Most distressingly, we start to assume that the world is falling apart: all strangers are potential threats, slaughter on our streets is to be expected, thousands are being killed in civil wars everywhere, tens of thousands are starving to death every day. *Everywhere there is danger and chaos, and there is nothing I can do about it.* We are narcotized into inaction. The media—both news reports and dramatic fiction—contribute to the numbing of America.

This sense of alienation and desensitization feeds on itself. We become increasingly convinced that the "mean world" is growing ever more hostile, and we turn to the media to confirm our fears. It becomes a self-fulfilling prophecy. In effect, we *ask* the media to corroborate our perceptions that society is falling apart. We seek out the news reports and documentaries that verify our social decay.

Desensitization does not lend itself to neat laboratory studies and quantifiable longitudinal research; but the phenomenon of desensitization explains better the effects of media in our demoralized, post-intellectual web culture than do the ambiguous findings about copycat crimes and modeling theory. Medved stresses that it is this desensitizing influence with which we need to be concerned, not the role-modeling function of the media: "The most profound problem with the popular culture isn't its immediate impact on a few vulnerable and explosive individuals, but its long-term effect on all the rest of us."[26]

The media do not stimulate us all to become criminals and social misfits; but the media do desensitize us to much of the violence and ugliness that is perpetuated by the criminals and social misfits. Rustigan writes,

Today, we have come to think that violence is normal. We are numb, desensitized, inured to the steady bombardment of cases and imagery. Office shoot-ups, carjackings, stalkers, drive-by shootings, children who kill, courtroom murders, child abductions, Jeffrey Dahmer, Joel Rifkin—ho-hum, that's life in the '90s.[27]

The politicians and trendy critics scurry to pacify the populace with a TV ratings system so that unsuspecting viewers can be warned about the amount of vulgarity they may be exposed to in some make-believe world. Such a panacea, however, will only obscure the real threats. The problem is not that we see too many obscenities on *NYPD Blue,* but that we see too many obscenities in Bosnia and Baghdad; not that we hear too many bad words on cable, but that we hear too many bad words from Washington and Wall Street; not that we see fictional bad guys beating up innocent good guys, but that we see genuine corporate thugs and legal rogues exploiting the innocent little guys; not that we witness too many cars crashing and buildings exploding, but that we are witnessing our intellectual institutions disintegrating before our glazed eyeballs.

The media today reflect and magnify a post-intellectual confusion that greatly exceeds anything society has experienced in the past. We are engulfed in a mediated web culture over which we have increasingly little control—a culture that renders us disoriented, desensitized, and narcotized. We are left without a set of values or cultural criteria, without a sense of direction or social purpose. The V-chip is not going to protect us from our cultural malaise.

NOTES

1. Cited in Garry Abrams, "Did We Rear a Bunch of 'Moral Mutants'?" *Los Angeles Times,* 11 October 1990, p. E1.

2. Figures are from the FBI, *Uniform Crime Reports* (Washington, DC: U.S. Government Printing Office, 1993).

3. Quoted in Ronald J. Ostrow, "Murders Drop 12% for Steepest Dip in 35 Years," *Los Angeles Times,* 18 December 1995, p. A33.

4. DiIulio, 1995, p. 56.

5. Bloom, 1987, p. 58.

6. Quoted in D'Antonio, 1992, p. 36.

7. Medved, 1992, p. 3.

8. Rustigan, 1993.

9. Sorokin, 1941, p. 97.

10. Lerner, 1990.

11. U.S. Center for Health Statistics, *Vital Statistics of the United States,* annual.

12. Quoted in Elaine Ciulla Kamarck, "Fatherless Families: A Violent Link," *Los Angeles Times,* 7 May 1992, p. B15.

13. See Elizabeth Shogren, "Traditional Family Nearly the Exception, Census Finds," *Los Angeles Times,* 30 August 1994, pp. A1, A18.

14. James Q. Wilson, "Shame," *Honolulu Advertiser,* 2 July 1995, p. B1.

15. Winn, 1985, pp. 101–02.

16. Al Martinez, "The King of All He Perceives," *Los Angeles Times,* 5 December 1995, p. B10.

17. See Medved, 1992, p. 100.

18. Ibid., pp. 27, 175.

19. William J. McGuire, "Possible Excuses for Claiming Massive Media Effects Despite the Weak Evidence," in Rothman, 1992, p. 143.

20. Kurt Andersen, "The Great TV Violence Hype," *Time,* 12 July 1993, p. 66.

21. Sapolsky and Tabarlet, 1991, pp. 505–06.

22. Medved, 1992, p. 242.

23. Quoted in Amy Harmon, "Fun and Games—And Gore," *Los Angeles Times,* 12 May 1995, p. A28.

24. See, for example, George Gerbner, "Scenario for Violence," in *Mass Media and Society*, 3rd ed., ed. Alan Wells (Palo Alto, CA: Mayfield, 1979), p. 352; and George Gerbner and Larry Gross, "Living with Television: The Violence Profile," *Journal of Communication*, 26 (Spring 1976): 173–99.

25. Moynihan [1993], 1994.

26. Medved, 1992, p. 243.

27. Rustigan, 1993.

PART 4

Political Consequences of Post-Intellectualism

The excess of liberty, whether in States or individuals,
seems only to pass into excess of slavery.

• Plato
Republic

Part IV is concerned with the question of survival of the republic. To establish and maintain a self-governing democratic nation-state is not a natural act. It requires a deliberate leap of intellectual commitment, based on reason and the abstract concept of a social contract. But in our post-intellectual web culture, we are finding this artificial construct increasingly difficult to maintain.

13

Retribalization:
Fragmenting the Global Village

Science advanced, knowledge grew, nature was mastered,
but Reason did not conquer and tribalism did not go away.

• Harold Isaacs
Idols of the Tribe

The pre-intellectual human grouping was the extended family, the clan, the tribe—small, closely knit communal bands who shared family, community, and ethnic ties. With the rise of the Industrial Age, these communal tribal ties were pulled apart by economic alliances, urbanization, the nation-state, mass media, legal contracts, and increasing vocational specialization. *Homo sapiens* today seek a way to regain this feeling of extended family, this sense of belongingness. Retribalization is *the post-intellectual process of merging a person's individual identity into the larger cultural consciousness of a group identity.*

One aspect of retribalization is the return to *an oral tradition of communication*—a nonliterate, intuitive means of experiencing and understanding the world. Marshall McLuhan and Quentin Fiore define the idea of the Global Village in terms of this concept of retribalization: "Ours is a brand-new world of all-at-onceness. 'Time' has ceased, 'space' has vanished. We now live in a global village—a simultaneous happening. We are back in acoustic space. We have begun again to structure the primordial feeling, the tribal emotions from which a few centuries of literacy divorced us."[1]

Joel Kotkin relates this return to tribalism with post-intellectual rejection of reason and rationality: "Such an embrace of tribalism or religion may seem a regression back to the instinctual, a celebration of the peculiarities and even the irrationality of our species."[2]

A second aspect of retribalization is *the breakup of today's political nation-*

states, a return to tribal loyalties that ignore twentieth-century political boundaries. The tribe is a pre-intellectual grouping. The nation is an intellectual idea. And the return to ethnic and provincial groupings is post-intellectual retribalization.

Newspaper headlines chronicle the prevalence of this tribal mentality: the unrest of a hundred different tribes within the dismantled Soviet Union; the balkanization of Eastern Europe and the emergence of traditional animosities among Serbs, Croats, Slavs, Moslems, and other ancient ethnic groups; the separatist movements of Quebec, Scotland, Northern Ireland; and the resurgence of Native American tribes. Even the inner-city gangs of American cities reflect a search for the cohesiveness and security of a tribal grouping.

Bernard Nietschmann, in the *Cultural Survival Quarterly*, analyzed 120 separate military conflicts that were ongoing in 1987. Of these, fully 75 percent involved ethnic animosities or tribal fights for independence. Azerbaijanis fight the Armenians over Nagorno-Karabakh; ethnic Kurds want their own state split off from Turkey, Iran and Iraq; Abkhazians and southern Ossetians seek separation from Georgia; Ukranians and Romanians fight each other in Moldova; Gypsies struggle for their liberties in Romania; seven million Tartars would like their own Crimean republic; Basque separatists continue their bloody confrontation in Spain; inter-tribal warfare in Rwanda and Burundi claims hundreds of thousands of lives in a couple months.

Nietschmann points out that *about one-third of the world's population identifies primarily with some tribal or native nation*—as opposed to geographically recognized political states drawn on global maps. There are some 3,000 such identifiable native nations in the world today.[3]

One malignant side of domestic retribalization is the emergence of militant groups based on racist or extreme religious or political ideologies. Americans are increasingly aware of the presence of armed splinter groups, from coast to coast and from Texas to Montana. There are an estimated eight hundred such "patriot" organizations in the United States—self-anointed militias, white supremacists, religious zealots, secessionists, separatists, and assorted clans declaring their opposition to the United States in one form or another.[4] The one trait common to all such groups is the anti-intellectual intolerance characteristic of cults and brain-washed fanatics. In their narrow-minded dogmatism, they represent the antithesis of an intellectual search for social cohesiveness. They represent post-intellectualism carried to the ugliest extreme.

RETURNING TO A TRIBAL MINDSET

Twenty years ago, Sociologist Harold Isaacs observed that we have not been able to replace our tribal allegiances with larger intellectual constructs:

For about two hundred years, the best and the brightest intellectuals in the Western world believed that with the advance of science, the growth of knowledge, the mastery of nature, reason would win and all earlier forms of human backwardness would just go away. . . . Science advanced, knowledge grew, nature was mastered, but Reason did not conquer and tribalism did not go away. . . . At its worst, our current retribalization signals the end of the illusion.[5]

The "best and the brightest intellectuals" were also exceedingly idealistic—holding on to this illusion that individuals could set aside their provincial and tribal loyalties to form a larger Lockean compact. Christopher Lasch points out that intellectuals *(or liberals)* have long underestimated the dynamics of tribal loyalties: "Liberals could not see that parochial attachments called forth an intensity of conviction unmatched by an abstract attachment to humanity as a whole."[6]

Despite our best intellectual efforts, we have not been able to replace tribal loyalties with a super-national intellectual federation of peoples—some sort of "abstract attachment to humanity as a whole." In his analysis of the role of modern global tribes, Kotkin points out that the reversion to tribal cultures escalates as the ideal of an intellectual international order fades: "Rather than the triumph of a rational and universal world order, we are witnessing a resurgence of popular interest in ethnic identities, religious roots and ancient affiliations that is shaking societies from the remnants of the former Soviet Empire to the streets of Los Angeles."[7]

Today, the hyphenated citizen—the African-American, the Italian-American, the Jewish-American, the Korean-American—finds him- or herself putting increasing emphasis on the tribal modifier *(African, Italian, Jewish, Korean)* rather than on the more abstract and intellectual nation-state identity *(American)*. A century ago, Irish, Greek, Chinese and Polish immigrants were eager to embrace the identity of "American." Today, however, many U.S. citizens are eager to embrace their ancestral roots and ethnic identity as their primary emotional security.

Writer Sam Fulwood observes, "Hundreds of thousands of black Americans, their patience worn thin by the lingering indignities of racism, are turning away from the centuries-old quest for inclusion in the mainstream of white society."[8] *Black is beautiful. Homosexuals are gay. I am woman. And our primary affiliation is with our tribal grouping.* Newt Gingrich sums up the dangers inherent in emphasizing such schisms: "America can absorb an amazing number of people from an astonishing range of backgrounds if our goal is assimilation. If people are being encouraged to resist assimilation, the very fabric of American society will eventually break down."[9] All separatist movements represent a post-intellectual trend.

Tribalism versus Individualism

Post-intellectual retribalization erodes our sense of individual identity. If there is one inalienable characteristic of an intellectual mindset, it is the concept of the *individual*—the independent, questioning, thinking, competitive, achieving individual. If a man or woman cannot think independently, if a person cannot rely upon his or her own reasoning skills, then that person has lost the concept of individual existence. Franco Ferrarotti writes, "Belief in the individual defines the modern world. . . . Individualism is the connecting thread that is found everywhere in the complex weft of the epoch stretching from Leonardo to the first decade of the twentieth century."[10] Intellectualism is individualism.

Expressing his concern that the modern *Organization Man* equates corporate identity with tribal belongingness—thus losing his or her individuality—William Whyte recalls the compelling observation of A. A. Bowman: "Of all the forms of wanton self-destruction, there is none more pathetic than that in which the human individual demands that in the vital relationships of life he be treated not as an individual but as a member of some organization."[11]

Individualism is the antithesis of tribalism. McLuhan states simply, "Tribal cultures cannot entertain the possibility of the individual or of the separate citizen."[12] As people lose their identity as an individual, they have a sense of existence only as they can be recognized as part of a tribe, a specialized trade, or a victimized group.

Analyzing the role of individuals in a liberal democracy, Stanley Rothman writes, "To become an American meant to see oneself primarily as a free individual, not as the member of some corporate group."[13] The political influence today of corporate PACs (political action committees) and other tribal lobbyists illustrates how far we have strayed from this intellectual ideal of the nation as a collection of individuals. We are today a nation of special-interest tribal pressure groups.

To be an individual is to value your personal identity above that of the tribe. To be an individual is challenging; it is scary; it means standing alone and being responsible for your own survival and well-being. It involves thinking and making decisions and being accountable for those decisions.

To belong to the tribe is to renounce your individuality in favor of a composite identity. To be part of a group or a tribe is to survive within the aggregate security of the larger entity. You subordinate your independence to a collective authority. It allows you to renounce responsibility.

Retribalization is not only anti-intellectual (de-emphasizing individual identity), but it is authoritarian in that the tribe is more important than the individual. Those who would accept the definition of Truth handed down by the authorities (tribal chiefs, priests, lawyers, political gurus, union officers, minority spokespersons) have retreated into the security of a non-intellectual collective mindset. Such tribal members have no need to think for themselves; they have but to heed the Truth as it is handed to them.

Electric Media and Retribalization

The electric media, because they are predominantly oral and pictorial, promote a tribal state of mind, a pre-literate, intuitive oral tradition. We are returning to an instinctive, tribal tradition of communicating with sounds and images.

Whether it is Koppel or Moyers guiding us through a political thicket, Barbara or Oprah interviewing a current celebrity, Liddy or Limbaugh inciting us to near-riot, the result is a shared nationwide tribal happening. We have an ongoing tribal talk experience, coast-to-coast, on multiple channels, twenty-four hours a day. The tribal radio and TV tube become a neighborhood bullhorn and community bulletin board. We deal today with what Howard Fineman labels the *cybertribe*—"bands of like-minded citizens 'threaded' together instantaneously, specifically, globally, sometimes obsessively."[14]

The committee is a form of tribal collectivism; and modern communications media have now given us the *electronic committee*—"collaborative computing," also labeled *desktop video conferencing* (as introduced in Chapter 5). This team-computing experience has a tribalizing or folk-art flavor to it in that individual inputs are lost in the synthesizing of the group effort. Individuality is assimilated in the cooperative output. This is not to say that such a collaborative effort does not result in a valuable end product; indeed, the group outcome may wind up with an excellent design/report/product. The point simply is that in the tribalized committee endeavor, one's individual creative effort and identity is sacrificed.

Retribalization and Openness. The tribal pictorial media also strip us of our privacy. The printed word, because it fosters reflective thinking and promotes individuality, was the enabling technology that defined civilization and created privacy. Ayn Rand defines the relationship of civilization and privacy with Howard Roark's declaration that "Civilization is the progress toward a society of privacy. The savage's whole existence is public, ruled by the laws of his tribe. Civilization is the process of setting man free from men."[15] But today we seem to value our privacy less and less.

McLuhan commented in 1974, "Before phonetic literacy, there had been no private identity—there had only been the tribal group." He elaborated in an interview two years later that when men and women view television "they become corporate, peer-group people—just by watching it. They lose interest in being individual private individuals. This is one of the hidden and, perhaps, insidious effects of television."[16] The electric media—from the telegraph to the satellite—integrate us into a tribal oral/pictorial "all-at-onceness." Television creates an open, instinctive, de-privatized, tribal culture.

Retribalization and Isolation. At the same time that electric media tend to strip us of our privacy, we also use the media to isolate ourselves. We seek out specialized content that helps us to identify with particular tribal groups— ethnic programming, religious experiences, cultural attractions, neighborhood gossip, or any other common ground that helps us to find some tribal identity. This is true with both print and electric media. Special-interest magazines and newsletters, professional journals, ethnic newspapers, youth-oriented movies, cable TV channels and LPTV operations (community-based low-power TV stations): these all provide us with specialized content for our particular cultural grouping.

Even while we use the media to search for a collective tribal identity, we isolate ourselves physically from other persons—we all have our separate receivers and segregated listening chambers. As our technologies—media, cities, specialized professions, bureaucracies and institutions—tend to isolate us and divest us of our human individuality, we grasp for something, some entity we can identify and connect with. Even as we sit isolated at our keyboards and terminals, we use the computer networks and on-line chat rooms to reach out to others of like mind. We are using the media to fragment McLuhan's Global Village into isolated tribes.

We use the electronic threads of our *web culture* to make temporary bonds with unseen thousands or millions of strangers, and then we shut off that particular link and turn to other connections. Retribalization is largely an instinctive *counter-intellectual* reaction to the sense of isolation fostered by *distended-intellectualism.*

THE NEW TRIBALISM AND AFFIRMATIVE ACTION

In a 1994 book review, Roger Kimball writes, "What killed liberalism in this country is a deeply misguided egalitarianism." Substitute the word *intellectualism* for *liberalism* and you have our current dilemma: *intellectualism has been killed by a misguided egalitarianism*—or at least seriously wounded. Intellectual liberalism embraces the idea of elitism: all shall compete equally and the best, the elite, shall rise to the top. Misguided or distended egalitarianism denies this intellectual competition. Kimball continues:

American democracy was founded on a dialectic between elitism and egalitarianism. Each is necessary to a healthy society that wishes both to be humane and to reward achievement. The problem today is that the dialectic has collapsed and "the unthinking and nonjudgmental egalitarian side has been winning."[17]

The "nonjudgmental egalitarian side" is represented by the affirmative action mindset.

Anticipating our contemporary affirmative action debate, Oliver Wendell Holmes delivered a Memorial Day oration a century ago in which he observed that "A misguided notion of justice had led humanitarians to the absurd conclusion that it was 'unjust that any one should fail.'"[18] He was referring, of course, to the libertarian idea that individuals in all fields should be allowed to compete in an open and fair contest—in the best intellectual tradition of Adam Smith. In a democratic society, some are going to win; others are going to lose.

However, to the extent that many of the non-winners have been denied equal training and opportunities due to their gender, race, religion, ethnicity, sexual preference, or physical disability, many would argue it *is* unjust that they should fail. Civil rights legislation and affirmative action programs evolved in a post-intellectual attempt to redress inequities based on these discriminations. Affirmative action is a manifestation of retribalization—sensitivity to a particular group's needs for special consideration and compensation.

Victimization of the Tribe

In his 1995 book, *The Good Life and Its Discontents*, Robert Samuelson analyzes our contemporary cultural malaise as the failure of the Age of Entitlements. We have come to expect more from both the private and public sectors than the economy or the government could deliver (the inability of linear growth to sustain our demands); therefore we are discouraged and malcontent. We then insist on even more entitlements from the government; and these demands are inevitably defined as benefits to be doled out to specific constituent groups. In a 1996 article, Samuelson writes, "The effect has been to strengthen a sense of group identity that transcends ordinary citizenship and at times is rivalrous. Personal responsibility is diminished and a culture of dependency and 'victimology' takes over."[19]

We have consequently created the institution of Victimization. Charles Sykes, author of *A Nation of Victims*, comments in an earlier article, "American life is increasingly characterized by the plaintive insistence: *I am a victim*. From the drug addicts of the ghettos to the self-help groups of the suburbs, the mantra is the same: *I am not responsible; it's not my fault*."[20] To a great extent, of course, it is true; many people—members of various tribes—have been victimized and deserve societal redress.

But others use the label of "victim" in order to extort whatever payment they can from a confused society. We hesitate to deny compensation to honestly wronged victims; we hesitate to probe too deeply into claims of victimization for fear of appearing insensitive—and politically incorrect. Therefore, we tend to submit to the claims of all those tribal groups who cry out that they have been wronged.

Thus, we strive today for sensitivity rather than competition, equality rather than excellence. These are our counter-intellectual egalitarian goals. People want their victimized group, their tribe, to be recognized and compensated as a whole, rather than having to fight the system as an isolated individual. But this diminishes the individual. Psychologist Judith Sherven points out, for example, how this works against the individual woman who is thus sheltered by feminist victimhood groups:

Women's leaders today are teaching victimhood as the primary identity for all women and powerlessness as strength. . . . The tragedy is that today's women, rather than being prepared to cope more effectively and powerfully with life's adversities, are being told to whine and sue because they have experienced some of life's troubles.[21]

Victimization and the No-Fault Society. As people lose their sense of individuality and self-reliance, we witness the rise of a "no-fault" society—the denial of responsibility for one's failures and shortcomings. If you are having trouble in school, it is because you suffer from some learning disability, or racial intolerance, or a poor home environment (it's not your fault). If you are not succeeding at work, it is due to sexual discrimination, unfair working conditions, or an unsympathetic boss (it's not your fault). If your marriage breaks up, it is because your spouse didn't understand you, or you were seduced by someone younger (it's not your fault). If your business went under, it was due to unfair competition from Japan, new traffic patterns, deterioration of the neighborhood, the bankers, or the weather (it's not your fault).

Any time anything goes wrong (it's not your fault), find a lawyer and sue somebody. Our litigious society exemplifies post-intellectualism—the abdication of personal responsibility: not understanding what is going on (ignorance), the inability to solve one's own problems (dumbth), buying into the technocratic legalistic culture (establishmentism), and hiring a lawyer (specialization).

One escalating trend is the "no-fault defense" in criminal trials. From battered wives to political terrorists, criminals claim not to be responsible for their own actions. They themselves are victims of a traumatic childhood, economic conditions, racism, peer pressures, substance addiction, or political subjugation. Headline cases have introduced defense arguments where the accused perpetrators were victims of child abuse, espousal abuse, mob psychology, and elevated blood-sugar levels—and therefore were not responsible for their actions.[22]

This post-intellectual redress of grievances and inequities has been broadened to the degree that the Americans With Disabilities Act of 1990 now encompasses those who suffer from *oppositional defiant disorder* ("negativistic, defiant, disobedient and hostile behavior toward authority figures"), *antisocial personality disorder* ("a pervasive pattern of disregard for the rights of others"), and *narcissistic personality disorder* ("grandiosity, need for admiration"). In other words, if you don't like your boss, and if you can't get along with your co-workers, *it's not your fault;* and society must make arrangements to compensate for your disability. Citing the work of G. E. Zuriff, George Will comments that "what once were considered faults of mind and flaws of character are [now] 'personality disorders' akin to physical disabilities that demand legal accommodation." Such a policy threatens "to undermine our culture's already fragile sense of personal responsibility."[23]

In an intellectual society, people are responsible for their own actions, their own destiny. Whether individuals succeed or fail depends on their own initiative and talents; if they do not succeed, it is their own doing. In this post-intellectual climate, individuals no longer are responsible for their own destiny; it is somebody else's obligation to take care of them—social agencies, government bureaus, insurance companies, affirmative action lawyers, the bankruptcy court, or the tribal leader.

Affirmative Action as a Remedial Measure

In a perfect intellectual society we would have, on one hand, a sense of individualism and competition, and, on the other hand, an attitude of fair play and concern for the needs and sensitivities of others. However, this ideal has never been achieved. For example, had the republic's founding fathers not condoned slavery, forcibly taken the land from the Native Americans, and denied women the vote, we would be living in a very different society today. There never would have been need for post-intellectual affirmative action programs.

If we were to treat all peoples truly fairly and provide equal opportunities for all, we would never need to agonize over affirmative action quotas and politically correct (PC) speech codes and regulations. When we have to set up equal-opportunity quota systems, we are in effect repudiating the intellectual concepts of competition and individual achievement. Affirmative action is a post-intellectual phenomenon. *Affirmative action is a counter-intellectual PC remedy to the inequities spawned by irresponsible pursuit of distended-intellectual libertarian concepts.*

Affirmative Action and the Loss of Individuality.
By turning to affirmative action in an attempt to rectify past injustices, a person must sacrifice his or her individual identity—making tribal or racial or gender identification the primary issue. The person is recognized not as an individual but only as a member of the victimized group. Michael Berliner and Gary Hull point out that it is affirmative action policies that actually represent racist thinking:

Racism is the notion that one's race determines one's identity. It is the belief that one's convictions, values and character are determined not by the judgment of one's mind, but by one's anatomy or blood.

The diversity movement claims that its goal is to extinguish racism and build tolerance of differences. This is a complete sham. One cannot teach students that their identity is determined by skin color and expect them to become colorblind. One cannot espouse multiculturalism and expect students to see each other as individual human beings. One cannot preach the need for self-esteem while destroying the faculty that makes it possible: reason. One cannot teach collective identity and expect students to have self-esteem.[24]

For example, in a hypothetical case, where individual identity and intellectual competition are paramount, we have a unique individual named Jones who has been hired as an engineer (and who happens to be an African-American). In another case, where equality and sensitivity and tribal identification prevail, we have an African-American tribal member who has been hired as an engineer to fill an affirmative action quota (and who happens to be named Jones). In the latter case, post-intellectual equality has been achieved—but not the intellectual goal of individual recognition. It may be a subtle distinction—but it does determine one's self-image. Recall Bowman's point that "of all the forms of wanton self-destruction, there is none more pathetic" than when an individual demands that "he be treated not as an individual but as a member of some organization."

Political Correctness on Campus

According to John Taylor, the ideologies of political correctness are rooted in the conviction that "the doctrine of individual liberties *itself* is inherently oppressive."[25] That is, the idea of allowing individuals to compete equally in an economic or intellectual foot-race is inherently unfair—because many persons of disadvantaged or victimized backgrounds are not able to begin the race at the starting line. Similarly, in his spirited attack on affirmative action, Dinesh D'Souza, in *Illiberal Education*, describes the PC curriculum in which students are taught that "standards and values are arbitrary, and the ideal of the educated person is largely a figment of bourgeois white male ideology, which should be cast aside; that individual rights are a red flag signaling social privilege, and should be subordinated to the claims of group interest."[26]

If (as discussed in Chapter 2) federally subsidized research techno-scholars represent the *distended-intellectual* element on today's college campuses, then the radical proponents of political correctness represent the *counter-intellectual* segment. Both are post-intellectual. Neither the narrowly specialized research professionals nor the PC proponents of disenfranchised tribes represent the liberal intellectual pursuit of knowledge.

Campus Speech Codes. In an attempt to curtail "hate speech" (racial slurs, gender slander, religious epithets, sexual harassment), many universities have instituted various forms of speech codes. Designed to halt any type of derogatory speech or "discriminatory conduct" in the classrooms, restrooms, locker rooms, hallways, and fraternity houses, over two hundred major public and private universities have adopted various hate-speech codes. But the problems of narrow minds and prejudice have not been resolved (and most of the codes have since been abandoned or declared unconstitutional).

Initiating a speech code (or any kind of censorship)—even if it is successful in maintaining a facade of law and order—can serve only to suppress the underlying problems. Applying an affirmative-action bandaid, or a PC tourniquet, is not going to cure the source of the infection. Speech codes cannot alleviate the problems of racial or gender animosities or intolerance. If we must guard against someone using the words "nigger" or "kike" on campus, then we have already lost the intellectual battle. *The need for speech codes is, in itself, an admission that we have not been able to handle responsibly the intellectual concept of freedom of expression.*

Self-Segregation of the Curriculum. In the post-intellectual wave of racial sensitivity spawned in the 1960s, liberals eagerly embraced the creation of Black Studies and Hispanic Studies departments—followed shortly thereafter by other curricular remedies to past injustices (Women's Studies, Jewish Studies). But questions persist about the academic legitimacy of such programs. At best, they represent a specialization that contributes to post-intellectual retribalization and parochialism. At the worst, they perpetuate the very problems they are established to correct.

It is important that every person should learn about and appreciate his or her heritage. *(Black is beautiful.)* But should one's cultural heritage dominate one's academic curriculum? Should not such a cultural perspective be transmitted by the family, the church, and other tribal institutions? Colleges and universities are charged with preparing the student to participate in today's intellectual environment—the economic, social, and political affairs of contemporary America. The schools are not set up to prepare students for being a member of an African tribe, a South Pacific culture, or a Native American way of life of three hundred years ago. Such a tribal emphasis only serves to perpetuate the schism that divides minority students from their contemporary environment. Thomas Short writes bluntly:

> Time spent on minority studies is time taken away from those traditional studies that prepare the student for a fuller participation in our society. Minority studies for minority students is a way of ensuring that minorities remain on—or get pushed out to—the margins of life, both in academia and in our society.[27]

By providing such multicultural curricula, there is a corresponding decline in traditional Western history and philosophy studies. Author Melvin Jules Bukiet points out that "Perhaps worse than the anti-European bias implicit in these curricular decisions is an anti-intellectual bias."[28] For in de-emphasizing the Western traditions of scientific research and rationalism, the academy is denying those intellectual attributes on which Western higher education is founded.

Multiculturalism should be an avenue for acceptance and appreciation of all cultures. (It is white students who should be taking Black Studies, men who should be enrolled in Women's Studies.) All too often, however, multiculturalism degenerates into an avenue for self-segregation and ethnocentrism— rejecting assimilation, even tolerance, in its embrace of tribal isolation. Integration is an intellectual ideal; let all peoples come together in a multicultural egalitarian setting and compete on an equal footing. Politically correct resegregation is a post-intellectual denial of equal competition; let us find refuge in the collective security of our tribal identity.

This is not to argue that Affirmative Action should be immediately discarded, that multicultural programs should be eliminated. *(Not all post-intellectual characteristics are to be considered negative.)* It is just to point out that retribalization, affirmative action, equal opportunity plans, and other PC programs indicate that we have failed in our attempt to make intellectualism and individualism the philosophical law of the land. Out of sensitivity for the disenfranchised and victimized, we have turned to post-intellectual remedies.

NOTES

1. McLuhan and Fiore, 1967, p. 63.
2. Kotkin, "Family Ties," 1993, p. 21.

3. Nietschmann, 1987.

4. Estimate is from Mike Reynolds of the Southern Poverty Law Center, Montgomery, Alabama, interviewed on KABC, Los Angeles, 19 April 1996.

5. Isaacs, 1975, p. 25.

6. Lasch, 1991, p. 384.

7. Kotkin, "Family Ties," 1993, p. 18.

8. Sam Fulwood III, "Black Attitudes Shift Away From Goal of Inclusion," *Los Angeles Times,* 30 October 1995, p. A1.

9. Newt Gingrich, "English Literacy Is the Coin of the Realm," *Los Angeles Times,* 4 August 1995, p. B11.

10. Ferrarotti, 1985, p. 17.

11. Quoted in Whyte, 1956, p. 59.

12. McLuhan, 1964, pp. 86–87.

13. Rothman, 1992, p. 39.

14. Howard Fineman, "The Brave New World of Cybertribes," *Newsweek,* 27 February 1995, p. 30.

15. Rand [1943], 1993, pp. 684–85.

16. Both quotations are taken from the film, *Marshall McLuhan: The Man and His Message* (McLuhan Productions, in association with the Canadian Broadcasting Corporation, produced and directed by Stephanie McLuhan, written and narrated by Tom Wolfe, 1984), broadcast on PBS.

17. Roger Kimball, "Some Things Are Better Than Other Things," *New York Times,* 16 October 1994, sect. 7, p. 30. The quotation is from William A. Henry III's *In Defense of Elitism,* 1994.

18. Oliver Wendell Holmes, "A Soldier's Faith" (1895), paraphrased and quoted in Lasch, 1991, p. 297.

19. Robert J. Samuelson, "Great Expectations," *Newsweek,* 8 January 1996, p. 31.

20. Charles J. Sykes, "No More Victims, Please," *Reader's Digest*, February 1993, p. 21.

21. Judith Sherven, "Feminism Sells Women Short," *Los Angeles Times,* 2 March 1994, p. B13.

22. The four representative cases were the following: Lyle and Erik Menendez, who shotgunned their parents into pieces; Lorena Bobbitt, who cut off her husband's penis; the men accused of beating trucker Reginald Denny (in the riots following the Rodney King verdict); and Dan White, who killed San Francisco mayor George Moscone and County Supervisor Harvey Milk.

23. George Will, "He's Not Disabled; He's Just Mad," *Los Angeles Times,* 4 April 1996, p. B13. Will is reporting on an article by G. E. Zuriff in a recent issue of *Public Interest Quarterly.*

24. Michael S. Berliner and Gary Hull, "Diversity of Ideas Is What's Really Needed," *Los Angeles Times*, 24 May 1995, p. B13.

25. John Taylor, "Are You Politically Correct?" in Beckwith and Bauman, 1993, p. 18.

26. D'Souza, 1991, p. 229.

27. Thomas Short, "'Diversity' and 'Breaking the Disciplines': Two New Assaults on the Curriculum," in Beckwith and Bauman, 1993, p. 101.

28. Melvin Jules Bukiet, "Exalting Tribalism over Athens," *Los Angeles Times,* 16 October 1995, p. B11.

14

Democracy and Responsibility:
The Freedom Dilemma

Those who profess to favor freedom, and yet deprecate agitation, are men who want crops without plowing up the ground, they want rain without thunder and lightning. They want the ocean without the awful roar of its many waters.

• Frederick Douglass
Frederick Douglass: The Clarion Voice

Democracy is collective decision-making. In our Enlightenment-launched system of participatory democracy, we have theoretically entrusted national decision-making to the people. In the words of Lewis Lapham, the founders of the American Republic "put their faith in the resourcefulness and self-discipline of the free citizen."[1] Inspired by the rhetoric of John Locke and Thomas Jefferson, we believed that an enlightened citizenry could enter into a rational social compact and demonstrate enough reason and responsibility to make the system work.

Universal participation means that the masses shall dominate; the average and mediocre shall provide the ruling voices. The result is government by an unenlightened citizenry. In our post-intellectual quagmire we are not doing a very good job of collective decision-making—or problem-solving. And a nation that does not make responsible decisions loses its freedoms; a citizenry that cannot solve its problems loses its liberties. I am concerned in this chapter specifically with the manner in which we misuse the media in our attempt at self-government.

THE QUEST FOR FREEDOM

The craving for freedom is innate in the human spirit. This is probably the strongest driving force behind the ideal of "the American Way." I mentioned in Chapter 3 that, when asked what they appreciate most about living in America, about 95 percent of my students in one course respond with some variation of freedom—liberty, civil rights, independence. But in this post-intellectual society, we are in danger of squandering that which we value most.

Freedom and Responsibility

Freedom demands intellect. Political freedom is an intellectual idea—an abstract goal derived from the libertarian underpinnings of the Enlightenment. Freedom can be maintained only as the citizenry *en masse* can exercise reason in running the nation's affairs—remaining informed, participating in the democratic process, and working as a unified body for long-term societal benefits (rather than immediate gratification).

As stressed throughout the book, *freedom demands responsibility.* Without external controls and regulation, we have only anarchy—unless there is some form of internal restraint, self-discipline, responsibility. Freedom gives us the opportunity to make our own decisions; but unless we accept responsibility for the consequences of our decisions, we cannot expect to hold on to our right to make independent decisions.

Freedom is not *license*—which implies a lack of responsibility. When we equate freedom with a never-ending license for the narcotic pursuit of earthly pleasures, we are attempting to turn our lives into one ceaseless materialistic orgasm. We distort the meaning of freedom when we use the word to mean license to overindulge (in drugs, liquor, rich food, sex), to bear personal artillery pieces, to get over our heads in debt, to discriminate against people because of their race or gender, to break commitments and contracts, and to exploit other individuals.

In the pursuit of unrestrained liberties, we have abandoned responsibility in numerous areas: our escapist use of the media, capitalistic manipulation of consumers, environmental abuse, runaway population growth. These are all post-intellectual excesses pursued without restraint, without self-control. We reject the twin pillars of freedom—reason and responsibility.

Freedom and Peace

We also misunderstand the inverse relationship between freedom and *peace or security.* Contrary to our wistful desires, freedom is not peaceful. Freedom demands stamina, exertion, agitation, and, often, conflict. Freedom dictates that we face a world of challenges and uncertainties—not serenity and security. Freedom and security are opposites. Peace and security exist when we allow others to make our decisions for us; we then do not have to worry about accepting any responsibilities. Freedom comes when we make our own decisions; and we have to accept the consequences of our decisions.

The phrase, "Eternal vigilance is the price of liberty," can be traced back to John Philpot Curran who in 1790 declared "The condition upon which God hath given liberty to man is eternal vigilance; which condition if he break, servitude is at once the consequence of his crime and the punishment of his guilt."[2] More poetically a century later, Frederick Douglass stated "Those who profess to favor freedom, and yet deprecate agitation, are men who want crops without plowing up the ground, they want rain without thunder and lightning. They want the ocean without the awful roar of its many waters."[3]

One interesting irony of the 1960s was the formation of the leftist Peace and Freedom Party. It sounds like a great slogan, but a moment's reflection will reveal the extent to which these two qualities are antithetical. Freedom entails vigilance, endurance, responsibility, and the willingness to fight to retain one's liberties. It is an intellectual goal based on individualism and independent decision-making.

Peace and security, on the other hand, imply acquiescence, compromise, a willingness to accept the dictates and directions of others. They are pre-intellectual (and post-intellectual) qualities resulting in shared responsibilities and the collective shelter of retribalization.

Freedom can be symbolized by the *jungle*. You are on your own, responsible for your own survival, with no one providing you food or shelter or protection from other predators. There are no traffic signals or pension plans. Peace and security, on the other hand, are symbolized by the *zoo*. The caretaker/Big Brother will provide for your every need—food, shelter, medical attention, and protection from the other animals. You are relieved of all responsibilities for your own well-being. To which does our society aspire—the freedom of the jungle, or the peace and security of the zoo? We cannot have both in full measure. Rousseau gives us an even darker comparison than the zoo: "Tranquillity is found also in dungeons; but is that enough to make them desirable places to live in?"[4]

Our forefathers could have accepted peace under George III and enjoyed a long and secure existence as the crown jewel of the British Empire. But they chose instead the violent and revolutionary road to liberty and the establishment of new freedoms. The question today is whether we can demonstrate the vigilance and responsibility to maintain those hard-won freedoms.

The unsettling theme of this chapter is that *a free people—unless they have sufficient intellectual strength—will willingly choose slavery over freedom;* we will readily embrace security in place of independence. We will voluntarily accept ignorance rather than pursue information; we want escapism rather than enlightenment. We will readily choose comfort over exertion, peace over vigilance. We will abandon the freedom and responsibilities of living independently in the jungle in order to enjoy the security and protections of the zoo.

MEDIA AND DEMOCRACY

We are specifically concerned in this section with the *media connection*. What are the consequences if we do not use our media in a rational and responsible way? What happens when a society does not make intelligent decisions regarding its use of a free press?

As diagrammed in Figure 14.1, *freedom* is dependent upon a *representative democracy;* such self-government demands an *enlightened citizenry;* an educated citizenry must be kept informed by a *free press;* a free press is paid for by *commercial support;* commercial media must aim at a *mass audience;* programming for the mass audience means primarily *trivia and escapist content;* such "lowest-common-denominator" content results in an *ill-informed citizenry;* and an ill-informed society leads to *authoritarianism*. This chain of reasoning results in the apparent contradiction of freedom eventually yielding to authoritarianism and slavery. This is America's Freedom Dilemma.

Figure 14.1
Media and the Freedom Dilemma

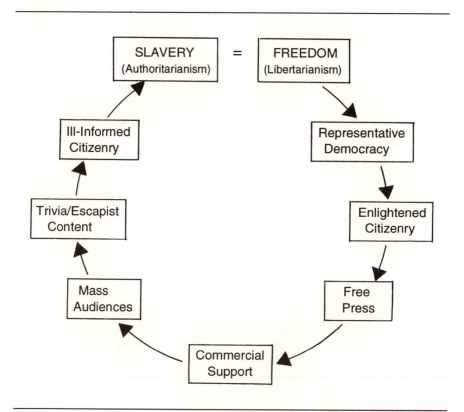

Without the specific reference to modern mass media, this was basically the pattern that Plato had in mind behind his observation that "The excess of liberty, whether in States or individuals, seems only to pass into excess of slavery."[5]

Freedom and a Representative Democracy

Political freedom exists only within a government elected by, and responsible to, the citizenry. If the people are to enjoy the freedoms of speech, assembly, religion, press, and a fair trial, the people must be in control of the government. Citizens must be able to elect their representatives and executive officers; they must be able to tell their leaders what they want and expect of them; they must be able to make laws directly through ballot propositions and initiatives.

However, if citizens choose to remain uninformed and indifferent, there is no way that we can expect the government to look out for our best interests. *We* must know our own best interests and *we* must act to ensure governmental action in those interests. If the citizen decides not to participate in the decision-making process, then the democratic decision-making process fails.

If you want someone else to look out for you—to protect your freedoms, to secure your livelihood, to make your decisions, to choose your government—you have, in effect, given up on the idea of a participatory democracy. You want "crops without plowing up the ground"; you want "rain without thunder and lightning."

Democracy and an Enlightened Citizenry

Inherent in a representative democracy is the assumption that each individual will be an enlightened, literate person who can keep abreast of the issues of the day. If we are to be in charge of our own political destiny, then we, as individuals, must be able to seek out evidence and evaluate conflicting arguments, think analytically and make independent decisions, discuss and debate governmental programs, decide on courses of action for society to follow, and exercise our democratic franchise in the voting booth. Without a literate, well-educated, responsible electorate, the idea of self-government is an illusion; democracy becomes merely a facade.

Jefferson was one of our most eloquent advocates of the enlightened citizenry's ability to maintain a free society. In his letter to Colonel Charles Yancey (6 January 1816), he explained "If a nation expects to be ignorant and free, in a state of civilization, it expects what never was and never will be." And he wrote to Du Pont de Nemours (24 April 1816), "Enlighten the people generally, and tyranny and oppressions of body and mind will vanish like evil spirits at the dawn of day."[6] In contemporary terms, Steve Allen voices the sentiment as clearly as anyone:

What is required for the fair, rational functioning of a democratic society, of whatever specific form, is an intelligent population. This is not to say that every citizen must be a scholar. But once the general level of intelligence falls below a certain minimum requirement, social chaos will result.[7]

Today—as we become more deeply entwined in the Progress Paradox—our obligation to gather information, analyze issues, and think independently becomes ever more crucial. We have to try to cope with the information explosion, computer advances, genetic engineering, convoluted economic arrangements, escalating urban anarchy, pollution and environmental deterioration, conflicting civil rights, population pressures, and increasingly turbulent international issues. However, in the late twentieth century, we see the populace settling deeper and deeper into the confusion and malaise of a post-intellectual web culture. We abandon our vigilance and sense of direction when we cannot figure out what to be vigilant about nor in which direction we should be headed.

The Role of the Free Press

If we citizens are to manage our governmental apparatus, we must have access to facts, reports, research data, opinions and ideas. What are the educational and informational channels available to us? *Schools* are usually viewed as having completed their task once the student reaches a designated age and has completed a given formal course of studies. We certainly cannot rely on *official government media* (broadcasts, reports, edicts, and other propaganda avenues) if we are to remain in charge of the government agencies and bureaucrats. *Institutions concerned with specific social and educational tasks* (religion, labor unions, business and professional associations, community organizations) are generally concerned only with narrow educational goals reinforcing their own moral or economic objectives. None of these institutional entities—schools, government channels, other agencies—really is able to satisfy the need to keep a mass populace educated on current social and political issues.

This leaves us with one overpowering omnipresent institution of mass education and widespread communication—*the mass media.*   Jefferson so strongly championed the importance of the free press that he wrote to Edward Carrington (16 January 1787), "The basis of our government being the opinion of the people, the very first object should be to keep that right; and were it left to me to decide whether we should have a government without newspapers, or newspapers without a government, I should not hesitate a moment to prefer the latter."[8]

One of the most perceptive social commentators of this century, Walter Lippman, writes 135 years later, "In the industrialized nations of the twentieth century the democratic polity cannot function as such without the institutional structure of independent mass media."[9] This statement was made when commercial radio broadcasting was just aborning. As our cultural environment becomes even more complex, the interrelated dependency of a democratic state, an enlightened populace, and an open and uncensored media system becomes increasingly apparent.

An educated citizenry is crucial for the maintenance of a free press. The mass media can fulfill their role only to the extent that an educated and involved populace demands a balanced, analytical, responsible, probing press. Walter Cronkite recently observed that education "lies at the very bottom of every problem that we have. If the people were truly well-informed, were truly philosophical, were truly aware of our associations with one another, [then] presumably our dialogue and our reporting would be considerably better than it is." He continues, "The tragedy is, we aren't educated to any degree. Education levels are so low that the public does not have a capability of making an informed judgment . . . so we're handicapped from the beginning."[10]

Mass Media and Commercial Support

It requires money—big money—to publish a newspaper or run a broadcast station. In the United States today it takes close to $200 billion a year to operate all of the newspapers, magazines, book publishers, television and radio stations, cable channels, and movie enterprises. Where is this money to come from?

Besides *voluntary donations* (which amount to less than 1 or 2 percent of the total cost of American media) and *government funding* (which accounts for less than 3 or 4 percent of our total media expenditures), the only viable source of money for media enterprises is *commercial* support. American mass media exist to make a profit. The media must be successful money-making operations; otherwise they fail. And all our idealistic libertarian goals disappear if the media go out of business.

This is what makes democracy in the United States a fascinating experiment—the reliance upon an information/media system based almost totally on profit-making enterprises. The informational and institutional foundation of the world's greatest democracy rests upon the bottom-line mercenary motivation of its profit-oriented capitalistic corporations. And it has worked—better than any system any other country has ever devised—for over two hundred years.

Nevertheless, there are many inherent problems with the system: heavier information loads imposed by a growing technological culture and data-saturated society, monopolistic mergers and corporate takeovers, interlocking boards of directors, government regulation and control, excessive profiteering, influence exerted on news content by advertisers, and the promotion of a consumeristic/materialistic frame of mind. The largest problem, however, may be the nature of the audience.

Mass Audiences

The entrepreneurial need to maximize one's profits leads inevitably to the struggle to reach the largest possible number of people. Reliance upon a *mass* media system inescapably means striving to reach a *mass* audience. This is what Plato referred to as the "tempers and tastes of the motley multitude," which "will oblige [the artist, poet, musician, or public servant] to produce whatever they [the masses] want."[11]   In contemporary terms, Melvin DeFleur and Everette Dennis define this as the *Law of Large Numbers:*

Newspapers, magazines, television, and radio depend on advertising revenue; advertisers in turn are looking for programs that will sell the largest possible quantity of beer or soup or soap. As a result, the American media are ruled by the *law of large numbers.* That is, whatever content will attract the largest number of consumers and produce the most advertising dollars will be the content provided. Content that can attract large numbers of consumers will tend to crowd out content that cannot.[12]

Even in the early nineteenth century, Tocqueville recognized this potential dilemma posed by the mass media: "In order to enjoy the inestimable benefits that the liberty of the press ensures, it is necessary to submit to the inevitable evils that it creates."[13]

Ratings services, marketing campaigns, audience research, and advertising strategies all are directed toward maximizing the numbers of readers, listeners, and viewers for each and every media outlet. No channel can ignore the obligation to its stockholders to reach the largest possible audience.

Even as more independent and specialized channels appear, breaking up the mass audience into smaller fragments, each channel still has to reach the largest possible number of consumers. Every public TV station, underground newspaper, special-interest magazine, religious pamphlet, and art film strives to maximize its audience. The history of media failures is littered with neighborhood newspapers, cultural cable TV channels, and specialized publishing houses that failed to reach enough of an audience to sustain themselves economically.

Trivia and Escapist Content

In this fight to attract the largest possible audience, the contest between competing mass media channels inevitably leads to providing attractive packages to the customers. And these attractive packages translate into what has been termed the "lowest common denominator" (LCD) content. DeFleur and Dennis explain that "It is no secret that people with unsophisticated artistic and intellectual tastes far outnumber people with highly developed tastes. Although there are exceptions to this crude law of large numbers, it generally accounts rather well for the low intellectual and artistic level that prevails in American mass communication."[14] As a result, commercial television has trivialized and sensationalized virtually every aspect of culture it has touched—drama, news, religion, politics, education, and sports.

Over the past decade I have conducted an informal content analysis in one of my media courses. The student assignment is to categorize all of the items in a one-hour local newscast. The results never fail to amaze the students—as they themselves identify only about one-sixth of the typical newscast as substantial news. The LCD content prevails not only in television and the movies, but in newspapers and news magazines as well. W. Russell Neuman in *The*

Paradox of Mass Politics observes,

In the newspapers, for example, where 60 percent of the content consists of advertising messages, the rest of the content consists primarily of human interest stories, horoscopes, sports scores, recipes, and movie reviews. . . . Roughly speaking, 10 percent of the editorial content, or 4 percent of the total newspaper content, consists of national and international news, and only a portion of that is political in nature.[15]

In criticizing the mass media, we must keep in mind that the media are essentially responding to the marketplace, fulfilling the basic free enterprise functions that are the core of the American system—making an honest profit by manufacturing a popular product and delivering it to as many people as possible. In our advertiser-supported free-enterprise commercial media system, the citizens get what they ask the media to deliver. And what they ask from the media is escapism, sensualism, trivia and sensationalism, cheap thrills, visual excitement, fast action, short and snappy messages, and content that requires no deep thinking.

In a 1995 essay, Neal Gabler writes that "we slide ever closer to a cultural abyss filled with trash and nothing but trash." The conservatives blame "a nefarious liberal media elite imposing its sybaritic values on an unsuspecting and upright populace" while the liberals blame "a nefarious conservative corporate elite reaping profits the only way it knows how—by pandering to our basest instincts." Gabler continues,

Whichever theory one buys, we ordinary citizens are not held responsible for devouring trash the way we do. We are either too malleable or too stupid to be accountable— malleable because we supposedly spend our money on things we really don't like; stupid because we supposedly like things we really shouldn't.

But if malleability and stupidity are the reigning theories of trash culture, it is probably because cultural critics find them preferable to the alternative. The alternative is that Americans have *deliberately* chosen the vulgar, the profane, the insipid, . . . [This excess of media trash] is a sobering exercise in democracy.[16]

An Ill-Informed Citizenry

As the pictorial media devote their channels to trivia and trash, we witness (as explored in Chapter 5) a continuing decline of enlightenment and literacy among the citizenry. In 1993, the U.S. Department of Education released the results of "the most comprehensive study of its kind," which indicated that literacy scores for people ages 21 to 25 have dropped significantly since 1985.[17] The study revealed that 23 percent of the adult population (44 million people) are illiterate or "can perform only the barest of tasks" (such as signing their name or adding a column of numbers). Another 26 percent (50 million people) can scarcely understand an appliance warranty or find an intersection on a map. Together, these two groups—almost one half of the adult American population—"are considered 'at risk' in today's rapidly changing economy."[18]

Nationwide polls and surveys continually reveal the lack of general knowledge and cultural information among the electorate. In a recent National Geographic poll, for instance, 53 percent of American adults could not find Britain on a world map; 23 percent could not find the Pacific Ocean; 19 percent had no idea where Mexico was; and 14 percent could not even find the United States!

Educators and critics used to fret about the fact that Americans were getting their news from television rather than from newspapers. Today, they are not getting their news at all. A 1990 Times Mirror poll revealed that only *41 percent* of Americans under age 35 said they watched TV news yesterday; the percentage was *52 percent in 1965.* And only *30 percent* said they read a newspaper yesterday; the figure was *67 percent in 1965!* Over the twenty-five-year period, this is a 21 percent drop in the number of people watching television news, and a 55 percent drop in the number of people reading newspapers for current events.

Perhaps the most damning indictment of our intellectual decline was voiced by one of America's most widely read futurists, John Naisbitt. Based upon his extensive trend-setting research, he made the somewhat shocking statement ten years ago that *"The generation graduating from high school today is the first generation in American history to graduate less skilled than its parents* [italics added]."[19]

There appears to be little hope that the situation will spontaneously get any better. Naisbitt observes that "In this literacy-intensive society, when we need basic reading and writing skills more than ever before, our education system is turning out an increasingly inferior product."[20] And Jonathan Kozol concludes, "There is reason to believe that all of this is going to get worse. Every bit of evidence we have at hand suggests that we will see an increase in the numbers of illiterate adults within another fifteen years."[21]

If increasing numbers of post-intellectual Americans cannot read well enough to comprehend the important social issues of the day, if the typical citizen gets his or her news summaries from *USA Today* and in-depth news analysis from the tabloid TV program *Hard Copy*, then the pretense of a participatory democracy grows thinner and thinner. As writer Robert Scheer sums up our situation, "Between having no education on the one hand, and listening to all this [media] nonsense on the other, you do not have Jefferson's enlightened electorate."[22] We do not have today an informed, responsible citizenry running the affairs of the country.

Embracing Intellectual and Political Slavery

As social and economic issues get increasingly complex, the individual citizen/voter concludes that it is impossible to deal with all the domestic and international problems facing us today. Joshua Meyrowitz emphasizes that "as our media lay bare more and more problems from around the world and push them into our consciousness, it has become impossible for an individual to assimilate or respond to all the issues raised."[23] As a consequence, large numbers of the electorate rarely or never participate in the political process (see Chapter 15). They opt out of the system. They choose to let others run their lives for them.

We return to the theme with which we started this chapter: a free people, when given the choice, will select entertainment and political ignorance over information; citizens will prefer to have someone else handle the responsibility for their lives rather than face the burdens of democracy; *we will willingly choose slavery over freedom*. Political and intellectual slavery are nothing more than accepting the security provided by a benevolent authority.

This is the difference between George Orwell's *1984* and Aldous Huxley's *Brave New World*. In Orwell's dark tale of Big Brother and the repressive totalitarian regime, society is controlled by fear of *pain*. It is from one of the three slogans of the Party, "Freedom Is Slavery," that the thesis for this chapter is taken. However, in Huxley's prophecy of genetic engineering and happiness drugs, the people are controlled not by pain but by the promise of *pleasure*. Neil Postman succinctly sums up the distinction between the views of *1984* and *Brave New World:* "Orwell feared we would become a captive culture. Huxley feared we would become a trivial culture, . . . Orwell feared that what we hate will ruin us. Huxley feared that what we love will ruin us."[24]

It is Huxley's vision, not Orwell's, that we should fear. The loss of freedom depicted in the authoritarianism of *1984* is an obvious threat that we can recognize and resist; indeed, we fairly successfully fought off Big Brother throughout the Cold War. However, the post-intellectual threat to freedom depicted in *Brave New World* is much more insidious and ultimately threatening. The pleasures and security provided in Huxley's world seduce us and enervate us; we welcome the benevolent technologies without recognizing that our fragile shell of independence is being gently dissolved. As we work to tame the fears and insecurities of the jungle, the comforts and safety of the zoo look increasingly attractive to us.

In summary, freedom allows us to use our media systems however we want, and we consistently choose to use our media channels to keep us amused and entertained—not informed. It is easier to let someone else make our decisions for us. As our technological society becomes increasingly complex and sophisticated, we members of that society appear to be decreasingly capable of remaining enlightened, vigilant, and in control. Therefore, given the choice between freedom and slavery, we willingly choose slavery.

NOTES

1. Lapham, "Modern Democracy," 1993.

2. Speech upon the Right of Election of the Lord Mayor of Dublin, 10 July 1790 (quoted in *Bartlett's Familiar Quotations*, 1980, p. 397).

3. Quoted in John W. Blassingame, *Frederick Douglass: The Clarion Voice* (Washington, DC: U.S. Department of the Interior, National Park Service, 1976), p. 46.

4. Rousseau [1762] (book 1, ch. 4), 1952, p. 389.

5. Plato (1942), book 8, p. 453.

6. Reprinted in *Bartlett's Familiar Quotations*, 1980, p. 389.

7. Allen, 1989, p. 195.

8. Jefferson, 1975, p. 415.

9. Quoted in Neuman, 1986, p. 133.

10. Quoted in Gay, 1996, p. 11.

11. Plato (1942), book 6, p. 379.

12. DeFleur and Dennis, 1988, pp. 90–91.

13. Tocqueville, 1835, ch. 9.

14. DeFleur and Dennis, 1988, p. 91.

15. Neuman, 1986, pp. 135–36.

16. Neal Gabler, "The Democratic Spirit's Romance with Trash," *Los Angeles Times,* 4 June 1995, p. M1.

17. Ralph Frammolino, "Federal Study Shows Adults Lag in Literacy," *Los Angeles Times,* 9 September 1993, pp. A1, A23.

18. Ibid.

19. Naisbitt, 1984, p. 25.

20. Ibid., p. 11.

21. Kozol, 1985, p. 57.

22. Robert Scheer, "Gore Vidal: Novelist of U.S. Past Sees an Empire Replacing Republic He So Admired," *Los Angeles Times,* 15 December 1991, p. M3.

23. Meyrowitz, 1985, p. 318.

24. Postman, 1985, pp. vii–viii.

15

Democratic Decline:
The Dream Grows Dim

*The voters think Washington is a whorehouse and every
four years they get a chance to elect a new piano player.*

• Peggy Noonan
Forbes Magazine

To what extent might they be right—those who warn about the demise, the
folly, the collapse of the America democratic venture? In his book, *Outgrowing
Democracy*, John Lukacs states gloomily that "it is quite possible that in the
history of mankind the democratic period may have been an episode."[1] *Harper's* editor Lewis Lapham laments, "I find myself wondering whether the
American experiment with democracy may not have run its course."[2] This
chapter looks at some of the signs of a faltering system.

THE BASIC REQUISITES

Democracy is an intellectual idea. There are at least three basic intellectual
prerequisites that any nation must have before it can sustain a true democratic
representative government. First, any country wanting to call itself a democracy
must demonstrate a *respect for individual human rights,* an egalitarian tradition
of observing civil liberties for all its citizens. This is the heritage our colonial
forefathers carried with them from the Magna Carta into the American Revolution. This was our foundation. And this is what is completely lacking in so
many Third World countries where we wish to force democracy into existence.
Retribalization works against this idea of equality and respect. The religious
zealot, the hyphenated-American racist, and the militant feminist all share this
intolerance in common: none are willing to respect and embrace those outside

their own tribe. Such separatism undermines the idea of democracy.

Second, any aspiring democracy must have a solid *commitment to universal education,* an unwavering dedication to the nourishment of an enlightened citizenry—a liberal arts curriculum that prepares the individual for responsible collective decision-making. Many nations espouse universal education; but too often, this consists of either establishment indoctrination (religious fanaticism, nationalistic jingoism) or specialized vocational and professional schooling that works against the enlightenment of the whole person. Without an intellectual commitment to the search for knowledge, analytic thinking, social criticism, and a broad cultural perspective, no citizen can participate in the democratic process.

Third, any country that wants to pursue self-government must have a *sound middle-class economy,* a history of free enterprise and an understanding of the relationship between a mercantile class and a self-governing people. No nation can maintain the schism between an aristocracy and a peasant class and expect to practice true democracy. There may be rich people and poor people, but the system must allow—indeed, encourage—the possibility of movement between the classes. Otherwise there is no incentive for making the system work.

Throughout the globe this truism holds: if a people cannot demonstrate true respect for human rights of all its citizens, if there is no universal educational system designed to instill democratic principles, if there is no working middle class—there can be no intellectual culture; there can be no hope for a stable democracy.

The American Head Start

The embryonic United States was fortunate in that we inherited these basic requisites from Mother England. For centuries, would-be Americans had been preparing for the day when they would establish their democratic experiment in the New World.

Additionally we had what, in retrospect, must be considered a combination of extraordinary advantages never before enjoyed by any new nation (and never to be enjoyed by any emerging nation in the future anywhere on the globe): a vast continent protected from foreign intervention on two sides by oceans, a preliterate native population easily subdued by advanced technologies, a robust economy based upon slave labor, seemingly limitless forests and mineral resources, the linear momentum of the Industrial Revolution, the intellectual and philosophical leadership of a remarkable group of founders, and religious faith in our Manifest Destiny to succeed and "subdue the earth."

We had an incredible head start in setting up our democratic demonstration project. Barbara Tuchman points out, however, that today we may have run out of these inherent advantages or "cushions against folly" with which we started: "Social systems can survive a good deal of folly when circumstances are historically favorable, or when bungling is cushioned by large resources or absorbed by sheer size as in the United States during its period of expansion.

Today, when there are no more cushions, folly is less affordable."[3]

With these requisites for a democratic society, we made the system work, sort of, for a while—until we ran out of the dream of unlimited linear expansion, until we used up our "cushions against folly." Today we see our three democratic requisites enervated. Retribalization has eroded our basic respect for the equality of all individuals. The ideal of universal education has been watered down to a mush of post-intellectual "feel-good" counselling and specialized vocational training. And belief in the vitality of a free enterprise system has been replaced by materialism, profiteering, an entrenched oligarchy, and a growing sense of despair within the permanently disenfranchised underclass.

If the viability of democracy can be questioned in America, what does this portend for the rest of the world? Time after time, in Latin America, Africa, the Middle East, Asia, the Caribbean, and most recently in Eastern Europe, we have charged into a country's internal affairs with gunboats, trade sanctions, supplications and threats, trying to impose the idea of democracy on a people who are no more equipped to handle such a responsibility than they are to send a space team to Mars. Stanley Meisler reminds us that "The Third World is strewn with tyrannies left behind by colonial powers that fancied themselves tutors of democracy."[4]

EMERGENCE OF THE ENFEEBLED GOVERNMENT

Inherent in any democratic government is the challenge of finding and electing a group of wise and responsible individuals to lead the state. There are two innate problems: one is the human tendency toward corruptibility, and the other is a distinct post-intellectual phenomenon—the weakening of authority due to the sharing of information.

The Corruptibility of Individuals

In the last year of the presidency of George Bush, his son Neil was involved in the conflict-of-interest scandal with Silverado Savings and Loan of Denver and was fined $50,000. Son Jeb was involved in an "unwitting" acceptance of improper political contributions from underworld figures. Son George, Jr., was in possible violation of SEC (Security and Exchange Commission) inside-trading regulations by dumping $848,000 worth of stock in the Harken Energy Company. Brother Prescott held a highly paid job as adviser to a Tokyo investment firm identified by Japanese police as a front for mob activities. Brother Jonathan's 1991 violation of Connecticut and Massachusetts security laws resulted in a relatively minor fine of $30,000.[5]

And shortly into his administration, Bill Clinton was plagued, not only by his own Whitewater investigation, but by probes into three of his appointed cabinet officials: Ron Brown (Secretary of Commerce), Henry Cisneros (Housing and Urban Development), and Mike Espy (Agriculture).

Political corruption has been part of the governmental scene since humans first began to gather in tribal councils. Criminal activity in the U.S. House of Representatives and the Senate has been going on for two hundred years. According to the *Congressional Quarterly*, a total of 91 members of Congress have been indicted since 1798 on a variety of criminal charges.[6] Two-thirds of these congressional indictments have occurred since 1960.

We can trace much of our current societal cynicism back to the political perversions of the 1960s and 1970s. Starting with the Johnson administration's lies to the public about our involvement in Vietnam, the White House has gotten bogged down in ever more serious deceptions and illicit activities. From Watergate to the Whitewater Affair, the people have hesitated to believe much of anything their chief executive tells them.

During the Reagan administration, the instances of wrong-doing escalated immensely: the Pentagon procurement uproar (cheating American taxpayers out of billions of tax dollars); the collapse of the savings and loan associations (which Mortimer Zuckerman, chair of *U.S. News and World Report*, called "the biggest financial scandal in American history");[7] the Bank of Credit and Commerce International debacle (involved with international terrorism, drug-money laundering, and domestic fraud); the Iran-Contra scandal (carried over throughout the Bush administration); and the Department of Housing and Urban Affairs influence-peddling (which "has joined the $300 billion savings-and-loan bailout and the ongoing Pentagon procurement investigation as a legacy of the freebooting Reagan years").[8]

Political corruption is not exclusive to the United States, of course. Many European countries have experienced their share of scandals over the past half century. Britain, France, and Germany all have their tales of dissolution. In recent years, governments in Italy, Japan, South Korea, and Mexico have collapsed as successive heads of state have been involved in scandals that make American transgressions look like college pranks.

Reflecting on the relationship between the public malaise and the nature of contemporary politics, David Brinkley in a 1992 interview looked back on his thirty-six years in front of the national news cameras and commented, "This country is really turned off on politics and politicians . . . and I know why. Because [the American people] have been lied to so much, and deceived so much. Cheated. Abused. Taken advantage of by pols. It would be surprising if they weren't turned off. They deserve to be turned off. I'm turned off."[9]

Weakening of Authority

Starting in the 1960s, two related information phenomena have contributed to a weakening of political authority and stability. One is the exposure of "backstage behaviors," putting everybody's business on display in public. The second is the widespread sharing of information among political leaders and the citizenry.

Exposure of Backstage Behaviors. Thanks to television, viewers now see what goes on in the back corridors of the police precinct, the corporate offices of law firms, the operating rooms of hospitals. Children now hear what parents are talking about in their bedrooms. Voters know what politicians are up to in their back rooms, what deals are being made in the halls of Congress. The previously hidden backstage worlds of different professions, sexes, races, and age groups are now brought into everybody's living rooms through the TV tube. We are saturated with images of what these people are doing when they are not on stage dealing with the public.[10]

Everybody in the tribe knows what everyone else is doing. Nothing is sacred; there are no remnants of any priestly or mysterious roles in our society. Everything becomes part of our public experience. Our post-intellectual loss of privacy extends to the backstage worlds of elected officials, celebrities, and business leaders. We have lost the distance between ordinary citizens and our public officials. We weaken the effectiveness of our elected leaders by encouraging an informality and familiarity that undermines their authority. Joshua Meyrowitz points out that,

> The current drive toward intimacy with our leaders involves a fundamental paradox. In pursuing our desire to be "close" to great people or to confirm their greatness through increased exposure, we often destroy their ability to function as great people. "Greatness" manifests itself in the onstage performance and, by definition, in its isolation from backstage behaviors.[11]

The more intimately we know our leaders, the more trouble we have maintaining a sense of awe and respect.

We have difficulty keeping our leaders on a pedestal when we see Lyndon Johnson showing us the scars of his abdominal operation, when we hear Richard Nixon's obscenities on the Watergate tapes, when we are invited into Gerry Ford's kitchen to watch him prepare breakfast, when we watch Bill Clinton answering questions about his undershorts on MTV. In the past, the public was shielded from the womanizing of Washington and Jefferson, the depression of Lincoln, and even the crippled physical condition of Franklin Roosevelt. Today, no intimacies are kept from the television lens.

We want strong powerful leadership—which demands a certain amount of reverence and mystery—but we also want open, fully accessible administrations. We cannot have both. And in recent years, thanks in large part to the probing and intimate nature of television, we have chosen the latter.

Sharing of Information. Those who have access to data and control of information sources have the power to make the best decisions, to solve their problems, to come out on top. *Information is power.* Conversely, by sharing all information equally among everyone, *no one has control.* Too much information access equals anarchy! If everyone has access to all the information, then all the people think that they know all the answers, that they can make all the right decisions.

Universal access to information weakens authority. Everywhere we turn we see increasing evidence of the breakdown of traditional control. Thanks to the immediacy of television, citizens now observe events firsthand—the dismantling of the Berlin Wall, the Los Angeles riots, the starving masses from Rwanda, the Oklahoma City bombing. Television viewers following the O. J. Simpson trial knew they had more information than the jurors themselves had; therefore the verdict was not acceptable.

We do not rely on our leaders to tell us what happened (they were watching CNN the same time that we were). Anchors Brokaw, Jennings, Rather, Shaw, and Lehrer have already showed us the event. Brinkley and Moyers have already analyzed the event for us. Increasingly, we do not believe what our leaders tell us about involvement in foreign countries, the safety of nuclear reactors, the dangers of certain drugs, the security of our economic system. We have too much information from other sources to accept the official line.

Gallup and Harris polls confirm that the American people have been consistently losing faith in their leaders in all fields. A 1993 report summarizes this trend: "The number of people saying they have a 'great deal' or 'a lot' of confidence in Congress, organized religion, the Supreme Court, public schools, big business and organized labor have all declined in those polls over the last 20 or 25 years."[12] How much of this loss of faith is correlated with the fact that we ordinary citizens are able to accumulate more and more information about what is going on in these fields?

Meyrowitz writes that this weakening of authority leaves us with a peculiar social enfeeblement.

Our increasingly complex technological and social world has made us rely more and more heavily on "expert information," but the general exposure of "experts" as fallible human beings has lessened our faith in them as people. The change in our image of leaders and experts leaves us with a distrust of power, but also with a seemingly powerless dependence on those in whom we have little trust.[13]

We entrust ourselves to Big Brother; but at the same time, we sense that Big Brother does not know any more than we do. Now that we have more access to information, do we have the confidence and the knowledge to know what to do with that dispersed power? Are we really intelligent and responsible enough to make the best decisions on our own? What do we do with the presidency once we have enervated or even dethroned the president? We have unmasked the Wizard of Oz. Where do we turn now for inspiration and guidance?

EMERGENCE OF CORPORATE GOVERNANCE

One major quandary is the intrinsic conflict between civic responsibilities and capitalistic motives. Much is said about the interrelatedness of democracy, capitalism, freedom, competition, and materialistic rewards. In the real world, however, the idealism of John Locke does not always fit hand-in-glove with the profit motives of Adam Smith.

This contradiction was apparent from the early years of the Republic. Roger Boesche writes, "It is difficult, Tocqueville concluded, to be simultaneously self-less citizen and self-seeking businessman."[14] The dedicated citizen must exercise the wisdom and responsibility to make decisions for the betterment of all society, thirty or fifty years into the future. The business executive, on the other hand, must be concerned with maximum profits for the next financial quarter—both for his or her own success and for the well-being of the stockholders. In attempting to strike the appropriate balance between these conflicting aims, most often the corporate interests win out.

Therefore, one of the most irksome issues we face is the intertwined nature of politics and Big Money—the symbiosis of government and Corporate America. Neil Postman comments that "the Founding Fathers did not foresee that tyranny by government might be superseded by another sort of problem altogether, namely, the corporate state."[15]

Government-Corporate Fusion

Self-government in America is governance by corporate interests. In effect, we have but one political party in the United States—the "Corporate Party"—with its Democrat and Republican factions. This control of government by big business (as introduced in Chapter 10) is a clear manifestation of distended intellectualism—an extension of free enterprise thinking without long-term societal responsibility or intellectual guidance.

One explanation for the corruption during the Reagan years (it is estimated that over one hundred high-level Reagan appointees came under suspicion and/or were forced to leave office during his two terms) was that Reagan was committed totally to the American business ethic—an unfettered *capitalistic, business-as-usual, profits-above-all-else, money-making-as-the-highest-good,* mindset. Therefore, a substantial percentage of his political appointments came from the corporate community—men and women schooled in the arts of making money, entrepreneurs whose primary motive had always been greed, those who would seize on any opportunity for personal enrichment. These were the success stories that Reagan wanted repeated in his administration.

Reagan's clear economic philosophy echoed the words of Charles Wilson, secretary of defense under Eisenhower: "What is good for the country is good for General Motors, and what's good for General Motors is good for the country."[16] This injection of business thinking and corporate greed into the political arena undoubtedly opens the doors to many more opportunities for gluttony and duplicity. In 1967 John Kenneth Galbraith was issuing the warning,

The industrial system, in fact, is inextricably associated with the state. In notable respects the mature corporation is an arm of the state. And the state, in important matters, is an instrument of the industrial system. This runs strongly counter to the accepted doctrine that assumes and affirms a clear line between government and private business enterprise.[17]

As our economic interests and governmental concerns become ever more entwined, we tend to lose sight of any value system other than the profit-oriented. Every social program is defined in terms of economic good. Our defense program becomes essentially a security blanket for the military-industrial complex. Our education system is judged by its success in making us economically competitive; students are viewed primarily as potential employees (not as potential citizens). Our homeless problem is defined in terms of how many bodies we can rehabilitate for the corporate world. All must be defined in terms of the bottom line of the financial profit-and-loss sheet.

In researching ancient Greece, author Joseph Heller came to some disturbing conclusions about our earliest democracy:

I found that as democracy was instituted, Athens became more chaotic, more corrupt, more warlike. . . . Commerce was important to Athens, so business leaders obtained control of the political machinery, and Athens became more and more warlike. . . . The government of Athens was completely chaotic from the time businessmen took over with the death of Pericles.[18]

The world's first democracy culminated in the same corporate-governmental death grip in which we find ourselves locked today.

Lobbyists and Special-Interest Groups

The influence of Washington (and state) lobbyists is one of the greatest indications of a post-intellectual mindset. The danger is that *special interests* are pursued to the detriment of the public *general interest*. A government cannot concern itself adequately with the pursuit of the general interest of the nation if it is constantly being splintered by hundreds of special-interest forces. Prior to the establishment of our Republic, Rousseau wrote,

When factions arise, and partial associations are formed at the expense of the great association [the State] . . . it may then be said that there are no longer as many votes as there are men, but only as many as there are associations. . . . It is therefore essential, if the general will is to be able to express itself, that there should be no partial society within the State, and that each citizen should think only his own thoughts.[19]

The writers of the Constitution envisioned a system in which enlightened citizens would be able intellectually to subordinate their immediate special interests in favor of the long-term best interests of the country as a whole. The ability to consider the greatest general good for the republic is an intellectual abstraction; to concern oneself primarily with special interests is a post-intellectual abdication of this democratic responsibility.

The monetary connection between corporate interests and politicians grows ever tighter. The problem was already so pervasive by 1935 that Senator (later to be Supreme Court Justice) Hugo Black declared: "The lobby has reached such a position of power that it threatens government itself. Its size, its power, its capacity for evil, its greed, trickery, deception and fraud condemn it to the death it deserves."[20] By 1993, Jeffrey Birnbaum was able to document the activities of a lobbying industry that had grown to some 80,000 persons (double what it was just ten years earlier).[21] Other sources claim there were over 90,000 paid lobbyists by 1994.

Fund-Raising Realities. The Federal Election Commission reports that more than $15 million was pumped into the 1992 campaigns by the six largest Political Action Committees (PACs)—National Association of Realtors, American Medical Association, International Brotherhood of Teamsters, Association of Trial Lawyers, National Education Association, and the United Auto Workers.

Perhaps the most insidious aspect of the government-corporate fusion is the fact that the one quality that defines successful politicians is their ability to raise funds from large business operations—and thus are held hostage to those financial interests. In an insightful column, Gore Vidal asks if these are the public officials who can best represent the interests of the individual citizen.

> Every four years the naive half who vote are encouraged to believe that if we can elect a really nice man or woman President, everything will be all right. But it won't be. *Any individual who is able to raise $25 million to be considered presidential is not going to be much use to the people at large. He will represent oil, or aerospace, or banking, or whatever moneyed entities are paying for him.* Certainly he will never represent the people of the country, and they know it. Hence, the sense of despair throughout the land as incomes fall, businesses fail and there is no redress [italics added].[22]

The government is becoming ever more estranged from its citizens while at the same time becoming more inextricably identified with corporate interests. Edward Abbey observes, "We call our system a 'representative democracy' but in fact our representatives, with honorable exceptions here and there, represent not the voters but those who finance their election campaigns."[23] We have evolved into a system of government by special interests. Establishmentism. Specialization. This is not an intellectual system.

EMERGENCE OF THE DYSFUNCTIONAL CITIZENRY

William Lederer writes over thirty years ago: "This is the law of functioning democracies. A nation operates honestly and well as long as citizens show interest. But when citizens become apathetic, then dictatorship, ignorance, and national decline take over."[24] To what extent has a dysfunctional citizenry emerged in contemporary America?

Political Perplexities and Soothing Images

At the beginning of the intellectual age, the average adult could be expected to understand his or her political environment—the economic institutions one had to deal with, the functions of an educational system, the governmental choices to be made. The voter was able to maintain a broad perspective; the typical citizen could still comprehend foreign policies and scientific advancements. But in our specialized, post-intellectual web culture, the issues and complexities overwhelm even the most conscientious citizen. How are we mere citizens to figure it all out?

In the midst of the 1992 presidential campaign, a survey by the Times Mirror Center for the People and the Press revealed that "About one-third of late-night viewers under 30 say they learn about the Presidential election from jokes told by stand-up comics."[25] We turn to television sketches, tabloid exaggerations, and sound-bite summaries to make our political decisions. Postman points out the dangers in relying on such pictorial representations:

On television, discourse is conducted largely through visual imagery, which is to say that television gives us a conversation in images, not words. . . . Television demands a different kind of content from other media. You cannot do political philosophy on television. Its form works against the content.[26]

Despite the best efforts of Ross Perot and his television charts, if we cannot communicate abstract theories through pictorial media, how then are we to discuss and understand the concepts of democracy, freedom, economics, the judiciary, legislative responsibility, and social reform? These are abstract ideas and they demand deliberation and consideration involving the printed word.

Since we cannot understand the issues, we elect those candidates who *appear* most capable of doing the job for us; we will vote for the leaders who provide us with the most sincere images of honesty, compassion, and competence. Postman continues: "We are not permitted to know who is best at being President or Governor or Senator, but whose image is best in touching and soothing the deep reaches of our discontent."[27] What becomes important in the media news and campaign coverage is not necessarily the *truth* (since that appears to be so difficult for the typical voter to discern for him- or herself) but, rather, *credibility*—the *appearance* of truth.

Thus, every presidential candidate since Harry Truman has used advertising agencies, television producers, public relations specialists, media handlers, image managers, and spin doctors to design the impressions and pictures that will stick in our collective consciousness. Indeed, the only president since Eisenhower to have been elected to two terms and successfully serve a full eight years was an actor. Larry Speaks, spokesperson for the Reagan administration, writes in his book, *Speaking Out,* that Reagan's image was manufactured and manipulated specifically for the pictorial media: "Underlying our whole theory of disseminating information in the White House was our knowledge that the American people get their news and form their judgments based largely on what they see on television. . . . We played entirely to the ratings, and made no bones about it."[28]

In a 1995 article, Fred Grandy, one-time TV star *(The Love Boat)* and former Congressional Representative from Iowa writes:

Running a campaign is now almost entirely a media event. It is primarily a war of attack ads and insidious sound bites designed more to confuse the average voter than to encourage an informed choice. Highly paid consultants who are rapidly becoming more important than the candidates they represent base their battle plans on up-to-the-minute polling data. Long-term solutions to complicated problems are usually sacrificed to the public passion of the moment. Winning is everything.[29]

The Mob's Perspective

In summarizing the American dilemma, Heller states that the Republic's Founding Fathers feared "that the mob—and that's a word they used—would not know how to vote, would not know where their interests lay." However, the opposite problem might be even more threatening: "The other fear was that the mob indeed would know where their interests lay, and they would vote for their interests."[30]

Elected representatives must be responsive to the demands of the electorate (Plato's "motley multitude"). Law professor and ethicist Michael Josephson observes that the people who are voting "are voting on self-interest. They say, 'As long as this guy gets me my piece of the pie, a little bigger than maybe I'm otherwise entitled, I'm putting him back in office.'"[31]

Therefore, elected office holders are driven by *two inevitable realities of popular politics*. First, they must try to get re-elected in just two to six years. Whatever good they intend to accomplish, it must be done within a short-term framework. No one in elected office can afford to consider long-range benefits a couple decades down the road; they must appeal to the voters right now. They may talk about the fouled environmental legacy we are leaving our grandchildren, they may lament the long-term implications of an increasing national debt; but they must appeal to today's voters now!

Second, representative officials must look after the welfare of their provincial constituents—which often are at conflict with the larger needs of society as a whole. Individual voters cannot perceive or identify with the larger abstract concept of society; the intellectual idea of the nation-state becomes increasingly blurry. Thus, we ask our representatives to fight for our local perceived needs—keeping open a military base, increasing our regional agricultural subsidies, building a new bridge or highway in our district, starting a neighborhood job-training program.

The Threat of Electronic Democracy. Political visionaries foresee a media millennium where we will have an electronic democratic forum that enables all citizens to participate in national debates and vote on every important issue on our law-making agenda. Whether it takes the form of a phone-in vote on *Larry King Live,* specialized satellite channels, CBS's *National Town Meeting* format, Ross Perot's electronic town meetings and referendums, interactive cable polling, or dedicated Internet lanes of the information superhighway, we are promised that eventually we will have a true democracy—with every citizen voting on every issue—rather than a republic with representatives handling the decision-making chores for us.

For many thoughtful observers, such a vision conjures up horror scenarios of emotional exploitation, knee-jerk arguments, irrational reactions, sensationalism, and mass manipulation. How can millions of ill-informed and self-centered voters possibly hope to make wise decisions in today's complicated social, scientific and economic environment? I doubt if even John Locke would wish that on a contemporary populace. The format of the New England town meeting of two hundred years ago simply cannot cope with our global entanglements in the late twentieth century.

At the very least, it would result in uninformed parochial legislation. At its worst, it would result in unprecedented control by lobbyists, special interests, and big-money players. Do we really want to try true democracy? Jonathan Alter writes, "The bigger problem is that direct democracy leaves no room for amendment, compromise and all of the other human elements that eventually lead to consensus and movement. Technology helps democracy by eroding secrecy; but technology hurts democracy by eroding reflection and time."[32] Cliff Stoll agrees:

Electronic referenda on current events would further shorten the event horizon for public policy. Instead of political changes every few years, policies would be voted on every few months. This is hardly the path to long-term planning. The electronic constituency would be a most fickle electorate.[33]

The pictorial media have diminished the mob's capacity to engage in sustained debate. Television has returned society to a pre-literate oral culture where we react intuitively and vote for candidates who smile a lot and make comforting promises. Pandering to the post-intellectual electronic electorate dictates that the messages be as cursory and simplistic as possible. Speaking of this trend toward political superficiality, Russell Neuman states "There is very little hope that the situation will improve as a result of improvements in the campaign process and media coverage, because the critical factor appears to be the *cognitive style of the electorate* [italics added]."[34]

We accept entertainers and teleprompter performers as leaders because we cannot handle complicated issues; we are uncomfortable with ideas and messages of substance. We want comforting images and soothing words of reassurance. We do not want our political candidates to explain intricate issues to us; we want to see them chatting on the *Today* show or clowning around with David Letterman. Postman sardonically observes, "Big Brother turns out to be Howdy Doody."[35]

The Growing Voter Apathy

The greater threat, however, is not that the citizens will clog up the machinery of the state by pursuing their parochial interests, but that they will give up entirely on trying to work with the machinery. They do not know how the machinery works. They are not sure what it is supposed to do. They do not know how to maintain it. And it is too much trouble to figure it all out.

We cling to the illusion of a participatory democracy in which an intellectual citizenry determines the direction of the government. In actuality, large numbers of the electorate rarely or never participate in the political system. The overall picture is one of increasing disenchantment with the political system. As Neuman succinctly sums up the situation, "Apathy dominates American mass politics."[36] To an increasing extent, moreover, the apathy turns to cynicism. Peggy Noonan, speech writer for Ronald Reagan and George Bush, sums up the attitude of many: "The voters think Washington is a whorehouse and every four years they get a chance to elect a new piano player."[37]

Research indicates that only about 15 percent of the electorate has ever written to their senators or legislative representatives. In fact, only 3 percent of the population accounts for two-thirds of all congressional mail.[38] And the situation promises to get no better with the upcoming electorate. Writing in *Newsweek* about his age group *(Generation X)*, twenty-two-year-old journalist Jonathan Cohn proclaims, "The problem is our perception of the political process itself. We see no connection between our concerns and the ballot box. National politics, for my generation, has become irrelevant."[39]

The most telling statistic, of course, is the percentage of voters turning out for elections. Except for presidential elections, well under half of the eligible voters show up at the polls. (The comparable figures for most European democracies average about 85 to 90 percent.) The percentage of the electorate that participates in the process is decreasing yearly.[40] Since 1960, when 62.8 percent of the eligible voters participated in the Kennedy-Nixon election, the percentage has decreased fairly regularly in almost every presidential election—declining to 50.2 percent in the 1988 Bush-Dukakis contest.[*]

At the local level, where voters can have the most relative impact, the percentage of citizens who are uninvolved is even more disturbing. For example, in April 1989, 23 percent of the registered voters in Los Angeles went to the polls to elect a mayor. This was during a period when the incumbent, Tom Bradley, was coming under increasing criticism for his role in several questionable banking relationships involving potential conflicts of interest. He was barely re-elected—with 52 percent of the votes cast. This means he was returned to office because about 12 percent of the populace voted for him!

The world gets more complex, the issues get increasingly arcane, the in-

---

[*] The increase in the voter turnout for the 1992 presidential election—up to 55.9 percent—can be attributed largely to the novel stimulus of the candidacy of Ross Perot.

stitutional technologies proliferate, the bureaucracies handle the maintenance of society for us, and the specialists assume more responsibility for running our lives. So we kick back, turn to our escapist media, and invite destiny to wash over us. We succumb to the three underlying determinants of the web culture—the failure of linear growth, the information overload, and technological determinism. Rousseau observes, "As soon as any man says of the affairs of the State *What does it matter to me?* the State may be given up for lost."[41] It is this disengagement of the populace that helps define our post-intellectual age.

NOTES

1. Lukacs, 1984, p. 7.
2. Lapham, 1990, p. 48.
3. Tuchman, 1984, p. 19.
4. Stanley Meisler, "Panama: Colonized and Corrupted," *Los Angeles Times,* 7 January 1990, p. M1.
5. This family portrait was compiled by Garry Trudeau, "Believe It. Not!" *New York Times*, 27 March 1992, p. A35.
6. See "Indictments—A Grand Congressional Tradition Since 1798." *Los Angeles Times,* 5 June 1994, pp. M2, M5.
7. Quoted in Richard Reeves, "They're Turning to a Minor to Deal With a Major Mess," *Los Angeles Times,* 19 April 1990, p. B17.
8. Nancy Traver, "Sam Pierce's 'Turkey Farm,'" *Time,* 18 September 1989, p. 20.
9. Quoted in Thomas B. Rosenstiel, "The Pol Watcher," *Los Angeles Times,* 20 August 1992, p. F1.
10. For a full discussion of this phenomenon, see Meyrowitz, 1985.
11. Ibid., p. 167.
12. David Shaw, "Distrustful Public Views Media as 'Them'—Not 'Us,'" *Los Angeles Times,* 1 April 1993, p. A18.
13. Meyrowitz, 1985, p. 324.
14. Boesche, 1994.
15. Postman, 1985, p. 139.
16. Charles Wilson, Testimony before the Senate Armed Forces Committee, 1952, quoted in *Bartlett's Familiar Quotations,* 1980, p. 817.
17. Galbraith, 1967, p. 304.
18. Quoted in Moyers, 1989, pp. 30–31.
19. Rousseau [1762], book 2, ch. 3 , 1952, p. 396.
20. Quoted in Rauch, 1994, p. 36.
21. See Birnbaum, 1993.
22. Gore Vidal, "Who Says the Republic Still Stands?" *Los Angeles Times,* 15 January 1992, p. B11.
23. Abbey, 1988, p. 169.
24. Lederer, 1961, p. 183.
25. "Scariest Statistic," *TV Guide*, 20 June 1992, p. 17.
26. Postman, 1985, p. 7.
27. Ibid., p. 135.

28. Quoted in Howard Rosenberg, "Keeping the Image Intact," *Los Angeles Times,* 20 April 1988, Calendar sect., pp. 1, 7.

29. Fred Grandy, "Re: My Capitol," *TV Guide,* 11 March 1995, p. 19.

30. Quoted in Moyers, 1989, p. 32.

31. Ibid., p. 25.

32. Jonathan Alter, "The Couch Potato Vote," *Newsweek,* 27 February 1995, p. 34.

33. Stoll, 1995, p. 33.

34. Neuman, 1986, p. 27.

35. Postman, 1985, p. 111.

36. Neuman, 1986, p. 9.

37. Noonan, 1992, p. 68.

38. Dye and Zeigler, 1978, p. 274.

39. Jonathan S. Cohn, "Can Clinton Rock the Vote?" *Newsweek,* 20 July 1992, p. 10.

40. Figures are taken from *Technical Report Number One: Federal Election Statistics* (Washington, DC: Federal Election Commission, Office of Election Administration: May 1995).

41. Rousseau [1762], book 3, ch. 15, 1952, p. 421.

16

Control and Manipulation: Alternatives to Anarchy

The body politic, as well as the human body,
begins to die as soon as it is born,
and carries in itself the causes of its destruction.

> • Jean Jacques Rousseau
> *The Social Contract*

In late 1991, Mikhail Gorbachev presided over the gradual dismemberment of the Soviet Union. He was replaced on the international scene by Boris Yeltsin, who assumed the burden of reform, only on a smaller scale—trying to hold together the pieces in his Russian republic. Within two years, however, Yeltsin saw his own nation besieged by the same tribal fragmentation that had destroyed the USSR.

In our own country, democracy today is but a shell of the idealism of the republic's founders. Writer Peter Leyden states, "It's become a standard lament among Americans of all political persuasions that our federal government simply does not work. No one seems to be able to figure a way out of the legislative gridlock and general paralysis."[1]

Maybe the Enlightenment was an aberration. Maybe the idea of human beings coming together to form large self-governing units—larger than community or tribal groupings—is too much of an intellectual leap. It demands that we think in abstract social contracts. It involves more of an intellectual commitment to long-range goals and a global perspective than we have been able to muster. Our institutions carry on by tradition. Institutional Momentum (Chapter 8) has perpetuated the illusion of a participatory democracy for the last half-century or so. The institutions, the bureaucracy, the technologies still stand. But for how long?

In today's post-intellectual retribalized culture, it is increasingly difficult to preserve any kind of stable government—communist or democratic. Rousseau explained over two hundred years ago that "The body politic, as well as the human body, begins to die as soon as it is born, and carries in itself the causes of its destruction."[2]

The sobering realization is that as society grows increasingly complex and as individual citizens increasingly accept less responsibility for self-government, we will have to rely more and more on big government for any semblance of order and security. But the irony of the late twentieth century is that elitist and authoritarian alternatives to representative government also flounder in the murky shoals of post-intellectualism.

Resurgent tribalism, widespread pictorial media, the end of linear growth and expansion, and the debilitating confusion of technological determinism all conspire to undermine any attempt at large-scale governance. Marshall McLuhan and Quentin Fiore observe simply, "The old civic, state, and national groupings have become unworkable."[3] But even as we grasp at governmental alternatives to democracy, other avenues of control and manipulation hover menacingly on the horizon.

ELITISM AND THE ILLUSION OF DEMOCRACY

Elitism has long been recognized as the de facto *modus operandi* throughout the globe. Writing in 1939, Gaetano Mosca defines this political reality: "In all societies, from societies that are very underdeveloped . . . down to the most advanced and powerful societies, two classes of people appear—a class that rules and a class that is ruled."[4]

Elitism in America

Only a small percentage of the American populace is really involved in political activities. Russell Neuman cites numerous research studies that explain "the theory of three publics." The bottom stratum of the public, about 20 percent, is an "abashedly apolitical lot." They have little idea as to what is going on; they do not care; they do not vote. The middle stratum, about 75 percent of the electorate, is "marginally attentive to politics." They may be aware of one or two issues that they consider personally important; they have but a superficial idea as to the actual debate over the issues; they may or may not vote in any given election. The upper stratum, the remaining 5 percent of the citizenry, are the political activists who "exhibit uniquely high levels of political involvement."[5]

This small group of political activists—highly motivated, well educated, and perpetually involved—are the movers and shapers, the opinion leaders who debate, twist arms, and mold our positions. They are the government officials, lobbyists, media moguls, educators, captains of industry, journalists, financial decision-makers, intellectual writers and researchers, influential celebrities, representatives of major movements (religious organizations, labor unions, environmental groups), and others who are most directly involved in the management of society. These are the political elites who run the country.

Thomas Dye and L. Harmon Zeigler begin their book, *The Irony of Democracy,* with the statement, "Elites, not masses, govern America."[6] They go on to describe the manner in which elitism in America functions:

> Democracy is government "by the people," but the survival of democracy in fact rests on the shoulders of elites. This is the irony of democracy: Elites must govern wisely if government "by the people" is to survive. If the survival of the American system depended on the existence of an active, informed, and enlightened citizenry, then democracy in America would have disappeared long ago; for the masses of America are apathetic and ill-informed about politics and public policy.[7]

Democracy survives because the elites, the handful of activists and idealists who make the system work, continue to defend the rights of the masses to enjoy the fruits and freedoms of representative government.

In terms of our post-intellectual paradigm, there is one important characteristic of political elitism in America: The *elites do not want to rock the boat*—this is the very definition of establishmentism. Elitism, is to that extent, an anti-intellectual phenomenon; meaningful social criticism and change come slowly and grudgingly. Lewis Lapham, in *The Wish for Kings,* describes this "presiding oligarchy" as "united in their devotion to the systems in place and the wisdom in office."[8]

Elites and the Media

The elites, in carrying out their problem-solving and decision-making responsibilities, must have the necessary information on which to base their decisions. As our societal issues become increasingly complex, it becomes more and more difficult for even the sophisticated elites to keep up with the technological and political environments that they are attempting to control. Where are the elites to get their information? Where are the conduits designed to keep the flow of substantial information circulating to the decision-making oligarchs?

There are three related questions. First, can the exclusive elitist channels— the academic journals, research reports, investment newsletters, trade magazines, and professional publications—carry enough material of a *broad perspective* to satisfy the needs for responsible decision-making? These channels are of necessity so specialized that they do not provide much of a common foundation for various elitist sub-groups to share a collective database in their self-governing efforts. How do the architect, chemical engineer, corporate lawyer, and brain surgeon get together to debate Third World debt policies?

Second, can those media channels that are shared by the elites and the populace provide enough substantial information if they must cater to the masses to any extent? After all, PBS stations still have to attract a large audience; the

Wall Street Journal has to reach enough readers to turn a profit. News magazines such as *Time* and *Newsweek* are but shadows of their former content; intellectual organs such as *Atlantic Monthly* have substantially reduced their in-depth analyses. Neil Postman writes, "*Harper's*, for example, has reduced the length of its stories and articles to suit its readers' impaired capacity for sustained concentration."[9] The *Christian Science Monitor* cut back substantially on its content and coverage in order to funnel more resources into its television operations.

Third—and this is a worrisome consideration—are today's elites as intellectual as their counterparts of two hundred years ago? How does the intellectual caliber of today's elites—the corporate kingpins and political manipulators—compare with the intellect of the political philosophers and idealists who founded the system? Are today's leaders as intellectual, as broad-minded, as far-sighted, as they need to be to run today's increasingly complex civilization? I am not questioning their intelligence or expertise or marketing savvy; but I am asking if they have the perspective and the intellectual breadth to grasp the totality of our contemporary environment—and the courage and responsibility to make decisions "for the seventh generation."

The bottom-line question therefore is, Can the elites—the activists and decision-makers who run the system—continue to govern wisely? The need to process ever-increasing amounts of ever-more sophisticated information will continue to escalate. What happens when the elites no longer are making responsible decisions? (Are they making responsible decisions today?)

THE AUTHORITARIAN ALTERNATIVE

Elitism pushed one step further becomes authoritarianism—the classic antithesis of libertarianism: *Human beings are essentially weak, ignorant, self-centered, dishonest, and driven by irrational emotional lusts; so therefore, a strong central authority is needed to govern the affairs of mankind.* We abdicate our intellectual responsibilities, we use the media primarily to keep ourselves anesthetized, we ask that society's problems be handled by the specialists and technocrats—we have already given up on running our own affairs. This is the essence of authoritarianism.

Robert Heilbroner foresees the possibility that democratic societies in the future may deliberately choose authoritarian regimes in order to better cope with the economic and environmental complexities of our technological culture: "If the issue for mankind is survival, such governments may be unavoidable, even necessary."[10] Recall that Adolph Hitler was freely elected into power by the people—people desperate for order and certainty. In the mid-1990s we see a resurgence of communist and ex-communist leaders winning elections in Russia, Belarus, Ukraine, Bulgaria, Poland, and Hungary. *Doonesbury* cartoonist Garry Trudeau has his character Duke proclaim, "It's happening all over the world—

dysfunctional peoples desperate for leaders who can deliver order, stability and—most important—scapegoats!"[11]

We decide to place ourselves in a *civil zoo* for safekeeping (letting the zookeeper/politicians look after us) rather than fighting to maintain our freedom in the *libertarian jungle* (where we would have to assume responsibility for our own well-being). This is the essence of the Freedom Dilemma (Chapter 14): a free people, when given the choice, will prefer to have someone else handle the responsibility for their lives rather than face the burdens of self-determination and independence; we willingly choose slavery over freedom.

Insidious Acceptance of Authoritarianism

People welcome and encourage the subtle incursion of authoritarianism—under the guise of security and convenience. We readily give up our independence and freedom of opportunity in return for product subsidies, protective tariffs, welfare programs, and more law enforcement. Robert Ekelund and Robert Hebert remind us that the state

derives its power and its existence from the fact that human beings are either incapable or unwilling to face head-on the problems that confront them in daily social interaction with one another. Over time, this monolithic structure called the "state" increases its power over people's lives, simply because *they allow it to do so* [italics added].[12]

Our political history during the twentieth century, certainly from the New Deal on, has been one of gradual acceptance of more and more federal intervention and control—expanding social programs, federal involvement in local education, government-sponsored research, affirmative action and equal opportunity programs, federal standards and bureaucratic regulation in all spheres of our daily community and business lives. James Madison warned us over two hundred years ago: "I believe there are more instances of the abridgement of freedom of the people by gradual and silent encroachments of those in power than by violent and sudden usurpations."[13]

As society digs itself deeper and deeper into a post-intellectual funk, it becomes more and more dependent upon the welfare state, the leadership of the specialists, and the perpetuation of the establishment. However, as Michael Novak writes, Benevolent Big Brother no longer can deliver on his promises: "Today, nearly all the world's social democracies and welfare states are in severe crisis. . . . Weighed down by the growing financial burden of the welfare state, and undermined by the moral corruption inherent in such a state, democracy will be hard-pressed to survive in the 21st century."[14]

Media and the Breakdown of Authoritarianism

The irony is that just as post-intellectual media may render democracy no longer feasible *(The Freedom Dilemma)*, so too might an abundance of media channels make authoritarianism untenable. We have seen numerous peoples' uprisings in the past couple decades. All were facilitated to some extent by increased access of the people—both as newsmakers and as consumers—to the media: international television, satellite broadcasting, shortwave radio (Radio Free Europe, Radio Liberty, the Voice of America, the BBC radio services), videotape machines, underground newspapers (an estimated 500 in communist Poland), camcorders, photocopiers, fax machines, and the computer. John Steinbruner observes simply, "Radical changes in the processing and transmission of information are restructuring economic and political patterns throughout the world."[15]

The people have access to too much information, too many channels of diversity, too many conflicting voices. Authoritarianism can succeed only when the flow of information can be controlled. Joshua Meyrowitz points out that the information transformation involves, not only access to sources of information previously kept from the masses (Chapter 15), but also the sharing of information horizontally by personal communication technologies such as the telephone and computer: "Such horizontal flow of information is another significant deterrent to totalitarian central leadership."[16]

The paradoxical consequence of a media-saturated post-intellectual culture is that an abundance of political information empowers the citizen, thus making totalitarianism impossible. *Television has made authoritarianism unacceptable.* But simultaneously, freedom allows people to immerse themselves in too much trivial information, thus making self-government impossible. *Television has made democracy unsustainable.*

By giving the people too many pictures, too much inside information, too much gossip and political half-truths—as well as too much diversion and trivia—*modern information media have made governance on a large scale hopeless!* We experience chaos. We return to a tribal state. Maybe.

INFORMATION CONTROL AND MANIPULATION

If any type of large-scale nation-state is to survive—democratic, elitist, or authoritarian—those who would attempt to govern must try to control and manipulate our information technologies. The more information that exists, the more it must be edited and structured to help us cope with our environment. Thus, we must rely ever more heavily on our *information-control systems*—which are themselves breaking down (Chapter 3).

However, the more we have to rely on others to edit our information, the more difficult it is for us to determine our own destiny. If individuals have to turn to outside agencies for assistance in coping with their personal information overloads—a favorite TV guru, church, schooling system, labor union, lobbying group, family, or government bureaucrat—they are surrendering some portion of their independence.

Think about your own sources of information. How do you find out about what is going on in Washington or Tokyo? The advantages and drawbacks of nuclear energy? Benefits of vitamin supplements? The direction of Latin American politics? Today's best investments? The impact of genetic engineering? The size of corporate profits? Consider who controls your sources of information on all these topics. Your parents? Teachers? Minister/priest/rabbi? Advertisers? Friends and fellow workers? Corporate PR officers? Administration bureaucrats? The mass press? Government censors? Whoever controls your information controls your way of thinking and your patterns of behavior. Back to Francis Bacon: *Information is power!*

If, for example, I were to have absolute control over your channels of information, I would have absolute power over your every action. If I could dictate what media you have access to—magazine articles, books, the movies you see, the news reports you hear, the lectures you would attend—you would be exposed only to my version of truth. You would know nothing except as it is filtered through me. You could make no independent decision about any aspect of your life—the clothes you wear, the places you would want to visit, the friends you would have, your opinions of Bill Clinton or Bob Dole, the very way you think. This is what brainwashing is all about—controlling all decision-making options. This is what cult living is. This is the basis of religious intolerance, nationalistic jingoism. You could never be aware of any value systems or courses of action except what I let you know about. *Information is control.*

This is one of the incongruities of the post-intellectual society. We cannot cope on our own and expect to comprehend everything. Neither can we rely on others to digest our information for us and expect to maintain our independence. With the promise of the information superhighway and the flood of electronic data into every sphere of our lives, the danger of information anarchy becomes even greater. And the need for more government intervention and control looms ever larger.

Marginalizing the Populace

Government agencies today employ a variety of devices to manage and manipulate our information sources: press conferences, news releases, controlled interviews, staged pseudo-events, classifying information, trial balloons, deliberate administration leaks, spin doctors, formal agency briefings, off-the-record briefings, official government reports, photo opportunities, press pools (to cover the invasions of Panama and Iraq), and so forth. The government's public relations front is a massive undertaking—one that can scarcely be countered by independent media channels or the underfunded efforts of non-profit environmental or peace groups. For example, during the Reagan years, the Pentagon's public relations operation ballooned to a $100 million annual budget and a staff of over 3,000, "which bombarded the American public and much of the world with endless rounds of official information."[17]

Theodore Roszak explains how information overload can be manipulated by establishment authorities to maintain their control.

Data glut is not some unforeseen, accidental fluctuation of supply, like a bumper crop of wheat. It is a strategy of social control, deliberately and often expertly wielded. It is one of the main ways in which modern governments and interest groups obfuscate issues to their own advantage; they dazzle and distract with more raw data than the citizenry can hope to sort through.[18]

Noam Chomsky sums up the attitude of those in control at the White House: "The Reagan Administration had a massive enterprise to control the public mind. In fact, when this was partially exposed during the Iran-Contra hearings, one high Administration official described it as the kind of operation that you carry out in enemy territory. That expresses the Administration's attitude toward the population—the population is the enemy."[19] Chomsky calls this the *marginalizing* of the general population—reducing voters to lethargy and obedience, allowing them to take part in the political system, but as spectators and consumers, not as true participants.

This has long been a technique of those concerned with brainwashing and mind control; keep each person isolated and quarantined from unauthorized information sources. Do not allow individual citizens, cult members, customers, patients, students, clients, or party members to have access to the same sources of information that those in control have. Keep all the fragmented specialists from coming into contact with each other; do not let anyone see the whole picture. Albert Speer points out how Hitler used this approach of isolation and information control within the Nazi party:

The ordinary party member was being taught that grand policy was much too complex for him to judge it. . . . Worse still was the restriction of responsibility to one's own field. . . . Everyone kept to his own group—of architects, physicians, jurists, technicians, soldiers, or farmers. The professional organizations to which everyone had to belong were called chambers (Physicians' Chamber, Art Chamber), and this term aptly described the way people were immured in isolated, closed-off areas of life. The longer Hitler's system lasted, the more people's minds moved within such isolated chambers. . . . What eventually developed was a society of totally isolated individuals.[20]

As government bureaucrats and technocrats intrude into more nooks and crannies of our daily existence, we are left increasingly defenseless. *They* know more than we do about what is good for us. We are debilitated by the expertise of the specialists who turn to their computers and data banks to confirm and sanctify their decisions and directions. We are told we do not have access to the fountains of knowledge. We do not have the expertise nor the information to make intelligent decisions.

The Computer as World Sysop

Jeremy Rifkin writes that "Computer programs introduce a new level of determinism into the social process. By automating the unfolding of future events, computer programs leave the individual a passive victim, forced to live within the narrow confines of preprogrammed scenarios laid out for him."[21] The structure of the coming "new world order" might be determined not by government authorities or corporate interests, but by information systems. As we proceed deeper into the computerized information environment, we may find that the information managers will emerge as the ultimate world powers.

The controller or custodian of a computer network or bulletin board is the system-operator—or *sysop*. In the coming World Information Order, Hugh Downs warns, the sysops would be the ultimate totalitarians: "In a very real way, world Sysops would be in a position to . . . hide or reveal information to whomever they chose."[22] As such, the sysops would exert complete control over all facets of our lives—economic and political. Downs continues by pointing out that the global computerized information system will eventually replace government.

The whole idea of governments, nations, and discrete grouping by geography become proportionally irrelevant, as the computer system expands. . . .

More importantly, as power shifts from armed forces and from the ownership of natural resources to information processing, new communities will emerge to control that information. These new communities will be gerrymandered across cyberspace, and across the world, in completely new configurations. Their dominion over certain types of crucial data will elevate these cyber-societies into new world powers; they will be the nation-states of the future—the nation-states of old, the ones we live in today, will wither and die.[23]

GENETIC CONTROL AND MANIPULATION

Finally, one ultimate means of control should be considered. This represents potentially the definitive alternative to anarchy. Vance Packard voiced the attitude of many research technologists and behavioral scientists two decades ago: "People are raw material that needs perfecting, modifying, or at least improving, either for their own good or to suit the wishes of others. Malleable people are more likely to be controllable people."[24] We need to monitor carefully the developments and progress in biotechnology—genetic and biological manipulation. As we abandon our intellectual heritage of self-reliance and individual identity, we must consider this consummate means of control.

Cloning Experiments

One dramatic speculation is that of *parthenogenesis* or cloning. In a 1993 "twinning" experiment—splitting an embryo into many single cells—researchers were able to create 48 identical human embryos. Viewed as a precursor to actual cloning, this experiment suggested that "researchers are approaching the day when they may attempt to alter the genes that control the development of a human embryo, changing the traits that would be passed on."[25] This is akin to what Aldous Huxley called Bokanovsky's Process in *Brave New World:*

> One egg, one embryo, one adul—normality. But a bokanovskified egg will bud, will proliferate, will divide. From eight to ninety-six buds, and every bud will grow into a perfectly formed embryo, and every embryo into a full-sized adult. Making ninety-six human beings grow where only one grew before. Progress.[26]

Huxley, writing in 1932, envisioned it would take us over six centuries to reach this stage. But here we are today. *Progress.*

What are the implications for behavioral control? Markku Linnoila of the National Institutes of Health is searching for "vulnerability genes" that cause low levels of serotonin which have been linked biologically with violent behavior. If such a genetic trigger can be found, how will society use such knowledge for human engineering? If youngsters who are certifiably prone to violence can be identified at an early age, how then will we handle them? Peter Breggin, founder of the Center for the Study of Psychiatry, is one who "envisions a frightening scenario in which government-funded genetic screening programs will label inner-city youngsters at risk for becoming violent, and then dope them up in what he calls 'a massive drugging of America's children.'"[27]

Genetic Half-Breeds

Another chilling possibility is the creation of human-animal halfbreeds or *chimeras.* Since 1989, when the first genetically altered animal cells were successfully implanted into a human being, the genetic creation of "designer animals" has become almost routine: rodents that carry human diseases such as arthritis, AIDS, and sickle-cell anemia; pigs born with human-like blood; dairy cows that produce milk with human proteins. One 1993 report stated that such *transgenic* technology had already resulted in at least 5,000 different strains of genetic chimeras in the past few years.[28]

The rationale for proceeding with gene insertion, like so many other technologies, is for undeniably positive purposes: a bacterium that produces ethanol from sawdust and grass clippings; potatoes that resist certain insects and freezing temperatures; a bacterium-spider hybrid that spits out huge quantities of silk; a fungus hybrid that produces a palatable chocolate substitute; pigs infused with genetically altered human growth hormone to create animals with leaner meat; and microbes that eat up oil spills. Scientists even assure us that they can insert "suicide genes" into these hungry mutant microbes so that "bugs that eat oil slicks would die off before they climbed out of the ocean and into your gas tank."[29] *What could possibly go wrong?*

All these genetic cross-breeds promise great social and medical progress. *Xenotransplantation* will enable medical teams to create transgenic animals with human genes inserted into pig hearts, kidneys, livers, and even brain cells, so that these animal-human organs can then be transplanted into human recipients with less chance of rejection. Successful techniques for freezing spermatogonia (the tissue that produces sperm) facilitate transgenic manipulation so that one species can be used to produce healthy sperm for another species—"although the specter of a mouse producing human sperm for human reproduction purposes triggers skepticism among some."[30]

Another scenario is the possibility of creating human-machine halfbreeds—men and women with computer implants, and androids with human components. Scientists at the Playsair Research Unit of the Toronto Western Hospital have successfully bonded a human neural brain cell, grown in a tissue culture, to a Motorola 68000 microprocessor. As rudimentary a step as this may be, the potential for continuing advances in human-machine interfacing presents incredible implications. *Homo sapiens* may no longer be evolving along an exclusively organic path.

The medical, legal, and religious communities struggle with numerous other issues raised in the late 1980s and early 1990s: Who gains legal custody of frozen embryos? Who has what legal rights when children are born with three or four genetic parents? Should new life forms be patentable? Should a person's genetic map be made available to one's insurance company, employer, or any federal agency? Should parents be able to modify genetic defects of their unborn children?

Increasing Acceptance of Biotechnology

In the Introduction to his book *Jurassic Park,* Michael Crichton paints a sobering picture of our whirlwind advances in biotechnology:

This enterprise has proceeded so rapidly—with so little outside commentary—that its dimensions and implications are hardly understood at all.

Biotechnology promises the greatest revolution in human history. By the end of this decade [the 1990s], it will have outdistanced atomic power and computers in its effect on our everyday lives. In the words of one observer, "Biotechnology is going to transform every aspect of human life: our medical care, our food, our health, our entertainment, our very bodies. Nothing will ever be the same again. It's literally going to change the face of the planet."[31]

One sober consideration is the extent to which the populace accepts this insidious surrender to technology and loss of self-determination. A 1992 Lou Harris poll revealed that 42 percent of American adults is in favor of genetic enhancement of intelligence levels.[32] We accept all manner of manipulation and control in the name of social betterment and advancement. Good purposes all. *Progress.* But we have little control over the long-term impact of what we are doing. We let the wonders and technologies propel themselves forward faster than our reason and common sense can keep up. Thus we surrender ourselves to the seductive pledge of medical miracles and technological paradise. This is our definition of technological determinism.

Bit by bit, byte by byte, gene by gene, we yield our individuality and our autonomy to the enticing promise of a technological Land of Oz—where wizards, scientists, lawyers and bureaucrats can make everything all right. In this post-intellectual wonderland, we can dispense with the pressure to understand science or think critically; we no longer have to negotiate the written word; we no longer need to assume responsibility for our own well being.

NOTES

1. Leyden, 4 June 1995, p. 5T.
2. Rousseau [1762], book 3, ch. 11, 1952, p. 419.
3. McLuhan and Fiore, 1967, p. 16.
4. Mosca, 1939, p. 50.
5. Neuman, 1986, p. 170.
6. Dye and Zeigler, 1978, p. 1.
7. Ibid., p. 2.
8. Lapham, *Wish for Kings,* 1993, p. 11.
9. Postman, 1988, "A Muted Celebration," p. 64.
10. Heilbroner, 1980, p. 130.
11. Garry Trudeau, *Doonesbury*, syndicated 6 February 1994.
12. Ekelund and Hebert, 1983, p. 230.
13. James Madison, Speech in the Virginia Convention, 16 June 1788, quoted in *Bartlett's Familiar Quotations,* 1980, p. 389.
14. Novak, 1994.
15. John D. Steinbruner, "A Crisis of Legitimacy Grips Emerging Commonwealth," *Los Angeles Times,* 22 December 1991, p. M2.
16. Meyrowitz, 1985, p. 322.
17. Lee and Solomon, 1991, p. 105.
18. Roszak, 1994, p. 164.
19. Interviewed in Moyers, 1989, p. 47.
20. Speer, 1971, p. 65.
21. Rifkin, 1987, p. 119.
22. Downs, 1993.
23. Ibid.
24. Packard, 1977, p. 11.
25. Robert Lee Hotz, "Embryo Splitting is Fertile Ground for Ethics Debate," *Los Angeles Times,* 27 October 1993, p. A1.
26. Huxley [1932], 1969, p. 3.
27. Sheryl Stolberg, "Fear Clouds Search for Genetic Roots of Violence," *Los Angeles Times,* 30 December 1993, p. A14.
28. Marla Cone, "The Mouse Wars Turn Furious," *Los Angeles Times,* 9 May 1993, p. A16.
29. Doug Stewart, "These Germs Work Wonders," *Reader's Digest,* January 1991, p. 86.
30. Thomas H. Maugh II, "Sperm Tissue Freezing Seen as Major Advance," *Los Angeles Times,* 30 May 1996, p. A21.
31. Crichton, 1990, p. ix.
32. Reported on Cable News Network (CNN), 21 October 1992.

PART 5

Prognosis:
Future Directions and Considerations

All the dangers we have examined are social problems, originating in human behavior and capable of amelioration by the alteration of that behavior.

● Robert Heilbroner
An Inquiry into the Human Prospect

There is essentially one reason for our present cultural dystopia: we are clinging to the framework of an intellectual society—but we have abandoned the intellectual requisites of reason and responsibility.

We tried a couple centuries ago to institute a society built on collective decision-making, universal liberal arts education of the populace, scientific critical thinking and problem-solving, the search for knowledge, and an economic system based upon rational competition. But we have forsaken the discipline and rigor of the intellectual mind needed to sustain such a society. Our intellectual lassitude today is best suited for a tribal culture, a society devoid of any technological enterprise, ruled by high priests and emperors, dedicated solely to materialism and pleasure-seeking. In short, there is nothing wrong with our culture that a strong dose of intellectual commitment could not help solve.

Although my purpose in this book is basically to explore the problem— to define post-intellectualism—it nevertheless would not be inappropriate in Part 5 to review a few unanswered questions (Chapter 17) and to glance briefly at some possible approaches to solutions (Chapter 18).

17

Concerns and Questions

People had better find new ways of acting, of relating,
of dealing with their environments. Just to survive,
it appears, we need a new human nature.

> • George Leonard
> *Education and Ecstasy*

Thomas Jefferson was, indisputably, one of the greatest intellectual minds in American history. The breadth of his intellect personified the highest hopes of the Enlightenment. However, his frustration and disappointment grew with his advancing years. Six years before his death, Jefferson wrote,

I regret that I am now to die in the belief, that the useless sacrifice of themselves by the generation of 1776, to acquire self-government and happiness to their country, is to be thrown away by the unwise and unworthy passions of their sons, and that my only consolation is to be, that I live not to weep over it.[1]

If Jefferson perceived such intellectual deterioration by 1820, where does that leave us today?

Walter Cronkite, 175 years later, comments, "I have believed all of my life . . . that this country is great and it has continuing potential to be the real model of democracy that we've always thought it would be. . . . But I'm getting less and less certain that that's the way it's going to be." Cronkite readily admits that he has "lapsed from skepticism into cynicism."[2]

REVERSING THE EFFECTS OF THE PROGRESS PARADOX

Human beings are not fit to be custodians of the planet if we cannot figure out how to structure our economic affairs without destroying our ecological resources, if we cannot comprehend the information we have generated, and if we cannot handle the power of the technology we have unleashed. Several difficult questions need to be asked—even if we have no glib answers.

Is Mankind Rational Enough to Govern Itself?

The American experiment was swept in on a euphoric wave of utopian expectations—not unlike the high hopes that ricocheted throughout the continent of postcolonial Africa some decades back, or the winds of freedom that swept across the plains and valleys of Eastern Europe a few years ago. We started out determined to be ruled by intellect; but we then discarded reason and responsibility. We must seriously ask, *Can human beings change?* This relates to the "primary consideration" we raised in Chapter 4—limitations of human intellect. George Leonard warns us that "people had better find new ways of acting, of relating, of dealing with their environments. Just to survive, it appears, we need a new human nature."[3]

Indeed, if we do not decide simply *to think better*, then we do not have a chance of maintaining an intellectually based self-governing society. If we cannot accept the responsibility for our decisions, then we cannot expect to hold onto the concept of individual freedom. And if we cannot moderate our own short-term greeds and gratifications to pursue the long-range good of society, then we have no chance to maintain an ordered and intellectual civilization. Robert Heilbroner reminds us that "all the dangers we have examined— population growth, war, environmental damage, scientific technology—are *social* problems, originating in human behavior and capable of amelioration by the alteration of that behavior."[4]

Can Society Resist the Lure of Infinite Growth?

Several questions must be asked about the three underlying determinants defined in Chapter 4. Our reliance upon perpetual growth and linear development is an extension of our commitment to progress and change—*distended intellectualism.* This has been the driving force behind most of our technological and material achievements of the past four hundred years. But how much longer can we maintain the nineteenth-century dictum that population growth and economic development will maintain a healthy society? In his 1980 *An Inquiry into the Human Prospect*, Heilbroner writes, "The industrial growth process, so central to the economic and social life of capitalism and Western socialism alike, will be forced to slow down, in all likelihood within a generation or two, and will probably have to give way to decline thereafter."[5]

How long can we maintain the illusion that all the peoples of the Earth will be able to enjoy increasing material standards as the planetary population approaches six billion people? As we indisputably are exhausting our global supplies of petroleum and mineral wealth? As we cannot deliver drinkable water to growing concentrations of population? As we continue to saturate our land-fills, rivers, and bays with billions of tons of garbage, toxic wastes, and radio-active leftovers?

Do we really think that genetic hybrids, algae farms, and miracle fertilizers are going to enable us to feed even more billions of mouths while also enabling them to enjoy the advantages of modern housing, the automobile, air condi-tioning, hair salons, and the information superhighway? This is one of the thorniest issues we face—how to reverse our long-standing commitment to continued linear expansion and growth. Sooner or later, global leaders will be forced to devise an economic theory based upon a stable population base.

Can Our Culture Handle the Information Overload?

Many of the problems we have examined relate directly to the information overload we are trying to deal with. The web culture is defined by informa-tion—too many data, too many choices, too much information in too many hands (loss of privacy), the accelerating rate of change, specialization and a loss of perspective, a loss of direction and self-sufficiency, information control and manipulation by bureaucratic forces.

How is the average mortal to deal with it all? How is the responsible citi-zen to participate in the collective decision-making enterprise of self-govern-ment when we are so inundated with mountains of data—both relevant and ir-relevant? How are we to sort through the clutter and focus on the meaningful? How are we to set up the filters and "information-control systems" that can give us some orientation and sense of purpose—while not surrendering our individ-ual freedoms and prerogatives?

Bill McKibben warns us that we are substituting trivia and drivel for in-formation of substance: "We also live at a moment of deep ignorance, when vital knowledge that humans have always possessed about who we are and where we live seems beyond our reach. An Unenlightenment. An age of missing information."[6]

Can Technological Determinism Be Reversed?

The relentless striving for more information and continued scientific prow-ess: this is the essence of technological determinism. There is no easy turning back. Each research success demands that we take the next step; each research failure dictates that we try again. Progress decrees that we push on. Technop-oly and post-intellectualism evolved out of the Enlightenment emphasis on the potential of the human mind. This is the irony of distended intellectualism.

Almost seventy years ago, Edward Arthur Burroughs, the Bishop of Ripon, issued a wistful, counter-intellectual appeal to curtail our drive for continued research and progress:

> After all we could get on very happily if aviation, wireless, television and the like advanced no further than at present. . . . The sum of human happiness would not necessarily be reduced if for ten years every physical and chemical laboratory were closed and the patient and resourceful energy displayed in them transferred to the lost art of getting on together and finding the formula for making both ends meet in the scale of human life.[7]

Such a pastoral counter-intellectual plea, of course, can never be realistically entertained. We are too busy pushing forward—progress, research, development, one technological achievement after another.

LIVING WITHIN THE WEB CULTURE

We point fingers at numerous scapegoats for our present cultural deterioration. *It's not my fault!* The problem lies with international banking cartels, crooked politicians, drug peddlers, industrial polluters, or some tyrant on the other side of the ocean. And, of course, with the media—those amoral purveyors of trash, trivia, sensationalism, and crass materialism. Many critics focus exclusively on TV and the movies as the source of all our societal woes. Politicians salivate as they stand in line waiting for their moment in front of the lens to condemn the same media they use for their own self-aggrandizement.

How Can We Co-Exist with the Electric Media?

Jerry Mander, in his 1978 *Four Arguments for the Elimination of Television*, insists he is serious in his campaign to make television disappear: "I finally faced the fact that television is not reformable, that it must be gotten rid of totally if our society is to return to something like sane and democratic functioning."[8] Few critics, however, entertain such a quixotic goal very seriously. The glowing kinescope screen has insinuated itself into the warp and woof of every aspect of our social fabric. The question to be asked is not "How do we get rid of it?" but rather, "How can we get along with it?" How can we add substance to the content? How can we provide intellect along with the pictures?

Attending to Substantive Content. One crucial question is, *Can we get the populace to pay attention to the serious content of the mass media?* How do we as a society discipline ourselves to use the popular media as vehicles for in-depth information and analysis of public affairs, as an institution for serious examination of crucial issues, as a forum for national discussion? William Lederer reminds us, "If your newspaper, television station, or magazine is inadequate (and the chances are that it is), then you share a large percentage of the guilt, Only if you express a demand for a more informed and informing American journalism will those who own the presses be seriously moved to provide it."[9]

Television would not have provided such saturated coverage of the O. J. Simpson affair, for example, unless there were an audience for such sensationalism. We watched and read every bit of scandal and hearsay we could get hold of. The one Los Angeles TV station to cover the Simpson trial gavel-to-gavel quadrupled its daytime ratings.[10] How are we to focus on the crucial issues of the day, how are we to function in a responsible democratic system, if we demand that we be entertained and titillated every waking moment?

Defenders and apologists for the media argue, with some justification, that the media will provide whatever the masses will pay attention to. *If the audience wants in-depth analysis and serious content, we will be glad to give it to them; but if they demand pap and pablum, that is what we will provide.* Even if the commercial media were suddenly to be spiritually infused with a moral obligation to dedicate themselves overwhelmingly to content of substance, what would make the populace pay attention? Only when the citizenry makes a willful decision to behave in an intellectual and responsible manner will the media be able to dedicate themselves to a higher purpose.

The Effects of Picturization. How can people be expected to handle complex ideas, engage in abstract reasoning, and negotiate political thickets, if they communicate only with pictures? In discussing the difference between reading and oral communication, Walter Ong makes the point that as our verbal style is changed by television, becoming looser and less structured, so, too, is our style of thinking. "Electronic verbalization, particularly through radio and even more through television, is affecting our present speaking and writing and printing styles, and thus *our modes of thought* [italics added]."[11]

We are being conditioned to think in a less organized and disciplined manner and to process information in a more spontaneous and intuitive mode. The longer we dwell in the land of pictures, the less able we are to think analytically and critically. Therefore, one of society's most perplexing questions remains, *How are we to counteract the nonlinear effects of picturization?* We must assure that future generations do not allow the pictorial content of our web culture to completely overpower the written word.

How Do We Strike a Balance with Post-Intellectualism?

As reiterated throughout the book, I am not advocating a complete rejection of everything non-intellectual, traditional, intuitive, and compassionate. The challenge is to find a way to balance an intellectual perspective with positive elements of post-intellectualism.

Perhaps we expected too much in assuming that all human beings could embrace an intellectual mindset, could master writing and reading. Speaking is instinctive; writing is not. Looking at pictures is easier than decoding printed symbols. Television is therefore a more natural way to communicate. Media theorist Paul Levinson argues that television presents more of an image of what is genuine and real—actual moving pictures and sounds. Humans "use media to recreate as 'natural' and as 'human' a means of communicating as possible."[12] Television represents reality; print is an unnatural, symbolic undertaking. Therefore—this line of reasoning would conclude—*intellectualism is not natural!*

An argument could be made for a return to an oral culture—a deliberate refutation of print and reason. Maybe we should just give up on any intellectual approach to the conduct of human affairs. Perhaps we are not rational enough. We should renounce any attempt at large-scale regional or national government, return to a tribal existence, live intuitively and instinctively. And abandon print. *We tried literacy and it didn't work!* Let us return to the fourteenth century—or at least to the 1960s, and we can all stand around in our love beads and sandals, hugging each other and passing out flowers.

As seductive as this line of argumentation may be, we cannot at this late stage return to the life of Rousseau's "natural man"—living in a world that had only a few million men and women roaming the planet, with their intuitive grasp of ecology and simpler lifestyle. Once we harnessed the energy of the internal combustion engine, generated electricity, split the atom, hurled satellites beyond gravity's pull, and committed our collective memory to a global computer database, we cannot put the technological genie back in the bottle.

And do we really want to give up on the idea of reason? Virginia Postrel, editor of *Reason* magazine, writes, "to be at war with modernity, at war with progress, at war with technology is not just to attack gadgets or advertising or even capitalism itself. It is to attack the life of the mind, the idea that human beings can, or should, understand the universe."[13]

Searching for the Synthesis. What we need is some sort of synthesis, a balance among the several underlying philosophical conflicts we have been exploring throughout the book: intellect versus intuition, print versus pictures, libertarianism versus authoritarianism, reason versus emotion, science versus religion, freedom versus security. We need a balance between intellectual and post-intellectual qualities, between long-term interests and immediate gratification, between nationalism and ethnic identity.

Between competition and cooperation. Cooperation is good, but everything that is worthwhile is achieved by competition, effort, and struggle—winning a mate, getting a job, earning a good grade, climbing a mountain, hitting a home run, getting a book published. To eliminate competition is to eliminate all sense of accomplishment. *Between capitalism and communal harmony.* Capitalistic enterprise is good; it results in better products, financial security, and progress. But a purely distended-intellectual capitalism also results in unsustainable exploitation of resources and manipulation of other peoples. *Between individualism and collective well-being.* Historian Francis Fukuyama states simply, "Clearly, all human societies must find some balance between group and individual interests."[14]

Fritjof Capra argues we have put too much emphasis on the "hard" or "macho" technologies that stress control and mastery—dominating nature, conquering time and space with communications and transportation technologies. We need to embrace instead a more benign science and technology—trying to understand the mysteries of our biosphere so that we may better fit in and define our complementary roles. We should strive for harmony with nature, not supremacy. "The natural order is one of dynamic balance between yin and yang."[15]

Throughout much of the book, I have been drawing parallels between pre-intellectualism and post-intellectualism—as if we were completing an inevitable cycle after a brief flirtation with an intellectual culture, as if our post-intellectual age were an unadulterated return to a pure pre-intellectual state. A more useful model might be to think in terms of our emerging post-intellectual culture as a merging or balance between positive intellectual qualities (search for knowledge, critical thinking, individualism, capitalism, self-government, and personal freedom) and some of the positive pre-intellectual qualities (communal welfare, tradition, and cooperation).

This is the essence of P. A. Sorokin's *idealistic* culture—blending the best of the *sensate* (scientific and rational) and the *ideational* (religious-oriented). It may be this idealistic balance between the pre-intellectual ideational and the intellectual sensate cultures toward which we are evolving in our post-intellectual fusion. To achieve such a synthesis would reflect the most optimistic prospect for humankind.

The danger is not simply that we are moving into an *affective* culture (with its emphasis on feelings and sensitivity), but that we are discarding our *cognitive* heritage (with its commitment to intellectual structures). What we should strive for is the idealistic blending of cognitive and affective values.

Balancing Tradition and Change. Nowhere is this need for balance more apparent than with the opposing qualities of tradition and change. Tradition is the cornerstone of the pre-intellectual *cyclical culture*. Nothing changes; every generation repeats the same cycle as its parents. On the other hand, change is the cornerstone of the *linear culture*—always moving, always advancing, always progressing. We are to question the establishment, not embrace it; we are to revise the status quo, not revere it. But in the *web culture* we are not sure what to change and what to throw out; so we wind up throwing out most everything without knowing what to replace it all with.

The challenge is to find the balance between Enduring Wisdom (tradition, eternal truths, moral directions, human values) and Change (flexibility, open-mindedness, unorthodoxy, adaptability). There is nothing sacred about preserving the status quo for the sake of holding on to everything from the past. But neither should we insist on always embracing change for change's sake. There are many aspects of our culture that should not be thrown out just because they are handed down from our elders—personal honesty, family loyalty, respect for others, civic responsibility. We need to adopt a modification of the traditional "Serenity Prayer":

> Give me the insight to hold onto what should not be changed,
> The intellect to change what needs to be changed,
> And the wisdom to discern the difference.

SEARCHING FOR MORAL DIRECTION

In our haste to reject the status quo, we have discarded many of our traditional sources of moral precepts—religious values, philosophical tenets, family traditions, literary guideposts, educational standards, and even humanist principles. Where, then, are we to find the moral guidelines and personal standards by which we can judge society and culture? Václav Havel reminds us, "Without commonly shared and widely entrenched moral values and obligations, neither the law, nor democratic government, nor even the market economy will function properly."[16] Can freedom be sustained in a society that has no sense of ethical direction?

What Is Our Basis for a Code of Values?

Our contemporary moral anarchy is summed up by the sheriff from the CBS television series *Picket Fences*. After an episode dealing with alleged child abuse, polygamy, an animal-sacrificing religious cult, and simultaneous intimate relationships with twins, Sheriff Jimmy Brock laments,

We live in a world without norms. Religion and family and law—there just are no norms any more. Society always pushed morality on us—good or bad, it was clear. Now, . . . I feel like the country is coming into a kind of moral adolescence. Sometimes freedom comes at the expense of structure. And that can be a little frightening.[17]

If the Generation Overlap has obliterated the definitions of truth, goodness, beauty, human dignity, *noblesse oblige,* virtue, and personal integrity, how are people to determine who they are and how they are doing? How are we to define happiness? How are we to judge human relationships? We are attempting to navigate the web culture without a moral compass. We have nothing to steer by, nothing to believe in.

Faith and Reason. By definition, *faith* is belief in that which cannot be verified by *reason*. Faith is the blind acceptance of an idea or doctrine without any rational evidence or tangible proof. Faith is non-intellectual.

Reason, on the other hand, is intellectual. The libertarian alternative to organized religion is *Humanism,* the doctrine that human beings have the rational ability to find truth and to determine their own destinies. Relying upon reason and enlightened self-interest, men and women can structure their governmental systems, establish a moral code, and provide for all their spiritual needs without recourse to a supreme being. Scientism and rationalism are both manifestations of humanism.

Reason is the antithesis of faith. Defending faith against reason, Martin Luther gives us this clear declaration, "Reason is the greatest enemy that faith has: it never comes to the aid of spiritual things, but—more frequently than not—struggles against the divine Word, treating with contempt all that emanates from God."[18] Voicing the opposite viewpoint, the intellectual mindset, we have Thomas Huxley, the eminent biologist: "The improver of natural knowledge absolutely refuses to acknowledge authority, as such. For him, skepticism is the highest of duties, blind faith the one unpardonable sin."[19]

Our moral confusion results, to a great extent, from the conflicting values of faith and religion versus reason and humanism. Traditional family/clan (pre-intellectual) religious values emphasize respect for authority and loyalty, conformity, and acceptance of the status quo. The libertarian democratic (intellectual) humanistic philosophy stresses independence, individualism, commitment to social criticism, and tolerance of alternate lifestyles. In our post-intellectual web culture, we are not sure which way to turn. To an alarming extent, we have rejected both faith and reason.

If a nation has faith in a higher authority—God, the king, the ayatollah, or Mao Tse-tung—the people can maintain a viable society. Although America still professes to be a religious country, for all practical purposes religion is not the driving force that determines the moral climate in the United States today. Social Critic Robert Bellah points out that much of the cultural decay of the past half-century or so has been due to a deterioration of our moral fabric in three areas identified by Tocqueville over 150 years ago: a decline in the integrity of family life, a decrease of participation in local government, and a loss of meaningful religious tradition.[20]

On the other hand, if individuals have intellectual confidence in a libertarian-based democratic form of rational self-government, the people then have a set of idealistic tenets and they can maintain a strong society. This is our heritage from the Enlightenment. But humanism has not resulted in the maintenance of an intellectual/democratic society. Christopher Lasch writes that "the myth of progress, which for a long time provided a substitute for religious faith, has now lost much of its plausibility."[21]

We can either accept religious faith or turn to human reason as our guiding principle—and we will have some sense of purpose, a value system by which to live. What happens, however, when a society loses both its religious belief system *and* its intellectual ideals? Humans must live either by faith or by reason (or a combination of the two). Either by Sorokin's ideational culture or sensate culture (or the idealistic combination of the two). There must be a cultural rule book with a set of either moral or intellectual instructions (or, ideally, both). Michael Novak writes, "Looking ahead to the 21st Century, the problem that worries me the most is the fragility of free societies that lose [both] their intellectual and moral roots."[22]

Materialism as Our Higher Purpose. If we abandon our sense of religious faith and also give up on our conviction that we can govern ourselves using reason and science, what then do we have left as our guiding principle? Satisfaction of our animal drives for food, sex, physical security—and what else? Especially in America where we have few alternatives to religion or humanism—no Old World cultural traditions, no centuries-old history of art and literature, no native mythology to explain our origins, no coherent ethnic or racial heritage. We have a conspicuous lack of alternative secular guidelines. We built a new nation on libertarian humanistic principles—and then abandoned its intellectual precepts.

What we have turned to in twentieth-century America for a value system is *Materialism*—money, power, prestige, image, conspicuous consumption. We have substituted material well-being for religion and for intellect. This is how we describe success, the Good Life, societal position. Our individual identities are defined by our salaries, our houses, and the cars we drive. *He who dies with the most toys wins.*

We have become so obsessed with the goal of *making money* that we have lost sight of what *living* is all about. The distended-intellectual glorification of monetary success is our greatest cultural goal; we have degraded all other social and human values. Thoughtful social critics question whether such secular materialistic values and goals are enough to sustain a culture. Harold Isaacs writes,

> The underlying issue is still: can human existence be made more humane, and if so, how? For a long time, answers to this question bore on varieties of the belief that the tribes of men would eventually, through Reason or Faith, come around to discover their One Humanity and would thereupon organize themselves to live more happily thereafter with one another. This belief survives only with the greatest difficulty in some of its religious versions. In its secular/political forms, whether in the humanistic tradition created by the Enlightenment or the materialistic tradition of socialism, it barely survives at all.[23]

Do We Have the Right Not to Be Responsible?

Kate Pierson of the rock group the B-52's was quoted in a *Rolling Stone* interview as saying, "As an American, I feel everyone has a right to be stupid."[24] She was talking specifically about "stupid consumers" who have the right to listen to the offensive lyrics of 2 Live Crew. However, she raises an interesting point. Do Americans have the right to be stupid, to remain uninformed and apathetic? Legally, yes. Morally—in an intellectual society—no. Citizens in a true democracy do not have the right to remain uninformed and uninvolved. Liberty is not license to remain ignorant.

Toward a Declaration of Responsibilities. In November 1990, *Harper's* magazine sponsored a seminar at Independence Hall, Philadelphia, to discuss the feasibility of creating a Declaration of Responsibilities.[25] In addition to the Bill of Rights, citizens also need a Bill of Duties, a citizens' compact to remind us of our obligations as members of a free society. Alongside the Pledge of Allegiance we also need a Pledge of Responsibilities.

It would, of course, be impossible to legally ordain specific civic duties. We cannot legislate responsibility. We cannot pass a law to create civic virtue. Legislating political participation is like censorship or affirmative action quotas: if you have to resort to it, then the system—the voluntary intellectual contract— is not working. The state, however, may assume a proper *educational* role— reminding people what their community responsibilities should be.

If we were actually to draft a Declaration of Responsibilities, the following are just *a few* of the considerations that I would suggest should be included. There obviously are many more.

- **The Family.** Marriage shall be undertaken only by those who view it as a lifelong commitment. No man shall father a child unless he is prepared to marry the mother and provide comprehensive family support.

- **Education.** Parents shall cooperate with the state to provide a thorough education for all children through their early adult years. All citizens will endeavor to complete as much schooling as they are capable of.

- **Human Dignity.** Every person shall demonstrate full and unconditional respect and appreciation for all other individuals—regardless of race, gender, age, physical disability, sexual orientation, national background, and religious preference.

- **Community Participation.** All citizens shall be active in local affairs—participating in and supporting school boards, civic associations, community organizations, service clubs, and the like.

- **Public Affairs.** All citizens shall keep themselves informed on all pertinent political and social issues, participate in appropriate meetings and forums, provide continuous feedback to their elected officials, and vote in all elections.

- **The Environment.** Each consumer shall avoid conspicuous consumption, show materialistic restraint, avoid all littering, recycle all materials possible, moderate all polluting activities, and reduce as much as possible the consumption of energy.

This is only a suggestion of some of the considerations worthy of inclusion in a Declaration of Civic Duties. Much more could be added—regarding employment obligations, personal and professional honesty, business ethics, crime prevention, labor practices, religious values, literary and artistic standards, creative leisure pursuits, self-improvement, and many other societal obligations. Think about what you would include in your own Bill of Responsibilities.

Throughout this chapter, I have raised several questions relating to the underlying determinants of post-intellectualism, the disorientation arising from the web culture, and the search for a value system. Many of these questions remain unanswered. However, in the final chapter I do try to outline a few considerations in searching for an approach to some answers.

NOTES

1. Letter to John Holmes, 22 April 1820, quoted in Jefferson, 1975, pp. 568-69.
2. Quoted in Gay, 1996, p. 10.
3. Leonard, 1968, p. 7.
4. Heilbroner, 1980, p. 77.
5. Ibid., p. 151.
6. McKibben, 1992, p. 9.
7. Edward Arthur Burroughs, Sermon to the British Association for the Advancement of Science, Leeds, 4 September 1927, quoted in *Bartlett's Familiar Quotations,* 1980, p. 776.
8. Mander, 1978, p. 46.
9. Lederer, 1961, p. 164.
10. Jerry Crowe, "2 Stations Gambling Big on the O. J. Trial," *Los Angeles Times,* 5 August 1995, p. F1.
11. Ong, 1982, p. 189.
12. Cited in Meyrowitz, 1985, p. 121.
13. Virginia I. Postrel, "Declaring War on the Pursuit of Knowledge," *Los Angeles Times,* 25 September 1995, p. B9.
14. Francis Fukuyama, "Is Happiness More Valuable Than Conformity? The New Asia Will Tell," *Los Angeles Times,* 12 February 1992, p. B11.
15. Capra, 1982, p. 35.
16. Havel, 1992, p. 19.
17. David E. Kelley, writer, *Picket Fences,* broadcast on CBS, 22 January 1993.
18. Martin Luther, *Table Talk,* 1569.
19. Thomas Huxley, *On the Advisableness of Improving Natural Knowledge,* 1866, quoted in *Bartlett's Familiar Quotations,* 1980, p. 595.
20. See Bellah, 1968, pp. 3–23.
21. Lasch, 1991, p. 386.
22. Novak, 1994.
23. Isaacs, 1975, pp. 217–18.
24. Kim Neely, "Rockers Sound Off," *Rolling Stone,* 9 August 1990, p. 27.
25. See "Who Owes What to Whom?" 1991.

18

Steps Toward Solutions

Humanity is at a major turning point. We live in a watershed era. One epoch has ended and a second is commencing. . . .

• Mikhail Gorbachev
1992 Speech

So we should make a decision to think better. It's a good start.

• Steve Allen
Dumbth

In *A Nation of Sheep*, William Lederer writes, "This book has been written in the conviction that something can be done . . . and that it must be the average citizen who does it."[1] This we must hold on to: we can reverse the self-destructive direction in which we are headed. Furthermore, our societal decline must be reversed by the populace at large. It cannot be left up to the elitists, the well educated, the rich, or those with special interests. We must find the ways to encourage the mass citizenry to become more open-minded, global in perspective, committed to reason and social responsibility.

TEN RECOMMENDATIONS

The purpose of this book is primarily to examine our contemporary cultural turmoil in the context of post-intellectualism. However, it might be fitting to close with a few proposals and recommendations. Some of these suggestions are rather general and sweeping; others present a more specific blueprint or program for action. Some are attempts to rekindle a sense of intellectual commitment; others are designed to build on positive post-intellectual realities. Some are innocuous and hortatory; others are more radical, certain to cause considerable opposition if ever seriously submitted for implementation. All are offered to stimulate discussion.

1. Emphasize Liberal Arts Education in Schooling

One problem with our present educational system is the *counter-intellectual* push toward self-esteem education, progressive "feel-good" curricula. Certainly youngsters need to have a healthy self-esteem. But is this not the job of the home? The church? Students should be rewarded in school when they meet scholastic objectives, not when they simply exhibit self-esteem. Schools should foster academic accomplishment, not mediocrity—excellence, not equality.

The second problem is the *distended-intellectual* thrust of specialized and vocational education, training future workers and professionals to keep the economy functioning. At the close of the 1989 "education summit" at the University of Virginia, President George Bush and the states' governors issued a "Jeffersonian Compact" that stated, "As a nation we must have an educated work force, second to none, in order to succeed in an increasingly competitive world economy." What we really need is a compact that states, *As a nation we must have an intellectual citizenry of poets and philosophers, historians and critical thinkers—so that we may understand where we are coming from, where we are today, and where we are headed.*

First, we must teach young people how to cope with today's information culture—analytic thinking and problem-solving skills, mastery of the written word, critical evaluation and decision-making abilities, research techniques and, yes, computer competencies.

Second, schools must emphasize more of a cultural and intellectual experience—examining what humankind is all about, what science is, how other cultures operate, the basics of self-government. Students need historical and geographic perspective; they need to know the great works of art and literature throughout the centuries. As Allan Bloom concludes in *The Closing of the American Mind*, "Our problems are so great and their sources so deep that to understand them we need philosophy more than ever."[2] Promoting a liberal arts perspective, Václav Havel writes,

> The role of the schools is not to create "idiot-specialists" to fill the special needs of different sectors of the national economy, but to develop the individual capabilities of the students in a purposeful way, and to send out into life thoughtful young people capable of thinking about the wider social, historical, and philosophical implications of their specialties.[3]

2. Rebuild the Family

One of the most serious causes of our social decay is the deterioration of the American family: about three out of every ten children born out of wedlock, more than 1.2 million divorces every year, increasing numbers of battered spouses and abused children, untold numbers of desertions and separations. Fredric Hayward writes, "both the left and the right are starting to notice that the social issue of our time is inadequate fathering. The best indicator of drug abuse, gang participation, promiscuity and academic failure is neither race nor income; it is fatherlessness."[4]

There is no substitute for the nuclear family. Amitai Etzioni, founder of the Communitarian Movement, makes this one of the themes of his campaign: "You can stone me if you want. But I have a moral duty to say that if parents don't bond with that child, especially during the first two years of life, under most circumstances there's going to be hell to be paid—and we're paying for it. If you want to have children, take care of them, dammit."[5] Despite all our assorted welfare and social programs (day-care centers, aid to dependent families, aid to single mothers, Head Start programs, and other community programs), there simply is no substitute for a caring, nurturing two-parent family. Of the children receiving Aid to Families with Dependent Children (AFDC) welfare assistance, over half are illegitimate.

The federal government and many states are trying to restructure social assistance programs so that family togetherness can be encouraged rather than penalized. States are beginning to require parents on welfare to sign social contracts, specifying the exact plan that they will follow regarding family arrangements, job training, continued education, and expected job placement. These binding contracts specify the particular responsibilities that welfare recipients have for themselves (self-support), for their families (especially their children), and for society in general.

Controversial political scientist Charles Murray argues that we should eliminate all welfare to unmarried mothers. The government should adopt a policy that says, "From society's perspective, to have a baby you cannot care for yourself is profoundly irresponsible, and the government will no longer subsidize it."[6] In any case, strengthening the family must be one of society's top priorities. All other reforms, remedial measures, health-care packages, and social security refurbishing is meaningless if the family does not survive at the heart of society.

3. De-Urbanize the Nation's Population

One promising area where communications and computer technologies can contribute to a more humane society is the repair and replacement of the disintegrating urban core. The information superhighway, computer networks, the Internet, sophisticated telephone and data services, efficient private mail services, faxes and modems: these all offer the opportunity to depressurize the centralized city.

Telecommuting can significantly cut down on congestion and pollution—as increasing numbers of professionals, sales representatives, consultants, freelance artists, corporate managers and government bureaucrats plug in their electronic umbilical cords to work at home. As robotics take over actual factory production work—and the planning, design, promotion and advertising, marketing and sales, personnel and other business functions are handled by computer terminals (which may be miles apart)—there is less need for centralized industrial squalor in the urban areas. Satellite links for videoconferencing and document conferencing tie together workers from all corners of the continent.

Distance learning provides higher education opportunities anywhere in the country. Direct-satellite broadcasting, video movie rentals, computer-linked video games, and CD and book clubs all offer a wide range of entertainment and cultural opportunities to provide art and diversion to the small-town resident and the rural recluse.

It becomes increasingly feasible to earn a living, educate one's family, and entertain oneself far from the madding crowd and urban disintegration. Alvin Toffler was writing about such decentralization and de-urbanization fifteen years ago. The *electronic cottage* "could shift literally millions of jobs out of the factories and offices into which the Second Wave swept them and right back where they came from originally: the home."[7]

The farm and cottage industries were a pre-intellectual culture. The urbanized factories and mills of the industrial age were indicative of an intellectual society. Hyper-urbanization and inner-city decay represent a *distended-intellectual* turn of events. And the halcyon desire to sever all urban links and adopt a pastoral, self-sustaining rural lifestyle symbolizes a *counter-intellectual* movement.

4. Promote Government Leadership on Population Control

The one issue underlying and complicating every other environmental and economic problem we face is that we are heading toward a global population of six billion people by the end of this decade. The net population growth of the planet is close to two million persons every week. Global population has increased almost fourfold during the twentieth century. We must intensify both domestic and worldwide programs dealing with population education and family planning; we must promote easy-to-use, reliable and affordable means of contraception. *There is no alternative!*

With less than 5 percent of the world's population, Americans consume 25 to 30 percent of the planet's resources and produce a third of its pollution. One U.S. citizen uses as much energy as do six Mexicans or 14 Chinese or 168 Bangladeshi.[8] America has both a moral responsibility and a heavy ecological obligation to lead the way toward population sanity. At the very minimum, the government can at least stop giving fertility drugs to women on welfare. In Massachusetts in 1994, for example, 58 percent of the 260 Medicaid patients who were receiving fertility drugs were being subsidized by AFDC.[9]

Large Family Tax Disincentive. One direct proposal would be this: *Eliminate the tax exemption for all but the first two children born in every family.* You can continue to get tax deductions for the first two children you have. But your third and subsequent children will not warrant any more tax breaks. Such a tax revision states, in effect, that we can no longer encourage couples to have large families.

To be fair, such a regulation should not take effect until a year after it has been promulgated; all current large families would have to be protected— "grandfathered in." Existing families with three or more children would continue receiving the tax deductions they have been promised in the past. If such a tax disincentive were to be implemented today, for example, it would apply only to third and subsequent children born to any given woman a year after next January 1.

Such a rational approach to population planning would not penalize any current large families; it would not violate any religious doctrines; it would not necessarily condone abortion or any specific means of birth control. It would simply be a practical way to say that it is plainly irresponsible for the government today to subsidize large families. It has to be done some time; our cities— our nation, our planet—cannot continue to expand forever. And the sooner we commit ourselves to a steady-state policy, the better off we all will be.

5. Advance the Concept of "No-Growth" Economic Planning

Patagonia, the sports clothing company, announced in its 1992 catalogue that it had decided to stop growing. The company underwent an internal environmental audit and decided that it could not conscientiously continue to expand its operations and exploit more and more resources. Yvon Chouinard, president of Patagonia, stated,

As a society, we've always assumed that growth is both positive and inevitable. When our economies sour, as they always do, we simply look for new customers and new resources. We hunt new export markets and new Third World sources for raw materials. But Third World resources are close to exhausted and many economies, burdened by debt, are no longer viable dumping grounds for our manufactured goods.[10]

The potential for expansion no longer exists. We need a free-enterprise economic model that does not rely on the illusory palliative of continued growth and development. We need a presidential commission on economic non-growth to immediately address this challenge: *Devise a new capitalistic model based on a stable and self-supporting economic system that is not predicated upon continual and perpetual physical growth.*

6. Fight for Stronger Environmental Protection

The overriding responsibility of human society, our primary and foremost obligation, is to leave the environment as we find it—to leave the planet intact for future generations. Virtually every ecological problem we face is the result of human intervention in the natural order of things. We must reverse our distended-intellectual attitude of exploitation and mastery over nature. There are many ways we could modify our abusive practices. For illustrative purposes, let me briefly look at just two areas—*international resources conservation* and *alternative energy sources.*

We must move toward more effective planetary cooperation in conserving global resources; no longer can pure water, oxygen, whales, or fish be considered the provincial resource of individual countries. One proposal is for a "Global Commons Trust Fund" which would charge fees for gathering fish from the high seas, harvesting minerals from the seabeds, dumping garbage and industrial wastes into the oceans, discharging carbons and other pollutants into the atmosphere, utilizing orbital space for satellites, and other similar uses and abuses.[11] How about paying for fresh air—through an international oxygen tax that developed nations pay to rain-forest countries in order to preserve what is left of the planet's oxygen-producing resources? Another possible approach would be debt relief for Third World countries; if developing nations agree to ease up on resources exploitation within their borders, the creditor nations can ease up on their $1.3 trillion debt burdens.[12]

We obviously cannot continue to rely indefinitely on consumable energy resources—oil, natural gas, coal, even uranium. There are numerous other alternative energy solutions that need to be developed and implemented *now:* solar, fusion, photovoltaic, wind power, geothermal power, and other exotic possibilities. One novel idea is *mantle power*—extracting heat from the planet's interior. One report indicates that "regions in the continental United States where partially molten magma rises to within six miles of the surface could provide 600 to 6,000 times as much energy as is annually consumed in this country."[13] Another possible source of non-polluting energy would be an *ocean thermal-energy conversion plant*—a floating power plant that would use the heat of tropical ocean water to vaporize propylene which could be used to spin turbines, steadily producing about 100 megawatts of electricity.[14]

These are just some illustrative examples—environmental remedies are possible. All it takes are two things: courageous and far-sighted political leadership, and an aroused and determined citizenry. Without either one, environmental sanity is forsaken. If we can find both, we can hold out hope for the future.

7. Adopt a Heavily Progressive Income Tax

On what principles is society to be based? The philosophies of classical Greece? The religious moralities of Moses, Buddha, Christ, and Mohammed? The visions of the Enlightenment thinkers? The political philosophies of our Founding Fathers? Or the principles and goals of the Ivan Boeskys and Donald Trumps of the world?

Ralph Nader points to one aggravating factor that contributes much to our cultural imbalance and turmoil: "Too much power and too much wealth in too few hands. One percent of the people in this country control over 35% of the wealth. . . . The top 10% control as much as the remaining 90%."[15] The other 90 percent of the population control next to nothing; they know it; and they resent it. Rousseau adds this footnote: "If the object is to give the State consistency, bring the two extremes [the affluent and the poor] as near to each other as possible; allow neither rich men nor beggars."[16] Steve Allen makes a complementary point: "We must inculcate a respect for wisdom and not put such heavy emphasis on material or financial accomplishment."[17]

Rather than debating the merits of a *flat-rate income tax* (actually most Americans would probably welcome a *simplified* tax system—not necessarily an even rate for rich and poor alike), we should be thinking about a heavily progressive tax. Sam Pizzigati, a trade-union journalist, argues in his 1992 book, *The Maximum Wage,* that the time has come for us to reconsider the idea of a maximum wage, a tax that would levy a 100 percent assessment on all income above a given rather-comfortable level. Today the highest tax rate is 39.6 percent (for income over $250,000). This is a legacy from the Reagan-Bush philosophy: *Wealth is to be coveted. Avarice is to be rewarded. Greed is good.* Such a policy says, in effect, our system is so philosophically bankrupt that we have no way of motivating people except to promise them they can become filthy rich. *We have no higher principles.*

A 100 percent tax bracket would create a maximum ceiling. Obviously if every executive were to be taxed of all income above, say, $500,000 (including bonuses, stock options, and other perks), no business would pay its executives any more than that. The idea behind such an extreme measure would not be to raise revenue; the idea would be simply to instill a moral climate that says, *Outrageous avarice and conspicuous consumption are not to be rewarded. Materialistic standards are not to be valued. Ostentatious displays of wealth are to be frowned upon.*

Even such a free-enterprise advocate as William F. Buckley agrees there may be a point beyond which executives are over-compensated. In a 1996 column, he writes of the "implications of preposterous salaries":

There is a point at which one stares at the salary and should ask oneself: Is this thing looking ugly? What do we have here, voluptuary greed? . . . The super-rich CEOs should pause just for a minute and ask whether, comparative advantage to one side, there isn't a sensibility in modern capitalism they'd just as soon not scorn.[18]

No one needs a million-dollar income in order to live well. There are other rewards that should motivate people to attain the top positions—even in a capitalistic society: power, self-image, prestige, social utility, the satisfaction of knowing that one is doing a job to the maximum of one's abilities. *A person whose highest goal is the acquisition of material possessions is a person who does not have very high goals.* And *a society whose highest rewards are based on materialistic success represents a culture whose values cannot long endure.*

Is such a proposal naive? Yes. It is just as naive as is the expectation that the masses can govern themselves by deciding to behave in an rational and responsible manner. Pizzigati asks, "An impossible pipe dream? The minimum wage must have once seemed equally fantastic. Yet today we take the concept for granted. Decency demands, we believe, a floor on income. Why not a ceiling? Why not a maximum wage?"[19]

8. Redirect Our National Research Efforts

How are we to reconcile continuing reason/intellectualism/scientific research with the need to curtail technological determinism? We must at least consider carefully toward what goals our research efforts should be directed. As recently as 1993, roughly two-thirds of the nation's research and development monies were spent on projects with direct military applications. Major research universities receive up to 60 percent of their research funding from the Pentagon. Do we really need bigger and more automated bombs and ballistic systems?

We should carefully rethink our research efforts in other areas. How about transportation and communication? Do we really need to perfect *ramjet* and *scramjet* technologies so that we can fly faster than five times the speed of sound? Do we really need to expand the carrying capacity of the information superhighway? Do we really need any more databases (with a new one being added to the Internet every ten minutes)? Do we need any more e-mail capacity (many recipients are now deluged with up to a thousand messages a day)?

On the other hand, several areas of civilian research certainly could be given higher priority. Medicine is undoubtedly an uppermost consideration. Environmental protection obviously should be pursued—alternative energy sources, pollution controls, recycling technologies, containment and disposal of nuclear and other toxic wastes. In the behavioral sciences, we should research what kinds of schooling systems offer the best hope for the future. What alternatives are there to our revolving-door prison systems? What kinds of population models can help to decentralize our cities? How can we build the non-growth, self-sustaining economic model called for in step five?

Could not federal research dollars that are pumped into higher education be funneled through the National Science Foundation and the National Institutes of Health—rather than through the Pentagon? Ironically, the research budgets of these institutions have been cut in recent years, while the Pentagon's research budget has remained largely untouched. Better yet, should not more of our federal support be channeled through the National Endowment for the Arts, the Smithsonian Institution, or the National Foundation on the Arts and Humanities? Possibly *(blasphemy of blasphemies)*, federal research dollars could even be scaled back? These are the questions, the priorities, the redirections, that must be addressed.

9. Work for Campaign and Election Reform

Michael D'Antonio, in discussing Etzioni's Communitarian movement, writes that "Almost every political conversation today begins with the assumption that idealism is dead and that most of our serious problems—health care, homelessness, economic decline—cannot be solved by the current political system."[20] One obvious area where we need substantial reform is the way we elect our government officials. Our campaign and election processes have gone dangerously astray.

Recall Gore Vidal's observation (Chapter 15) that "Any individual who is able to raise $25 million to be considered presidential is not going to be much use to the people at large." Vidal's 1992 figure is already outdated. Competing for a California Senate seat in 1994, Diane Feinstein and Michael Huffington spent a total of almost $30 million. Alexander Cockburn asked after the 1990 elections, "How can you beat the corporate dollar, which runs more or less everything, without public campaign funding? The answer is that you can't, and if Americans don't want public campaign financing, they'll end up with corporate fascism."[21]

With public campaign funding, the contest for every office would be financed solely with public tax dollars. (Perhaps, as in the quixotic presidential campaigns of Jerry Brown, individual contributions of no more than $100 could be allowed.) As soon as you allow any major campaign contributions, you open the door to relentless influence from lobbyists, corporate giants, religious coalitions, miscellaneous PACs, unions, professional associations, and other special-interest groups.

Limitations must also be placed on the amount that candidates can contribute from their private fortunes. Otherwise, the Rockefellers, Kennedys, Perots, Huffingtons, and Forbeses have a major head start on the rest of the candidates. A 1994 survey by *Roll Call*, the Capitol Hill newspaper, indicated that almost one out of every five members of Congress is a millionaire—seventy-two representatives and twenty-eight senators. How representative can such politicians be when they are so far removed from the economic realities faced by their constituents?

Provisions should also be made for fair and equitable media coverage of each candidate's campaign. Every radio and television station would provide free a given amount of air time to each qualified candidate. Major candidate debates would be presented on PBS and public radio stations. CNN and C-SPAN would also provide extended coverage.

10. Further the Idea of World Federalism

I have no doubt but that if an expeditionary force of extra-terrestrial aliens were to actually visit Earth in their flying saucers, their first observation would be, *What in heaven's name are you earthlings doing by carving your planet up into 200 separate sovereign nations? For Jupiter's sake, you have but one people, one race, inhabiting one small celestial body. Why do you draw all these political jurisdictions all over your globe?* Why, indeed? It has to do with our tribal identities, our pre-intellectual territorial cravings (and post-intellectual insecurities). The reason has to do with our inability to grasp the abstract idea of a social contract and larger form of rational governance.

The intellectual idealism of the Enlightenment called for the creation of nation-states where individual citizens would put aside their local parochial concerns and work for the greater common good. In the twentieth century, such intellectual idealism would be expanded to encompass the entire planet. Transportation advances, instantaneous global communications, multinational commerce and financial webs, intertwined environmental concerns, and the need for international law and order all demand that we create a supernational world-wide federation of some sort. Common sense dictates that we do no less.

The twenty smallest nations in the world have a *combined* population less than that of the greater Milwaukee area—about 1.6 million.[22] With all due respect for the sensibilities and identities of the residents of Andorra and Tuvalu, one must ask what intellectual justification there is for the independent sovereign status of such nations. But let us ask also what intellectual justification there is for the independent sovereign status of Switzerland, Ethiopia, Brazil, India, France, or the United States.

Despite their provincial defensiveness, many world leaders sense the day is approaching when the logic of a global federation can no longer be ignored. In his last public reflections on the role of the United Nations, in September 1988, Ronald Reagan said, "A change that is cause for shaking the head in wonder is upon us . . . the prospect of a new age of world peace. The U.N. has an opportunity to live and breathe and work as never before."[23] And Mikhail Gorbachev, in 1992, spelled out his vision of a new world government:

Humanity is at a major turning point. We live in a watershed era. One epoch has ended and a second is commencing. . . . No one yet knows how concrete it will be. . . . What is emerging is a more complex global structure of international relations. An awareness of the need for some kind of global government is gaining ground, one in which all members of the world community would take part.[24]

What is it we really must preserve—the symbols and icons of America, the flag, the bald eagle, the *Star Spangled Banner*? Or the values and principles for which those symbols stand—human dignity and justice, freedom of speech and religion, respect for all persons, equal economic opportunities for all, citizen participation in self-government, individualism, and freedom of thought? Why support democratic objectives only for citizens of the United States? Do not human beings in Mexico, Estonia, Cambodia, or Rwanda deserve the same human freedoms and opportunities that we embrace? Why not pursue such goals on a global scale? Should not the United States of Earth be even a more noble goal than the United States of America or the United Counties of Michigan? Let us work for the betterment of all peoples.

SUMMARY

Plato stated that *the excess of liberty seems only to pass into excess of slavery.* This excess of liberty, an intemperate and irresponsible license, is distended-intellectualism—intellectual ideas pushed beyond the bounds of reason and self-restraint. An excess of universal education seems only to pass into an excess of esteem-building; an excess of pictorial media seems only to pass into illiteracy. Such excesses are what lead to the three underlying determinants of post-intellectualism. An excess of linear growth and development results in unrestrained exploitation and ecological devastation; an excess of research results in information overload and loss of knowledge; and an excess of scientific progress seems only to pass into technological determinism and innumerable social problems.

As mentioned in Chapter 2, perhaps the concept of *democracy* is an oxymoron—a contradiction in one word. Maybe the very idea of *self-government* is unattainable; self-government means self-restraint, a commitment to *responsibility.* Such an obligation, along with a commitment to reason, is what we have lost in the late twentieth century. Perhaps governance can only be superimposed from the outside. Perhaps there is an inherent incongruity in the idea of people willingly coming together and establishing a collective society—while holding onto some degree of individuality and freedom. But nevertheless, we must try.

In our attempt to remedy our cultural dystopia, there are several attributes of an *intellectual culture* that we must restore: a liberal arts perspective, a commitment to critical thinking and a scientific attitude, media responsibility, individualism, privacy, restoration of the nuclear family, democratic participation, and the idea of global federalism. Most importantly, and simply, we need to decide that we will restore reason and responsibility to our cultural affairs. In Steve Allen's book *Dumbth,* his first Rule is "Decide that in the future you will reason more effectively." He concludes that bit of advice by stating, "So we should make a decision to think better. It's a good start."[25]

Also (as pointed out in Chapter 17), we need to establish a balance with several positive post-intellectual qualities we have identified. In reaffirming our cognitive commitment to reason, we need not abandon the affective virtues of beneficial emotions and good feelings. There are several traits of *counter-intellectualism* to be encouraged: sensitivity and cooperation, some elements of affirmative action, a holistic-intuitive environmental ethic, respect for tradition, and perhaps even religious faith.

Just as importantly, there are many elements of *distended-intellectualism* that we need to reject: illiteracy and heavy reliance on pictorial media, materialism and capitalist exploitation, hyper-urbanization, mediated reality, an overemphasis on specialization, and technological determinism.

Closing with a Hint of Optimism

We must not allow ourselves to despair and subscribe to the nihilistic philosophy of the Unabomber: "The industrial-technological system has got to be eliminated, and to us almost any means that may be necessary for that purpose are justified."[26] On the contrary, there *are* peaceful, positive steps that can be undertaken. When all is said and analyzed, *we have little choice but to persevere and make the system work.* Lewis Lapham reminds us, "The hope of democratic government descends from the ancient Greeks by way of the Italian Renaissance and the Enlightenment, but no matter how often it has been corrupted and abused (simply by reason of its being such a difficult feat to perform), it constitutes the only morality currently operative in the world."[27] Paul Kennedy, concluding his *Preparing for the Twenty-First Century,* writes,

> Thus, despite the size and complexity of the global challenges facing us, it is too simple and too soon to conclude gloomily that nothing can be done.
> . . . The pace and complexity of the forces for change are enormous and daunting; yet it may still be possible for intelligent men and women to lead their societies through the complex task of preparing for the century ahead.[28]

Among all our contemporary tribulations, there are some positive signs, some indications of hope for an intellectual reawakening.

Breakup of the East European Communist Bloc: Arguably the most heartening event of the late twentieth century has been the disintegration of the monolithic communist model; the idealistic egalitarian doctrine turns out to be a totalitarian fraud.

Formation of the European Union: A most encouraging sign for the possible beginning of a true multinational compact, the initiation of the European Union holds the hope of serving as one of the cornerstones for a true international federation.

Worldwide Environmental Reawakening: Although we have a long way to go, there are signs that among the developed nations, there is emerging an awareness of the perilous situation of our biosphere (despite the United States' foot-dragging at most of these international conferences): The Helsinki Accord of 1989 and the London Ozone Conference of 1990, both following up the Montreal Protocol of 1987; the Rio Environmental Summit of 1992; and the 1994 U.N. Conference on Population and Development in Cairo.

However, despite these encouraging signs and occasional moments of intellectual renaissance, we face a difficult task in proving that the citizenry— Plato's *motley multitude*—is indeed capable of self-government. The masses have yet to demonstrate that they can exercise the intellectual discipline and responsibility needed to maintain our freedoms in this complex cultural environment.

I would like to believe that human beings can surmount the problems we are facing. Lederer affirms this position: "The final and vital point of this book is that the state of the nation depends upon individual citizens."[29] I believe in the strength and ultimate potency of truth and reason to prevail. However, this does not mean that truth and reason inevitably *will* prevail. We cannot simply decree that Freedom is Good, and Right has Won. If men and women do not *choose* to act with intelligence and responsibility and long-range wisdom in the coming years, we can be assured that truth and reason will *not* prevail, our freedoms *cannot* be maintained. It is our choice. Donella Meadows reminds us, "I know that war and mayhem run in our blood. [But] I refuse to believe that they must dominate our lives. . . . We know how to restrain ourselves, if we choose to do so. We know how to build fences and bridges and churches and peace—if we choose to do so."[30]

The peoples of the planet face an immense challenge during the next half century or so. Havel's closing plea resonates throughout our culture: "We must—as humanity, as people, as conscious beings with spirit, mind, and a sense of responsibility—somehow come to our senses."[31] If we are to persist in the pursuit of an intellectual society—democratic self-governance, a capitalist economy, universal education, civil rights and individual liberties for all—then we must deliberately decide that reason shall prevail; we must commit ourselves to the maintenance of our intellectual infrastructure.

NOTES

1. Lederer, 1961, p. 8.

2. Bloom, 1987, p. 382.

3. Havel, 1992, p. 117.

4. Fredric Hayward, "Properly Honoring Our Fathers," *Los Angeles Times,* 19 June 1994, p. M5.

5. Quoted in D'Antonio, 1992, p. 36.

6. Quoted in Harry Stein, "Our Times," *TV Guide,* 1 January 1994, p. 39.

7. Toffler, 1980, p. 194.

8. Figures are according to Rose Hanes, executive director of Population-Environment Balance, cited in Joseph Alper, "A Crowded Planet," *Los Angeles Times Health Horizons,* 29 March 1992, p. 14.

9. As reported by State Representative Ronald Gauch, in "That's Outrageous," *Reader's Digest,* August 1994, p. 97. Massachusetts has since abandoned the fertility assistance.

10. Quoted in Donella H. Meadows, "A Company Decides Not to Grow," *Los Angeles Times,* 27 December 1992, p. M5.

11. See Christopher D. Stone, "Tax Nations to Repair the Earth," *Los Angeles Times,* 25 August 1989, pt. 2, p. 7.

12. See Michael D. Lemonick, "What Can Americans Do?" *Time,* 18 September 1989, p. 85.

13. "Fahrenheit 932," *Discover,* August 1988, p. 12.

14. Andrew C. Revkin, "Tapping the Sea," *Discover,* July 1989, p. 40.

15. From a speech at the University of Redlands Convocation-Lecture Series, 21 September 1993, quoted in "Speaking Up," *Los Angeles Times*, 24 September 1993, p. B10.

16. Rousseau [1762], book 2, ch. 11, 1952, p. 405n.

17. Allen, 1989, p. 117.

18. William F. Buckley, "CEO Salaries, Like Sausages, Aren't Pretty." *Los Angeles Times*, 11 April 1996, p. B15.

19. Sam Pizzigati, "How About a *Maximum* Wage?" *Los Angeles Times*, 8 April 1992, p. B11.

20. D'Antonio, 1992, p. 34.

21. Alexander Cockburn, "The Losing Idea Is 'Moderation,'" *Los Angeles Times*, 12 November 1990, p. B9.

22. Andorra, Antigua and Barbuda, Belize, Dominica, Grenada, Kiribati, Liechtenstein, Marshall Islands, Micronesia, Monaco, Nauru, Saint Kitts and Nevis, Saint Lucia, Saint Vincent and the Grenadines, San Marino, São Tomé and Principe, Seychelles, Tonga, Tuvalu, and Vanuatu.

23. Quoted in Jonathan Power, "United Nations Moving Toward a New Age," *Los Angeles Times*, 19 January 1990, p. B15.

24. Quoted in Eric Harrison, "Gorbachev Backs World Government," *Los Angeles Times*, 7 May 1992, pp. A1, A38.

25. Allen, 1989, p. 129.

26. Excerpted from the Unabomber's "manifesto," as reprinted in the *San Francisco Examiner*, 1 July 1995, p. A14.

27. Lapham, *Wish for Kings*, 1993, p. 188.

28. Kennedy, 1993, pp. 348–49.

29. Lederer, 1961, p. 190.

30. Donella H. Meadows, "Good Will to Sheep--And Men," *Los Angeles Times*, 25 December 1994, p. M5.

31. Havel, 1992, pp. 115–16.

Selected Bibliography

Abbey, Edward. *One Life at a Time, Please.* New York: Henry Holt and Company, 1988.

Adler, Mortimer J. *Six Great Ideas.* New York: Macmillan Publishing Co., Inc., 1981.

Agee, Warren K., Phillip H. Ault, and Edwin Emery. *Introduction to Mass Communications.* 6th ed. New York: Harper & Row, 1979.

Allen, Steve. *Dumbth: And 81 Ways to Make Americans Smarter.* Buffalo, NY: Prometheus Books, 1989.

Ardrey, Robert. *The Territorial Imperative.* New York: Atheneum, 1966.

Bagdikian, Ben. "Economics and the Morality of Journalism." In *Readings in Mass Communication: Concepts and Issues in the Mass Media*, 6th ed. Edited by Michael Emery and Ted Curtis Smythe. Dubuque, IA: Wm. C. Brown, 1986.

Bandura, A., and S. A. Ross. "Transmission of Aggression through Imitation of Aggressive Models," *Journal of Abnormal and Social Psychology*, 63 (1961): 575–82.

Bandura, Albert. *Social Learning Theory.* Englewood Cliffs, NJ: Prentice-Hall, 1977.

Barlow, John Perry. "Jackboots on the Infobahn." *Wired,* April 1994, pp. 40, 44–47.

Barnes, Fred. "Communism's Incredible Collapse: How It Happened." *Reader's Digest*, March 1990, pp. 105–10.

Barnes, Fred, and Rachel Flick Wildavsky. "Is Washington for Sale?" *Reader's Digest*, February 1993, pp. 45–50.

Bartlett's Familiar Quotations. 15th ed. Edited by Emily Morison Beck. Boston: Little, Brown and Company, 1980.

Beck, Melinda, Mary Hager, Patricia King, Sue Hutchinson, Kate Robins, and Jeanne Gordon. "Buried Alive." *Newsweek*, 27 November 1989, pp. 66–76.

Becker, Gary S. "As Role Models Go, Sweden Is Suspect." *BusinessWeek,* 9 July 1990, p. 14.

Beckwith, Francis J., and Michael E. Bauman, eds. *Are You Politically Correct? Debating America's Cultural Standards.* Buffalo, NY: Prometheus Books, 1993.

Bellah, Robert. "Civil Religion in America." In *Religion in America,* edited by W. G. McLoughlin and R. Bellah. Boston: Houghton Mifflin, 1968.

Bellow, Saul. "There Is Simply Too Much to Think About." *Forbes*, 14 September 1992, pp. 98–106.

Bennett, Ralph Kinney. "Why Los Angeles Burned." *Reader's Digest*, October 1992, pp. 74–80.

Bennett, W. Lance. *News: The Politics of Illusion.* 2nd ed. New York: Longman, 1987.

Berman, Paul, ed. *Debating P.C.: The Controversy Over Political Correctness on College Campuses.* New York: Laurel Trade Paperback/Dell Publishing, 1992.

Berry, Wendell. *The Unsettling of America: Culture and Agriculture.* San Francisco: Sierra Club Books, 1977.

Birnbaum, Jeffrey H. *The Lobbyists: How Influence Peddlers Get Their Way in Washington.* New York: Times Books, 1993.

Bloom, Allan. *The Closing of the American Mind: How Higher Education Has Failed Democracy and Impoverished the Souls of Today's Students.* New York: Simon and Schuster, 1987.

Bodley, John H. *Victims of Progress.* 2nd ed. Menlo Park, CA: Benjamin/Cummings Publishing Co., 1982.

Boesche, Roger. "The Real Reason Americans Don't Vote." *Los Angeles Times,* 12 June 1994, p. M5.

Brand, Stewart. *The Media Lab: Inventing the Future at M.I.T.* New York: Penguin Books, 1987.

Bronowski, Jacob. *The Ascent of Man.* Boston: Little, Brown and Company, 1973.

Brown, Lester, ed. *State of the World 1989: A Worldwatch Institute Report on Progress Toward a Sustainable Society.* New York: W. W. Norton and Company, 1989.

Brownstein, Ronald. "America's Anxiety Attack." *Los Angeles Times Magazine,* 8 May 1994, pp. 14–20, 36–37.

Caldicott, Helen. *Saving the Planet.* Westfield, NJ: Open Magazine Pamphlet Series, 1991.

Calleo, David, and Benjamin Rowland. *America and the World Political Economy.* Bloomington, IN: Indiana University Press, 1973.

Campbell, Jeremy. *The Improbable Machine: What the Upheavals in Artificial Intelligence Research Reveal About How the Mind Really Works.* New York: Simon and Schuster, 1989.

Capra, Fritjof. *The Turning Point: Science, Society, and the Rising Culture.* New York: Bantam Books, 1982.

Carson, Rachel. *Silent Spring.* Boston: Houghton Mifflin Co., 1962.

Cassirer, Ernst. *An Essay on Man.* Garden City, NY: Doubleday/Anchor, 1956.

Charren, Peggy, and Martin W. Sandler. *Changing Channels: Living (Sensibly) with Television.* Reading, MA: Addison-Wesley Publishing Company, 1983.

Chomsky, Noam. *The Chomsky Reader.* Edited by James Peck. New York: Pantheon Books, 1987.

————. *Deterring Democracy.* New York: Hill and Wang, 1991.

Clark, Kenneth. *Civilisation: A Personal View.* New York: Harper and Row, 1969.

Cline, Victor. *The Desensitization of Children to Television Violence.* Bethesda, MD: National Institutes of Health, 1972.

Cloud, Stanley W. "The Can't Do Government." *Time,* 23 October 1989, pp. 28–32.

Cohen, Joel E. "How Many People Can Earth Hold?" *Discover,* November 1992, pp. 114–19.

Colson, Chuck, and Jack Eckerd. *Why America Doesn't Work.* Dallas, TX: Word Publishing, 1991.

Commission on Obscenity and Pornography. *Report of the Commission on Obscenity and Pornography.* Washington, DC: Government Printing Office, 1970.

Commission on Population Growth and the American Future. *Population and the American Future.* New York: Signet Book, New American Library, 1972.

Commoner, Barry. *The Closing Circle: Nature, Man, and Technology.* New York: Alfred A. Knopf, 1971.

Comstock, George, ed. *Public Communication and Behavior.* Orlando, FL: Academic Press, 1986.

Comstock, George, Steven Chaffee, Natan Katzman, Maxwell McCombs, and Donald Roberts. *Television and Human Behavior.* New York: Columbia University Press, 1978.

Comte, Auguste. *The Positive Philosophy* [1830–1842]. Translated by Harriet Martineau. London: George Bell and Sons, 1915.

Congalton, David. "ALL IS orWELL: Privacy and the New Technology." *Earlhamite* (Earlham College), 109, no. 3 (Spring 1989): 8–10.

Crichton, Michael. *Jurassic Park.* New York: Ballantine Books, 1990.

Crockett, Norman L., ed. *The Power Elite in America.* Lexington, MA: D. C. Heath and Company, 1970.

Dahlburg, John-Thor. "The Atom Sows Crop of Sadness." *Los Angeles Times,* 2 September 1992, pp. A1, A8–A9.

D'Antonio, Michael. "Tough Medicine for a Sick America." *Los Angeles Times Magazine,* 22 March 1992, pp. 32–37, 50.

Davis, Kingsley. "The Urbanization of the Human Population." *Scientific American,* 213, no. 3 (September 1965): 41–53.

DeFleur, Melvin L., and Sandra Ball-Rokeach. *Theories of Mass Communication.* 5th ed. New York: Longman, 1989.

DeFleur, Melvin L., and Everette E. Dennis. *Understanding Mass Communication.* 3rd ed. Boston: Houghton Mifflin Company, 1988.

Devall, Bill, and George Sessions. *Deep Ecology.* Salt Lake City: Gibbs Smith, Publisher, 1985.

Diamond, Jared. "The Worst Mistake in the History of the Human Race." *Discover,* May 1987, pp. 64–66.

DiIulio, John J., Jr. "Crime in America: It's Going to Get Worse." *Reader's Digest,* August 1995, pp. 55–60.

Dixon, Lloyd S., Deborah S. Drezner, and James K. Hammitt. *Superfund: Private-Sector Expenditures and Transaction Costs.* Santa Monica, CA: RAND Corporation, January 1993.

Dorris, Michael. "A Desperate Crack Legacy." *Newsweek,* 25 June 1990, p. 8.

Downing, John, Ali Mohammadi, and Annabelle Sreberny-Mohammadi. *Questioning the Media: A Critical Introduction.* Newbury Park, CA: Sage Publications, 1990.

Downs, Hugh. "Greater Ganglia." Broadcast on *Perspective,* ABC Radio News, 12 December 1993.

Drucker, Peter F. *Post-Capitalist Society.* New York: HarperCollins Publishers, 1993.

D'Souza, Dinesh. *Illiberal Education: The Politics of Race and Sex on Campus.* New York: The Free Press, 1991.

Du Bois, W. E. B. "The Talented Tenth" [1903]. In *A W. E. B. Du Bois Reader.* Edited by Andrew G. Paschal. New York: Macmillan Company, 1971.

Dubos, René. *Mirage of Health: Utopias, Progress, and Biological Change.* New Brunswick, NJ: Rutgers University Press, 1987.

Dye, Thomas R., and L. Harmon Zeigler. *The Irony of Democracy: An Uncommon Introduction to American Politics.* 4th ed. North Scituate, MA: Duxbury Press, 1978.

Eaton, S. Boyd, Marjorie Shostak, and Melvin Konner. *The Paleolithic Prescription: A Program of Diet and Exercise and a Design for Living.* New York: Harper and Row, 1988.

Ebenstein, William. *Great Political Thinkers: Plato to the Present.* 3rd ed. New York: Holt, Rinehart and Winston, 1963.

Ehrenfeld, David. *The Arrogance of Humanism.* New York: Oxford University Press, 1978.

Ehrlich, Anne H., and Paul R. Ehrlich. *Earth.* New York: Franklin Watts, 1987.

Ehrlich, Paul R. *The Population Bomb.* New York: Ballantine Books, Inc., 1968.

————. *The Machinery of Nature.* New York: Simon and Schuster, 1986.

————. *New World New Mind: Moving Toward Conscious Evolution.* New York: Doubleday, 1989.

Ekelund, Robert B., Jr., and Robert F. Hebert. *A History of Economic Theory and Method.* 2nd ed. New York: McGraw-Hill Book Company, 1983.

Elfstrom, Gerard. *Moral Issues and Multinational Corporations.* New York: St. Martin's Press, 1991.

Ellul, Jacques. *The Technological Society.* Translated by John Wilkinson. New York: Vintage Books, 1964.

Elmer-Dewitt, Philip. "Rich Vs. Poor." *Time,* 1 June 1992, pp. 42–58.

————. "Taking a Trip into the Future on the Electronic Superhighway." *Time,* 12 April 1993, pp. 50–55.

Emerson, Ralph Waldo. "Self-Reliance" [1841]. In *American Literature: An Anthology and Critical Survey,* Vol 1: *From the Beginning to 1860.* Edited by Joe Lee Davis, John T. Frederick, and Frank Luther Mott. Chicago: Charles Scribner's Sons, 1948.

Emery, Michael, and Ted Curtis Smythe, eds. *Readings in Mass Communication: Concepts and Issues in the Mass Media.* 7th ed. Dubuque, IA: Wm. C. Brown Publishers, 1989.

Englebardt, Stanley L. "Get Ready for Virtual Reality." *Reader's Digest,* December 1993, pp. 127–31.

Entman, Robert M. *Democracy without Citizens: Media and the Decay of American Politics*. New York: Oxford University Press, 1989.

Evans, Christopher. *The Micro Millennium*. New York: Viking Press, 1980.

Ewen, Stuart, and Elizabeth Ewen. *Channels of Desire: Mass Images and the Shaping of American Consciousness*. New York: McGraw-Hill Book Company, 1982.

Ferrarotti, Franco. *The Myth of Inevitable Progress*. Westport, CT: Greenwood Press, 1985.

————. *The End of Conversation: The Impact of Mass Media on Modern Society*. Westport, CT: Greenwood Press, 1988.

FitzGerald, Frances. *America Revised*. Boston: Atlantic Monthly Press Book, Little, Brown and Company, 1979.

Fore, William F. *Television and Religion: The Shaping of Faith, Values, and Culture*. Minneapolis: Augsburg Publishing House, 1987.

Forster, E. M. "The Machine Stops" [1914]. In *The Eternal Moment and Other Stories*. New York: Harcourt, Brace and Company, 1928.

Freedman, David H. "If He Only Had a Brain." *Discover*, August 1992, pp. 54–60.

Freedman, Warren. *The Right of Privacy in the Computer Age*. New York: Quorum Books, 1987.

Friedman, Milton. *The Essence of Friedman*. Stanford, CA: Hoover Institution Press, 1987.

Fukuyama, Francis. *The End of History and the Last Man*. New York: Free Press, 1992.

Galbraith, John Kenneth. *American Capitalism: The Concept of Countervailing Power*. Rev. ed. Boston: Houghton Mifflin, 1956.

————. *The New Industrial State*. New York: Signet Books, 1967.

————. *The Affluent Society*. 4th ed. Boston: Houghton Mifflin, 1984.

Garrett, Laurie. *The Coming Plague: Newly Emerging Diseases in a World Out of Balance*. New York: Farrar, Straus and Giroux, 1994.

Gay, Peter. *Age of Enlightenment*. New York: Time, 1966.

Gay, Verne. "Is Walter Cronkite the Last Trustworthy Man in America?" *Los Angeles Times Magazine,* 21 January 1996, pp. 9–11, 34.

Gibbs, Nancy. "How America Has Run Out of Time." *Time,* 24 April 1989, pp. 58–67.

Gilder, George. "Into the Fibersphere." *ASAP: Technology Supplement to Forbes Magazine*, 7 December 1992, pp. 111–25.

Gill, Stephen. *American Hegemony and the Trilateral Commission*. New York: Cambridge University Press, 1990.

Goffman, Erving. *Behavior in Public Places: Notes on the Social Organization of Gatherings*. New York: Free Press, 1963.

Gore, Al. "The Power of Technology." *Discover,* October 1993, pp. 54–55.

Greene, Bob. "Society's Crumbling, and We're Watching." *Chicago Tribune*, 27 June 1994, sect. 5, p. 1.

Gupta, Udayan. "Hungry for Funds, Universities Embrace Technology Transfer." *Wall Street Journal,* 1 July 1994, pp. A1, A5.

Habermas, Jürgen. *Jürgen Habermas on Society and Politics: A Reader*. Edited by Steven Seidman. Boston: Beacon Press, 1989.

Hamakawa, Yoshihiro. "Photovoltaic Power." Scientific American, 256, no. 4 (April 1987): 86–92.

Hansen, Christine Hall, and Ranald D. Hansen. "Constructing Personality and Social Reality Through Music: Individual Differences among Fans of Punk and Heavy Metal Music." Journal of Broadcasting and Electronic Media, 35, no. 3 (Summer 1991): 335–50.

Hardison, O. B., Jr. Disappearing through the Skylight: Culture and Technology in the Twentieth Century. New York: Viking Penguin, 1989.

Harris, Marvin. America Now: The Anthropology of a Changing Culture. New York: Simon and Schuster, 1981.

Havel, Václav. Summer Meditations. Translated by Paul Wilson. New York: Vintage Books, 1992.

Hayes, Brian. "Machine Dreams." Discover, October 1989, pp. 82–87.

Heilbroner, Robert L. The Economic Problem. 3rd ed. Englewood Cliffs, NJ: Prentice-Hall, 1972.

————. An Inquiry into the Human Prospect: Updated and Reconsidered for the 1980s. New York: W. W. Norton and Company, 1980.

Henry, Jules. Culture Against Man. New York: Random House, 1963.

Henry, William A., III. In Defense of Elitism. New York: Doubleday, 1994.

Herrnstein, Richard J., and Charles Murray. The Bell Curve: Intelligence and Class Structure in American Life. New York: Free Press, 1994.

Heyer, Paul. Communications and History: Theories of Media, Knowledge, and Civilization. Westport, CT: Greenwood Press, 1988.

Himmelfarb, Gertrude. "A De-moralized Society?" Forbes, 14 September 1992, pp. 120–28.

Himmelstein, Hal. Television Myth and the American Mind. 2nd ed. Westport, CT: Praeger Publishers, 1994.

Hirsch, E. D. Cultural Literacy: What Every American Needs to Know. Boston: Houghton Mifflin, 1987.

Hofstadter, Richard. Anti-Intellectualism in American Life. New York: Alfred A. Knopf, 1963.

Holden, Richard. "America: Life, Liberty and the Pursuit." Earlhamite (Earlham College), 108, no. 1 (Fall 1987): 6–12.

Hollinger, David A. In the American Province: Studies in the History and Historiography of Ideas. Baltimore: Johns Hopkins University Press, 1989.

Hoobler, Dorothy. Your Right to Privacy. New York: Franklin Watts, 1986.

Howard, Philip K. The Death of Common Sense. New York: Random House, 1994.

Huxley, Aldous. Brave New World [1932]. New York: Harper and Row, 1969.

Illich, Ivan. "The Institutionalization of Truth." In Tradition and Revolution. Edited by Lionel Rubinoff. Toronto: Macmillan of Canada, 1971.

Innis, Harold A. Empire and Communications. Oxford, U.K.: Clarendon Press, 1950.

————. The Bias of Communication. Toronto, Canada: University of Toronto Press, 1964.

Isaacs, Harold R. *Idols of the Tribe: Group Identity and Political Change*. New York: Harper and Row, 1975.

Iyer, Pico. "History? Education? Zap! Pow! Cut!" *Time*, 14 May 1990, p. 98.

Jacoby, Russell. *The Last Intellectuals: American Culture in the Age of Academe*. New York: Noonday Press/Farrar, Straus and Giroux, 1987.

————. *Dogmatic Wisdom: How the Culture Wars Divert Education and Distract America*. New York: Doubleday, 1994.

Jamieson, Kathleen Hall, and Karlyn Kohrs Campbell. *The Interplay of Influence: Mass Media and Their Publics in News, Advertising, Politics*. 2nd ed. Belmont, CA: Wadsworth Publishing Company, 1988.

Jefferson, Thomas. *The Portable Thomas Jefferson*. Edited by Merrill D. Peterson. New York: Penguin Books, 1975.

Jeffres, Leo W. *Mass Media Processes and Effects*. Prospect Heights, IL: Waveland Press, 1986.

Kantrowitz, Barbara. "An Interactive Life." *Newsweek*, 31 May 1993, pp. 42–44.

Katz, Elihu, and Paul F. Lazarsfeld. *Personal Influence: The Part Played by People in the Flow of Communication*. Glencoe, IL: Free Press of Glencoe, 1955.

Kelly, Kevin. *Out of Control: The Rise of Neo-Biological Civilization*. Reading, MA: Addison-Wesley Publishing Company, 1994.

Kennedy, Paul M. *The Rise and Fall of the Great Powers: Economic Change and Military Conflict from 1500 to 2000*. New York: Random House, 1987.

————. *Preparing for the Twenty-First Century*. New York: Random House, 1993.

Key, V. O., Jr. *Public Opinion and American Democracy*. New York: Alfred A. Knopf, 1961.

Kidder, Rushworth M. *An Agenda for the 21st Century*. Cambridge, MA: MIT Press, 1987.

Kilpatrick, William K. *Why Johnny Can't Tell Right From Wrong*. New York: Simon and Schuster, 1992.

King, Stephen. *Danse Macabre*. New York: Berkley Books, 1981.

Knoke, William. *Bold New World: The Essential Road Map to the Twenty-First Century*. New York: Kodansha International, 1996.

Koberg, Don, and Jim Bagnall. *The Revised All New Universal Traveler: A Soft-Systems Guide to Creativity, Problem-Solving, and the Process of Reaching Goals*. Los Altos, CA: William Kaufman, 1981.

Kosinski, Jerzy. *Being There*. New York: Harcourt Brace, 1971.

Kotkin, Joel. "Family Ties in the New Global Economy." *Los Angeles Times Magazine*, 17 January 1993, pp. 18–21.

————. *Tribes: How Race, Religion, and Identity Determine Success in the New Global Economy*. New York: Random House, 1993.

Kowinski, William Severini. "Do the Eyes Have It?" *Metamorphoses*, Spring 1988, pp. 18–25, 46–48.

Kozol, Jonathan. *Illiterate America*. Garden City, NY: Anchor Press/Doubleday, 1985.

Kubey, Robert, and Mihaly Csikszentmihalyi. *Television and the Quality of Life: How Viewing Shapes Everyday Experience.* Hillsdale, NJ: Lawrence Erlbaum Associates, 1990.

Lacayo, Richard. "A Threat to Freedom?" *Time,* 18 September 1989, pp. 28, 32.

————. "Nowhere to Hide." *Time,* 11 November 1991, pp. 34–40.

Lamm, Richard D. "A Prodigal Father Confesses." *Boston Globe,* 21 June 1987, pp. A1, A4.

Lapham, Lewis H. "Democracy in America?" *Harper's Magazine,* November 1990, pp. 47–56.

————. "Modern Democracy: A State of Being Artfully Deceived." *Los Angeles Times,* 21 November 1993, p. M2.

————. *The Wish for Kings: Democracy at Bay.* New York: Grove Press, 1993.

Lasch, Christopher. *The Culture of Narcissism: American Life in an Age of Diminishing Expectations.* New York: W. W. Norton and Company, 1978.

————. *The True and Only Heaven: Progress and Its Critics.* New York: W. W. Norton and Company, 1991.

Lasswell, Harold D. "The Structure and Function of Communication in Society." In *The Communication of Ideas,* edited by Lyman Bryson. New York: Harper and Brothers, 1948.

Lazarsfeld, Paul F., and Robert K. Merton. "Mass Communication, Popular Taste and Organized Social Action." In *The Communication of Ideas,* edited by Lyman Bryson. New York: Harper and Brothers, 1948.

Leach, William. *Land of Desire: Merchants, Power, and the Rise of a New American Culture.* New York: Pantheon Books, 1993.

Lederer, William J. *A Nation of Sheep.* New York: W. W. Norton and Company, 1961.

Lee, Martin A., and Norman Solomon. *Unreliable Sources: A Guide to Detecting Bias in News Media.* New York: Carol Publishing Group, 1991.

"The Left in Western Europe." *The Economist,* 11 June 1994, pp. 17–19.

LeMond, Alan, and Ron Fry. *No Place to Hide.* New York: St. Martin's Press, 1975.

Leonard, George B. *Education and Ecstasy.* New York: Delacort Press, 1968.

Lerner, Michael. "Psychodynamics of the Status Quo." *Los Angeles Times,* 17 January 1990, p. B13.

Levinson, Marc. "Everyone's Magic Bullet." *Newsweek,* 21 September 1992, p. 44.

Levy, Steven. "TechnoMania." *Newsweek,* 27 February 1995, pp. 24–29.

Leyden, Peter. "On the Edge of the Digital Age." Minneapolis *Star-Tribune* [four-part supplement], June 4, 11, 18, and 25, 1995.

Linowes, David F. *Privacy in America: Is Your Private Life in the Public Eye?* Urbana: University of Illinois Press, 1989.

Linton, Ralph. *The Tree of Culture.* New York: Alfred A. Knopf, 1964.

Lippmann, Walter. *Public Opinion.* New York: Macmillan, 1922.

Lock, James Joseph. "The Internet as Mass Medium: The Media Enter the World of Cyberspace." *Feedback,* 36, no. 4 (Fall 1995): 7–10.

Locke, John. *Concerning Civil Government, Second Essay.* 1690.

Lowe, Janet. *The Secret Empire: How 25 Multinationals Rule the World.* Homewood, IL: Business One Irwin, 1992.

Lowenstein, Jerold M. "Genetic Surprises." *Discover,* December 1992, pp. 82–88.

Lukacs, John. *Outgrowing Democracy: A History of the United States in the Twentieth Century.* Garden City, NY: Doubleday and Company, 1984.

Lynch, Kevin. "The City as Environment." *Scientific American,* 213, no. 3 (September 1965): 209–19.

Macmurray, John. *Reason and Emotion.* New York: Barnes and Noble, 1962.

MacNeil, Robert. "The Trouble with Television." Speech at the President's Leadership Forum, State University of New York at Purchase, 13 November 1984. Reprinted in *Reader's Digest,* March 1985, pp. 171–74.

Mahler, Richard. "While You Wait: TV Marketers Hunt Captive Viewers." *Electronic Media,* 30 December 1991, pp. 1, 4, 29.

Malthus, Thomas Robert. *An Essay on the Principle of Population, as It Affects The Future Improvement of Society.* London: J. Johnson, in St. Paul's Church-Yard, 1798. New York: Reprints of Economic Classics, Augusts M. Kelley, Bookseller/Sentry Press, 1965.

Mander, Jerry. *Four Arguments for the Elimination of Television.* New York: William Morrow and Company, 1978.

————. *In the Absence of the Sacred: The Failure of Technology and the Survival of the Indian Nations.* San Francisco: Sierra Club Books, 1991.

Mann, Charles C. "How Many Is Too Many?" *The Atlantic Monthly.* February 1993, pp. 47–67.

Marx, Karl. "Economic and Philosophic Manuscripts" [1844]. In The Marx-Engels Reader, edited by Robert C. Tucker. New York: W. W. Norton and Company, 1972.

————. "Capital" [1891]. In *The Marx-Engels Reader,* edited by Robert C. Tucker. New York: W. W. Norton and Company, 1972.

McKibben, Bill. *The End of Nature.* New York: Random House, 1989.

————. *The Age of Missing Information.* New York: Random House, 1992.

McLuhan, Marshall. *Understanding Media: The Extensions of Man.* New York: New American Library, Signet Books, 1964.

McLuhan, Marshall, and Quentin Fiore. *The Medium Is the Massage: An Inventory of Effects.* New York: Bantam Books, 1967.

Meadows, Donella H., Dennis L. Meadows, Jorgen Randers, and William W. Behrens III. *The Limits to Growth: A Report for the Club of Rome's Project on the Predicament of Mankind.* New York: Signet Book, New American Library, 1972.

Medved, Michael. *Hollywood Vs. America: Popular Culture and the War on Traditional Values.* New York: HarperCollins Publishers, 1992.

Meeks, Brock N. "The End of Privacy." *Wired,* April 1994, pp. 40, 50–51.

Merchant, Carolyn. *The Death of Nature.* New York: Harper and Row, 1980.

Meyrowitz, Joshua. *No Sense of Place: The Impact of Electronic Media on Social Behavior.* New York: Oxford University Press, 1985.

Miles, Rufus E., Jr. *Awakening from the American Dream: The Social and Political Limits to Growth.* New York: Universe Books, 1976.

Mill, John Stuart. *On Liberty* [1859]. In *Great Books of the Western World,* Robert Maynard Hutchins, general editor. Vol. 43: *American State Papers, Federalist, J. S. Mill.* Chicago: Encyclopædia Britannica, 1952.

Mills, C. Wright. *The Power Elite.* New York: Oxford University Press, 1956.

Milton, John. *Areopagitica* [1644]. In *Great Books of the Western World,* Robert Maynard Hutchins, general editor. Vol. 32: *Milton.* Chicago: Encyclopædia Britannica, 1952.

Mirabito, Michael M., and Barbara L. Morgenstern. *The New Communications Technologies.* Boston: Focal Press, 1990.

Mosca, Gaetano. *The Ruling Class.* New York: McGraw-Hill Book Co., 1939.

Moser, Leo J. *The Technology Trap: Survival in a Man-Made Environment.* Chicago: Nelson-Hall, 1979.

Moyers, Bill. *A World of Ideas: Conversations with Thoughtful Men and Women about American Life Today and the Ideas Shaping Our Future.* Edited by Betty Sue Flowers. New York: Doubleday, 1989.

Moynihan, Daniel Patrick. "A Cry For My City." Speech delivered to the Association for a Better New York, 15 April 1993, reprinted in *Reader's Digest,* January 1994, pp. 77–79.

Mumford, Lewis. *Technics and Civilization.* New York: Harcourt, Brace and World, 1934.

Naisbitt, John. *Megatrends: Ten New Directions Transforming Our Lives.* 2nd ed. New York: Warner Books, 1984.

National Commission on Excellence in Education. *Nation at Risk.* Washington, DC: U.S. Government Printing Office, 1983.

National Institutes of Mental Health. *Television and Behavior: Ten Years of Scientific Progress and Implications for the Eighties.* Rockville, MD: U.S. Department of Health and Human Services, 1982.

Neuman, W. Russell. *The Paradox of Mass Politics: Knowledge and Opinion in the American Electorate.* Cambridge, MA: Harvard University Press, 1986.

Nietschmann, Bernard. "The Third World War." *Cultural Survival Quarterly,* 11, no. 3 (1987).

Noble, David. "Intellectuals Endangered, Expert Says." *Albuquerque Journal,* 5 April 1987, p. F5.

Noonan, Peggy. "You'd Cry Too If it Happened to You." *Forbes,* 14 September 1992, pp. 58–69.

Novak, Michael. "The Urgent Need for Virtuous Capitalism." *Los Angeles Times,* 13 March 1994, p. M5.

Ong, Walter J. "Reading, Technology, and Human Consciousness," In *Literacy as a Human Problem,* edited by James C. Raymond. University, AL: University of Alabama Press, 1982.

Orwell, George. *1984* [1949]. New York: New American Library, 1961.

Packard, Vance. *The People Shapers.* Boston: Little, Brown, 1977.

Parachini, Allan. "Probing the State of Our Minds." *Los Angeles Times,* 1 November 1988, pt. 5, pp. 1, 3.

Parkes, Henry Bamford. *The Divine Order: Western Culture in the Middle Ages and the Renaissance.* New York: Alfred A. Knopf, 1969.

Pask, Gordon, with Susan Curran. *Micro Man: Computers and the Evolution of Consciousness.* New York: Macmillan Publishing Co., 1982.

Paulos, John Allen. *Innumeracy: Mathematical Illiteracy and Its Consequences.* New York: Hill and Wang, 1988.

————— . *A Mathematician Reads the Newspaper.* New York: BasicBooks/HarperCollins, 1995.

Perse, Elizabeth M., and Alan M. Rubin. "Chronic Loneliness and Television Use." *Journal of Broadcasting and Electronic Media,* 34, no. 1 (Winter 1990): 37–53.

Peter, Laurence J., and Raymond Hull. *The Peter Principle.* New York: Bantam Books, 1969.

Picard, Robert G. *The Press and the Decline of Democracy: The Democratic Socialist Response in Public Policy.* Westport, CT: Greenwood Press, 1985.

Pizzigati, Sam. *The Maximum Wage: A Common-Sense Prescription for Revitalizing America—By Taxing the Very Rich.* New York: Apex Press, 1992.

Plato. "Republic." In *Five Great Dialogues.* Translated by B. Jowett. Edited by Louise Ropes Loomis. New York: Van Nostrand Company, 1942.

Pool, Ithiel de Sola. *Technologies of Freedom.* Cambridge, MA: Belknap Press, 1983.

Postman, Neil. *Television and the Teaching of English.* New York: Appleton-Century-Crofts, 1961.

————— . *The Disappearance of Childhood.* New York: Delacorte Press, 1982.

————— . *Amusing Ourselves to Death: Public Discourse in the Age of Show Business.* New York: Penguin Books, 1985.

————— . *Conscientious Objections: Stirring Up Trouble about Language, Technology, and Education.* New York: Vintage Books, 1988.

————— . *Technopoly: The Surrender of Culture to Technology.* New York: Alfred A. Knopf, 1992.

Postman, Neil, and Charles Weingartner. *Teaching as a Subversive Activity.* New York: Dell Publishing Company, 1969.

Powers, Ron. *The Newscasters.* New York: St. Martin's Press, 1977.

Quigley, Carroll. *Tragedy and Hope: A History of the World in Our Time.* New York: Macmillan Company, 1966.

Rand, Ayn. *The Fountainhead* [1943]. 5th ed. New York: Signet Novel/Penguin Books, 1993.

————— . *Atlas Shrugged* [1957]. New York: Signet Book/Penguin Books, 1985.

Rauch, Jonathan. *Demosclerosis: The Silent Killer of American Government.* New York: Times Books, 1994.

Revel, Jean-Francois. *Without Marx or Jesus: The New American Revolution Has Begun.* Translated by J. F. Bernard. Garden City, NY: Doubleday and Company, Inc., 1970.

Rheingold, Howard. *The Virtual Community: Homesteading on the Electronic Frontier.* Reading, MA: Addison-Wesley Publishing Company, 1993.

Rifkin, Jeremy. *Entropy: A New World View.* New York: Bantam Books, 1981.

——— . *Time Wars: The Primary Conflict in Human History.* New York: Simon and Schuster, 1987.

Rivers, William L. *Ethics for the Media.* Englewood Cliffs, NJ: Prentice-Hall, 1988.

Rogers, Everett M., and F. Floyd Shoemaker. *Communication of Innovations: A Cross Cultural Approach.* New York: Free Press, 1971.

Rogers, Michael. "Smart Cards: Pocket Power." *Newsweek,* 31 July 1989, pp. 54–55.

Rosenberg, Bernard, and David Manning White, eds. *Mass Culture.* Glencoe, IL: Free Press, 1957.

Rosenstiel, Thomas B. "Someone May Be Watching Us." *Los Angeles Times,* 18 May 1994, pp. A1, A12.

Rossi, Peter H. *Down and Out in America: The Origins of Homelessness.* Chicago: University of Chicago Press, 1989.

Roszak, Theodore. *The Making of a Counter Culture.* New York: Doubleday/Anchor, 1969.

——— . *Person/Planet: The Creative Disintegration of Industrial Society.* Garden City, NY: Anchor Press/Doubleday, 1979.

——— . *The Cult of Information: A Neo-Luddite Treatise on High Tech, Artificial Intelligence, and the True Art of Thinking.* 2nd ed. Berkeley: University of California Press, 1994.

Rothfeder, Jeff. "Nothing Personal." *Netguide,* 1995, pp. 61–62.

Rothman, Stanley, ed. *The Mass Media in Liberal Democratic Societies.* New York: Paragon House, A PWPA Book, 1992.

Rousseau, Jean Jacques. "The Social Contract Or Principles of Political Right" [1762]. Translated by G. D. H. Cole. In *Great Books of the Western World,* Robert Maynard Hutchins, general editor. Vol. 38: *Montesquieu [and] Rousseau.* Chicago: Encyclopædia Britannica, 1952.

Rubin, Bernard. *Media, Politics, and Democracy.* New York: Oxford University Press, 1977.

——— , ed. *Questioning Media Ethics.* New York: Praeger Publishers, 1978.

——— , ed. *When Information Counts: Grading the Media.* Lexington, MA: Lexington Books, 1985.

Rubin, David M., and David P. Sachs. *Mass Media and the Environment: Water Resources, Land Use, and Atomic Energy in California.* New York: Praeger Publishers, 1973.

Rubner, Alex. *The Might of the Multinationals: The Rise and Fall of the Corporate Legend.* New York: Praeger Publishers, 1990.

Rustigan, Michael. "The Excesses of 'Getting Even.'" *Los Angeles Times,* 2 August 1993, p. B13.

Sale, Kirkpatrick. *Dwellers in the Land: The Bioregional Vision.* Philadelphia: New Society Publishers, 1985.

————— . "In Industrial Revolution II, Information Rules." *Los Angeles Times*, 11 June 1995, p. D2.

————— . *Rebels Against the Future: The Luddites and Their War on the Industrial Revolution*. Reading, MA: Addison-Wesley Publishing Company, 1995.

Salvaggio, Jerry L., ed. *The Information Society: Economic, Social, and Structural Issues*. Hillsdale, NJ: Lawrence Erlbaum Associates, 1989.

Sampson, Anthony. *Company Man: The Rise and Fall of Corporate Life*. New York: Times Books, 1995.

Samuelson, Robert J. *The Good Life and Its Discontents: The American Dream in the Age of Entitlement 1945-1995*. New York: Times Books, 1995.

Sanoff, Alvin P. "The Greening of America's Past." *U.S. News and World Report*, 19 October 1992, pp. 68-69.

Sapolsky, Barry S., and Joseph O. Tabarlet. "Sex in Primetime Television: 1979 Versus 1989." *Journal of Broadcasting and Electronic Media*, 35, no. 4 (Fall 1991): 505-16.

Schell, Jonathan. *The Fate of the Earth*. New York: Alfred A. Knopf, 1982.

————— . "Our Fragile Earth." *Discover,* October 1989, pp. 44-50.

Schlesinger, Arthur M. [Sr.]. *The Birth of the Nation: A Portrait of the American People on the Eve of Independence*. New York: Alfred A. Knopf, 1968.

Schlesinger, Arthur M., Jr. *The Cycles of American History*. Boston: Houghton Mifflin Company, 1986.

Schramm, Wilbur. *Responsibility in Mass Communication*. New York: Harper and Row, 1957.

————— . *Men, Messages and Media: A Look at Human Communication*. New York: Harper and Row, 1973.

Schwartz, John. "How Did They Get My Name?" *Newsweek*, 3 June 1991, pp. 40-42.

Siebert, Fred S., Theodore B. Peterson, and Wilbur Schramm. *Four Theories of the Press*. Urbana: University of Illinois Press, 1956.

Siegel, Ronald. *Intoxication: Life in Pursuit of Artificial Paradise*. New York: E. P. Dutton, 1989.

Signorielli, Nancy, and George Gerbner, eds. *Violence and Terror in the Mass Media*. Westport, CT: Greenwood Press, 1988.

Silver, Gerald A. *The Social Impact of Computers*. New York: Harcourt Brace Jovanovich, 1979.

Skousen, W. Cleon. *The Naked Capitalist: A Review and Commentary on Dr. Carroll Quigley's Book, Tragedy and Hope*. Salt Lake City: Author, 1970.

Slack, Jennifer Daryl, and Fred Fejes, eds. *The Ideology of the Information Age*. Norwood, NJ: Ablex Publishing Corporation, 1987.

Smith, Adam. *An Inquiry Into the Nature and Causes of the Wealth of Nations* [1776]. In *Great Books of the Western World,* Robert Maynard Hutchins, general editor. Vol. 39: *Adam Smith*. Chicago: Encyclopædia Britannica, 1952.

Sorokin, Pitirim A. *The Crisis of Our Age: The Social and Cultural Outlook*. New York: E. P. Dutton and Co., 1941.

Speer, Albert. *Inside the Third Reich*. Translated by Richard and Clara Winston. New York: Avon Books, 1971.

Stavrianos, L. S. *The World to 1500: A Global History*. 3rd ed. Englewood Cliffs, NJ: Prentice-Hall, 1982.

Stephens, Mitchell. "The Theologian of Talk." *Los Angeles Times Magazine,* 23 October 1994, pp. 26–30, 44, 46.

Stoll, Cliff. *Silicon Snake Oil: Second Thoughts on the Information Highway*. New York: Doubleday, 1995.

Strieber, Whitley, and James Kunetka. *Nature's End: The Consequences of the Twenti-eth Century*. New York: Warner Books, 1986.

Surgeon General's Scientific Advisory Committee on Television and Social Behavior. *Television and Growing Up: The Impact of Televised Violence*. Washington, DC: U.S. Government Printing Office, 1971.

Sykes, Charles J. *A Nation of Victims: The Decay of the American Character*. New York: St. Martin's Press, 1992.

Thibodaux, David. *Political Correctness*. Lafayette, LA: Huntington House Publishers, 1992.

Thoreau, Henry David. *Walden: or, Life in the Woods* [1854]. New York: New American Library of World Literature, 1942.

Tocqueville, Alexis de [Charles Henri Maurice Clerel]. *Democracy in America, Part I.* 1835.

Toffler, Alvin. *Future Shock*. New York: Bantam Books, 1970.

———— . *The Third Wave*. New York: Bantam Books, 1980.

———— . *Powershift: Knowledge, Wealth, and Violence at the Edge of the 21st Century*. New York: Bantam Books, 1990.

Tönnies, Ferdinand. *Gemeinschaft und Gesellschaft,* 1887.

Toynbee, Arnold. *America and the World Revolution and Other Lectures*. New York: Oxford University Press, 1962.

Tuchman, Barbara W. *The March of Folly: From Troy to Vietnam*. New York: Alfred A. Knopf, 1984.

Turow, Joseph. *Media Systems in Society: Understanding Industries, Strategies, and Power*. New York: Longman, 1992.

Vande Berg, Leah R., and Lawrence Wenner. *Television Criticism: Approaches and Ap-plications*. New York: Longman, 1991.

Van Evra, Judith Page. *Television and Child Development*. Hillsdale, NJ: Lawrence Erlbaum Associates, 1990.

Vartabedian, Ralph. "Eye in the Sky," *Los Angeles Times,* 1 May 1994, pp. D1, D4.

Ventura, Michael. *Letters at 3AM: Reports on Endarkenment*. Dallas: Spring Publications, 1993.

Vogel, Jennifer. "Computers Know a Lot about You; Databases Cut a Wide Swath through Personal Privacy." *Utne Reader,* May/June 1994, pp. 30, 32.

Wachtel, Paul L. *The Poverty of Affluence: A Psychological Portrait of the American Way of Life*. Philadelphia: New Society Publishers, 1989.

Ward, Barbara. *Spaceship Earth*. New York: Columbia University Press, 1966.

Watson, Russell, with Sharon Begley, Ginny Carroll, Daniel Glick, Mark Hosenball, Sherry Keene-Osborn, John McCormick, Susan Miller, and Andrew Murr. "America's Nuclear Secrets." *Newsweek,* 27 December 1993, pp. 14–18.

Weber, Max. Max Weber on Capitalism, Bureaucracy and Religion: A Selection of Texts [1889–1924]. Edited by Stanislav Andreski. Boston: George Allen & Unwin, 1983.

Weizenbaum, Joseph. *Computer Power and Human Reason: From Judgement to Calculation.* San Francisco: W. H. Freeman, 1976.

"Who Owes What to Whom?" *Harper's Magazine: Forum,* February 1991, pp. 43–54.

Whyte, William H., Jr. *The Organization Man.* New York: Simon and Schuster, 1956.

Winn, Marie. *The Plug-In Drug: Television, Children, and the Family.* Rev. ed. New York: Penguin Books, 1985.

Wolfson, Lewis W. *The Untapped Power of the Press: Explaining Government to the People.* New York: Praeger Publishers, 1985.

Wood, Donald N. *Mass Media and the Individual.* St. Paul: West Publishing, 1983.

————. *Designing the Effective Message: Critical Thinking and Communication.* 2nd ed. Dubuque, IA: Kendall/Hunt Publishing Company, 1996.

Wurman, Richard Saul. *Information Anxiety.* New York: Doubleday, 1989.

Wylie, Philip. *The End of the Dream.* Garden City, NY: Doubleday and Company, 1972.

Index

About the Author

DONALD N. WOOD is Professor of Radio-Television-Film at California State University, Northridge. He is author of *Educational Telecommunications* (1977), *Mass Media and the Individual* (1983), *Designing the Effective Message* (1989), and co-author of *Television Productions: Disciplines and Techniques* (1978, and Sixth ed. 1995).

ISBN 0-275-95421-8